S0-BAJ-554

George Washington's Beautiful Nelly

Eleanor Custis Lewis by John Trumbull c. 1825, after Gilbert Stuart, c. 1800. Wood-lawn Plantation, a Property of the National Trust for Historic Preservation.

George Washington's Beautiful Nelly

The Letters of Eleanor Parke Custis Lewis
to Elizabeth Bordley Gibson
1794–1851

edited by Patricia Brady

University of South Carolina Press

Women's Diaries and Letters
of the Nineteenth-Century South

Carol Bleser, Series Editor

Cover portrait:
Eleanor Custis Lewis by Trumbull c. 1825,
after Gilbert Stuart, c. 1800. Woodlawn Plantation,
a property of the National Trust for Historic Preservation.

Copyright © 1991 Patricia Brady

Published in Columbia, South Carolina, by the
University of South Carolina Press

Manufactured in the United States of America
99 98 97 96   05 04 03 02

Library of Congress Cataloging-in-Publication Data
Lewis, Nelly Custis, 1779–1852.
  George Washington's beautiful Nelly: the letters of Eleanor Parke
Custis Lewis to Elizabeth Bordley Gibson, 1794–1851 / edited by
Patricia Brady.
      p.   cm. — (Women's diaries and letters of the nineteenth
  century South)
  Includes bibliographical references and index.
  ISBN 0–87249–754–2
  1-57003-124-x (pbk.)

  1. Lewis, Nelly Custis, 1779–1852—Correspondence.   2. Gibson,
Elizabeth Bordley—Correspondence.   3. Presidents—United States—
Children—Correspondence.   4. Women—Southern States—
Correspondence.   I. Brady, Patricia, 1943–.   II. Title.
III. Series.
E312.19.L49   1991
973.5′0922—dc20   91-4797

For Colin and Elizabeth

Contents

Illustrations

George Washington's Beautiful Nelly is the fourth volume in an ongoing series of women's diaries and letters of the nineteenth-century South. In this series being published by the University of South Carolina Press will be a number of never before published diaries, some collections of unpublished correspondence, and a few published diaries that are being reprinted—a potpourri of nineteenth-century women's writings.

The Women's Diaries and Letters of the Nineteenth-Century South Series enables women to speak for themselves, providing readers with a rarely opened window into Southern society before, during, and after the American Civil War. The significance of these letters and journals lies not only in the personal revelations and the writing talents of these women authors but also in the range and versatility of their contents. Taken together these publications will tell us much about the heyday and the fall of the Cotton Kingdom, the mature years of the "peculiar institution," the war years, and the adjustment of the South to a new social order following the defeat of the Confederacy. Through these writings the reader will also be presented with firsthand accounts of everyday life and social events, courtships and marriages, family life and travels, religion and education, and the life and death matters which made up the ordinary and extraordinary world of the nineteenth-century South.

George Washington's Beautiful Nelly is the story of Eleanor Parke Custis Lewis (1779–1852), told in a series of letters written over nearly a lifetime to her best friend, Elizabeth Bordley (later Gibson). Eleanor Parke Custis, called Nelly, was born into the planter elite of Virginia and was in many ways the quintessential Southern lady. But Nelly, having been adopted by George Washington, her grandmother Martha Washington's second husband, had life experiences that transcended those of most women of the planter class. Nelly's father, John Parke Custis, called Jacky, was Martha Washington's son by her first marriage. Childless themselves, the Washingtons had dearly loved Martha's two children by her earlier union. By 1781, both of Martha's children were dead and the senior Washingtons reached an agreement with Jacky's widow to adopt her two youngest children, Nelly and George Washington Parke Custis.

Nelly reveled in being a member of the president's family. She grew to womanhood during Washington's presidency and despaired at being separated from the Washingtons for a time in 1795. She wrote to Elizabeth that this was the first separation from them since she was two years old and that Martha had "been ever more than a Mother to me, and the President the most affectionate of Fathers. I love them more than any one."

Despite Nelly's excellent connections as part of the first president's family, what emerges through her correspondence with Elizabeth covering nearly sixty years from 1794 to 1851 is the picture of Nelly's transformation from fortune's darling and young wife to that of the dissatisfied matron who wrote that she looked to the future without hope. Her letters to Elizabeth attest to the limitations imposed on even the most privileged eighteenth- and nineteenth-century American women.

Carol Bleser
October 1990

Eleanor Parke Custis Lewis (1779–1852) was in many ways the quintessential Virginia lady, emblematic of the southern planter class. But her experiences as a girl and young woman transcended those of most southern women: being adopted by George Washington, her grandmother's husband, gave her very unusual advantages—a thorough education, an extended residence in New York and Philadelphia during Washington's presidency, and an intimate acquaintance with the leaders of the early republic. Her later disappointment with her life shows poignantly the ultimate limitation of opportunities for even the most privileged eighteenth- and nineteenth-century American women.

These letters, written by Nelly Custis Lewis to her girlhood friend Elizabeth Bordley Gibson form a sizeable, largely intact collection, spanning nearly a lifetime. They are generally both lengthy and unguarded, revealing the myriad details of a long life; they are an excellent source for the study of southern social history. Housed in the library at Mount Vernon, the 189 letters cover nearly sixty years. They begin in 1794 when Nelly was a flighty schoolgirl of fifteen and continue through 1851, a few months before her death, when she was seventy-two, incapacitated and partially paralyzed by a stroke. Apparently Elizabeth saved almost every letter that Nelly wrote to her; only a few that are mentioned in other letters appear to be missing. The letters remained in the hands of family members until their sale to Mount Vernon in 1951.

By blood or marriage, Nelly was related to half the tidewater aristocracy of Virginia and Maryland—Parkes, Custises, Dandridges, Calverts, Burwells, Lewises, Carters, Robinsons, Randolphs, Lees, Fitzhughs, Washingtons. These letters bring to life the web of family connections and shared concerns of southern planters. Births and deaths, marriages (happy and unhappy), the rearing and education of children, family dynamics, the omnipresence of illness, the role of women in nursing the family, neighborhood scandals, propriety and religion, family tragedies, the rhythms of the agricultural year, weather, household concerns, slavery, mourning customs, political views and the use of influence, fashion, social events, travel, the deep friendships among women—all are illuminated here. Emotional openness and a degree of introspection mark the letters.

As part of the first president's family, Nelly was something of an American celebrity, almost a little princess. Because of that position, her visiting list in middle age read like a Who's Who of the Revolution and early republic. She valued and maintained friendships with members of the older generation who had been aides, friends, secretaries, and political allies of Washington.

Like others of her class in the nineteenth century, she looked back to those early days as purer and finer than the present. One of the most telling series of letters encompasses the 1824–25 return of Lafayette to America. His visit occasioned hysterical adulation from the American public: for a year, Nelly's attention was focused on being with Lafayette. To her, he was a living link to Washington and the hallowed past—the days of her own reflected importance.

Though not intensely interested in politics, Nelly often commented on current events: the various manifestations of the French revolution, Jackson's 1824 electoral defeat, the scandal made of his marriage by political enemies, the nullification controversy, the colonization movement and abolitionist debate, the Mexican War, and more. She knew all the presidents of her lifetime, but was on good terms only with Andrew Jackson and Zachary Taylor. She had a considerable acquaintance among politicians, the military, and foreign diplomats and visitors, about whom she frequently commented at some length.

The introduction to Nelly Custis Lewis's letters is a brief account of her life and her views. Intended for the general reader, the introduction is not footnoted though all sources used may be found in the bibliography. There are 189 extant letters from Nelly, of which 119 are published here. They were selected to tell the story of her life as it unfolded. The criteria used for inclusion of a letter were: inherent interest; illumination of social, intellectual, political, or familial matters; maintenance of chronological balance; and continuation of a particular story line. Annotation of the letters is spare; standard reference works—biographical directories, encyclopedias, and dictionaries—are not cited.

A superior education included extensive lessons in penmanship, but Nelly was never a credit to her teachers. As a girl, she wrote fairly legibly, but with none of the style which characterized Elizabeth's hand. As a woman, her handwriting deteriorated drastically, becoming a difficult-to-decipher scrawl for which she frequently apologized. In general, the transcription of these letters is literal. Spelling, capitalization, and punctuation have been retained as written with the following exceptions: each sentence begins with a capital letter and ends with a period, and raised letters are brought down to the line with a period.

To save paper and postage, Nelly seldom indented paragraphs but wrote from edge to edge of the paper and frequently crosshatched the pages—that is, after writing a page, she turned the paper and wrote across her lines perpendicularly. For the convenience of the reader, paragraphing that is implicit in the text is rendered according to modern conventions. Square brackets indicate editorial intervention: to provide missing datelines and places (derived from the cover of the letter or from internal evidence), to supply words where the text is torn or illegible, to expand abbreviations, to translate foreign phrases, or to define period slang.

Acknowledgments

Mr. and Mrs. Richard C. Plater, Jr., of Acadia Plantation in Thibodaux, Louisiana, introduced me to the Custises. Their donation of the Butler Family Papers to the Historic New Orleans Collection included Eleanor Custis Lewis's housekeeping book, which I edited for publication. Mr. Plater is a direct descendant of Nelly Custis; both Mr. and Mrs. Plater are longtime supporters of historic research and preservation. Their sympathetic interest in my work on the Custis family has always been very important to me.

Buddy Frazar, for many years director of the Historic New Orleans Collection, shepherded me through the transition from teacher to editor and encouraged me to write social history. Like all those touched by Buddy's extraordinary gift for friendship, I treasure the memory of the years spent under his leadership.

Working at Mount Vernon is like going home. Neil Horstman, the director, and his staff have gone to great lengths to be helpful. Their cooperation has been essential to the completion of this book. John P. Riley, assistant librarian/archivist, never grew impatient, even at the hundredth telephone call to check a transcription or a date. He is delightful to work with, as is Christine Meadows, curator, who has shared her perceptive understanding of the Washington family, the fruit of a lifetime's career at Mount Vernon. Both of them were kind enough to read the manuscript; their careful comments helped me to avoid egregious errors and to clarify the complexities of Nelly's adoption. Ellen McCallister Clark, Mount Vernon's former librarian, was most helpful in the early stages of work on Nelly's letters.

When I first visited Woodlawn in 1981, Margaret Davis was curator. Our friendship—professional and personal—has grown through the years. Though she has retired, Margaret's interest in Nelly is as consuming as ever, and the manuscript benefited from her close reading. Anne Huber Gorham, the present curator at Woodlawn, has given invaluable assistance, from fact checking to arranging for illustrations. Linda Cunningham Goldstein, acting director, has been very supportive, and former curator Kathleen Huftalen was also helpful during her tenure. Barbara Martin, curator at the National Trust for Historic Preservation, who is doing the furnishing plan for Woodlawn, provided useful information about the Lewis household.

In tracing Nelly's family and friends in Virginia, Maryland, the District of Columbia, Pennsylvania, New York, Louisiana, and South Carolina, I have had the pleasure of working with researchers who know the past as intimately as the present. Constraints on time and travel have meant that much of this research was done by telephone or mail. Many people have gone to a great deal of trouble in assisting me with long-distance research, sending piles of photocopies to meet the most pressing deadlines. Sara B. Bearss, associate editor at the Virginia Historical Society and biographer of George Washington Parke Custis, has guided me through the convoluted byways of Virginia family relationships. Jeffrey A. Cohen, associate editor, Benjamin H. Latrobe Papers, helped with architectural and geographical questions about Philadelphia and did a tedious newspaper search for me. T. Michael Miller, research historian at Lloyd House in Alexandria, knows more and has written more about Alexandria than anyone else; he has been very generous about sharing that knowledge. Eleanor C. Preston, curator of Tudor Place, searched through boxes of uncatalogued papers for Peter family information; she also took me on a thorough tour of the house and grounds, helping me to picture an important part of Nelly's world. Roy E. Goodman, reference librarian at the American Philosophical Society (surely one of the most pleasant libraries in America), helped considerably in identifying Philadelphia people and places and has answered many phone enquiries since. F. James Dallett, retired archivist of the University of Pennsylvania and a professional genealogist, is compiling an incomparable master file of information on French emigres; he was kind enough to provide considerable information—almost impossible to obtain otherwise—about Nelly's many French friends and acquaintances. Jane W. McWilliams, despite her own deadlines as director of research for the Legislative History Project at the Maryland State Archives, always managed to answer just one more query—at considerable length. Wylma Wates, retired senior archivist of the South Carolina Department of Archives and History, untangled the branches of the Izard/Manigault/Deas family for me. Celeste Walker, associate editor, The Adams Papers, unearthed Nelly's Boston acquaintances from the records of the Massachusetts Historical Society. On her own time, Lynn D. Adams, researcher at the Historic New Orleans Collection, used her finely honed research abilities to find Louisiana connections and to do general library research.

Very grateful thanks for research assistance are owed to Pamela D. Arceneaux and Jessica Travis, reference librarians, Historic New Orleans Collection; Trudi J. Abel, New Jersey Historical Society; Gladys E. Bolhouse, curator of manuscripts, Newport Historical Society; Margaret N. Burri, curator of collections, Historical Society of Washington, D.C.; Nancy Davis, director, The Octagon; Patricia Kahle, assistant director, Shadows-on-the-Teche; Jon Kukla, curator of collections, Historic New Orleans Collection; Charles H. Lesser, senior historian, South Carolina Department of Archives and History; Henry G. McCall, New Orleans banker and descendant of Nelly's friends, the McCall family of Philadelphia; Tamara Moser Melia, fleet liaison, and Christine Hughes, historian, Naval Historical Center; Richard Newman, publications officer, New York Public Library; Stacia G. Norman, curator, Kenmore Association; Linda Stanley, manuscripts archivist, Dan Rolph, genealogist, Ellen Slack, manuscripts and archives librarian, and Peggy Suckle, research assistant, of the Historical Society of Pennsylvania, a genealogical treasure house; Mariam Touba, reference librarian, New-York Historical Society; Sandra Gioia Treadway, senior editor, Virginia State Library; Dorothy Twohig, associate editor, Papers of George Washington; Lawrence E. Walker of Cincinnati, historian by avocation; and the Howard-Tilton Library of Tulane University.

Most of the illustrations in this volume are from Woodlawn, Mount Vernon, and Kenmore. For assistance in arranging for additional illustrations, I would like to acknowledge the following: Julie Cline, Washington and Lee University; Jennifer F. Goldsborough, chief curator, Maryland Historical Society; Melanie F. Harwood, senior registrar, Baltimore Museum of Art; Bryden B. Hyde of Baltimore, a collateral descendant of Elizabeth Bordley Gibson; Melissa Marsh, acting collections manager, National Trust for Historic Preservation; Deborah L. Sisum, deputy keeper, Catalog of American Portraits, National Portrait Gallery; Jo Anne Triplett, assistant to the coordinator, Inventory of American Paintings, Research and Scholars Center, National Museum of American Art.

The title of this book was originally used by the late Donald Jackson, editor of the Papers of George Washington, in an article for *American Heritage*. Though I disagree with his conclusions about Nelly, I am grateful for the very descriptive title.

Working at the Historic New Orleans Collection, with its fine collections and talented staff, helps provide the stimulus to do research and to write. I am very appreciative of the consideration given me by the board and the director in arranging an extended research trip to Mount Vernon.

I have benefited a great deal from the editorial suggestions of Carol Bleser, general editor of this series, and of Warren Slesinger, acquisitions manager, University of South Carolina Press. It has been a pleasure working with them.

I offer grateful thanks to my friends for their support: to my sisters Melissa and Jane Brady, to Janice Richolson for a place to stay in Virginia, to Dee Manning for house sitting during my frequent absences, and to the members of the Association of American Georges—Lynn and Dave Adams, Lou and Don Hoffman, Rosanne and Charlie Mackie, Martha Anne Swayze and John Treen, and Peggy and Howard Estes.

Eleanor Parke Custis Lewis

GRANDPARENTS ——————————————

Martha Dandridge (1731–1802) married

1) 1749 Daniel Parke Custis (1711–1757)

        John Parke (Jacky) (1754–1781)
        Martha Parke (Patsy) (1755–1773)

2) 1759 George Washington (1732–1799)

PARENTS ——————————————

Eleanor Calvert (Nelly) (c.1757–1811) married

1) 1774 John Parke Custis (Jacky) (1754–1781)

        Elizabeth Parke (Eliza) (1776–1832)
        Martha Parke (Patty) (1777–1854)
        Eleanor Parke (Nelly) (1779–1852)
        George Washington Parke (Wash)
          (1781–1857)

2) 1783 Dr. David Stuart (1753–c.1814)

        Ann (Nancy) (b.1784)
        Sarah (Sally) (b. 1785)
        Arianne (b. 1789)
        William Shalto (b. 1792)
        Charles Calvert (b. 1794)
        Eleanor (b. 1797)
        Rosalie Eugenia (b. 1802)

Elizabeth Parke Custis (Eliza) (1776–1832) married

1796   Thomas Law (1756–1834), divorced 1811

        Eliza (1797–1822)

Martha Parke Custis (Patty) (1777–1854) married

1795   Thomas Peter (1769–1834)

        Martha Elizabeth Eleanor (1796–1800)
        Columbia Washington (1797–1820)
        John Parke Custis (1799–1848)
        George Washington (1801–1877)
        America Pinckney (Mec) (1803–1842)
        Britannia Wellington (Brit) (1815–1911)

Eleanor Parke Custis (Nelly) (1779–1852) married

1799   Lawrence Lewis (1767–1839)

        Frances Parke (1799–1875)
        Martha Betty (1801–1802)
        Lawrence Fielding (1802)
        Lorenzo (1803–1847)
        Eleanor Agnes Freire (Agnes) (1805–1820)
        Fielding Augustine (1807–1809)
        George Washington Custis (1810–1811)
        Mary Eliza Angela (Angela) (1813–1839)

George Washington Parke Custis (1781–1857) married

1804   Mary Lee Fitzhugh (1788–1853)

        Mary Anna Randolph (1808–1873)

Eliza Law (1797–1822) married

1817   Lloyd Nicholas Rogers (c. 1787–1860)

        3 children

America Pinckney Peter (Mec) (1803–1842) married

1826   William George Williams (c. 1801–1846)

Martha Custis (1827–1899)
4 other children

Britannia Wellington Peter (Brit) (1815–1911)
married

1842   Beverly Kennon (1793–1844)

Martha Custis (1843–1886)

Frances Parke Lewis (1799–1875) married

1826   Edward George Washington Butler
(1800–1888)

Edward George Washington, Jr.
(1826–1827)
Edward George Washington, Jr. (Sonny)
(1829–1861)
Eleanor Angela Isabella (Sissy)
(1832–1866)
Caroline Swanwick (Caro) (1834–1876)
Lawrence Lewis (1837–1898)

Lorenzo Lewis (1803–1847) married

1827   Esther Maria Coxe (1804–1885)

George Washington (Wassy) (1829–1885)
John Redman Coxe (1834–1898)
Lawrence Fielding (twin, 1834–1857)
Edward Parke Custis (1837–1899)
Charles Conrad (1839–1859)
Henry Llewellyn Daingerfield (1843–1893)

Mary Eliza Angela Lewis (Angela) (1813–1839)
married

1835   Charles Magill Conrad (1804–1878)

Angela Lewis (1836–1837)
Charles Angelo Lewis (1837–1892)
Lawrence Lewis (Lewis) (1839–1883)

Mary Anna Randolph Custis (1808–1873) married

1831   Robert Edward Lee (1807–1870)

7 children

Elizabeth Bordley Gibson

PARENTS ————————————————————————————————

John Beale Bordley (1727–1804) married

1) 1751 Margaret Chew (d. 1773)

Thomas (b. 1755, d. at school)
Matthias (b. 1757)
Henrietta Maria (b. 1762)
John (b. 1764)

2) 1776 Sarah Fishbourne Mifflin (1733–1816)
Elizabeth (1777–1863)

Sarah Fishbourne had married

1) 1758 John Mifflin (1714 or 1715–1759)

John Fishbourne (1759–1813)

FIRST GENERATION ————————————————————————

Matthias Bordley (b. 1757)

1799 married Susan Heath

John Beale (1800–1882)
12 other children

Henrietta Maria (b. 1762)

1781 married David Ross

several children

John Fishbourne Mifflin (1759–1813) married

1788 Clementina Ross (1769–1848)

Sarah (1789–1872)
Elizabeth (1797–1885)
4 other children

Elizabeth Bordley (1777–1863) married

1817 James Gibson (1769–1856)

no children

George Washington's Beautiful Nelly

Introduction

Recalling "the dear scenes of our youth . . . where the *Sun always appears to shine* as it did in our hearts in those happy days," Eleanor Custis Lewis wrote, "M & I used to sit up until 2 oclock generally trying to write a novel in *letters*. She writes the sentiments, I the witty, very *poor* stuff I must acknowledge."

Rather than that youthful novel, Nelly unintentionally wrote her own life in letters. For nearly sixty years, beginning as a young girl and continuing until shortly before her death, she corresponded with a friend, Elizabeth Bordley (later Gibson). In frank and intimate detail, nearly two hundred of Nelly's letters—carefully preserved by Elizabeth and now at Mount Vernon—reveal her life with the immediacy of a diary.

Eleanor Parke Custis, Martha Washington's granddaughter, was born into the planter elite of the upper South, a descendant of the Custis, Parke, and Dandridge families of tidewater Virginia and of the influential Calverts of Maryland. Nelly's father, John Parke Custis, called Jacky, was Martha Washington's son by her first marriage. An impetuous and romantic young man, Jacky married the even younger Eleanor Calvert; they had four small children by the time of his death.

George Washington was the central figure in the lives of all the Custises. He had been a careful stepfather to his wife's two children, but both had died by 1781. For the four grandchildren, descending in age from six to infancy, Washington at first attempted unsuccessfully to convince Martha Washington's brother to serve as guardian. Then, as the Revolution neared an end and the Washingtons faced the prospect of returning to a childless home, they decided instead to adopt the two younger grandchildren.

So they reached an agreement with Jacky's young widow: they would adopt Nelly (b. 1779) and George Washington Parke Custis (b. 1781), called Wash, and rear them as their own. There were no formal legal proceedings, but the adoption was considered binding by the family. The elder daughters, Elizabeth Parke

Custis (b. 1776) and Martha Parke Custis (b. 1777), remained with their mother.

For the Washingtons and for Eleanor Calvert Custis, the children's mother, many considerations, emotional and practical, must have determined this complex decision—Martha Washington's love of children, the Washingtons' childlessness, the fondness of the two women for each other, the perceived need of a little boy for masculine authority, the more deeply rooted attachment of the older girls for their mother. Perhaps the decisive factor was that, since birth, Nelly and Wash had lived largely at Mount Vernon, often in the care of an overseer's wife, because their mother was so ill after their births.

Fostering—taking in the orphaned children of relatives or friends—was a commonplace of domestic life in the early days of the republic, the result of high birth and death rates. Even when one parent survived, children were often parceled out because the financial or emotional burden was too great for one parent alone. Very frequently, too, couples with several children allowed a childless relative to adopt one of their children, particularly a twin. In many cases adopted children were reared in more privileged conditions than the sisters and brothers who stayed with their parents. Adoption was not a secret: comparisons between the children's circumstances were obviously made.

Commonplace as such adoptions were, they still exacted a psychic toll. Regret and envy in varying degrees were experienced by all the children, those who stayed with their parents and those who were adopted. The older Custis girls—Eliza and Patty—lived on an isolated plantation "in the windings of a forest obscured" (Nelly's words) under the guardianship of a dour stepfather and a perpetually pregnant mother. After her remarriage in 1783 to Dr. David Stuart, Eleanor Calvert Custis Stuart produced a seemingly endless stream of half-sisters and brothers. In her two marriages, she gave birth to at least twenty children; only eleven survived. In contrast, Nelly and Wash were cosseted by devoted grandparents who gave them every advantage of education and society. They enjoyed the glamour and celebrity of being the adopted children of the most important man in America.

Relations between the Mount Vernon family and that at Hope Park, the Stuarts' home, were cordial. The Stuarts were welcome guests at Mount Vernon, the older Custis girls arrived there at regular intervals for long visits, and the younger children frequently visited their mother at Hope Park.

Though Nelly was fond of her mother in a rather conventional manner, the adoption, perhaps inevitably, created an emotional distance between them. In 1795, when compelled by Martha Washington to spend the winter with her mother, Nelly was aghast—and spent much of the time moping. Her overwhelming adult obsession with mother love seems a reflection of the severity of the subconscious wound she had suffered.

The focus of Nelly's deepest love and loyalty was the Washingtons. She revered her Grandpapa, whom she also referred to as "the General," as though there were only one in America. In return, he found his beautiful Nelly a constant joy. She doted on her Grandmama, the person who cherished her and was her emotional anchor. She wrote, "she has been more than a Mother to me. It is impossible to love any one, more than I love her."

Whatever her hidden insecurities, Nelly reveled in being a member of the president's family. She grew to womanhood during Washington's presidency: the little girl of ten became the polished belle of seventeen. The capital, at first in New York City, was soon moved to Philadelphia, the leading city of the nation. Commercially and intellectually bustling, Philadelphia had no real rival for preeminence; the city's leaders were rich, well-educated, sophisticated, very social, and much given to entertaining. The elegant lifestyles of such families as the Powels, Binghams, and Morrises attracted and engaged the presidential family—to the disapproval of republicans, who feared their conservative political influence.

Congressmen and government officials from throughout the nation gathered in Philadelphia to rule the new republic. Washington's Federalist political supporters—wealthy landowners, merchants, lawyers, Revolutionary officers—tended to be on social terms with the president and each other, forming what was sometimes called a "Republican Court." Visits and outings with the families of the nation's leaders were regular events for Martha Washington and the children.

More intriguing—especially to Nelly, who developed a lifetime affinity for foreign visitors—were the exotic (to American eyes) Europeans who lived in Philadelphia. French emigrés, both aristocrats and revolutionaries who had fled subsequent phases of the French Revolution, were attracted to the city, where there was a sizeable Gallic colony. European diplomats were on visiting terms with the Washingtons, and in some cases, enjoyed their friendship. Nelly was the special pet of two envoys' wives—Henrietta Liston of England and Agnes Freire of Portugal.

Ever after, Nelly looked back on the years in Philadelphia as the golden period of her life, the passing of which she bitterly regretted. Philadelphia in the early national period was an exciting and dynamic city. More important, those were the days of her girlhood, before she took on the cares and disappointments of adult life. When she bemoaned the loss of Philadelphia, she was really mourning the loss of youth.

Though they enjoyed an active social life, the education of the Custis children was carefully attended to throughout the presidential years. Nelly was far better educated than most southern girls. From the time she was very small, George Washington had insisted that she, along with her brother, be well taught, arranging for his secretaries at Mount Vernon to double as tutors. In New York and Philadelphia, select young ladies' academies and private masters taught the basics as well as the frills—music, dancing, drawing, and foreign languages—for all of which she had a decided talent.

Manners and decorum, household management, home remedies, fashion and style, plain and fancy sewing, vocal and instrumental music, and proper religious observance—these were the stuff of life for a southern lady, and Martha Washington trained her granddaughter rigorously. Nelly's very conventional social attitudes as an adult were the result of her strict girlhood training.

Many members of the Washingtons' social circle had young daughters or granddaughters who became Nelly's friends. Several of these friendships were lifelong; her closest friend in Philadelphia was Elizabeth Bordley (b. 1777), to whom she wrote these letters. Elizabeth was the daughter of John Beale Bordley, one of Philadelphia's leading citizens. An eminent jurist and wealthy landowner with large holdings on the eastern shore of Maryland, Bordley also wrote important works on scientific agriculture. Washington's great interest in experimental farming drew the two men together, and the families became close during the presidential years.

Elizabeth had spent her early life on her father's estate at Wye Island, Maryland, where she was taught by her parents. When she was thirteen, the Bordleys moved to Philadelphia to a spacious red brick townhouse on Union Street close to the riverfront. Both newly resident in the city, Elizabeth and Nelly shared masters who taught the girls at the Bordleys' house and at the president's rented mansion on Market Street. Elizabeth was a little over a year older than Nelly, and they had a great deal in common. The child of a late second marriage for both her mother and her father, Elizabeth too was being reared by elderly parents: the Bordleys were much of an age with the Washingtons. The only girls in old-fashioned, traditional households, they were expected to be dutiful companions to their mothers.

Very few eighteenth- or nineteenth-century American lives can be told solely in terms of individuals. Rather, the subject, particularly a woman, should be seen as enmeshed in an immense spider web of family relationships. In becoming friends with each other, Nelly and Elizabeth committed themselves also to a concern for the many members of their respective families.

The full extent of an extended family is often obscured by the many different surnames of close relatives. This complexity of family relationships in early America was caused by frequent deaths and remarriages and very large families. Elizabeth's family illustrates such familial convolutions. She had two sets of adult half-siblings: two Bordley half-brothers and a half-sister, her father's children by his first marriage, and a half-brother named John Mifflin, her mother's son by her first marriage and stepbrother to the Bordleys; John Mifflin also had older half-brothers by *his* father's first marriage, who were the stepsons of his and Elizabeth's mother and reared by her, but who were not related to Elizabeth or the other Bordleys. From the Mifflin brothers to Elizabeth Bordley the ages of these interconnected siblings spanned some thirty-five years.

Numerous nieces, nephews, cousins, and in-laws added another layer of family: in-law relationships of women are especially difficult to detect because of women's married names. One of Elizabeth's important relationships was with the sisters of her sister-in-law, a relationship not immediately apparent.

These letters reflect the importance of the family network. Nelly and Elizabeth sent greetings and inquired at length about each other's families, exchanging news about the most tenuously related members. This was not mere politeness but a recognition of the centrality of family to both women.

Nelly, Elizabeth, and their other friends—daughters of prominent Federalists and wealthy Europeans—formed a tight little group. They giggled and chattered constantly—to the distraction of the Washingtons who were unused to the company of lively adolescent girls. Jokes, secrets, and fantasies illuminated their lives. They wrote poetry, sang, played musical instruments, and flirted with the young men of their social circle. A leader in their games and foolery, Nelly saw herself as harum scarum and "cracked brained."

As the girls reached their mid-teens they began attending assemblies and dances. Elizabeth, tall with a fine figure and a strong face, had several admirers. Slender Nelly with her masses of dark curls and large dark eyes was quite lovely. Her quick wit, vivacious manner, and willingness to dance the night away were much admired by the beaux of the day. Young men wrote poems extolling her beauty, but she was heart-whole at nearly eighteen when Washington relinquished the presidency at the end of his second term.

Back at Mount Vernon, though Nelly pined for her friends and the bustle of Philadelphia, the Washingtons' social life was not humdrum. George Washington had become a national icon— the object of interest and admiration at home and abroad. A pilgrimage to the home of the venerable statesman was *de rigueur* for visitors to the nation's capital. Former colleagues in arms, acquaintances, and those strangers who could scrape up an introduction came to Mount Vernon to pay their respects and frequently stayed for days. Generous Virginia hospitality called for their entertainment, sometimes to Washington's exasperation. Nelly, singing and playing the harpsichord, conversing amiably, helped to entertain her grandparents' guests. Visitors inevitably commented on her charm and beauty.

But it was time for a southern girl to settle down to the real business of her life: marriage. Nelly attended balls and parties in Alexandria and Georgetown where she met many eligible young men. Her popularity sent rumors flying of an imminent engagement, but no desirable suitor declared himself.

Marriage was a frequent subject in Nelly and Elizabeth's letters, as they quizzed each other about rumored fiances. Both young women were highly eligible—attractive, well-connected, and well-off. For all their lighthearted jokes about the desirability of the spinster's life, they clearly wanted to marry. A married woman's household authority and position in society were attractive; their elder sisters had married wealthy men and enjoyed elite social status.

For Elizabeth, though, family duty intervened. In 1799, her father, in his seventies, began to fail rapidly; he was no longer able to visit his beloved experimental farm. Elizabeth gradually withdrew from society, caring for her father until his death in 1804 and then nursing her mother through twelve years of increasing invalidism. Until she was thirty-nine, Elizabeth was closely tied to home and parents. Her life fell into a pattern of churchgoing and good works, with the mild amusement of quiet social gatherings with family and a few congenial friends.

The Washingtons, though, were still vigorous in their late sixties and wanted Nelly to marry. The unmarried woman in the South was the object of slightly scornful pity, a woman outside the natural order of things. A spinster could look forward to life in her father's house, followed by the protection of her brother or other male relative, at the beck and call of the mistress of the household. To remain unmarried was not a decision to take lightly. Nelly also had a strong maternal urge. She doted on her little nieces, writing tenderly and devotedly about them—"the sweet Toads." She was very anxious to set up her own nursery.

Propinquity provided an acceptable candidate for husband and father. In 1798 Washington invited his nephew, Lawrence Lewis, to join the Mount Vernon household as an unpaid secretary cum deputy host to the press of visitors.Twelve months after Lawrence's arrival, he and Nelly became engaged. Nelly, at least, seems to have been in love, delighted to be marrying a Virginia gentleman of high principles, so acceptable to the Washingtons. Lawrence, a widower twelve years Nelly's senior, had much to recommend him. As a family member, his honorable and serious character was known and respected; Washington may have felt that he would be a good balance for Nelly's flightiness, and a marriage within the family simplified inheritance.

Lawrence remains a shadowy figure without the verve and personality of his young fiancee. A brief early marriage had left neither children nor inheritance when his first wife died in childbirth. Though he had inherited some land and slaves from his father, he did not himself farm. Commissioned by Washington, he saw only brief peacetime military service, but (as was the custom of the day) he was styled "major" for the rest of his life.

Washington was concerned by Lawrence's lack of occupation: even though unattended by vice, idleness, he believed, was a disgrace in itself. This very idleness, however, made Lawrence amenable to Nelly's wish to remain at Mount Vernon. Closely tied to her Grandmama's apron strings, Nelly found any separation from her very painful. Martha Washington was extremely attached to Nelly, accustomed to her constant company; she had a lifelong habit of depending on the companionship of young married women in the Washington household—nieces and the wives of secretaries and aides.

Though the young couple had discussed living on Lawrence's

land in Frederick County, they soon decided to continue living indefinitely at Mount Vernon after their marriage. Lawrence would farm the land, part of the Mount Vernon estate, that would be Washington's legacy to Nelly, and they would begin building a house there.

Washington legally became Nelly's guardian in January 1799 so that he could authorize the license for her wedding. Nelly and Lawrence were married on Washington's birthday in 1799 and began the traditional round of visits to relatives and friends. Their journey was marred by Lawrence's falling prey to an eye inflammation; for four weeks he lay in bed in a darkened room. This was the first instance of a significant pattern in their marriage. Lawrence suffered from lengthy illnesses during which he retired to his bedroom for weeks at a time.

For the most part, however, their wedding trip was successful; Nelly enjoyed being feted by their many hosts although she missed her grandmother severely. On their return to Mount Vernon in the fall, she was happily pregnant, fond of her husband, and looking forward to a life that would be an extension, enriched by marriage, of her girlhood. After a week's labor, Nelly gave birth to a daughter, Frances Parke, in late November 1799. Shortly afterward the mainspring of life at Mount Vernon, George Washington, suddenly became ill and after a brief and hideous struggle, died on December 14, 1799.

Life was never the same. For Martha Washington the reason for existence had gone, and she became a shadow of the cheerful, efficient consort she had been. The Lewises remained with her, though they began work on their own house, Woodlawn, some three miles from Mount Vernon. Nelly was her grandmother's constant companion, helping her to cope with life without Washington; she gave birth to a second daughter, Martha Betty, who was her great-grandmother's delight. In 1802, Nelly was heavily pregnant again, when Martha Washington fell ill and died. At the same time, Nelly and both her daughters broke out with measles. They were very sick, and little Martha Betty died soon after Martha Washington.

Distraught at the double loss and still in very shaky health herself, Nelly faced an immediate, practical problem. George Washington had left his wife a life tenancy in Mount Vernon; on her death, it became the property of his nephew, Bushrod Washington. The Lewises had to vacate Mount Vernon, but the central block at Woodlawn, their new house, was still under construction, and even the two dependencies—story-and-a-half cottages—were not yet habitable. With their surviving daughter, they went to the home of Lawrence's sister, Betty Carter. There Nelly gave birth to a son who died shortly after birth.

Soon afterward, the Lewises moved to Woodlawn, living in one of the dependencies while construction continued. Two rooms up and two down: it was quite a comedown for George Washington's beautiful Nelly, accustomed to the elegant Morris mansion in Philadelphia and to gracious Mount Vernon.

This period of her life is difficult to document. The young woman struggling under the burden of heavy misfortunes had little time or heart for letter writing. Having been fortune's darling, Nelly found the litany of deaths and misfortunes following Washington's demise unbearable. She fell into a serious decline (the nineteenth-century term for depression); for months it was feared that she would not recover.

Gradually, however, Nelly emerged from the depths. In 1803 she gave birth to a son, Lorenzo. Agnes Freire, born in 1805, was named for her admired Portuguese friend. Around this time, the mansion was completed, and the family moved into the main house, a beautiful red Georgian brick, elegantly designed by William Thornton, one of the architects of the Capitol.

Nelly's correspondence with Elizabeth lapsed after her marriage in 1799; when she took it up again in 1804, the tone of her letters, her attitude toward life, indeed even her handwriting had altered dramatically. The happy young bride had become the dissatisfied matron: "I look back with sorrow, & to the future without hope." Lawrence Lewis, the husband she had believed would ensure her happiness, she now referred to as Mr. L., in a respectful, but dry tone; his frequent illnesses, stinginess, and opposition to her wishes figured largely in her letters. She no longer indulged her youthful passion for dancing. Frequent pregnancies and mourning for the infants who died were not conducive to that pleasure. No longer did she ride horseback, and she claimed with some exaggeration to have given up "music & painting, for pickling, preserving, & *puddings.*"

Nelly ran her large household to the exacting standards set by Martha Washington. Mirrors shone, chandeliers sparkled, mahogany glowed softly. Woodlawn was rich with antiques and keepsakes, many of them heirlooms from Mount Vernon. Guests—relatives, acquaintances from the capital, old friends of the Washingtons, military officers from the nearby fort—were welcomed graciously. Evenings were spent in music and conversation. Nelly set a notable table, serving elegant foods and imported wines. Though a staff of slaves did the work, to oversee the cleaning of such an establishment and to keep it supplied with both necessities and luxuries was an administrative job of no mean proportions.

Evidence of her attitude toward Woodlawn's slaves is fragmentary. Many southerners mentioned individual slaves regularly in letters and diaries and pondered the institution of slavery; this was not the case with Nelly. Very occasionally, she referred to female house servants, usually in the context of their domestic roles. Only one letter to Elizabeth gives an indication of her thinking about slavery in these early years. She contemplated taking a seamstress and nurse with her to Philadelphia, but did not delude herself that the slaves valued loyalty over freedom. She wrote, "There is no certainty of retaining them by wages, if they fancy they could be happier elsewhere." This did not appear to her a human problem, but one of management. Her solution was to leave the women in Virginia. Apparently, at this point she saw slavery as an inevitable feature of plantation life.

In later life, during the rising abolitionist ferment of the 1830s, she freely criticized both northern and southern zealots: "all this uproar creates discontent, & induces insurrection and murder." In principle, she believed in gradual emancipation for the "*dark* torments of our lives," but in fact did not free the Lewis slaves. Like many conservatives North and South, she subscribed to the idea of African colonization for "these ignorant people."

Besides the household, the health of the family and probably of the slaves was also her responsibility. In serious cases, a doctor was called; Nelly considered their Alexandria doctor, Henry Daingerfield, one of her best friends. She carried out his instructions explicitly, administering his prescriptions of cathartics, emetics, and mercury, and carefully nursing her children and husband when they were ill.

Less serious cases Nelly herself treated with home remedies, the secrets of which she collected from family, friends, and neighbors. Unlike the doctors' prescriptions, these remedies did no harm (not a small virtue in the days of heroic medicine) and frequently had curative or ameliorative powers. She served up medical advice in her letters—homely recipes for horehound syrup and slippery elm jelly—and sang the praises of her favorite cure-alls, Seidlitz powders (effervescing salts) and the leaves of the American poplar.

One cure she could never have enough of: travel. Change of air was, she believed, a sovereign remedy for whatever ailed her and her beloved children. She always longed to be elsewhere: if she were only in Philadelphia, Newport, Boston, Saratoga, White Sulphur Springs, or a hundred other places, she would be well and happy. From the lumbering coaches of her youth to the railroad cars of her old age, traveling assuaged her restlessness; she ventured forth, happy in the belief that things would be better somewhere else.

When at home without company, though, Nelly passed her time agreeably after her housekeeping duties were finished. She loved to read. Her favorite books were history, biography, and, of course, travel. Her artwork was her most constant resource. She did fine needlework, making all manner of things—fire screens, bookmarks, pincushions, purses—which she frequently gave as gifts to her friends and relatives; another artistic pleasure was painting on velvet, a fashionable diversion of the day.

Through the years, two more sons were born and died as toddlers. Her last child, Angela, born in 1813, survived to grow up. After the baby's birth, sexual relations between Nelly and Lawrence apparently ceased, although she was only thirty-four. From the time Angela was born until she married, she shared her mother's bed. Not surprisingly, Nelly, who had been regularly pregnant since her marriage, had no more children.

Certainly her attitude toward her husband had hardened. Although Nelly would never follow her sister Eliza's shocking course in leaving an uncongenial husband, the Lewises were temperamentally unsuited to each other. Nelly loved company, society, gaiety, travel, gossip, the arts, music, foreign languages. Lawrence, twelve years older than his wife, was quiet and retiring. He was irritated by her enthusiasms and found it nonsensical that she should study velvet painting or Spanish as an adult. His poor health contributed to the couple's differences. He suffered from "flying gout," a mysterious ailment that painfully attacked various parts of his body, as well as recurring eye problems; during his lengthy confinements he depended frequently on opium pills. In a letter of 1823 Nelly censured the marriage of a young woman to an older man, probably thinking of the problems of her own marriage.

Perhaps Lawrence's greatest failing in Nelly's eyes was that he did not measure up to George Washington. He was a private man without any ambition to figure largely in the world. Both his health and his nature precluded his taking a major role in the affairs of the day.

Nelly wrote in another context: "a woman's consequence depends so much on the respectability of her Husband." In her middle years, her disappointment with her life (read: her husband) was acute. Her education, family connections, and intelligence fitted her for public service, but her sex precluded that ambition. For a woman as socially conservative as she, a career was impossible. She despised—perhaps with a touch of envy—social rebels like Fanny Wright who flouted society's expectations for women. The only thinkable role to her was helpmeet to her husband. His success in life would determine hers.

Had she married a man who was active in public affairs, her life would not have been so shadowed by regret. Furthering her husband's career, as for many political wives, might have become, in effect, her own career. As the years passed, she found the life of a planter's wife increasingly dull; she pined for the days when George Washington was at the center of national discourse, and she had felt a reflected importance. Frustrated in her ambitions, she blamed Lawrence for not being other than he was. Dissension between them was sharp, but despite their incompatibility, the Lewises maintained a solid public facade. Both mindful of social appearances and devoted to their children, they put a good face on things.

Nelly's children were her constant preoccupation. As she wrote—with decided insensitivity—to the childless Elizabeth, "*you cannot conceive* a Mothers trials." She constantly worried about their health and happiness. Her terrors about their survival might seem obsessive, but life was chancy in nineteenth-century America: she buried seven of her eight children; only her oldest daughter outlived her.

To educate her children as well as she and her brother had been was her desire, but her situation was quite different from the Washingtons'. The Lewises' exchequer did not run to resident tutors. Nelly taught the children herself when they were small and did well as a teacher. As they reached adolescence, she longed to set up housekeeping in Philadelphia and to have the children attend school as day students. Lawrence opposed that plan, and

instead they sent the older children to boarding schools in Philadelphia.

There in 1814, when Nelly brought Parke to Madame Grelaud's select boarding academy, she and Elizabeth renewed their
friendship, which had weakened over the past fifteen years. Their
correspondence had become desultory as the circumstances of
their lives had diverged so widely. Now, meeting again after the
years of separation, they found that their "Hearts [were] the
same that they formerly were." They picked up the loosened
strands of friendship, and that friendship ended only with Nelly's
death.

While Parke was at school, Elizabeth's elderly mother died.
The following year, in 1817, Elizabeth married James Gibson, a
middle-aged attorney from a respected family. Nelly stayed with
the Gibsons at their home on Walnut Street during her visits to
Philadelphia, never frequent enough to suit her. Elizabeth served
as an unofficial godmother to Parke, Lorenzo, and Agnes Lewis in
their Philadelphia school days.

The death of fifteen-year-old Agnes at Madame Grelaud's—
her daily sinking chronicled in a series of hastily scrawled
notes—gave Nelly a horror of letting her children spend time
away from her. Angela, the adored baby of the family, was not
sent away to school; instead she and Nelly moved to a small house
in Alexandria during the school year.

Once they were educated, proper marriages for her children
became her principal concern. For her elder daughter Parke,
Nelly desired a wealthy, socially prominent husband, not a south-
erner, marriage to whom—paradoxically—would entail no separation from her mother. Parke was unable—or perhaps unwilling—to charm one of the sprigs of the Philadelphia elite her
mother found so desirable. Elizabeth showed a sensible realism
about Nelly's daydreams for her daughter, and Nelly sometimes
bridled at her comments.

Though Parke was courted by men both worthy and successful—an army officer, a senator, a wealthy merchant—she
remained stubbornly unattached until she met Lieutenant Edward George Washington Butler, a former ward of Andrew Jackson and aide-de-camp to General Edmund Pendleton Gaines. The
young lieutenant was handsome, hot-tempered (a trait that made
his relations with his mother-in-law eventually disastrous), and
financially dependent on his salary. His lack of an independent

fortune concerned both the Lewises, and Nelly was further opposed to the match because marriage to a serving officer would mean continual separations from her daughter. The young couple prevailed, though, and Parke became an army wife in 1826.

Lorenzo, with the independence enjoyed by men, was able to conduct his own affairs with less maternal interference. He pursued a career of enjoyable flirtations in Philadelphia, Washington, and Alexandria, indulging in one ill-advised engagement which was soon broken off. The year after his sister's marriage, he married the very down-to-earth Esther Maria Coxe, daughter of a prominent Philadelphia doctor.

The newlyweds came to make their home at Woodlawn, their bedroom furnished by Esther—an old Philadelphia custom. Lorenzo increasingly took over the management of the land from his father, but the heyday of healthy profits from tidewater plantations such as Woodlawn and Mount Vernon was rapidly ending. Audley, a second Lewis plantation in western Virginia, became the main source of income for the family.

Money—always a source of conflict between Nelly and Lawrence—became a central issue in the late 1820s. A planter because of his wife's inherited land, Lawrence never emulated George Washington's success in farming. Neither healthy nor energetic, he had not managed the plantation as effectively as possible in the good days. Hard times had now come. Soil exhaustion, increased production costs, rising competition from the west, the decline of Alexandria as a port—all contributed to the Lewises' financial woes.

The combination of a lifetime's expensive habits and an increasingly pinched purse did not sit well with Nelly in middle age. Her belief that there should always be enough money for an elegant lifestyle and an expansive generosity was typical of the Virginia planter class. She resisted practicing unpleasant habits of economy, and Lawrence was incensed by her lack of frugality. They blamed each other for improvidence and selfishness.

The 1830s began the dissolution of their life at Woodlawn. Lorenzo and his growing family spent most of their time at Audley as revenues from Woodlawn dropped steadily. Edward Butler resigned his commission (opportunities for promotion were slim in peacetime) and bought a sugar plantation in Iberville Parish, Louisiana. Most of the Woodlawn slaves were divided among the Lewis children as part of their inheritance.

Nelly and Lawrence made extended visits to the Butlers at

Dunboyne, their plantation, and for a time seriously considered buying land and moving to Louisiana themselves. Though they decided against the move, on one of their visits Angela met Charles Magill Conrad, an ambitious New Orleans attorney from a planter family. Despite Nelly's intense dislike of Louisiana, she was charmed by the young man. Angela and Charles married in 1835, and Nelly moved with the newlyweds to New Orleans. Her elderly husband visited Louisiana, but he lived primarily in Virginia at Audley and at Woodlawn, which was becoming increasingly neglected as the family scattered. The Lewises did not publicly separate, but they were clearly happier spending most of their time apart.

In 1839, while Nelly was visiting in Virginia, Angela died following childbirth. Nelly was distraught: she had made Angela and her family the focus of her love. Two months later, Lawrence, who, despite a lifetime of ill health had survived to seventy-two, also died. A brief attempt to live with the Butlers ended with a thunderous quarrel and her hurried departure by steamboat. She never returned to Dunboyne and hated Edward Butler for the rest of her life; Parke she considered a martyr to his selfishness and bad temper.

Nelly then went to live at Audley with Lorenzo and Esther and their sons. Plantation society in the Shenandoah Valley was pleasant; relatives and friends visited regularly, particularly her favorite niece, Mary (Mrs. Robert E.) Lee. She was a doting grandmother, boasting proudly of her twelve grandchildren. Three of the Butler children came east to school—the girls to Virginia, the eldest son to South Carolina—and they visited at Audley. Closest to her heart were the Conrad boys, Angela's sons, Charley and Lewis. They lived with her at Audley for awhile after their mother's death and again while their father traveled abroad. Throughout the remainder of her life, they came to Audley for extended stays. Charles Conrad, who never remarried, became a successful politician, serving in Congress and in Fillmore's cabinet; he remained his mother-in-law's fast friend.

For the last several years of Nelly's life, she and Elizabeth did not meet, but the old friends continued to write faithfully. Elizabeth and James Gibson, now retired, lived quietly, the mainstays of their many nieces and nephews and of the Episcopal church. Elizabeth suffered from frequent headaches and was almost totally deaf.

Nelly, too, suffered from the complaints of old age—rheumatism and deafness—but her health was generally good. With glasses, she could see quite well, and she passed many hours with needlework and reading. Travel, though not very frequent, continued to be a delight.

By no means a politically astute woman, she took a spectator's interest in politics, commenting from a personal and social, rather than an intellectual, perspective. Thomas Jefferson and James Monroe—political opponents of Washington—she had despised. She had also disliked both the Adamses. Andrew Jackson she had supported and admired, but the emergence of Zachary Taylor into national politics provided, in her opinion, a worthy successor to Washington. For the first time in years, she felt that she was given proper respect by the occupant of the White House.

Her old age was deeply saddened by the sale of Woodlawn in 1846, by that time fallen into considerable disarray, and the death of her son Lorenzo in 1847. Her only surviving child, Parke, was far away in Louisiana and was unable to come to Audley for the extended visit that her mother craved.

Nelly's consolation for all the disappointments and sorrows of her life was religion. Brought up by her grandmother as a devout Episcopalian, she was genuinely and unselfconsciously religious all her life. She frequently expressed a "proper sense of my obligations to the giver of all good, for his unmerited favours." When she suffered a stroke in 1850, she wrote: "I felt that great as was my trial I had often *deserved greater*, & that it might have been far worse."

For the last two years of her life, she was partially paralyzed and spent much of each day in a wheeled chair. She still took pleasure in reading, correspondence, and visits. In her letters to Elizabeth she harked back constantly to their youth, referring often to Andrew Allen, the young beau whom she might have loved. She wrote of the happiness of those shining days, musing wistfully: "how like a magic lantern now appear to me the years & the persons I once knew so well."

Chapter One

The President's Daughter
1794–1799

" . . . those Beloved Parents [George and Martha Washington] whom I
loved with so much devotion, to whose unceasing tenderness I was
indebted for every good I possess'd . . . "

Germantown,[1] September 8th [1794]

My Dearest Elizabeth

Our friend Susan Randolph[2] came to see me yesterday and as
she told me, she intended writing to you today, I could not resist
this opportunity of giving you a few lines; allthough, to tell you
the truth I am rather jealous of your writing to her, & not me. I
should have wrote to you long before this, but did not know of an
opportunity. I have not seen our dear Elizabeth[3] since I left Philadelphia for Morrisville. I am very anxious to see her. She is at
Landsdown[4] & very well I have heard. I hope soon to see her. I can

---

1. In 1794 frontiersmen defied the authority of the government to tax the whiskey they made. Rather than summering as usual at Mount Vernon, Washington stayed in the capitol to put down this Whiskey Rebellion. The family,
however, moved to a rented house in Germantown, a resort village a few
miles northwest of Philadelphia, because Washington feared a repetition of
the previous summer's devastating yellow fever epidemic in the city. George
Washington, *The Diaries of George Washington*, ed. Donald Jackson and Dorothy Twohig, 6 vols. (Charlottesville, 1976–79), 5:182, hereafter cited as
GWD; Elswyth Thane, *Potomac Squire* (Mount Vernon, 1963), 260–61;
James T. Flexner, *George Washington*, 4 vols. (Boston, 1965–69), 4:160–71.
2. Susan Beverly Randolph (b. 1782), Elizabeth Bordley's cousin, was the
daughter of Elizabeth Nicholas Randolph and Edmund Randolph (1753–
1813), Washington's secretary of state 1794–95. GWD, 5:41.
3. Elizabeth Allen (b. after 1768), was the daughter of former Attorney General of Pennsylvania Andrew Allen and Sarah Coxe Allen, both members
of prominent Philadelphia families. Edward F. Delancey, "Chief Justice
William Allen," *Pennsylvania Magazine of History and Biography* 1 (1877):
202–211.
4. Lansdowne was the country house of John Penn (1729–1795), last proprie-
tary governor of Pennsylvania. At this time, he was living in political retirement on the estate with his wife Ann Allen Penn, Elizabeth Allen's aunt.
GWD, 5:158, 160.

not tell how I have supported the absence of my two dear friends. If it had not been for the hope of seeing them, I fear it would have been too much for me.

I have learnt to ride on horseback my dear; & am very much delighted with it I assure you. I have rode thrice—not the least fear beleive me. I have some intention of riding this afternoon. It is very fine weather for it. I wish you were here to go with me. I am sure I need not tell you how happy it would make me. I [am] very much pleased with Germantown, & have no desire to quit it for Philadelphia. However I beleive we shall return the last of this month. I spent ten days very agreeably at Morrisville & had the honour & glory of teaching our pretty green pet to sing Pauvre Madelon. You may guess what kind it was. A master peice of thorough Base[5] (in music spelt Bass, but I thought Base would give you a better idea of his harmonious voice) he is vastly improved I assure you—more than ever like what we compared him too. In Germantown we have a most plentifull scarcity of Beaux— only a few pinks & carnations [exquisites, members of the elite]. My dearest Elizabeth breakfast is ready & I must now take leave of you for this time.

Grandmama the President & E P C desire their compliments to Mr Mrs and Miss Bordley.

Your's most sincerely.
Eleanor Parke Custis

My love to dear little Snipe[6] I wish very much to see her. I forgot to tell you the name of my nag—it is Rozinante—myself harum scarum sans soucie [carefree scatterbrain]. We propose haveing a grand cavalcade when we go to P[hiladelphia]—You Venus—E P A—S B R and E P C—the three graces—to the exclusion of everyone else—such as cupid's, Adonis's and green monkey's.

Excuse this terrible writing.

---

5. Thorough Bass, usually called continuo, is an instrumental part for a keyboard instrument. It consists of a succession of bass notes with numerals and other marks placed under each note according to a system that indicates the required chords, but leaves the actual arrangement of notes in each chord to be filled in by the player. Judith S. Britt, *Nothing More Agreeable: Music in George Washington's Family* (Mount Vernon, Va., 1984), 22–23.
6. Probably Sarah Mifflin (1789–1872), Elizabeth Bordley's niece. John H. Merrill, *Memoranda Relating to the Mifflin Family* (Philadelphia, 1890), 56.

[Philadelphia 1794?]

Dear Elizabeth

Your charming note which I received yesterday gave me infinite pleasure. I am afraid there was some fairy in the business as I never received the cake. However I am as much obliged to you for your attention to me as if I had received it. I send you the note for our dear Elizabeth. I am very much obliged to my dear friend for furnishing me with an opportunity of writing to her. I got up this morning at a quarter before five—and sat myself soberly down to get a long Italian lesson—and after that took pen in hand to write to you good ladies. I shall be very happy to go to Landsdown with Mrs Bordley whenever it is agreeable to her.

Grandmama's compliments, and my respects to her if you please.

Here I remain my Dear Elizabeth your grave and affectionate friend

Eleanor Parke Custis
Votre tres humble servante.

———————— ❦ ————————

Mount Vernon October 13 1795

My Dear Elizabeth,

You must have been accusing me of neglect, before this time, in not answering your very acceptable, entertaining, & instructive letter, & really appearances are very much against me, however as it is the custom for criminals to be heard before they are condemned, you must hear (or rather see) my defence before you pass judgement. Well then—I did not receive your letter untill more than a month after you wrote it. & probably should never have received it had I not seen it advertised in the Alexandria paper as a dead letter. Upon this, I immediately sent, & got it. I was very near dubbing you a lazy girl before I received your letter, but soon acquitted you, when I cast my eye upon the date & found you were not in fault. Soon after this I went with Mama to Hope Park[7] (her place of residence) and there—in the windings of a forest obscured—I staid ten days; since I came back I have often intended writing but something or other has allways prevented

me. However I determined to do it today as my Dearest Grandmama sets off for Philadelphia tomorrow.

You will no doubt be surprised, (and I flatter myself much
disappointed) when you expect to see me, to receive this letter. I
take up my residence for this winter in Virginia—& the greatest
part of it, at Hope Park. No one beleived I should be left behind.
However it is so. To part from Grandmama is all I dread. I have
lived with her so long—& she has been more than a Mother to
me. It is impossible to love any one, more than I love her, & it will
grieve me extremely to part from her. She thinks it right for me
to spend a winter with Mama, after being so long seperated from
her. The amusements of Philadelphia I do not at all regret. I shall
often think of Union & Pine Street's, & the happy hours I have
spent with you, & Elizabeth. Grandmama returns early in the
Spring, & I shall return to her as soon as she arrives here & next
winter if nothing prevents, I shall meet you again in Philadelphia.

I request that no one may see these scrawls, as I am in a great
Hurry, & they are wrote extremely bad

To E Bordley
Yet never let our hearts divide
Nor death dissolve the chain
For love, & joy were once allied
& must be joined again
Has she no fault then (Envy says) Sir!
Yes she has one I must aver:
When all the world conspires to praise her
The Womans deaf, & will not hear

Eleanor Parke Custis
Mount Vernon Virginia

Allways send your letters to Grandmama & she will inclose
them to me with hers. If you do not—it is very probable I shall not
receive any of them.

———————————— ❦ ————————————

Hope Park October 19th 1795

My Dearest Elizabeth—

Before this time you have undoubtedly accused me of neglect,
remissness, & forgetfullness. But as a Criminal is generally

heard, before being condemned—you must hear my defence (or rather see it) before you pass judgement. 1*st* I did not receive your letter untill more than a month after you wrote it—& perhaps never should have got it—had I not seen it advertised in an Alexandria paper, as a dead letter—then I sent & got it. This My Dear, was a little your fault—as had you directed it, under cover to the President—I should have had it immediately. After that a number of unlucky circumstances prevented my writing. The day before My Dearest Grandmama set off for Philadelphia. Although suffering most severely with the tooth ach—I took up my pen determined to write to you. But after writing one page—I was in such agony of pain—that I was obliged to give up all thought of doing anything but laying down. I assure you I wished very much to write to you but I think you will excuse me, since I have told you the cause, of my seeming neglect.

I have gone through the greatest trial, I ever experienced—parting with my beloved Grandmama. This is the first seperation for any time, since I was two years old. Since my fathers[8] death she has been ever more than a Mother to me, and the President the most affectionate of Fathers. I love them more than any one. You can guess then how severely I must feel this parting, even for a short time. I have been so long from My Mama, that Grandmama thought it proper & necessary for me to spend this winter with her & as my Sister Peter[9] expects a little one, in a few months, I think it is right for me to stay. She is now settled in the Federal City [Washington, D.C.] very charmingly—her husband the best and most affectionate. She is perfectly happy. You can form an idea, how thankfull, & happy I am to see her so. I expect to spend part of the Winter with her—as she wishes me very much to do so. I flatter myself you will be a good deal disappointed, in not seeing me this winter—as I do not intend glading the eyes of my northern friends for this winter. However—since we cannot see each other—we must write long, & frequent letters to beguile the time of separation away. I expect very long ones from you—& shall write every thing I stumble upon, (if worth writ-

7. Hope Park, an estate located ten miles west of Alexandria in an isolated area of Fairfax County, was the home of Nelly Custis's mother, Eleanor Calvert Custis Stuart (c. 1757–1811) and her husband, Dr. David Stuart (1753-c.1814). GWD, 5:291, 6:250.
8. John Parke Custis (1754–1781) was Martha Washington's son by her first husband, Daniel Parke Custis (1711–1757).
9. Martha Parke Custis (1777–1854) married Thomas Peter (1769–1834), son of a wealthy Georgetown merchant and landowner, in 1795.

ing about). I received a letter from our beloved Elizabeth a week past. She mentions writing to you by the same opportunity. Her letter was rather short but I was happy to find by it that she was safely landed in England. I shall write to her very soon. Poor little Frisk [Nelly's dog] is very well in Philadelphia. My Brother[10] has promised to take great care of him this winter—& Grandmama will bring him with her in the spring.

I am afraid Eliza, that your brain was in a bad state when you wrote last—or I must have been out of my senses when I wrote to you. You say—as I went through Bristol, I must have called on Miss Ann Allen[11]—now you must know, (if you were ignorant of it before), that Bristol is on the road to New York—& as I was bound to Virginia I could not have passed through it. I am very glad to hear Miss Allen is well, as I have a regard for her. I should like to have been with you when you visited the Panorama[12] as it must have been very amusing. My love to Ann Allen—& compliments and congratulations to Mrs Hammond[13] on the birth of her daughter. That affair of A H's turned out pretty much as I expected. After the terror I saw in his countenance, when coming from Gray's[14]—I did not expect much from him. However as I was in some measure the cause of his being spoke to. I thought it right to request he would accomodate it as well as he could without coming to *blows* (he has proved that he is of a very peaceable disposition). After such cowardly behaviour, I am surprised he is not ashamed to shew his face—poor little sly[boots?].—a little milk & water monkey. So much & no more for him.

I have just come across the letter I began to you and intended sending by Grandmama—& shall therefore send it with this—

---

10. George Washington Parke Custis (1781–1857).
11. Ann Allen (b. after 1768) was one of Elizabeth Allen's sisters.
12. First patented in London in 1787, panoramas were large circular paintings, lit from above and behind, which were displayed in circular buildings. Spectators, who stood on a central platform, found the effect startlingly realistic. Edward Savage brought the *View of Westminster and London* to Philadelphia in 1795, where it was displayed in a rotunda he had erected at the corner of High and Tenth streets. John F. McDermott, *The Lost Panoramas of the Mississippi* (Chicago, 1958), 1–2, 5–6; Karin H. McGinnis, "Moving Right Along: Nineteenth Century Panorama Painting in the United States" (Ph.D. diss., University of Minnesota, 1983), 30.
13. Margaret Allen (d. 1838), another of Elizabeth Allen's sisters, married George Hammond, first British minister to the United States, in 1793. Charles P. Keith, "Andrew Allen," *PMHB* 10 (1886): 364–65.
14. Gray's was a public amusement garden on the Schuylkill River. GWD, 5:159.

that you may judge of both. I have a fine opportunity of being romantic here if I was inclined. However thank heaven I do not deal much in the romantic stile.

I hope your conversations with the wood nymphs will be both amusing, & instructive to you. I am in no danger of being captivated by any one here, as we seldom see a living creature except the family. You must know—I am grown very industrious—& shall shortly be as grave as any quaker, or baptist of your acquaintance. A great change—methinks I hear you cry—(holding up your hands, & turning your eyes inside out with astonishment). What will this world come to—since my cracked brained friend is growing grave. Ah! my Dear when people are growing old, & infirm—it is necessary to cast off all vanities—&c &c. I suspect you will think I am still more crazy than ever if possible.

I expect to go to the Anapolis races the thirtieth of this month. If any thing worth telling happens, you shall have it in full. Sister Betsey[15] joins me in love to you. Mine to your Mama, Papa, Sister Mifflin & all enquiring friends. Compliments to Your Brother.[16] Love & congratulations to Lana Ross.[17] I hear she is going to be married.

Avec tout le respect qui est necessaire et convenable. Je suis votre tres sincere amie, et affectionee servante [With all necessary and proper respect, I am your very sincere friend and affectionate servant].

Eleanor Parke Custis

———————————❦———————————

Washington February 7th [1796]

My Dear Elizabeth,

It is now three weeks since I received your affectionate letter. I am really ashamed that I have not answered it before, but I will

---

15. Elizabeth Parke Custis (1776–1832).
16. Elizabeth Bordley's half-brother, John Fishbourne Mifflin (1759–1813), was an attorney; he and his wife, Clementina Ross Mifflin (1769–1848), and their four (eventually six) children lived next door to the Bordleys in Union Street. Merrill, 56; Frank W. Leach, "Philadelphia Families," Historical Society of Pennsylvania, 65.
17. Anna Helena Amelia Ross (1776–1846), Clementina Mifflin's sister, married George Plumsted (1765–1805) on December 3, 1795. Leach, "Philadelphia Families," 24, 37.

waive all excuses, & tell you the real truth. I set down to answer it
a fortnight ago, & wrote allmost one side, when company coming
in, prevented me from finishing it. Two or three times since, I
have attempted answering your letter, but was prevented. This
evening I was determined to devote to you—& as yet luckily no
interruption. I shall just give you a sketch of my present situation. In Sister Peters room Patty & the child asleep. Thomas
reading—& your humble servant—writing to E. Bordley for
whom (between ourselves) I have a kind of friendship. Since I
wrote last I am become an *Aunt*, two or three inches taller upon
the strength of it (as you may suppose.) My Dear Sister has been
very ill, but is now thank God pretty well again—& my little
neice, a very fat, handsome good tempered, clever toad. Its nose &
forehead very like its fathers. & its mouth & chin like Patty's. *I*
think its eyes are very deep blue, but Sister Peter insists upon it,
that they are hazle. It has a great deal of beautifull brown hair.
Her name is to be Martha Eliza Eleanor Peter—& to be called
Eleanor. Martha is after Grandmama, & Sister Peter. Eliza after
Mama's Mother,[18] Old Mrs Peter,[19] Grandmama's Sister,[20] Mr.
Peter's eldest Sister,[21] & My Sister—& Eleanor after Mama &
your most obedient, very humble Servant Eleanor Parke Custis.
Thus all the names of its nearest relations are taken in at once
without giving offence to any. I approve very much of this way of
getting quit of all the family names at once. You also approve of it
no doubt. You must know that I am housekeeper, Nurse—(and a
long train of Etcetra's) at present. Mama & Sister Eliza went
from this to Hope Park yesterday, & left *me* here, to take care of
My Sister Peter, young neice—& the house. I assure you I am
quite domesticated—stay constantly at home, & am an excellent
manager, Nurse, & housekeeper. I have been out but twice since I
came here (which is three weeks.) to one assembly which was a
very agreeable one, & once to see Cousin Lear[22] who was sick, &
sent for me.

---

18. Elizabeth Calvert (1730–1798), the daughter of former Governor Charles
    Calvert of Maryland, married Benedict Calvert, the natural son of Lord Bal-
    timore, in 1748. *Maryland Genealogies*, 2 vols. (Baltimore, 1980), 1:160, 164.
19. Elizabeth Scott (1744–1821) married Robert Peter (1726–1806), a prominent
    merchant and developer who was the first mayor of Georgetown. Charles
    Moore, *The Family Life of George Washington* (Boston, 1926), 117, 120.
20. Elizabeth Dandridge Henley (b. 1749). GWD 6:251.
21. Elizabeth Peter Dunlap (1771–1831). Genealogical files, Tudor Place.
22. Frances Bassett Washington Lear (1767–1796), Martha Washington's niece,
    had first married George Washington's nephew, George Augustine Wash-

I have a peice of information to give you, which I think will surprise you a *little*. I shall be—Miss Custis[23]—in two, or three months as my Sister Eliza is engaged to Mr Law[24] (whom I suppose you have seen) & will be married in a short time. *Strange most passing strange*—quite unaccountable (you will cry!) 'tis strange my Dear but nevertheless quite true beleive me—E Custis & E Bordley Spinsters—& so likely to remain to the end of time. What say you to this—agreed? Well be it so—de tout mon coeur. Uncle Edward Calvert is to [be] *tied* the first of March—to a very amiable, handsome girl of eighteen—a Miss Biscoe of Nottingham.[25] I have told you all the news—therefore must now conclude with my love to your Mama & Papa. Patty & Brother Peter desire to be remembered to you. Excuse & burn this very badly written scrawl—& beleive me your sincere & most affectionate friend,

Eleanor Parke Custis

Hope Park March 30th 1796

My Dearest Elizabeth,

For sometime I have waited in the hopes of hearing from you. Now I begin to fear you are either sick or offended at my apparent neglect in not answering the letter I received two months ago, sooner than I did.

If either of these fears are true I shall be very sorry—but I

---

ington, who died young. Though suffering from consumption, in 1795 she married Tobias Lear (1762–1816), Washington's private secretary and onetime tutor to the Custis children. She died later in 1796. William Miles Cary, "The Dandridges of Virginia," *William and Mary Quarterly* 5 (1896): 38.

23. The eldest unmarried daughter of a family was known simply as Miss Surname; younger daughters were addressed by their given names as well. Nelly was at this time styled Miss Eleanor Custis; with the marriage of both her elder sisters, she would become Miss Custis.

24. Thomas Law (1756–1834), an Englishman who made a fortune in India, came to the United States in 1794 and became a real-estate speculator. Members of Eliza Parke Custis's family objected to the marriage because of his age and eccentricity. GWD, 6:238–39.

25. Edward Henry Calvert (1766–1846), brother of Eleanor Calvert Stuart, married Elizabeth Biscoe (1780–1857) March 1, 1796. *Maryland Genealogies*, 1:161.

hope you will very soon write to me & inform me, the reason you have not wrote, since my last letter. Since I have wrote last—I have been to two balls—& my Sisters wedding. The balls were very agreeable—& I danced a good deal. Dancing you know has allways been my delight—& I prefer balls to any other amusement. After staying two months with my Dear Sister Peter—I left her, & my Sweet little niece very well a fortnight ago—and came up with Brother Law in his charriott. Sister Eliza was married the twenty first—and left us on Thursday. She has every chance for happiness—a good hearted affectionate husband—one most sincerely attached to her—& She is the same to him.

They are fixed in the City, four miles from Sister Peter. Mama & self expect to go to the City in two, or three weeks. I am now Miss Custis, & as you may suppose not a little proud of the title, & have determined within myself that I will allways be called *Eleanor* as Nelly is extremely homely in my opinion. To-morrow I am seventeen.

Before I left George Town I had the pleasure of seeing Miss A Stuart she made many enquiries after you. She told me little *Snipe* was very well. I should like very much to see her. Miss Stuart says she often speaks of me. I was introduced to Mrs. Charles Lowns[26] at the last ball I was at. She made many enquiries after you. When have you heard from our Dear E Allen? I have not had a letter from her for three or four months. When do you intend writing to her—if you will inform me—I will write, & send the letter to you, to inclose for me. I have never heard of, or from our little friend Susan since she came to Virginia.[27] Sister Law desired me to remember her to you whe[ne]ver I wrote. Sister Peter also.

Remember me to your Mama, Papa, Sister, & Brother Mifflin. Also Mrs. Smith[28] of Roxbury. I hope she enjoy's better health

---

26. Eleanor Lloyd (1776–1805) of Wye, Maryland, married Charles Lowndes in 1794. *Maryland Genealogies*, 2:189.

27. In 1795 Edmund Randolph had resigned as secretary of state after being falsely accused of impropriety in dealing with France. He returned with his family to Virginia, where he became one of America's leading attorneys.

28. Frederick Smythe, a former English colonial official, and his wife were fixtures of Philadelphia's elite society; they lived alternately on Union Street and at their country estate, Roxborough. Thompson Westcott, *A History of Philadelphia*, 5 vols. (Philadelphia, 1886), 5:1308, 1322.

than when I left Philadelphia. Love to H McCall[29]—Mrs. Plumsted, & M Ross.[30]

> With truth, & sincerity, Your faithfull friend—
> *Eleanor Parke Custis*

P.S. This is wrote so bad I fear you will be scarcely able to read it. Write to me very soon—a very long letter.

------------------ ❦ ------------------

Hope Park May 13th 1796

My Dear E Bordleys acceptable letter arrived safe to my hands last week & here accordingly am I seated to answer it & without further perambulation I will proceed to the first head of my discourse. (But first a query.) Is not a letter (such as the one I am now writing after receiving yours) *sometimes* (and I think I may say, *generally*) improperly called an *answer*? Not one *question* is *answered*—& they are nothing but an uninterrupted series of questions and *query's* without one proper reply, or reasonable solution.

Inclosed is a letter to our Dear Elizabeth which you will send with yours. I was much pleased at hearing from her. She says she is very well except a bad cold which I have at present also and which is by no means agreeable. It is allmost a year since Our Dear E Allen left us. I am afraid it will be many years before she will visit us again. However necessity has no law. We must therefore make a virtue of it & be contented to *hear* from her, instead of *seeing* her. I think I could spare her some of *my plumpness* without detriment to myself, as I have a very great portion of *that* article—although not enough to *incommode* me or to prevent me from dancing, & walking with satisfaction.

I am in the hope of seeing my Beloved Grandmama soon. She wrote me some time since that she expected it would not be long now before she should see me. I wish more & more every day to

---

29. Harriet McCall (1777–1847) was the daughter of Archibald McCall, a leading Philadelphia merchant, and Judith Kemble McCall. Charles McCall, "The Chronicles of the McCall Family" (Philadelphia, 1873), 29.

30. Mary Ross was Clementina Mifflin's youngest sister. Leach, "Philadelphia Families," 65.

see her. We have been seperated now near seven months, & that is very long for a first seperation.

We all return thanks to your Mama & self for your congratulations on my Sister Eliza's marriage. It was quite a private wedding, & we have had no dancing or parties of any kind. My Sister wished it to be as private as possible. We have just returned from paying her a visit in the City & have brought Sister Peter & her darling little Daughter Martha Eliza Eleanor with us. Sister Law is fixed in a charming situation, with an elegant, & commanding view of the Potomac river.

Present My love & thanks to your Mama for her love & good wishes. Tell her that I hope she will bring you to Mount Vernon this Summer, as I am very anxious to see you, & shew my lovely fat Neice. I am sure you will both agree that she is the greatest beauty & the best child you have ever seen.

If you will come to Virginia I shall be very glad. I expect to be perfectly happy this summer at M.V. with My Dearest Grand Mama, Mama, Sisters, Brothers, & little Neice. We shall agree very well I expect, you & myself.

The spirit of *Matrimony* seems to reign in Philadelphia I think of late years. I never heard of so many marriages as have taken place, for the two or three years last past. I never heard of Mr Kemble or either of the Read's. Pray from whence did they spring.

When you see M[aria] Morris,[31] give my love to her, & tell her she is a very sad scrub for she has not wrote to me for a length of time, & every post I have expected a letter.

The spring with smiling face is seen. The Country is now delightfully pleasant—but this has been the most backward spring which has been known for sometime. The fruit is much injured from the unseasonable weather.

I suppose you will soon be retiring for the summer. Let me advise a trip to Mount Vernon before you settle yourself at your Country residence. I hear Mr & Mrs Morris intended visiting the City soon. I shall be much pleased to see Maria. Sister Peter's compliments to your Mama [&] self. Miss Stuart told me sometime ago

---

31. Maria Morris (1779–1852) was the daughter of Mary White Morris and Robert Morris (1734–1806), an immensely wealthy merchant, financier of the American Revolution, and friend of George Washington. GWD, 5:326.

that my little friend *Snipe* was well. Love to your Sister Miflin H McCall &c. Congratulations to Mrs Breck[32] & Mrs Plumsted.

Without further preface—I remain your ever sincere affectionate friend

Eleanor Parke Custis
alias
Deborah Bridget muckle weaver Tackabout a votre service

———————❦———————

Mount Vernon September 6th 1796

Dearest Elizabeth,

I wrote you a few lines by Mr Taylor,[33] but as they were badly written & very stupid I have made an attempt to write something better, but strongly suspect I shall not succeed. However I know you will excuse it, & therefore I shall make no more excuses. My Beloved Grandmama missed her ague yesterday, & I hope will soon be entirely restored. I am tolerably well, & hope I shall continue so.

Many thanks to My Friend for her solicitude on my account. Be assured I shall never forget it—& allways pray fervently for every blessing for you. I wish very much to see you, & should be delighted if you could come here. I am more, & more attached to this place, & in spite of the ague & fever, prefer it to all others. I should pity you very much being obliged to stay in Philadelphia all summer if you had no other troubles. But I am indeed very sorry that your Papa has been so very much indisposed as to prevent your enjoying country air at this season. I most sincerely hope he will soon be quite restored—& You eased of the anxiety which I am sure you feel on his account. I have not received a letter for several months from our Dear, and lively friend Elizabeth—& have not written to her for sometime, I wish much to hear from her, & intend writing very shortly. I will send the letter

---

32. Jean Ross Breck (1774–1858), another of Clementina Mifflin's sisters, was married to Samuel Breck (1771–1862), a prominent merchant and civic leader. Leach, "Philadelphia Families," 65.

33. Perhaps Thomas Taylor (1743–1833), one of the original commissioners of the District of Columbia. GWD 6:144.

to you, if you will inclose it to her. Write to me allways when you feel disposed to do so. Your letters allways afford me pleasure.

My Mother & Sisters have spent several weeks with us. They are all gone home. My Neice is the sweetest child I ever knew. It is impossible to express to you how much I love her.

I am as happy as a mortal can wish to be when they are all here. I ride sometimes on Horseback, walk, read, write french—work, play & sing & always think the weeks go off too fast. By the bye, I had a fall from my horse sometime ago—from which however I received no injury. I was riding on, not looking where I went. A branch of a tree took me across the breast & I fell—came off very easy, the moment I was on the ground I jumpt up had my horse carried to a stump got up again & rode home—& never felt the least inconvenience from it although I fell on stony ground by the side of a ditch & the horse trod on my foot. Grandmama & Mama were very much frightened & would not permit me to ride for sometime, however at last I persuaded them my neck was not to be broken yet awhile—& I have rode several times since. It has given me more courage, & more caution also. Present my respect-full love to your Mama. Grandmama sends affectionate regards to your Mama, & Self. Accept for votre meme My most sincere love, & Friendship—& Beleive me in Sincerity and Truth Yours—

Eleanor Parke Custis

You will agree with me that this letter is the most intolerable pen-scratching you ever saw.

————————————❦————————————

Mount Vernon March 18th 1797

My Dearest Elizabeth,

We arrived here last Wednesday after a tedious & fatiguing journey of seven days. The roads from Philadelphia to the Head of Elk were very good, from thence to this place they are very bad. But as they have been much worse than they are at present, we were very well satisfied to make the best of them.

We encountered no adventures of any kind, & saw nothing uncommon, except the light Horse of Delaware, & Maryland, who insisted upon attending us through their states, all the Inhabitants of Baltimore who came out to *see*, & *be seen* & to Welcome My Dear Grandpapa—some in carriages, some on Horseback, the others on foot. The gentlemen of George Town also attended us to the River, & four of them rowed us over in a barge.[34] Tuesday we arrived in New Jersey Avenue [the Laws' residence] where I had the pleasure of finding both My Dear Sisters, & Neices. My Sisters are both extremely thin, & look very sick. Sister Law is not well. Her child is the prettiest, & sweetest infant I have ever seen, her mouth & nose are finely formed, her skin remarkably fair, fine, & soft—her eyes large & dark. I think they will be hazle, her countenance very mild & sweetly interesting, & I think her disposition will be grave & sedate.

My Neice Eleanor has grown very much, walks very well, will soon talk, has many teeth, & is the fattest, most saucy, charming, entertaining, mischevious little monkey, of my acquaintance.

We left the City on Wednesday, & arrived here without accident at four o'clock.

The weather untill today has been very damp and disagreeable, but this has been a charming morning—& every thing appears to be revived. The grass begins to look green. Some trees are in blossom, others budding. The flowers are coming out—& the numerous different Birds keep up a constant serenading. Next month every thing will look charmingly. When I look at this noble river, & all the beautifull prospects around—I pity all those who are in Cities, for surely a country life, is the most rational & the most happy of any—& all the refinements of art & luxury are nothing in comparison to the Beauties of Nature.

Since I left Philadelphia every thing has appeared to be a dream, I can hardly realise my being *here*, & that Grandpapa is no longer in office. If it is a dream I hope never to awaken from it—for although I shall ever remember my friends with regret yet I am delighted to be once more settled here, & surrounded by my Dearest relatives. I passed last winter very happily in Philadelphia but I do not regret its amusements, & shall be much happier *here* without them.

I have not yet seen my Dearest Mother, but hope soon to see

---

34. John Adams was inaugurated president March 4, 1797; the Washingtons set off by coach for Mount Vernon on March 9. Many of their belongings, including Nelly Custis's harpsichord, were sent by water. The journey took on the quality of a triumphal procession as militia troops and delegations of citizens turned out to honor Washington on his journey home. Flexner, 4:338–39; Thane, *Potomac Squire*, 362–63.

her here. My Brother comes in April, & then all our friends will come to meet him.

My Beloved Grandmama has a very bad cold & cough—but I trust that she will be soon entirely recovered.

Grandpapa is very well, & has already turned Farmer again. I am on Monday to begin gardening. I hope to make some proficiency in it.

I am also deputy Housekeeper, in which employment I expect to improve much, as I am very partial to it. When my Harpsichord comes, I shall practice a great deal, & make my Sister sing your parts of our Duetts. I think you had better come here to sing them with me. I do not despair of seeing you, & I shall be very much disappointed if you do not visit us.

My love, & respects to your Papa, & Mama & tell them that the air of Mount Vernon would be of infinite service to them I am sure. Love & every good wish to our Dear Elsina. She cannot doubt that I should be highly gratified in seeing her here, with her parents, to whom pray offer my respects.[35]

Compliments to our Master, Signor Trisobio[36]—& inform [him] that I shall endeavour to learn all the *Graces* &c &c, contained in his book of instructions, although I fear my endeavours will not be crowned with success—as the *Graces* are not fond of visiting or staying with me.

Miss Eliza Ross was married last Thursday to Mr Jeremiah Smith.[37]

My Grandparents join in affectionate regards to your Parents, & yourself.

Heaven bless My Friend, prays her sincerely attached,
Eleanor Parke Custis

---

35. Frederick Frank de la Roche (b.1857), a German baron with large landholdings in France, had fought in the American Revolution. His wife, whose maiden name was Marcus, was born in Holland (1761); Elsina Espinasse (b. 1778) was her daughter by a previous marriage to a French nobleman. The family had fled France in 1792; in Philadelphia they were well received by both the emigré community and American society. The de la Roches had two children, Sophie and George. In her will, Elizabeth Bordley left lots in Washington, D.C., to George Frank de la Roche. [Médéric-Louis-Elie] Moreau de Saint-Méry, *Voyage aux États-Unis de L'Amérique, 1793–1798*, ed. Stewart L. Mims (New Haven, 1913), 154–56; *Last Will and Testament of Elizabeth Bordley Gibson, Deceased* (Philadelphia, 1863).

36. Filippo Trisobio, an Italian singer and voice teacher who arranged and published music, taught Nelly Custis to sing in Italian. Britt, 54.

37. Jeremiah Smith (1759–1842) of New Hampshire was serving in Congress when he met and married Eliza Ross of Maryland. He went on to become governor and chief justice of New Hampshire.

P S. direct your letters under cover to General Washington—
M-t V-n Virginia, & I shall be sure of getting them directly.

———————————— ❧ ————————————

Washington April 24th 1797

My Dearest Elizabeth—

I received your very affectionate letter today, & to prove to
you how much I was gratified in the receipt of it—I have now
taken pen in hand to write an answer. I must acknowledge that I
have for sometime been expecting to hear from you, but I very
readily excuse you as I am sure you had good reasons for not writing sooner. I am very glad you have lately heard from our Dearest
E Allen—that she is well and happy. Pray when you write again,
say every thing affectionate to her from me. I was much pleased
with her kind remembrance, I shall allways love her very sincerely & fervently. & wish her every happiness. To our amiable
Elsina, offer my sincere love, & assure her that I shall allways be
greatly interested in her happiness.

I left Mount Vernon last Monday & my Dearest Grandparents well. My Beloved Grandmama was for sometime much indisposed with a violent cold & cough but I had the satisfaction of
hearing that she is perfectly well. It is the first visit I have paid
my Sisters since I came home, & they had often written for me,
but I could not leave my Grandmama when she was so much
indisposed. I went also to see my Mother for a day or two, she is
getting pretty well again. But looks very badly from her long confinement. My Sisters expect her tomorrow to spend some weeks
with them, & change of air will certainly restore her. She has a
fine little girl, another Eleanor.

My Dearest Brother is very much grown, & astonishingly
improved I think. We are delighted to observe the change & he is
perfectly well & happy. I am sure he will be much gratified by
your remembrance. I came up last week to the races here where
there has been company from every part I believe.

On Tuesday there was a match race between Mr Tilghman's[38]

————————————

38. Several members of the Tilghman family of Talbot County, Maryland,
   owned racehorses.

horse & General Ridgely's[39]—the former won—& made fifteen hundred dollars. On Wednesday morning as the ground was very muddy they postponed the racing—but in the evening we had a charming Ball at the Union Tavern in G Town. I staid untill after one o'clock, danced six dances with Mr C Carroll of Carrollton[40] & two with your acquaintance Mr Ben Ringold[41] who made many enquiries after you, & I gave him all the information in my power.

I was told that Mr Paca[42] went to Philadelphia to pay his addresses to you, & some beleived that you would perhaps accept his sweet person. Pray inform me if it is true—I can keep a secret. On Thursday morning we went again to the race ground—there was another match race but I care not a fig for racing & if it was not for the sake of the company one meets I should never go to such places.

Mrs C Lownes came in the morning to see me & begged me to go that evening to a dance at her house. I went accordingly with Sister Peter, & spent a charming evening—danced with Mr B. Ringold. Mrs. Lownes made many enquiries after you, & appeared much interested in your happiness. I saw her Sister Miss Loyd—& her Brother Edward—he is not yet eighteen—& as great a fop as I have seen.[43] I was invited to a party at Mr Scott's[44]

39. Charles C. Ridgely III (1762–1829), militia general, planter, and later governor of Maryland, was the dictator of the turf along the Potomac, Patapsco, and Chesapeake rivers. John Hervey, *Racing in America, 1665–1865,* 3 vols. (New York, 1944), 2:6–10; *Biographical Directory of the Governors of the United States, 1789–1978,* ed. Robert Sobel and John Raimo, 4 vols. (Westport, Conn., 1978), 2:654.

40. Charles Carroll (1775–1825), later of Homewood, was the son of the extremely wealthy Marylander Charles Carroll of Carrollton. GWD 6:288, 336.

41. Benjamin Ringgold (1774–1798) was the son of Thomas and Mary Galloway Ringgold of Kent County, Maryland. The Ringgolds were wealthy merchants and landowners. *Biographical Dictionary of the Maryland Legislature, 1635–1789,* ed. Edward C. Papenfuse, Alan F. Day, David W. Jordan, and Gregory A. Stiverson, 2 vols. (Baltimore, 1979).

42. John Philemon Paca (1771–1840) of Talbot County, Maryland, was the son of William Paca (1740–1799), a governor of Maryland and federal district judge, and his second wife, Anne Harrison of Philadelphia (d. 1780). *Biographical Dictionary of the Maryland Legislature.*

43. Elizabeth Lloyd (1774–1849) and Edward Lloyd (1779–1834) of Wye, Maryland. Later a successful Republican politician, Edward Lloyd was elected to the state legislature, the U.S. House and Senate, and the governorship of Maryland. *Maryland Genealogies,* 2:178.

44. Probably Gustavus Scott (1753–1800), one of the commissioners for the District of Columbia since 1794. Julian U. Niemcewicz, *Under Their Vine and Fig Tree,* trans. and ed. Metchie J. E. Budka (Elizabeth, N.J., 1965), 310.

on Friday, but as I had engaged to come to Sister Law—I refused it. I expect to return to Mount Vernon on Saturday or Monday, My Sweet Neices are perfectly well & more charming than ever. I was sorry to hear of the *trist accident du povero Cavaliero* [sad accident of the poor horseman]—& am sincerely glad to hear of his recovery. I should be very sorry if I could not feel for any ones misfortunes. But do not think it necessary to inform him that I was at all sorry for it—as vanity (so universal with men) might make him suppose I felt more for him than I should have done for any other in the same situation. However every thing happens for the best & he may console himself with thinking that it might have been worse. I presume he will never again attempt to excel in *Equestrian* exercise.

How goes on your *mad Beau*—Bleakly[45]—is he as *entertaining* & constant in his attendance as ever. They say every person is like some animal. If so he resembles a Spaniel—for the more ill treatment he receives the more attentive & ridiculously troublesome he is. I am much obliged to Signor Trisobio for his good' wishes & return them very sincerely. I do not at present want any music but when I do I will write to you to select for me. The "Call of Honor" I have been practising a good deal. I like it much—& often wish for you to sing it for me. Pray present my respectfull love to your Papa & Mama. My Sisters & Brothers join affectionate remembrance to you—kisses from My two Darlings. Mr Lafayette[46] desired me when ever I wrote to remember him very particularly to you. I fear you can hardly read this sad scrawl. My Candle is allmost out & I must bid you good night,

Addio cara Amica—Tutto a voi—alias My lovely Friend yours in sincerity, truth & faithfullness

Eleanor P Custis

---

45. Probably John Bleakley (d. 1802), a very wealthy Philadelphian. He never married, reportedly because he had been disappointed in love. Henry Simpson, *The Lives of Eminent Philadelphians Now Deceased* (Philadelphia, 1859).

46. George Washington Lafayette (1779–1849) was the son of the marquis de Lafayette. His father had been imprisoned by the Austrians in 1792; when his mother was able to leave France in 1795, she took her daughters with her to join Lafayette in prison and sent her son, accompanied by a tutor, to America. Though at first Washington feared the political repercussions of welcoming so famous an exile, in April 1796 young Lafayette came to Philadelphia to live with the Washington family, returning with them to Mount Vernon in 1797. John S. Penman, *Lafayette and Three Revolutions* (Boston, 1929), 221–40; GWD, 6:237

Mt Vn May 30th [1797]

My Dearest Elizabeth,

Yours of May 15th I received with pleasure, read with increased satisfaction, & prepare to answer as well as in my power. *All* of your *faults* which I have discovered (or you have pointed out to my observation & consideration) I freely forgive as they are not many or manifold, & I am sure are unintentional.

The circumstance which raised your interest & curiosity my Dear—is by no means an uncommon instance—as it is, & has allways been the custom in Maryland, & Virginia to dance all the evening at the *Assemblies* with the same partner. Therefore instead of being particular because I danced *six* dances with the same partner, I deviated from the general rule by dancing the two others with another person. I can give you very little information with respect to the *intrinsic merit* of the *happy* youth, as I was only introduced to him the morning of the Ball, & met him at a private dance the evening after—which was Thursday, & he left the City on Friday morning early.

He is not very tall, well made—fair, blue eyes, fine light hair, & is altogether a pleasing young man. His character is generally allowed to be very amiable, sensible, well informed, studious, a dutiful son, & a generous good Heart. So says report—unfortunately he has been too often told of his merit & accomplishments, & it has given him more affectation than is by any means agreeable. When I *have* any thing to impart I shall rely upon your secrecy. At present it is unnecessary. I have contradicted the report concerning you, I was certain it could have no foundation, as I have too good an opinion of you to suppose for a moment that such a conceited, disagreeable fop could have any chance of captivating you.

I was much pleased to receive a letter from our Dear Elizabeth, as I began to think she neglected me, I enclose you an answer for her. Mr & Mrs Rigal, Mr Beeker Mr Hope[47] & Mr Bearing[48] have been here lately, also Mr Emille & Don S. Sanchez two

---

47. Henry Philip Hope, a member of the Amsterdam banking firm Hope and Company, traveled in America with Alexander Baring. Frederick S. Allis, Jr., ed., "William Bingham's Maine Lands, 1790–1820," in *Publications of the Colonial Society of Massachusetts*, vols. 36–37 (Boston, 1954), 847–49, passim.
48. Alexander Baring (1774–1848) was a member of a very important British

homely Spaniards whom you may have seen perhaps they were at Mr Trisobio's concert. They neither of them speak English or understand it, & Mr Emille speaks but very bad French. Don S. Sanchez is a crazy count—(quite deranged & terrifying to behold) he appears to be (as Pindar says) "madder than the maddest of March Hares". They staid one night here & I had the felicity of playing & singing more than an hour to endeavour to attune their souls, but failed in the attempt. "Music had not charms sufficient to soothe *their* savage breasts."

My Dear Mother & all my younger Sisters & Brothers are with us at present, she is much better but still pale & thin.

My Beloved Grandmama is well also Grandpapa. Sister Law's child is innoculated for the small pox, & as soon as she recovers they are all to be here with us. I am glad you are not going to Como[49] as it is so far from Elsina, & I should not perhaps hear as often from you as I hope to hear now.

Present my Best love & respects to your Papa & Mama love to our Dear Elsina & respects to Mrs La Roche, & Mrs. Smith. Grandmama & Grandpapa join in regards to your Papa & Mama & self & good wishes.

Addio cara Elisabetta tutto gli giorni vostra amica [Goodbye, dear Elizabeth, always your friend]

Eleanora Parke Custis

My young Friend La Fayette thanks you for your good wishes & begs you will accept of his sincere regards.

———————————— ❦ ————————————

Mount Vernon, August 20th [1797]

After having nearly exhausted *all* my *few ideas* in forming three *immense long letters*, I proceed to spend the *remainder* of

financial house; he was sent to the United States to extend the firm's business operations. In 1798 he married Anne Louisa Bingham, daughter of William and Anne Willing Bingham of Philadelphia.

49. John Beale Bordley purchased a farm in Chester County for agricultural experimentation; the family spent summers there in the 1790s. Bordley named the farm Como for the birthplace of Pliny, one of his favorite authors. Elizabeth Bordley Gibson, *Biographical Sketches of the Bordley Family of Maryland* (Philadelphia, 1865), 137–38.

them in answering my Dearest Eliza's charming & affectionate letter. Be assured My Friend *'tho last, thou art not the least* in my affections. By the bye *that* you I am sure know full well, therefore to repeat my sentiments of regard for you, will not here be deemed necessary I hope. Many thanks for your kind epistle, but send me no more *excuses*, allways remember our *covenant*, make yourself easy, & write whenever convenient & agreeable to you. I hope you do not think me so ceremonious as not to write another letter, because I had not received an answer to the first. I am sure you *cannot*, because it would be an unjust opinion. I intended writing today if I had not received yours before, & should have written last week, but my *Brain* was so much disordered, & stupified by a weeks indisposition that I could not write a sentence. I have been sick all the past week, but being pretty well today—I have *rallied* my *deserting wits*, & determined to devote this day to *five* of my Dear Friends. I am afraid the fickle creatures (*my wits*) will yet leave me in the lurch, as it is a trick they often play me as you can answer for, from the experience you have had of *their odd flights, & fancies*.

I am glad you are so much pleased with your new residence, & wish I could take a peep at you & our Dear Elsina. I am not at all surprised that you have constantly company—as (to use an *old* saying & perhaps *you* may think it a *homely* one) where *sweet flowers* are, there will the *Butterfly's* go. Not but that I suppose you have more *edifying company* generally than *those gentry*. However you know My Dear it is impossible to prevent a *forward pert Butterfly* from sometimes slipping in, amongst the crowd.

I am very happy to hear that your Dear Papa is so much better, long may you know the blessing of a kind & most indulgent Father. Mine, I was too young to know the loss of as I was only two years & six months old when he died. But I often think how much I should have loved him, & how happy his society would have made us, but no doubt all is for the best. And My Beloved Mother & particularly My Beloved Grandmama have been the most excellent Friends, & tender Parents to me. Whilst they are preserved to me I can regret nothing.

I am astonished my Dear at the report you mention that I had hurt myself by falling from a Horse. Madame Freire[50] wrote me that she was assured I had bruised & hurt my face extremely by falling from a Carriage. Who can be the inventor of such false-

---

50. Agnes Freire was the wife of Portugal's minister to the United States, Chevalier Cypriano Ribeiro Freire (d. 1825). Charming and well-educated,

hoods & for what purpose can they have been fabricated? I have never received any hurt, no accident. I wish the world would not be so extremely busy, & impertinent. E P Custis desires not its notice, & would thank those meddling *reporters* never to mention her name. I wish they would also allow her to *marry who* she *pleases, & when she pleases* without perpetually *engaging her to those whom she never had a chance of marrying, & never wished* to be united to. The opinion of the *wise* (that *friendship alone* cannot exist between two young persons of different sexes) is very *erroneous & ridiculous*. I know it by *experience*, which is by far a better teacher than any of those, who pretend to know so much. I shall ever feel an interest & sincere regard for *my young adopted Brother* [George Washington Lafayette]—but as to being *in love with him* it is entirely out of the question. Therefore I *shall certainly never* be *engaged or married to him*—as *whoever* is my *Husband* I must *first* love him *with all my Heart*—that is *not romantically*, but *esteem & prefer him before all others, that Man* I am *not yet* acquainted with—perhaps *never* may be, if so—then I remain *E P Custis Spinster for life.*

I am a good deal surprised at the *matrimonial news* but Wonders never will cease. *You* are right not to think of making your choice this year as you have had so many bad precedents. The people of this earth how sadly have they degenerated—the next generation I think, & hope will be better (*because they can hardly be worse than the present*).

All our regards, and good wishes are offered to your Parents & self. My love & respects to your Papa & Mama—& love to Our Elsina. Tell your Papa I am studying his book on Farming.[51]

Heaven Bless you My Dearest Eliza prays your friend in sincerity.

E P Custis

——————————— ❦ ———————————

Mount Vernon November 23rd [1797]

My Dearest Eliza,

Yours of the 1st instant I received a fortnight ago when I was suffering severely with the Toothach, your reasons were very sat-

---

the Freires were very popular in Philadelphia. Innocencio Francisco da Silva, *Diccionario Bibliographico Portuguez,* 22 vols. (Lisbon, 1858–1919), 2:116.

51. Probably John Beale Bordley's *Sketches on Rotation of Crops and Other Rural Matters*, which was published in 1797.

isfactory & I hope you do not think me so ceremonious as to have waited an answer to mine of August 20th, before I wrote again to you. I should certainly not have deferred writing untill this time for such a reason as that, but I have several times determined to write to you & have been prevented by constant company, & many other hindrances. I have been I confess extremely anxious to hear of your health & that of your parents, & could not avoid being a little surprised that I should not receive any tidings for so long a time. I am much indebted to you for releiving me so kindly from my fears on your account.

Soon after I wrote last, my Cousin[52] & self went on a visit to my Sisters at the City of Washington, where we remained allmost four weeks, were very sedate, had no Balls, no entertainments of any kind, most of my time was taken up in nursing & playing with my sweet Neices, I wish you could see the sweet Toads, I am sure you would be much pleased with them. My Sisters are not very well, Sister Law looks very thin & badly, she has been very ill lately, but is now tolerably well, & we expect her here this week to spend sometime with us. Sister Peter staid a few days here some weeks ago, she is now confined at home, as she expects every day an addition to her family; I hope in my next to inform you that I have a fine *Nephew*, as I have now Neices enough for some years at least.

Soon after we came home, our amiable & esteemed friends Messrs La Fayette & Frestel[53] left us for New York, from whence (as they informed us by letters) they sailed for Havre de Grace, the 25th October in the Brig Clio. We regretted very much that they left us, although their prospects were then very favorable, & they left us in the hope of soon meeting their excellent & suffering friends, restored to liberty & happiness. Since they sailed the newspaper accounts have been so very unfavorable, that I fear their voyage will not meet the success they expected, or their Friends desired. It does not appear that the Marquiss is yet liberated by the last accounts,[54] & the late events in France I fear will act rather against them.[55] By the bye Dear Eliza excuse me for

52. Frances Dandridge Henley (1779–1856) was the daughter of Martha Washington's sister Elizabeth Dandridge and Leonard Henley. In 1803 she became Tobias Lear's third wife. GWD, 6:251; Ray Brighton, *The Checkered Career of Tobias Lear* (Portsmouth, N.H., 1985), 197, 333.

53. Felix Frestal was George Washington Lafayette's tutor. GWD, 6:236.

54. Lafayette was released September 19, 1797.

55. Radical members of the Directory, the five-man executive that ruled France, had staged a coup September 4, 1797.

troubling you with a political opinion, but although I am no politician I can assure you, yet I cannot avoid expressing my opinion of the *French.*

Were I drowning & a *straw* only in sight, I would as soon think of trusting to that *slender support* (which in fact could not save me) as place the smallest dependance upon the stability of the *French republican* government. Neither would I trust the life of a *Cat* in the hands of a sett of people who hardly know religion, humanity or Justice, even *by name.* Do not think me so narrow minded or prejudiced as to judge a whole nation by a few individuals. Some frenchmen I esteem highly—but those barbarous *democratic murderers,* or rather *Demons,* I shall ever abominate. I pity those poor misguided multitudes who follow every phantom with avidity—who whilst they hear the cry of *liberty* forget how they are to smart for it & whilst they follow with eagerness the *shadow*—lose the *substance* beyond recovery.

I am afraid you will think this digression rather malapropos, but when I am writing to a friend whatever thought strikes me must appear on paper immediately, without ever considering whether it will be interesting or entertaining to my readers.

We have had company in abundance lately, very pleasing to us some of them, & others not disagreeable. There were races in the City sometime ago. I did not attend them—one race a year is quite enough for me at one place. I only go for the company, & as I am not much interested in any that would attend at those times, I should be tired of them, were I to see them very often in a year.

I had business a fortnight ago in Alexandria, & for a frolic went up one morning with my Brother on Horseback. My beast is a pretty Iron grey, 4 years old, 15 hands high, gentle, goes well except starting—called Sir Edward Pellew. The morning was fair but very damp, before we got far from home, it began to rain, however as I never like to give up any undertaking after once engaging in it, & wished also to accustom myself to riding in all weathers, I kept on, two mile[s] from Alexandria the rain poured violently, my Brother & self rode to town full gallop, & got our faces very nicely washed before we could get to a place of shelter. I wore a cloth dress, which was wet, my hair like rats tails, beaver hat & feather compleatly soaked. Sat sometime without a fire, but did not expect to suffer any inconvenience—& determined to return home in the evening, in spite of the war of elements but the rain continued without intermission all that night—& the good people with whom I dined laid violent hands on me & insisted that we should stay all night. I was detained until Monday

which was a damp windy day. Then returned & changed my cloth
for a thin cottin dress. Two days after I was taken with the toothach, for three days & nights I suffered severely, & could get neither ease or sleep. & for five days I ate nothing but a little broth &
tea. Unluckily my face was very much swelled & inflamed & I
was obliged to have it tied up all the time Mrs Liston[56] staid here,
which was three days. For two or three days after her departure
my face was quite well & I was in hopes that I should suffer no
more. But one of the back teeth in my left jaw, in order to try my
patience to its utmost extent—has aked unmercifully for three
days past. Last night it was very painful. It is tolerably easy
today, & I hope as I have now had pain in *both sides*, that I shall
have no more visits from the toothach this Winter.

I am delighted with Mrs Merchant, she is a sweet beautiful
engaging woman, her husband very pleasing & entertaining.[57]
I am really sorry that his health is so very precarious. A Mr
Atheil[58] from Antigua came with them, he is a sensible agreeable
man. All who have seen Mrs Liston must love her kind & friendly
manners. Mr Brown[59] is a very genteel young man, I am sorry he
has left Philadelphia, as I am sure the Belles will feel his loss. He
was in my opinion one of the most elegant & pleasing young men
last Winter. They went by Water to Norfolk, from whence Mr &
Mrs Merchant Mr Brown & Mr Atheil will embark immediately
for Antigua & Mr & Mrs Liston will return to Philadelphia by
land, I fear they will have a very disagreeable time as the season

---

56. Henrietta Marchant (bapt. 1752) was the daughter of Nathaniel Marchant;
    the Marchants were one of the leading families of Antigua. In 1796 she mar-
    ried Robert Liston (1743–1836), British minister to the United States (1796–
    1800). The Listons were generally popular with Americans and became very
    friendly with the Washingtons. Mrs. Liston admired Nelly, writing 6 Sep-
    tember 1796 that she was "one of the prettiest girls I have seen." GWD,
    6:268; Flexner, 4:283; Vere L. Oliver, *The History of the Island of Antigua*, 3
    vols. (London, 1894–99), 2:237; Bradford Perkins, ed., "A Diplomat's Wife in
    Philadelphia: Letters of Henrietta Liston, 1796–1800," *William and Mary
    Quarterly* 11 (Oct. 1954): 603.
57. The Listons were accompanied to Mount Vernon by her brother Dr. Nathan-
    iel Marchant (1754–1804), a member of the Council and justice of the peace
    in Antigua, and his wife Mary Weston Brown (m. 1784). Oliver, 1:74–76,
    2:237.
58. Dr. Samuel Byam Athill (1758–1832), a member of another important Anti-
    guan planter family and friend of Nathaniel Marchant, was president of the
    Council of Antigua. Oliver, 1:10–11.
59. Mary Marchant had two sons by her previous marriage to Antiguan mer-
    chant Joseph Brown—Francis Frye Brown (1775–1842) and Samuel Martin
    Brown (bapt. 1776). Oliver, 1:74–76.

is so far advanced. Mrs. Liston very kindly pressed me to spend a few weeks with her this Winter—assuring Grandmama that I should meet with every care & attention from her. I am sure I should be happy under her protection & should have every reason to be pleased with my reception. But it is utterable impossible I beleive to avail myself of her kindness this Winter, for although I wish much to see my good friends in Philadelphia yet I could not think of leaving home so soon again, I have not spent a Winter here for eight years. I wish to try one again, & I could not leave my Beloved Grandmama so lonesome & to go so far from her to a place where I have so long been accustomed to stay with her entirely.

My *thoughts* will often hover round you, & be your attendants wherever you go—& I shall expect an accurate account of all that pleases & interests you. I am now settled here for the Winter, & except two or three Balls in Alexandria & a short trip to the City I shall remain entirely at home, the family now consists of my Grandparents, Brother & self. My Cousin left me this morning for her Home. I regret the loss of her society much, as she was great company for me, she is an affectionate amiable girl. We expect Mr Lewis[60] a nephew of Grandpapa's to spend the Winter here, he will make our number five in all.

We have had some Winter weather, the Trees, grass, houses &c all covered with ice. The appearance is beautiful, & the river looks so wide & desolate—the Maryland shore so bleak & sublimely horrifying that I am quite delighted—& in better trim than ever to enjoy the beauties of *Ossians Poems* & the *Mysteries of Udolpho*.[61] I am sadly afraid my poor pericranium will be rather the worse for my Country residence this Winter—what with the *Blues* in rainy weather—& the *extacies* from seeing all nature dressed in *snow* & *ice*. When any *reality* distresses or displeases me I immediately dress up some *idea* in the gayest & most pleasing colours, fancy a thousand things which may never happen, & make myself happy by the force of imagination.

60. Lawrence Lewis (1767–1839), son of Washington's sister Betty Washington Lewis, had been invited by his uncle to live at Mount Vernon as deputy host and part-time secretary. Merrow E. Sorley, *Lewis of Warner Hall* (Baltimore, 1979), 202–3.

61. *Fingal* and *Temora*, known collectively as Ossian's poems, were published in the 1760s by James Macpherson. These tales of the Irish poet-hero Ossian were a central influence in the early Romantic movement. *The Mysteries of Udolpho*, published by Ann Radcliffe in 1794, was one of the more popular Gothic romances.

I sincerely congratulate you, & all the inhabitants of your distressed City, that the Yellow fever has taken its leave of you & hope you may never again be visited with that dreadful epidemic.

I rejoice that your Dear Father has his health so much better & that your kind Mama is so well. Do present my most affectionate respects to them, thank them for remembering me so kindly, & assure your Papa that any Book of his composition will allways be highly acceptable to Eleanor P. Custis. I have studied the one he gave me last Spring & hope with his instructions to become a *great Farmer* in time.

I condole with you my Dear Eliza on the departure of our amiable friend Elsina. I was told by Madame Cottineau[62] (who spent a day with us last month) that Madame La R[oche] & her family had left Philadelphia but did not mention any of the circumstances that occasioned it. I am sincerely sorry for the distresses of the worthy Madame La R. & her charming children & hope she will enjoy that happiness with them & her Sister which she so well deserves, & her Husband has so cruelly interrupted. I thank our Dear Elsina for remembering me so affectionately, I was allways happy in her society, & very much pleased with her Mother & little Sister, I allways thought myself lucky in being among their acquaintance. I allways thought before that La R. was a respectable man, good Father & affectionate husband— how dreadfully deceitful are appearances in general! I am sometimes allmost determined to adopt the opinion of Mrs Littleton in the Fille de Chambre[63]—i.e. "think ill of every person, until long experience has convinced you they deserve the contrary." However I think it is better to be sometimes deceived than to judge harshly of those who deserve better.

Vous avez entendu quelque chose de drole en verite. Vous avez vu recentemente le Philosophe n'est pas. Il faut qu'il est comme un autre, quelque fois sage et serieux, mais plus souvent il aime à badiner, folatrer comme un enfant. Il a beaucoup de vanité sans doute. Il pense qu'il est le *plus sage*, et le *plus agreeable* dans la monde, il est passablement agreeable pour deux ou trois

---

62. Luce Moquet, a sister of the marquis de Montalet, married Denis Nicholas Cottineau de Kerloguen (1745–1808), a Breton officer who served with the Continental navy during the Revolution and later settled in America. GWD, 6:265–66.

63. *La Fille de Chambre*, a novel by Mrs. Rowson, was first published in the United States in 1794.

jours, mais après cela—il devient tedieux, et J'etois ennuyé à la morte. Il demeure chez Monsieur Law trois semaines. C'etoit trop long pour Moi.[64]

Many thanks to you for the Anthem, which I am learning & like very much. I am glad to hear our Dear Elizabeth enjoys her health & spirits so much, remember me most affectionately to her when you write. For fear you should think I intend writing a volume instead of a letter to you I will now conclude, hoping soon to receive an answer of nearly if not quite the length of this.

My Grandparents offer their kindest regards to your Parents & self. My Brother sends his respects.

With every wish for the continued happiness of my Dearest Eliza I subscribe myself her affectionate Friend

Eleanor Parke Custis

———————— ❦ ————————

Mount Vernon March 20th 1798[65]

I am really so much ashamed My Dear Friend of my long silence, that I can scarcely muster up resolution enough to write now, but knowing your goodness, & affection for me, I must rest my hopes of pardon of them, as I am certain you will not accuse me of loving you less than I have ever done; no, My Dear Eliza however neglectful I may *appear*, be assured my affection for you will last until Time shall be no more. Your accusation of *ceremony* on my part is unjust indeed, my delay in answering you, was sometimes occasioned by a number of different circumstances, & sometimes by an indolence which I could not conquer, the last is certainly an unpardonable excuse, but it unhappily is too often

---

64. Probably a reference to Constantin-François de Chasseboeuf, comte de Volney, a philospher, economist, and historian, who was in exile in the United States from 1795 to 1798. *Trans.*: You have truly heard something humorous. Haven't you recently seen the Philosopher? He, like anyone, is sometimes wise and serious, but often enough he loves to joke, fooling like a child. Without doubt he is quite vain. He thinks he is the wisest and most agreeable man in the world. He is passably agreeable for two or three days, but after that—he becomes tedious, and I have been bored to death. He has stayed at Mr. Law's three weeks which has been too long for me.

65. Elizabeth Bordley Gibson penciled a note on the verso of the last sheet: "April 19. 1851 I cut off superscription with Genl. Washington's frank on it, for M. Plumsted, for the Church Fair. N.B. It sold for $3."

the case with me; as I have now made a full confession of my faults to you, I will hope for absolution, & in that hope, I will now proceed to inform you of the manner in which I have spent part of my time since my last letter.

Not long after I had written it, I went to Alexandria, & remained there five days with My friends Mrs Harrison,[66] & Mrs Potts.[67] In that time I attended one Assembly which I found very agreeable; & two private dances which I found charming. The other two evenings I spent at sober small tea parties, where I *spoke little, & laughed still less*, however they did very well then for a little variety as I had been highly entertained, & in admirable spirits the two preceding evenings. After that frolick I staid at home until the eleventh of February, when my Grandparents & self went up to Alexandria to attend the celebration of the Birth night. The room was crowded, there were twenty five or thirty couples in the two first setts, I danced with our little Friend G. W. Craik[68] whom you may well remember, I engaged him for a partner at the Birth night in Philadelphia where you & I were flourishing away so much to our own, & each others satisfaction. My other Partners were Mr Robert Peter,[69] a Mr Fitzhugh[70] (an old married man), & Mr Gibbs[71] of Rhode Island. You have probably seen him in Philadelphia, in case you should not have had that *felicity*, I will give you a short description of him, that you may know the *Beau* when you see him, his face is fat, fair, & rather pallid, his eyes light blue, full, & very unmeaning, he keeps them generally cast downwards, as if afraid of trusting them to gaze at

---

66. Ann Craik Harrison was the daughter of Dr. James Craik of Alexandria, one of Washington's closest friends; her husband was an auditor. GWD, 6:265; F. L. Brockett, *The Lodge of Washington* (Alexandria, 1876), 113.

67. Probably Eliza Ramsay Potts, whose husband, John Potts, Jr., was secretary of the Potomac Company. GWD, 5:22, 217.

68. George Washington Craik (1774–1808), the youngest son of Dr. James Craik, served Washington as private secretary during the last year of his presidency. Returning to Alexandria to practice law, he often visited Mount Vernon as one of Nelly's circle of friends. GWD, 6:222; Thane, 276, 278; Brockett, 108.

69. Robert Peter (1774–1809) was the younger brother of Nelly's brother-in-law, Thomas Peter. Genealogical files, Tudor Place.

70. Probably Washington's friend, William Fitzhugh (1741–1809) of Chatham and Ravensworth; his daughter, Mary Lee Fitzhugh, later married George Washington Parke Custis. GWD, 5:24.

71. Probably George Gibbs (1776–1833) of Newport who became a well-known mineralogist. Wealthy, cultured, and hospitable, he was particularly noted for his brilliant conversation. George Gibbs, *The Gibbs Family of Rhode Island and Some Related Families* (New York, 1933), 28.

the objects around, or rather, in *affectation* of extreme *Diffidence*, the which quality he has not the *smallest pretentions* to,—a pug nose, ugly mouth, which *he* thinks pretty, & therefore distorts in all manner of ways, he has tolerable teeth, a *so so* person rather likely than otherwise, not tall, a little embonpoint [stoutness]. *Lisps* much naturally, & *adds* a little to it of his own accord, *is*, or *pretends* to be very near sighted, and in consequence, adorns his *pug*, & *optics* with a pair of *large green spectacles*, except when he goes to Balls, &c, & wishes to cut a dash.

The *furniture* of his *pericranium* I cannot give you an inventory of, as I have seen too little of him, to fathom his *scull*, yet,— his conversation to *Ladies* is composed of, *little Cupids* by wholesale, with *Hearts, darts, hopes, fears, heartachs*, & all the etcetera superfluous, of the *tender passion*. I do not know what subjects he discusses with *Gentlemen*, more probably the *weather, roads*, the *last fashions*, &c. I have now given you a picture of the delectable Gibbs, that you may not mistake him, whenever he may chance to meet your anxious eyes—which I am sure will be for ever *stretched* as wide as their *sockets* will allow, that he may not be unregarded.

We danced until two o'clock, I went with Mrs Potts to her house & sat up until five, got up on Tuesday morning at nine, breakfasted at eleven, dined there with company & went to the *Theatre* where I was very well entertained, with the house & its inhabitants,—the *Theatre* is a long *work shop*, very roughly done, wooden, & small, there are four or five *benches*, one above another (like the seats in the Assembly room) which are called the *Boxes*, then there is a kind of board partition made, and those seats beyond the partition, is the Pit. The *gallery* is made by laying a few boards across the *rafters* of the house; on which the *Gods* & *Goddesses* mount at the hazard of their bones being fractured, in case of the boards giving way, there, they make noise enough in all conscience;—the stage is very near to the *first row of boxes*, one row of candles illumines the whole, in the *Pit* the glimmering light, only serves to make "darkness more visible". The scenery is execrable, what I have seen; the performers very indifferent, except Mrs *Shaw*[72] whom you must remember in

---

72. Mrs. Shaw was an accomplished English actress, a large woman who generally played supporting roles. Brought to America by Thomas Wignell, she played two seasons in Philadelphia at the New Theatre (1794–1796) and then joined the West and Bignall Company, headquartered in Richmond,

Wignell's company.[73] I saw your old master for singing Mr Shaw, he performed with the band at the Birth night, & his clarinet sounds as sweetly as ever.[74] They have met with great encouragement from the Alexandrians, I went twice, the last time I was disgusted; the Child of Nature,[75] was performed, I do not like the play, I saw Mrs Merry[76] perform Amanthis, & even then I was not well pleased; it does not act well I think, Mrs. Shaw performed infinitely better than I expected, she made a pretty Amanthis enough, but she was not supported at all by the others, one in particular, who performed the Marquiss Almanza, was the most horrid, stiff, ugly, inanimate Blockhead I ever beheld, his countenance never changed at all, & in the most affecting parts he "grinned (with all might)—horribly a ghastly smile."

One o'clock was my resting hour that night, & eight in the morning of Wednesday found me ready for breakfast, I was out in the morning shopping, dined at Mr Andrew Ramsay's,[77] & returned to Mr Potts's after dinner, that night Mrs Potts gave me a charming dance, I danced twenty four dances, setts, cotillions, reels &c, sung twelve songs & at five went to *roost*, got up at seven; dined at Mr Wilson's,[78] danced until twelve; Friday dined

---

which in the off-season performed in coastal towns such as Alexandria. Thomas C. Pollock, *The Philadelphia Theatre in the Eighteenth Century* (Philadelphia, 1933), 60, 202–4; George O. Seilhamer, *History of the American Theatre*, 3 vols. (Philadelphia, 1891), 3:144; Martin S. Shockley, *The Richmond Stage, 1784–1812* (Charlottesville, 1977), 113, 119–26, 130, 139–40.

73. Thomas Wignell (1753–1803) was an English actor and theatrical manager. In partnership with Alexander Reinagle, Nelly's onetime music teacher, he built a theater in Philadelphia with a permanent theatrical company; their productions were the most professional and popular in the United States.

74. Mr. Shaw, the husband of the actress, was a musician of some accomplishment who had played at Drury Lane. Brought by Wignell to America in 1794, he played in the New Theatre's orchestra under Alexander Reinagle and then in West and Bignall's orchestra from 1796 until 1798. In Virginia he also directed and played in concerts and occasionally took a part in a play, as did the Shaws' son. Seilhamer, 3:144; Shockley, 119–26, 129.

75. *The Child of Nature*, a two-act romance first performed and published in late 1788, was written by Elizabeth Inchbald, a successful actress and dramatist. It was one of the staples of the Philadelphia theater in the 1790s.

76. Ann Brunton Merry (1769–1808) was an outstanding English actress brought to Philadelphia to perform by Thomas Wignell in 1796. She married Wignell in 1803, and after his death, continued in theatrical partnership with Alexander Reinagle. Merry played Amanthis, the "child of nature," twice in December 1796. Pollock, 312, 317.

77. Andrew Ramsay, brother of Eliza Potts, was an Alexandria merchant. GWD, 6:306.

78. Probably William Wilson (d. 1823) of Alexandria, a partner in a mercantile and shipping firm. GWD, 4:122.

at Mr Fitzhugh's with a large company, went to the Theatre, not at all pleased with the performance—roosted at twelve. Saturday dined out & drank tea also, returned at night at eleven to Mr. Fitzhughs. Sunday—ditto—except that I went to Church in the morning. Monday Mr Wilson gave me a dance, vastly agreeable it was too, a great variety of partners, some passable enough; four, was my resting hour, & seven next day, the rising.

I intended going that day to George Town to celebrate the Birth night there, was prevented by bad weather, & worse roads, passed two *sedate days*. Thursday went to a Ball given to Me by Mr Hodgson[79]—sat up until five, danced a great deal, on Saturday I danced again until eleven. Sunday could not go out on account of wet & dirty walking, & besides that, not a very pleasant day. Monday went post to George Town, staid there a fortnight, no dancing, no gaiety, & at last after four weeks absence returned joyfully home again, not any the worse for my late hours, & immoderate exercise. Brought Sister Peter & her two sweet children with me, they are now here, fat, sweet, & good, the youngest—yclept—Columbia Washington Peter, after the *City*, & district of Columbia. Do you not think the name pretty? It is one of My sisters & my chusing, & I am to be her Godmother.

& so you would not allow me as much credit as the little Don wished to give me, you were right my Dear. I did not deserve it. I am generally remarked as a person who is *much given* to *deep reflection*—& certainly even if I *prefered* a City life, I could make myself happy here, with my friends. But I can claim no merit from it, I allways have & do now, prefer the Country infinitely, & particularly this place to all others in the world. But I can thank Heaven be happy any where when in society. I enjoy it, & gaiety as much as any one, but I can leave it without a moments regret, & find myself quite as happy in retirement. I expect sometime in this or the next month to visit my Mother at Hope Park, & shall remain at this place allmost constantly this Summer.

I am much delighted to hear of your Father's present good health, pray present my respectful love to him & your Mama, with the assurance, that I wish them heartily, long life health & every happiness, in which all here join me, & you are not forgotten in any of our good wishes, I wish you could persuade them to bring you here this Summer, the ride would be of service to all of you, & how delighted I should be to see my Dear Bett again. I am

---

79. William Hodgson (1765–1820) was a prominent Alexandria merchant who married Nelly's cousin, Portia Lee, in 1799. GWD, 5:341, 6:306.

happy to hear that Madame La Roche & Elsina had arrived safe, when you write, remember me in the most affectionate manner, & give them on my part good wishes innumerable.

I suppose you have now seen my Sister and sweet Neice, give the latter a few dozen kisses for her Aunts sake. We have heard nothing of our Friends La Fayette & Frestel since their arrival, we expect the Marquiss & family this spring in America. I am so much hurried as the Post Boy waits, that I can only add, all our regards to your family & self. Remember me to Mr & Mrs Smith of Roxbury. I fear you cannot read this scrawl, if you should find yourself at a loss—Borrow *Cupid Gibbs's green spectacles* & you will decypher it immediately.

God bless My Dearest Eliza prays her affectionate Friend
Eleanor Parke Custis

Have you heard from E Allen lately & how is she.

———————————— ❧ ————————————

Hope Park May 14th 1798

My Dearest Eliza's most acceptable favour of May 3rd I received two days since, from Mount Vernon, whither the Mail carried it, & from whence I came ten days ago. I hasten to thank you for this, & your former epistles & to request that you will continue to write to me as often as you can conveniently, without ceremoniously waiting for an answer, as you may believe me My Dear Friend when I assure you, that you can never write too often, your letters are allways a source of real delight to me, & if I do not *allways* return letter for letter, it is not from want of inclination or affection. I have, as you requested, contradicted positively the report of your engagement with Mr Holker[80] wherever I have heard it mentioned, at the same time giving the young man credit for *all* the good qualities he now possesses or may hereafter possess.

And now, to releive your suffering Ladyship from the tenter

---

80. ——— Holker (b. c. 1771) was the son of John Holker, a former French consul who was involved in private commercial enterprises with Robert Morris. George Washington, *The Writings of George Washington*, 39 vols., ed. John C. Fitzpatrick (Washington, D.C., 1931–40), 13:184; Samuel Breck, *Recollections of Samuel Breck*, ed. H. E. Scudder (London, 1877), 85–86.

hooks of impatience, curiosity, &c &c—on which you are so un-
comfortably dangling no doubt, even at this *present writing*, my
superabundant delicacy would not have kept my tongue tied until
this time, when I know the interest you take in whatever concerns me, if there was any truth in this report, this second part of
last spring's rumour, & with as much foundation as then existed
for it. I cant think *who* the *wiseacre* is who lately left Mount Vernon, & who vouches for the authenticity of the affair, or how Mr
Craik[81] (the *most honorable member*) could know that the young
persons in question have had since last spring an *excellent opportunity* of knowing each other. To *my* certain knowledge (who you
will allow should know something of the matter) they have never
directly, or *indirectly* set eyes on each other but *once* since the
races in April twelvemonth, of which I gave you information.
Report has often informed me that he was attached to a certain
Eleanor Parke Custis, an *oddity* of these parts, but as *he* has
never told it to *her* by *tongue*, or *pen*, therefore she is yet in the
dark as to the *truth* of the surmise & consequently she is not, nor
has been engaged to said Charles Carroll, therefore of course
your impatience, anxiety, & all that, goes for nothing; there is at
present no shadow of the event; clouds and darkness rest upon it,
& you or any one else know as much of the business as I do. Mr
Carroll was at Mount Vernon in March, staid one day & night,
nothing more than common civility passed on either side, & he
marched off as he came. Since when I have neither seen him, or
heard anything of his movements. You will excuse my not de-
scribing *said youth*, his *external* appearance I pourtrayed to you
last Spring, my acquaintance since, being only of one day's standing, does not authorise me to speak of his *internal* qualities. By
all accounts they exceed his *personal attractions*, which are not
very great, although quite equal to *most* of the youths of the present day. If I should ever be engaged to *him* or any other person,
you may rely upon having the earliest, & most candid, information, without being necessitated to interrogate me.

I left Mount Vernon with My Sister Law to come here on a
visit to My Dearest Mother whom I had not seen for several
months; I left my Beloved Grandparents & Sister Peter well, &

---

81. William Craik was the eldest son of Dr. James Craik. At this time a member
of Congress, he later served as a federal judge and Chief Justice of the
County Court of the Fifth Judicial District of Maryland. GWD, 6:265;
Brockett, 113.

found the family here in perfect health, Mr & Mrs Law left us last week, with my charming neice Eliza who is very much improved. My Sister & Brother were much pleased with their visit to Philadelphia, & the kind attentions they met with there. Sister Peter has returned to the City, her sweet children were dangerously ill for two days, but they had recovered allmost when I came away.

I have never been out since I returned from the City, have seen few persons, & heard no news.

Many thanks My Charming Friend for the song sent, I sing it every day with *strong patriotic feelings*, & think it very fine.

I am full as patriotic as you can be *Bett*, & to speak truth, I am becoming an outrageous politician, perfectly *federal*, & determined even to lend a hand to extirpate the *Demons* if their unparellel'd impudence, & thirst of conquest should make them attempt an invasion of our peaceable happy Land.

Have you courage enough think you to turn *Soldier* on such an occasion? If you have, let me know it, & I will enroll you in *my* corps of *independent volunteers*, if occasion suits, we may perhaps *dub* ourselves *knights*. You must procure a black dress, the *fashion* of it we will settle hereafter, we shall have black helmets, of morocco leather, ornamented with black bugles, & an immense Plume of black feathers. You have no idea how becoming it will be, "we shall tow'r above the rest"—our arms shall be, Lances, Pistols, Bows & arrows. & I shall take especial care to provide *burnt corks*, or *charcoal* sufficient to furnish amply the whole association of valorous *knights* with immense *whiskers*, & *mustachios*, of uncommon magnitude, to strike with awe the beholders. "My Ambition fires at the thought", & I feel chok full of fight. Think child how glorious, to be celebrated as the *preservers* of our *Friends & Country*, "In such a cause a Womans vengeance tow'rs above her Sex!" We shall perform wonders I am sure, & our fame will be transmitted to latest posterity. I have already engaged several of the sisterhood to be ready at a moments warning, I am *Commander in Chief* of the corps. I am at present quietly seated in this still retreat, free from noise & bustle, enjoying the present, & keeping myself in readyness for, & prepared to meet anything that may come round in the course of events. I do not wish to dance again until next Winter. I allmost lamed myself last Winter. I am not at all surprised that you wish for retirement, I would not exchange mine, for all the pomp & Vanity of this wicked world.

I expect to remain here some weeks longer, if you write to me in the interim, direct your letters to Mount Vernon, & I shall get them regularly as heretofore. You will have some difficulty to read this scrawl I fear, I have copied part of it, but it is still hardly legible. I beg you will remember me with great respect & affection to your Parents, friendly greetings to your Brother Mr Miflin—& compliments to all our old friends who are kind enough to remember me.

Be assured My Dearest Eliza of the firm & lasting attachment of your

Eleanor Parke Custis

———————— ❦ ————————

Mount Vernon July 1st 1798

My Dearest Eliza,

Six weeks have elapsed since I last wrote to you, My friend has perhaps been a little surprised, that I could be so long silent, after the hint she wrote me on being ceremonious; I am rather faulty I confess, but not so much so as you may suppose. My letter was dated from Hope Park, where I remained four weeks with My Dear Mother, very happy in her society, & surrounded by my younger Sisters, the day after my return to Mt Vn—my Sister & Brother Law arrived, accompanied by my lovely Neice, and Mr Niemcewicz, a Polish gentleman & great friend to General Kosciusko.[82] & two days after My Mother & Co came, & we had the satisfaction of having their society ten days.

My Sister has recovered her health & good looks entirely, Brother Law has been indisposed two or three times this Summer,

---

82. Tadeusz Kosciusko (1746–1817) was a Polish officer who served in the American Revolution. He led the unsuccessful 1794 Polish insurrection against Russia; one of his companions and supporters was Julian Ursyn Niemcewicz (1758–1841). Both were imprisoned by the Russians and, on their release, came to the United States, arriving August 19, 1797. Despite Kosciusko's sudden return to Europe in May 1798, Niemcewicz continued his travels and observations of America. He returned Nelly's good opinion, writing, "This was one of those celestial figures that nature produces only rarely, that the inspiration of painters has sometimes divined and that one cannot see without ecstasy. Her sweetness is equal to her beauty . . . ." Niemcewicz, xix, xxiv-xxvii, 97.

he is pretty well at present, & My Neice is very sweet & entertaining. Mr Niemcewicz you may have seen perhaps, no doubt you
have heard of him. He is not hansome, but his countenance is
mild & pleasing, & is so expressive of great sensibility & unhappiness, that I was very much interested, & I think no one can
know him, without feeling for his past severe sufferings, & an
interest in his future wellfare. He appears to be very amiable, his
manners are diffident, perfectly polite, without that disgusting
ceremony & obsequiousness that most foreigners think the *quin-
tessence* of gentility, but which has allways been very disagreeable & troublesome in my opinion. We were all pleased with his
society, I beleive he has received a very finished education, & his
understanding very cultivated.

I was very much disappointed in not seeing General Kosciusko. His great character & his sufferings have made me very
desirous of his acquaintance. We hope to see him here this Summer. Our friends left us three weeks since, & we have no one with
us at present but Miss Portia Lee a distant relation of mine. A
very fine sensible Woman, she will return to her Guardians next
week, & then My Grandparents & self will compose the Mount
Vernon family. I have not seen Sister & Brother Peter for nine
weeks, they are well, also my Neices. I shall stay at home all the
Summer. My Brother will come home in August to pass his vaca-
tion. He is much pleased with Annapolis,[83] & studies very well.
I should not be thus minute in respect to my family, did I not
beleive my Dearest Eliza feels an interest in whatever contrib-
utes to my happiness.

Since I returned to this place I have anxiously expected to
hear from you, without considering that you would probably wait
until I informed you of my arrival here. I have deferred writing
from post to post, in the hope of receiving an answer to my last.
But I will no longer defer the gratification of writing, & proving
to you that I do not stand upon ceremony.

Last week Mr LeGuin & Mr Flamend[84] dined with us, they
are genteel men I think, the former I like very well, I think his
conversation very entertaining, & his manners rather pleasing,

---

83. In the spring of 1798, Washington, hoping for an improvement in Washington Custis's studies, sent him to St. John's College in Annapolis. In
   August, however, young Custis gave up his studies and returned home for
   good. GWD, 6:259–60, 284, 311–12.
84. Thomas Law frequently brought foreign visitors to Mount Vernon. LeGuin
   may have been the Louis LeGuen who came to America in 1794 and went

Mr Flamend is neither as entertaining or pleasing as the other. Mr Law speaks highly of both, they are old friends of his. I heard of you from them, & that Our amiable Young Friend Elsina Espinasse, was with her Mother and Aunt at Bordeaux. Have you lately heard from her, or Our Dear Elizabeth Allen? When you write to them, be so kind as to present my most affectionate regards, & good wishes to them, & to Madame La Roche & Mrs [Ann Allen] Penn, my respects. I suppose Elizabeths Sister the pretty & sweet Ann has changed her name before this time, if she has, add my congratulations, to the regards & good wishes you will offer to her, from me.

Have you lately seen my Friend Maria Morris, I have written repeatedly to her but received no answer. I love Maria, & sincerely feel for the change herself & family have experienced[85]— & was I not induced from her long silence (a twelvemonth) to beleive She wishes to discontinue a correspondence begun under happier circumstances, or could I believe that my letters would afford her the smallest degree of pleasure, I would write continually. As it is, I know not what to do, I wish to prove to her what is perfectly true, that no change whatever in her situation could make me for a moment slight her, or diminish in the smallest degree my affection which has lasted nine years, on the contrary, I think she is far more entitled now to every affectionate attention, than when her Father possessed millions. For *myself* I know, that were I by misfortunes reduced *even* to the necessity of working to procure a scanty subsistance, without having done anything that could deserve contempt—I should not feel at all humbled, nor should I care for the slights of the world. The attentions of my real friends I should allways value. *Innate worth* is not diminished by loss of *wealth*. I fear to continue writing to her, I know her feelings must be very acute at the change so sudden & so great—& I would not do any thing that would hurt her feelings or be disagreeable to her. I suppose she does not feel in sufficient spirits to keep up a correspondence. If you see her My Dear Betsy, pray remember me most affectionately to her, & her family.

into trade in New York and Philadelphia. Niemcewicz also mentioned a friend in New York named LeJuin. Washington recorded the second visitor as Clarmont, rather than Flamend; a Flamin visited Kosciusko in Philadelphia. GWD, 6:303; Niemcewicz, 129; Moreau de Saint-Méry, 257.

85. Land speculation and overextension by Robert Morris caused a financial disaster. In February 1798 he was arrested for debt and remained in debtors prison until August 1801. Broken by his failure, he lived on his wife's annuity until his death.

I hope your Dear Parents are quite well. I was rejoiced to hear that your Father has recovered his health very much. Present my sincere respects & love to them, remember me to Mr & Mrs Mifflin Mr & Mrs Smith—Mrs Powel,[86] Mrs FitzSimons,[87] & all my Old Friends in Philadelphia—& assure them that Eleanor P. Custis can never forget their kindness to her. Were you not pleased at General Marshall's reception?[88] *I* was delighted at it— he has richly deserved every attention. I hope General Pinkney[89] will soon return, his family are very amiable & his character is very respectable indeed. His friends in Charleston must be very uneasy on his account—he has two daughters there with Mrs Horry his Sister, they are fine accomplished Women.[90] You have heard me mention Miss Horry my friend, she has married Mr Frederick Rutlege,[91] he is, I am told an amiable young man, and

86. Elizabeth Willing Powel (1742–1830) was one of Washington's closest women friends. Intellectual and witty, she and her husband, Samuel Powel, one of the wealthiest and most cultivated men in Philadelphia, were social and community leaders. Flexner, 2:314–21; Carl Bridenbaugh and Jessica Bridenbaugh, *Rebels and Gentlemen: Philadelphia in the Age of Franklin* (New York, 1962), 207–12.

87. Catharine Meade, daughter of Philadelphia merchant Robert Meade, in 1761 married Thomas Fitzsimons (1741–1811), an Irishman who made his fortune in the West Indian trade. He was an ardent patriot and supporter of Washington's policies. GWD, 6:23.

88. John Marshall (1755–1835), attorney, brigadier general of the Virginia militia, and future Chief Justice of the Supreme Court, had been appointed in 1797 as one of three American commissioners to France; the others were Charles Cotesworth Pinckney and Elbridge Gerry. Their purpose was to bring an end to the undeclared naval war that existed between the United States and France, but Talleyrand, newly named foreign minister by the Directory, refused to receive them without the payment of bribes and loans. They refused and Marshall returned to America. When the American people were informed of what became known as the XYZ Affair, public sentiment became even more violently anti-French. Marshall was greeted by cheering crowds on his return to New York. In Philadelphia on June 23, a huge celebration dinner was given in his honor. GWD, 6:314; Frances N. Mason, *My Dearest Polly: Letters of Chief Justice John Marshall* (Richmond, 1961), 67, 118–19.

89. Charles Cotesworth Pinckney (1746–1825), Revolutionary War general and political supporter of Washington, remained in France until August because his daughter Eliza was too ill to sail for America. Marvin R. Zahniser, *Charles Cotesworth Pinckney* (Chapel Hill, 1967), 182–90.

90. Pinckney's elder daughters, Maria Henrietta (d. 1836) and Harriott (1776–1866), had remained in South Carolina with their aunt, Harriott Pinckney Horry (1748–1830), the widow of Col. Daniel Horry, a very wealthy planter. Mabel L. Webber, "The Thomas Pinckney Family of South Carolina," *South Carolina Historical and Genealogical Magazine*, 39 (1938): 24; GWD, 6:126.

91. Daniel and Harriott Horry's daughter Harriott Pinckney Horry (d. 1858) married Frederick Rutledge (1768–1821), a member of another leading

the cleverest in Charleston; she is a charming Woman, & her Mother is remarkably so.

Do you leave town this Summer? Write a long letter you *Scrub*, & let me have a just and minute account of all that is interesting to you. All your movements, &c. When you see Mrs Liston, pray present my respectful regards. Also to Mrs McHenry, & kind greetings to the entertaining & good little *Secretary of the War Department* [James McHenry], he must have his hands full at this important crisis. What think you *Bett*, of the delectable Apostate Bishop of Autun,[92] what an intolerable wretch he is, I could positively hang *him*, the five Directors, & *Monsieur* le *Philosophe* Chasseboeuf de Volney—without the smallest remorse, I should rather glory in ridding this earth of such *fiends*. Does not your wrath often kindle at the recollection of Talleyrand, & Volney, when with their smooth tongues & woe begone faces, they excited the sympathy of the Americans, & were treated with so much kindness—that they were both Spy's, and are doing all in their power to injure those who befriended them.[93] However I hope if the insolent french should dare to come here, that the Americans may humble them compleatly, I would not care a pin for any relation of mine, who could do it, if he would hesitate one moment to fight will all his Heart & strength, and lay down his life & fortune for the service of his country.

My Beloved Grandparents are well, & unite with me in kindest regards to your Parents & self.

Adieu ma tres chere Amie, soyez persuadez que Je serois pour toujours Votre sincere et affectionée [Good-bye my very dear friend, be assured that I will always be your sincere and affectionate]

Eleanor Parke Custis

South Carolina family, October 11, 1797. Mabel L. Webber, "Dr. John Rutledge and his Descendants," *South Carolina Historical and Genealogical Magazine*, 31 (1930): 17.

92. Charles-Maurice de Talleyrand-Perigord (1754–1838) had been appointed Bishop of Autun shortly before the beginning of the French Revolution. A leading revolutionary deputy, he resigned the bishopric in 1791 and served the new government as a diplomat and negotiator. As different factions succeeded to power, he first fell from favor, going into exile in 1794, and then returned in 1796. He was named foreign minister in the fall of 1797 and was the particular object of American hatred because of his actions in the XYZ Affair.

93. Both Talleyrand (1794–96) and Chasseboeuf (1795–98) had been exiles in the United States.

Mount Vernon February 3rd 1799

My dearest Eliza,

How shall I address my ever loved Friend, after a silence so long, so unjustifiable, so unpardonable; & particularly when I have now *two* of her kind and acceptable letters to answer. Be assured I am overwhelmed with deep contrition for this my fault, & scarcely dare hope for your forgiveness, if you do accord it to me, it will be entirely *your own goodness*, & not, I am sorry to say, *my deserts. Why* I have not answered you months ago, I could not tell. Beleive me, Neglect and want of affection is not, and never will be a reason for my silence to you, what is it then? *Laziness, unconquerable indolence, absence of mind, giddiness, desertion of reason. One* and *all* of those I beleive you must be contented with for I cannot think of any *better* reasons. Certain it is, that every day, of every week, since I received your first letter by Mr Harper I have determined to answer it—but another and another came and no answer could I accomplish. Then Grandpapa, Mr Lewis & Mr Lear were taken sick—very dangerously ill, I being *deputy Doctor* had my *hands* full generally, & my *Heart* constantly filled with uneasiness on their accounts. During all that time, I do not remember sending the scrape of a Pen to any mortal. When I heard of my Dear E Bordley's illness, I was sincerely sorry for it, very anxious to hear from you, & offered up daily, most fervent prayers for your speedy recovery—*then* I was resolved to write, & when your second letter arrived I was extremely rejoiced to find you had recovered your Health entirely. You were in a very good way of having an answer, but alas, How shall I speak it. However *truth* will come to light.

Cupid, a small mischeivous Urchin, who has been trying sometime to humble my pride, took me by surprise, when I thought of nothing *less* than him, & in the *very moment* that I had (after mature consideration) made the *sage* and prudent resolve of passing through life, as a *prim starched Spinster*, to the great edification of my Friends in particular, & the public in general— when I had abused & defied him, & thought my Heart impenetrable he slyly called in Lawrence Lewis to his aid, & transfixed me with a Dart, before I knew where I was. It was sometime I assure you before I could reconcile myself to giving up my favourite scheme, but resistance was vain, I had to contend with perseverance, & at last was obliged to submit & bind myself to become that old fashioned thing called a *Wife* & *now, strange* as it may seem—I am perfectly reconciled & neither think "the day *evil*, or the Hour *unlucky*," that witnessed my solemn promise to become *Mrs Lewis*, & take said *Lawrence* for better for worse.

That promise will soon by ratifyed—the 22nd of this month is the day which will fix my future destiny. My present prospects are the most pleasing. The Man I have chosen to watch over my future happiness, is in every respect calculated to ensure it. I have long known & regarded him highly, he is universally esteemed for those virtues which do honour to the Head and Heart. & in devoting my life to him, to make him happy, I have not one anxious thought in regard to myself—confident of his sincere and unalterable attachment, & that every wish of his Heart tends to promote my felicity.

He has been absent from me with my Brother four weeks. We expect them every day to return here. My Friend will make some allowances for my remissness when she considers the various events which have occurred since I last wrote. I hope you never will again have cause to remark my silence, should it happen unavoidably, you will I am sure always exculpate your Eleanor who has so long considered your affection as invaluable, from the charge of neglecting you. You may expect a letter from *Mrs Lawrence Lewis* soon after she becomes so—& I need not add how happy a letter from E Bordley will make her. My residence will be in Frederick County thirty miles from Bath, I indulge the pleasing hope that I shall one day or other, (the sooner the better,) have the happiness of seeing my Dear Betsy in a House of which I shall be the mistress, & in which, every exertion will be made by its owners to render her stay agreeable, & to induce her to make it lengthy. Mr Lewis is not unacquainted with Miss Bordley. I have often spoken of you to him, & he wishes very much for the pleasure of your acquaintance personally. & now my Dear as I have so candidly communicated to you, will you not be as sincere in informing me whether *you* have not a *penchant* for some one of your numerous admirers, & who is the person who is so happy? I hear often that you are engaged, or about to be so. & nothing would please me more than to know that you have found a Person worthy of your heart and Hand, one, to whom your excellent & tender parents could resign you with the pleasing assurance of ensuring your Happiness, that such an one may soon be found & that every felicity may be yours which frail mortality will admit of, is my fervent Prayer.

For me, my prospects of happiness although very great are yet clouded when I think of leaving My Beloved Grandparents who have been everything to me hitherto, & this dear spot— which has been my constant *Home*, since my first remembrance—to which I must ever feel the strongest attachment. I hope to pay frequent visits however to My Parents, Mr. Lewis being Grandpapa's Nephew, will have the same inducement—affection—& will I am sure be ever ready to accompany me here. The part of Virginia to which I am going is remarkably fertile, the neighbourhood excellent, & the situations & views, sublime and beautiful. The life of a Farmer was allways my delight. I pity those who can prefer the Dissipations of a City life, & artificial beauties to the simplicity cheerfulness & content of a Country residence, & to the contemplation of the innumerable Beauties of Nature. I have not been to any entertainment this Season, or spent one night in Alexandria since last February. I have but lately returned from a visit of three weeks to my Dearest Mother in the Forest. Nearly twelve months have elapsed since I visited my Sisters in the City. The Winter has passed away imperceptibly & I have felt no inclination to go from Home at all. The weather has been generally very mild, particularly the last month. I should have liked very much to accompany Grandpapa & Grandmama to Philadelphia when *he* went this Winter but as She could not go, *I* could not think of leaving her. My Dear and Kind Friends in Philadelphia I often think of with heartfelt pleasure, their kindness I can never forget—& happy should I be to see them again, which I hope will one day be the case.

I was sincerely sorry for their distresses during the last dreadful Summer, I hope not, but I fear they will be liable to the Same again.

I am happy to inform you that my Dearest Grandparents, Mother, Sisters and other Friends enjoy uninterrupted Health. I hope soon to have the pleasing assurance that you have recovered yours perfectly, & that your Dear Parents are quite well. Do present my most affectionate respects to them, & every wish for their continued Health and Happiness. My Grandparents offer affectionate regards and best wishes to them & you. Remember me particularly to Your Sister & Brother Mifflin, Mr & Mrs Smith of Roxbury, Mrs Fitzsimons, Mrs Powell, & all others of my Friends in Philadelphia.

Please to thank your good Father for his little Book,[94] I received it by Mr Harper[95] & ought long since to have returned my acknowledgements for it.

I fear you will scarcely be able to make out this letter it is so badly written, my hurry must plead my excuse, & as it is now late at night I conclude with

Assuring my Dearest Eliza, that she has not a Friend more sincerely attached to her—than

Eleanor Parke Custis

———————————— ❧ ————————————

Mount Vernon November 4th 1799

My Dearest Elizabeth's acceptable & affectionate letter is now before me, in it you accuse me of never having informed you of the change in my situation. The letter probably miscarried for I am allmost certain I wrote soon after my marriage. However that may be, yet I acknowledge myself extremely culpable in not writing oftener to my beloved Friend. Constant occupations, frequent journeys, the confinement of my beloved Husband with an inflamation in one of his eyes, occasion'd by a violent cold, I might offer as excuses, and could my Dear Eliza review the scenes we have passed through she would I am sure readily pardon my silence. My affection & the most unfeigned interest in your wellfare are and ever will be unalterable. Be assured I should experience the sincerest delight in embracing you & enjoying your valued society, & my Spouse is equally anxious for the pleasure of your acquaintance. Your congratulations could never be unacceptable & my Dear Friend I know will rejoice in the confirmation of her wishes for my happiness. In the tenderness & unceasing solicitude of the best of Husbands I experience that perfect content & unalloy'd felicity which renders the marriage state so bless'd. I have not a wish beyond domestic retirement, and complying with every wish of my Husband. My lot has been extremely fortunate. I am united to one who is in every respect calculated to ensure my happiness—the only person I ever

---

94. Probably John Beale Bordley's *Essays and Notes on Husbandry and Rural Affairs*, which was published in 1799.
95. Perhaps Robert Goodloe Harper (1765–1825), a congressman from South Carolina, who had business connections in Philadelphia.

thought I could be happy in a union with & I thank Heaven constantly for uniting us.

Sometime hence I shall have an additional source of happiness to acquaint you with I hope. The idea of being a Mother, of watching over & forming the mind of Our little infant is a source of delight which none but those in similar situations can experience. I have been busily engaged in providing little trappings for the sweet stranger & anticipating the delight I shall experience when presenting it to its Dear Father. My Belov'd Grandmama has also been employ'd for sometime for her little great grandchild. Think My Dear Eliza what a pleasure I shall have in seeing her fondle my child. You will smile I am sure when you read the foregoing, & recollect the *writer*, is the once rattlepated, lazy Eleanor P Custis who was generally stiled a thoughtless giddy mortal extremely fond of going to Balls;—now a sedate matron attending to domestic duties, & providing for a young stripling who will call her Mother. "Tis she, the same person, & instead of saying with Hamlet! "But oh! how *fallen*" I may say with truth that she is by the late circumstances, *exalted*. & converted into a rational being.

We left this, in May after having visited my Mother & Sisters, & gone through the routine of ceremonious dinners, parties, visits; some agreeable, others tiresome. I left my Beloved & revered Grandmama with sincere regret, & it was sometime before I could feel reconciled to travelling without her. We passed a fortnight in Culpeper County, at a charming little seat belonging to Mr Charles Carter who married My Husbands Sister.[96] With them we were very happy & I have constantly experienced from them & Mr Lewis's Brother's every affectionate & tender attention. From thence we proceeded on a party of pleasure to Richmond, & Shirley, the elegant mansion of Mr Carter's Uncle[97] 25 miles from Richmond. With them we passed a pleasant fortnight. Mr L. & self paid a short visit to the Estate belonging to my Brother, where my *Grandfathers* lived in New Kent.[98] I had never been there & was very anxious to see their old dwelling.

---

96. In 1781 Betty Lewis (1765–1830) had married Charles Carter (1765–1829); the couple made their home at Western View, near Stevensburg in Culpeper County. Sorley, 186.

97. Charles Carter (1732–1806) of Shirley, located at the confluence of the James and Appomattox rivers, shared with Washington a keen interest in experimental farming. GWD, 3:215.

98. The White House was the estate of Daniel Parke Custis, Martha Washington's first husband, in New Kent County; she and Washington were married there. Thane, 41.

We returned then to Marmion near Fredericksburg where Brother George Lewis[99] resides, & intended staying but a fortnight as we wished to pay My Grandparents a short visit before we proceeded to the upper Counties. But Mr Lewis was confined for four weeks to a dark room with an inflamation in one of his eyes, & we were detain'd six weeks which oblig'd us to hasten to Culpeper as soon as possible to avoid the Ague & Fever. I suffer'd very much anxiety during the confinement of My Belov'd Husband whose sufferings were severe. In the warmest weather we were obliged to exclude the air entirely, that the light might not be admitted. The remainder of the Summer we divided between Our Sisters & Brothers of Culpeper & Fauquier.[100] Our House in Frederick not being ready for our reception as Mr Lewis could not travel there to superintend. I had the influenza severely for 4 weeks, reduced so much & from constant fevers & pain [in] my breast & side, my Friends apprehended a decline. Fortunately however by good nursing I am entirely restored to health. Mr Lewis is perfectly well, his eye is free from inflamation, & the sight nearly as good as ever. I met with Our Old Friend Susan Randolph in Richmond, she is very much grown & improv'd, a very fine person, & her face is rather hansome. She made many enquiries concerning you.

We returned here two or three weeks since & shall remain during the Winter. My Belov'd Grandmama had been extremely ill a few weeks before my return, but I was never informed of it until my arrival or I should have hastened to pay her every dutiful affectionate attention in my power. She is now thank Heaven quite well & recovers her good looks fast. Grandpapa is quite well. We rejoice that your excellent Father has recover'd, & that your Mama is in good Health. Pray tender them my thanks for their good wishes, my respect & affection. My Grandparents, Mr Lewis & my Brother unite in the most sincere regards & best wishes for your Parents & self. The intelligence concerning our amiable Friends Elizabeth, & Elsina afford me sincere pleasure. When you write to them remember me in the most affectionate manner. At all times your letters My Dearest Eliza with what-

---

99. Major George Lewis (1757–1821), one of Washington's nephews who was closely associated with him, had moved to Marmion in King George County in 1796. Sorley, 153–57.

100. Betty Lewis Carter and Howell Lewis (1771–1822) lived in Culpeper County; Robert Lewis (1769–1829) received a farm in Fauquier County from George Washington. Sorley, 229, 232, 248–50.

ever interests you will be highly gratifying to me, & I hope you will not have so much cause to complain of me, as lately.

Remember me with affection to those Friends whose regard will induce them to mention me. And Be assured Dear Eliza that I shall ever be with prayers for the Happiness of yourself & Parents

Your sincerely affectionate Friend
Eleanor P. C. Lewis.

Chapter Two

The Young Matron
1804–1811

" . . . sickness and sorrow, are not very favorable to epistolary
communications."

Woodlawn December 4th 1804

Many years have elapsed since I had the happiness of seeing
my Dearest E Bordley, and nearly seven years have passed since
we corresponded; but neither time or the variety of changes I have
experienced, has diminish'd the sincere affection I have felt for
you since our first acquaintance; & I feel persuaded, that you my
Dearest Elizabeth, will not easily forget one of your most attached friends. Believe me, I think of you incessantly. Most ardently do I wish to see you again; and I take this opportunity of
introducing my amiable Sister[1] to you, that I may hear particularly how you are, and whether I still hold a place in your remembrance; also to assure you, how constantly I regret the distance
between us, which deprives me of the society of my most valued
young friend.

We have both experienced the most severe distress in being
deprived of affectionate Parents,[2] whose loss can never be repair'd. In addition to this, I have lost two children, one of them the
most lovely & engaging little Girl I ever saw.[3] I have had very bad
health since my marriage until the two last years, I have now
recover'd my health, and have two charming children. The Eldest
is five years old, a Daughter [Frances Parke Lewis], the youngest,

---

1. Mary Lee Fitzhugh (1788–1853), the daughter of William and Anne Ran-
   dolph Fitzhugh of Chatham and Ravensworth, married George Washington
   Parke Custis in 1804. GWD, 6:291.
2. George Washington died in 1799; Martha Washington, in 1802; and John
   Beale Bordley, in 1804.
3. Martha Betty Lewis was born in 1801; she fell ill with measles the night of
   Martha Washington's death and died shortly afterward. Lawrence Fielding
   Lewis died soon after birth in 1802.

a charming Boy [Lorenzo Lewis] of twelve months; remarkably lovely & healthy. I have commission'd my Sister, to give you an excellent description of them, and hope you will reserve a portion of your affection for these precious babes, to whom my life is devoted. I often wish you could see them, is there no prospect of your ever visiting this state My Dearest Elizabeth, most sincerely should I rejoice to wellcome you here, and your Dear Mama, Will you assure her, of my most respectful and affectionate remembrance of her former kindness to me. I shall ever retain the most heartfelt gratitude for the friendly attentions I recieved in Philadelphia, when blest in the society of the best and most Beloved Parent that any one could possess. To all our intimate friends I hope you will offer my affectionate regards, to Mr & Mrs Smith of Roxbury, your Brother & Sister Mifflin particularly. Do you ever hear from our friend E Allen now, I hope she is well and happy. My love to her allways when you write, & to Elsina.

My Brother will have the pleasure of presenting his Wife to you, and I will bespeak for her a share in your regard, for she is truly deserving of every one's affection. She is in great distress at present on her poor Mother's account, who is confined in Philadelphia with a cancer. Mrs. Fitzhugh is one of the best and most valued of our society—and is so far advanced in years, that I much fear she will never recover. Any little attentions to her & her excellent Husband, I shall consider as being confer'd upon me.

My Sister will answer all your enquiries respecting My Children & myself, & I shall impatiently expect an account of your health & all that is interesting to you. My Husband requests your acceptance of his best wishes for your health & happiness, & is extremely anxious for a personal introduction to you.

My Daughter often speaks of Elizabeth Bordley and is prepared to love you.

May every blessing attend My Dearest Elizabeth. Prays her faithfully attach'd friend

E P. Lewis.

———————————— ❦ ————————————

Woodlawn March 23rd 1806

My Beloved friends affectionate letter of December 4th of which Mr Pedersen[4] was the bearer I have been unavoidably, and

---

4. Peder Pedersen was named chargé d'affaires for Denmark in 1803. Like many

painfully prevented answering until now. Although I cannot experience a more sincere and lively pleasure than the affectionate remembrance of my much loved friend excites; yet I am so unfortunate as to be prevented expressing it in person altogether, and very often, the same ill fortune attends my assuring her of it by letter.

I wrote to you in July a long letter, which I fear you never received; and I have made enquiries of every one I have seen, but could gain no intelligence of you, until I met with Mr Hamilton[5] at the City races. I intended writing by him, but he was prevented calling at my Brothers as he intended, and I lost the opportunity. I staid four weeks with my Brother and his amiable Wife, in which time I dined once with Mrs Merry,[6] and was in company with her 2 or 3 times afterwards; I think her manners extremely affable and friendly, and she a *little*, resembles my ever beloved and regretted Madame de Freire; I should be very much pleased to cultivate her acquaintance, but we are eighteen miles apart, and I seldom go to the City. I have never left home since I came from my Brothers in October, and have been by that means deprived of the pleasure of Mr Pedersen's acquaintance which I regret I assure you, I have heard the most exalted character of him, from many persons, but I have two reasons in particular, to ensure my most favorable opinion of his merits—viz—My Friends good opinion of him, and *his* respectful and devoted admiration of, *Miss Bordley*, are not then sufficient to convince me that I should form the most correct impression of him? I hope however, that I may yet be fortunate enough to make an acquaintance, which you recommend so much by your introduction.

You were misinformed in regard to my dining at the *Presidents*, I have not the honor to be in that *great mans* good graces, nor can one who knew so well the *first President*, ever wish to be noticed by the present chief magistrate [Thomas Jefferson]. Ah my Beloved friend, how sadly times are changed to us all, but to *me* more than anyone, deprived of those Beloved Parents whom I loved with so much devotion, to whose unceasing tenderness I was

---

diplomatic representatives, he lived in Philadelphia and traveled to Washington only to conduct business. Charles Lanman, *Biographical Annals of the Civil Government of the United States* (Washington, D.C., 1876), 615; Westcott, *History*, 5:1155.

5. Perhaps Alexander Hamilton's son, James Alexander Hamilton (1788–1878), a lawyer and politician.

6. Elizabeth Death Leathes Merry (d. 1824) was the wife of Anthony Merry (1756–1835), British minister to the United States from 1803 until late 1806. Malcolm Lester, *Anthony Merry Redivivus* (Charlottesville, 1978).

indebted for every good I possess'd, and forever separated from
other friends, from my Beloved Mde. de Freire whom I must ever
love and regret, whether remember'd by her or not; and from you
my intimate and Dear friend. I look back with sorrow, & to the
future without hope. It appears to be a dream long passed away, so
heavily has time passed to me. And believe me my friend, the
anxiety and fears of a Mother, are beyond anything you can con-
cieve; when our children are sick we are miserable, and should
they recover, we constantly fear that they may be again ill, and
when we see them suffer without the power of relieving, and
often unable to discover what it is which afflicts them, happiness
is out of the question. My darling Parke has sufferd with an
imposthume [abscess] under one arm and on the shoulder since
the first of January. It was very painful part of the time, and was
lanced under the arm, since that time, the shoulder and arm continued swelled hard, & inflamed, without being at all changed, by
the variety of applications recomm[end]ed by the Physician, at
last the mercurial ointment[7] was rubbed on, and this, continued
every night and morning, at last removed the complaint; affected
the system as the Physician wished, without having occasion'd a
sore mouth; we have ceased the last week to rub with the ointment, and by the assistance of tonics, I hope she will acquire a
better state of health, than she has ever had. Her constitution is
very delicate and my fears are continually excited for her.

My Lorenzo is very healthy, he is a sweet Boy, I have made
him Turkish dresses of red flanelle this winter, and he looks very
manly in them I assure you.[8] Since I wrote you my friend, I have
had an addition to my little family. A fine fat girl, who was born
in August, & to whom I have given the name of *Agnes Freire*, in
remembrance of my much valued friend. From whom I have received some letters since her departure from America, but not one
for the last two years. Indeed I have not been a regular correspondent myself, for sickness and sorrow, are not very favorable to
epistolary communications. I have the pleasure to hear by a
friend, that my last letter was received and I will hope that there
is a letter now on its way to me, I should be sincerely grieved to
loose a particle of that affection which Mde. de Freire has so

---

7. Mercury, mistakenly believed to be a sovereign remedy, was one of the most
frequently prescribed medicines of the nineteenth century. Since mercury is
poisonous, painful symptoms and even death resulted from its use.
8. Boys under the age of five or six generally wore dresses; fashionable Scottish-
and Turkish-styled dresses were considered particularly masculine.

often professed for me, for my attachment to her is so immoveably fixed, that nothing will ever diminish it.

My children shall be allways taught to love those who were the friends of their mother, and my Dearest E Bordley is often mentioned by them, and they shall be constantly reminded of you. I teach my Parke to read, & she can read tolerably, but I believe I am not well calculated for an instructress, and her ill health prevents her attending as she ought to do. She is a child of fine genius, and an excellent memory, but she has no application, and being entirely alone in lessons, she has not that spirit of emulation so necessary to make her exert her talents; I cannot trust her away from me, and so far from a city as I am, it is impossible to procure day teachers which I think much the best. I am very anxious she should excell in every thing, but I do not know how to accomplish this favorite object. I have purchased Miss Edgeworth,[9] and am sure your opinion of her work is perfectly correct, but I fear I shall never succeed as I wish.

I will now conclude my Beloved friend with a hope that I shall soon, and often, be favour'd with your letters. My Husband and children unite in most sincere affection for you, and your dear and respected Mama.

With your faithfully attach'd friend
Eleanor Parke Lewis.

My sister Custis remembers you with sincere regard and admiration, as does Mrs Craik,[10] who is perfectly well. My sister is not well, she expects to be confined in June, or July, and her spirits are not good. I hope she will be more fortunate than she was the last summer. Poor Mrs Fitzhugh suffer'd extremely before her death, with a *cancer* which appeared in her throat, in spite of Doctor Tates[11] assurances that the cancerous virus was totally eradicated. I fear there is no cure for this dreadful malady. After her death, cancers appear'd in several parts which proves that the whole system was affected.

---

9. Maria Edgeworth (1767–1849) was a popular British writer. At this time, her series, *Tales of a Fashionable Life*, had begun to appear.
10. Anne Fitzhugh Craik (1784–1806), the elder sister of Mary Lee Fitzhugh Custis, was married to William Craik; she died seven months later in October 1806. GWD, 6:291; Ralph Happel, *Chatham: The Life of a House* (Philadelphia, 1984), 22.
11. John Tate practiced at 167 Walnut St. in Philadelphia. Philadelphia City Directory, 1806. (City directories will hereafter be cited as PCD, along with the year of publication.)

Will my Dearest E B. be so good as to assure the Friends of my deceased Parents, and myself, of my constant and affectionate remembrance—amongst those, is Miss Bond.[12]

Can you inform me how my old friends, the Morris family are? I have never heard from Maria since her marriage.[13] Will you offer my affectionate and sincere regards to them all. Write often my friend, and tell me how you and your dear family are, and all our old intimates.

God bless you.

E P L

———————————— ❦ ————————————

Woodlawn August 25th 1811

Your most acceptable letter my Dearest Eliza of April 9th & July 3rd dates (that is, the "Duplicate") I received a fortnight since, I have this long delay'd my answer because I hoped to have the pleasure to assure of the former letter being safe in my possession. I have waited in vain, after sending repeatedly to the post offices in Washington, G Town, & Alexandria. I must resign myself to the loss. Curiosity, or inattention in Postmasters I suppose is the cause of my disappointment. I cannot describe to you my anxiety before I received the "Duplicate".

I fear'd you might not have received my letter, or that you consider'd it too violent to deserve an answer, and my joy was extreme when I found by your friendly expressions that you did justice to the *only* motive I had in writing. Your reputation & happiness & not a little *pride* did I feel in the power of proving to those who were inclined to believe the reports, that a friend known and loved by me steadily for twenty years, would never lessen my regard for her, by departing from those principles which ensure to her the love & respect of all who are so happy as to be acquainted with her. The reports I mentioned in my last had been often contradicted by me, and I had frequently intended to write to you on the subject, but thought them too ridiculous to trouble you with. When the *Divorce* was concluded, & [Thomas]

---

12. Perhaps a daughter or sister of Thomas Bond (1712–1784), a distinguished Philadelphia physician and acquaintance of the Washingtons.
13. Maria Morris married Henry Nixon, a Philadelphia attorney, in 1802. GWD, 5:326.

Law in the *eyes of many* free to make a new choice, I thought it more necessary to attend to those reports as they might be supposed to [be] justified by circumstances.[14] They became too, more serious and more injurious I thought to you, and I cannot believe that Mr Law or his Sons are entirely innocent of their origin. I have heard so many circumstances to justify my doubts of their perfect veracity on this subject. I am very happy to find that he has been called on to deny or acknowledge them as it may prevent any farther inventions on this subject. If he should be disposed to think me influenced by a spirit of malice or revenge, or by the instigations of his enemies he will be pleased to recollect that I have never been a "puppet" to be moved by any ones influence, against my serious ideas of right. & that, when no member of my family would speak to him or countenance him in the smallest degree, Mr Lewis and myself were his active friends, invited him to our House, & endeavour'd to make his stay with us as happy as we could—because we could not see the propriety of becoming his enemies merely because, our sister & himself could not be happy together, when difference of dispositions induced them to seperate. I always opposed their seperation, and endeavour'd to reconcile them for their childs sake. For your kind attentions to my Beloved and favourite Niece, accept my best thanks, she is most truly deserving of them.[15] A more affectionate grateful heart no one ever possessed. She has fine talents and an amiable temper. May she be as happy as she deserves, I shall ever love her with the affection of a mother, & rejoice in her improvements.

Will you permit me to encroach upon your kindness by asking your kind countenance for my Dear Niece & Godchild Columbia Washington Peter. My Sister has determined to send her to Mrs Rivardis School[16] in a month or two. She will be entirely a

---

14. Thomas Law and Eliza Custis separated in 1804. In 1810 Law established residence in Vermont and received a divorce in 1811. Apparently Law was rumored to be courting Elizabeth Bordley; the earlier letter mentioned here is not at Mount Vernon. Moore, 107–8.

15. Eliza Law (1797–1822), the Laws' only child, was in her father's custody. She lived in Philadelphia, residing alternately at Mrs. Grelaud's school and with one of Law's friends. Moore, 106, 111–12.

16. An Austrian widow, Mme. Rivardi kept an elite girls' school in Philadelphia in the early part of the nineteenth century. The trustees of her school included some of the most important men in the city. Overreaching herself financially, not least by leasing the elegant "Gothic Mansion" on Chestnut Street, she was imprisoned for debt and later returned to Europe. Joseph Jackson, *Encyclopedia of Philadelphia*, 4 vols. (Harrisburg, 1932), s.v. "Gothic Mansion"; B. Hoff Knight, Mullanphy Family Data, Historical Society of Pennsylvania; PCD 1803–1814.

stranger in Philadelphia, and has always been so much with her Mother, that she will feel very lonely for sometime. She is of an affectionate disposition, very industrious and neat with her needle, and appears anxious to improve. I wish it was in my power to visit you, & to give my children such advantages as are to be found in Philadelphia—but I fear this must never be. Farmers are too busy to leave their homes, and I cannot part with my daughters. If I lived in Philadelphia, I should prefer having my daughters taught at home. We are preparing to leave Home for our Farm in Frederick County, where we shall remain until the 1st of Novr. Our Dear Children require a change of Air & the limestone water will I hope make them perfectly healthy.

My darling Parke begins to improve a little on the Harpsichord, and I hope will have industry & perseverance to make her excel in time. She is very ingenious, and I think would justify all my wishes & hopes in every department, if she could be properly instructed. Her health is very delicate, and she grows very fast. Mr. Provost told me a great deal about your singing, and it gratified me very much. I often wish you could sing with me our favourite Duetts. Would it fatigue your revered Mother too much to visit Washington? I think she would be gratified in seeing that City, of which so much has been said for and against. Mount Vernon is only one days ride from the City, I am sure you must wish to visit that venerable Mansion, and I am only 2½ miles farther. With what delight I should receive and wellcome your Dear Mama and her Beloved Daughter. I shall think of it frequently between this and Novemr., and hope you will bestow a thought on the subject occasionally. And let me at least meet with a long letter from you when I return here from Frederick County. Direct to me always at, Woodlawn, near Alexandria, Virginia.

Can you inform me where, & how, my kind friends the Morris family are. I never hear from my dear Maria now. I hope to see her Sister when in Fred[eric]k.[17] I knew not that our good old Friend Mr Smith of Roxborough was alive until Eliza mention'd him in a letter to her Mother. Will you offer my respectful regards to him, and tell him that I shall never forget our happy visits to his delightful Seat, and the pleasure I had in admiring his beautiful drawings. I have preserved the Rose he was so good to paint for me, and my daughter will try to copy it when she

17. Esther Morris (1774–1816) married James Markham Marshall (1764–1848), a Virginian, in 1795. GWD, 5:326.

knows how. She has an excellent talent for drawing, if she could study the art with an experienced master, I have forgotten my small stock of knowledge, and my music very much. Indeed am becoming a very humdrum character. Do rouse me from this state of apathy by your exhilarating presence. This epistle will prove that I have forgotten how to write *legibly*, although I undertake to *teach writing*. Excuse all deficiencies in consideration of the sincere love I now and ever will bear you.

Accept our united loves, present our most affectionate respects to your Beloved Mother and believe me to be as I always was, yrs truly

Eleanor P Lewis

Love to Mrs & Miss Mifflins, Eliza speaks highly of their kindness to her.

Chapter Three

Philadelphia Schoolgirls
1815–1820

" . . . it is a severe trial to part with my children. My happiness
depends on them & to have more than a hundred miles between us is
almost too much for my fortitude."

Woodlawn 3rd Janry 1815

My Well Beloved,

With Joy & thankfulness do I perform my promise, to "continue the correspondence which you have so kindly commenced"—
and I hope that it will not be again so sluggishly carried on as it
has been for years past. In truth my Friend, our late happy meeting has proved to us that our Hearts are the same that they formerly were, and we can have no fears that time or circumstances
can effect a change, since *matrimony* on my part, and *absence* on
both sides failed to disunite us. I know that it is a received opinion
that a married woman can have no secrets from her Husband, &
therefore, her female friends are afraid to make any communications lest the Caro sposo [dear husband] should be the wiser for
them; but in the *first* place, *we* were always Honest hearted fe-
males who had no *secrets* to disclose, & in the second, if we should
perchance stumble upon a subject improper for *vulgar eyes*, we
will recollect that it is proper "to keep a Friends counsel when we
are in trust."—and this settles the business at once.

With infinite delight I have read your dear letter over already four times, and it has not been four hours since I received
it. It is to me like the face of an old Friend, then I pray you my
Well Beloved, to gratify me with a sight of your *handwriting*,
whenever you can conveniently spare so much time from your
superior duties to the best of Mothers. Most gladly would I assist
you to nurse and cherish her, if I could be so happy as to reside
near you. When my Beloved Child is at liberty to leave school, I
am sure she would willingly do anything in her power to amuse

my much loved & respected Mrs Bordley.[1] If she can assist you in any way, will you gratify me by calling on her to do so.

Does your Dear Mother use the jelly of the slippery elm? It has been found to be beneficial in many cases of debility. Is it to be had in Philadelphia of the Apothecaries? The Bark is cut into narrow slips, wash'd, then put into a bowl which is filled with boiling water and cover'd close with a plate. When the water is cold you will find the Bark cover'd with a jelly, which must be scraped off and season'd with nutmeg, wine & sugar if required. I have it dried every summer in Fred[eric]k. County, & bring down quantities for my patients in this neighbourhood, should it not be in Phi[ladelphi]a, I will send some to my Sister Peter, & beg her to forward it to you soon as possible.

It was indeed a severe trial to part with my darling Daughter who was my companion & friend, but to comply with her earnest wish, & to benefit her, as I trust it will in every respect, I could submit to any sacrifice. I cannot suppress my anxiety about her. She is ever in my thoughts, at the most trying period of her life, to make so great a change, from retirement to a splendid City. Unaccustomed to the voice of flattery which has turned wiser heads than hers, will she now be able to resist its syren voice. You my Beloved must assist me in guarding *our* Daughter against those shoals & quicksands which she will encounter in the perilous voyage of life. My Blessing be upon you for all your kind attentions to her, and for that friendly & maternal solicitude which will ever influence you in her favour I am persuaded. I am charmed with the account you give me of her, will you endeavour as far as you can, to learn how she conducts herself in large companies, and what is the general opinion of her deportment. Excuse the anxiety of a Mother, who is much more ambitious for her Daughter than she ever was for herself. But [in addi]tion to her claims on me as her Mother, she has [one] equally great, if not more so, she was the *darling of my first best Friend, my rever'd Grandmama*, & ought I not to wish that she may ever deserve that early and mark'd preference?

I feel most grateful to my old Friends for all their attention to my child, she speaks with pleasure of her visits to you, & to them all. My inestimable Friend Charles Hare[2] has really per-

1. In 1814 Parke Lewis became a boarder at Madame Grelaud's School in Philadelphia.
2. Charles Willing Hare (1778–1827), a member of the powerful Willing and

formed the part he has undertaken for her, that of a *careful Father*; *absent* as he is, he has never neglected her, & his lovely Wife has been extremely kind. May every blessing attend them. I am very much gratified by your attention in introducing my daughter to Mr & Mrs Smith, & their friendly reception. I hope that you may be more fortunate when you again visit Mrs Manigault[3] & Miss Peters,[4] Mrs Manigault I have the highest respect & admiration for, & from the Parents of Miss Peters I received much friendly attention formerly. I think that I could recognise Mr Smith, although those beautiful light curls which I admired so much formerly, have been replaced by the *frost of age* or rather displaced. I dare say he would find as much difficulty in recognising me, since the *curly honours of my head* have fallen, never to rise again.

We have a report here, that the dreadful *Typhus fever*, or bilious pleurisy as it is sometimes called, is in Phi[ladelphi]a. Is it indeed so, & is my child in danger? She must not go where there is the least risk, or out in bad weather. To the Almighty I commit her, and will endeavour to conform to his decrees. I trust she will be preserved for happiness here and everlasting bliss hereafter. My excellent sister Mary Custis offers her most affecte. regards to you & your dear Mother, she has a sweet child, whom I wish you could see, as well as my little ones. I sent a letter to my child today before receiving hers, which I will answer on Sunday. Love & respects to your Mother, love to Miss Ross & the Miss Mifflins.

Ever truly yrs E P Lewis.

Will you excuse this miserable scrawl, in consideration of the love I do bear you, and the time of the night. 2, o'clock on my *veracity* & I have just signed my name.

Shippen families, was a distinguished attorney, professor of law at the University of Pennsylvania, and active Federalist politician who had served on the city council and in the state legislature; his wife, Anne Emlen Hare, was Elizabeth Bordley's cousin. Leach, "Philadelphia Families"; Frank W. Leach, "The Philadelphia of Our Ancestors: Old Philadelphia Families," *The North American*, scrapbook of articles arranged alphabetically by surname, Historical Society of Pennsylvania, s.v. "Hare"; Thomas P. Cope, *Philadelphia Merchant*, ed. Eliza C. Harrison (South Bend, Ind., 1978), 486.

3. Margaret Izard (1768–1824), daughter of Senator Ralph Izard and Alice DeLancey Izard of South Carolina, married Gabriel Manigault (1758–1809) in 1785; they moved to Philadelphia in 1806. Betty-Bright P. Low, "The Youth of 1812: More Excerpts from the Letters of Josephine du Pont and Margaret Manigault," *Winterthur Portfolio* 11 (1976): 175.

4. Sarah Robinson Peters (1785–1850) was the daughter of Richard Peters (1744–1828), judge of the U.S. District Court of Pennsylvania. Leach, "The Philadelphia of Our Ancestors," s.v. "Peters."

Woodlawn 1st of March 1815

The *Blessed tidings*, contained in the affecte. letter of my Well Beloved, in regard to my darling child, gave me a foretaste of what was to happen and that *Peace* which then cheer'd my Heart—Now gladdens the Hearts of Millions.[5] Thanks, Thanks, my Friend, for the kind assurances, that I need feel no anxiety in regard to my childs propriety of conduct—and for the pleasing information of her improved health. I have read your letter so often that it is fixed in my memory, and I am persuaded you would have been gratified, to see us congratulating each other on the approbation you expressed of our Parke. May she ever continue to deserve it, I require no stronger or more convincing proof of her merit. This, by the bye though, is rather a hasty assertion, and one which might lead *me* into the error of thinking well of *myself*, since *you* tolerate *me* with all my faults and failings. But then, there is much to be said on that side of the question. I crept into your heart slyly, when you were very young, and not so prudent as you now are, and having once gained possession, I would not suffer you or *any one else* to dislodge me. Nor will I give place to any other (unworthy as I am of the blessing) unless my precious girl be permitted to *reign* in my stead. To her, I would resign all the advantages I ever possessed, and be happy in witnessing her felicity. I am always charmed when I read that she has been with you, and find her growing upon your affection. Oh my Well Beloved! cherish this affecte. feeling toward her, you will obtain the grateful prayers, and the everlasting affection, of two Hearts deeply impressed with your excellences, and with the favours already confer'd. Do not, however, permit her to interrupt you in those moments when a far more sacred duty calls you. Your Dear Mother must not be incommoded on any account. And when My Beloved Child is with you, instil into her mind those feelings of right which may guard her when removed from your protecting care.

I have (like those divines who *preach* better than they *practice*) written volumes, almost, of advice to her, but a practical illustration would be far more impressive, & that I must make over to my E Bordley. It is drole enough that you should ask, why I do not reprove you for your sad scrawl! To tell the truth my dear, I am not *entirely* divested of modesty, and cannot with any pro-

---

5. The Treaty of Ghent, ratified by the Senate in February 1815, ended the War of 1812.

priety reprove you, when I am so much more to blame myself. Verily I fear, that my scrawl will defy your utmost skill to decipher—and in that case, what an escape you will have! I once flatter'd myself, that I possessed some small portion of Lady Delacours l'eloquence de Billet, but, time, care, vexation and *what not* have bereft me of all claims to this talent. Now *Peace* irradiates our Country once more, we may hope that the night of folly, and wickedness is over, and when the cheering influence of a *new* day breaks in upon us, will not our ideas brighten in proportion! Look forward then my Beloved, to the time when the spirit of dullness will emancipate my brains, and then, perhaps, I may make you amends, for your patience in wading through *puddles* of ink, for my sake.

Last week I employed myself in looking over, and assorting, the letters of my ever dear Friends; several of yours, and of our charming, and lamented Elizabeth's, I read, and lost myself compleatly, in recurring to those scenes, and those events, which happen'd in those happiest days of our lives. Could I be permitted to reside near, and in Phi[ladelphi]a again, the society of my surviving Friends there, would console me for all I have lost. I delight to retrace in imagination those days of unclouded felicity; and often, when alone, I enjoy in perfection the "Pleasures of memory."[6] I can never forget that "those things were, and that they were most precious"—and even when a cloud comes over my mind, when I feel the "Pains of memory" for a moment, from the recollection of my heavy deprivations by the deaths of those, most revered, most honour'd, most Beloved, the reflection that "The Lord gave, & the Lord taketh away," and that my Friends have exchanged *temporal* for *eternal* happiness, makes me bow in submission to the decrees of an all wise, all merciful Providence.

I have lately experienced the goodness of the Almighty in the preservation of my three little darlings, and in my own safety. The epidemic of which you have heard accounts so alarming, and which has been a very fatal visitation indeed in Alex[andri]a, and the lower counties; came to us also, but in so mild a form, that we have not lost one person by it. Most of our negro's have had it, and have recover'd, my three children had every symptom of the dis-

---

6. "The Pleasures of Memory" was a long poem by Samuel Rogers (1763–1855), whose work was highly respected by Byron and Wordsworth. Published in 1792, the poem was immensely popular; by 1806 it had gone through fifteen editions. Nelly and Elizabeth shared this book with pleasure in 1796: throughout the years Nelly returned to its themes in her letters.

ease, and are now perfectly well, I had a very sore throat for nearly four weeks, and was obliged to take some simple medicine every day or two to ward off the other symptoms (as I cannot bear to nurse *myself*) and am perfectly well again, Mr L escaped with a very slight attack. Added to these favours, my eldest darling is, I trust, out of the way of it entirely, improving in health, & becoming, I flatter myself, all that the fondest Mother can desire.

To these, could I add, a residence near this Beloved Child, at least for the next three years, I should have nothing to desire but a proper sense of my obligations to the giver of all good, for his unmerited favours. It is my most earnest wish to accomplish this plan, but I fear it will not be in my power. Virginians have everything in greater abundance than money, which is the one thing needful, for procuring food, and raiment in a far Country. We have small crops, expensive families, and, this year, very heavy taxes, the *State* tax is equal to the United States tax. Mr L is not the most energetic of men, of course, cannot be expected to struggle much against these difficulties—loves to be a *genuine Virginian*, that is, to have plenty of servants for every purpose, he thinks that we should be in a lamentable predicament in this respect in Phi[ladelphi]a.

I do not wish to keep house, two neat retired rooms near Madame Grelauds[7] (for the convenience of seeing Parke, and sending Agnes to school) is all I ask. I could see my Friends in a family way, give them a sincere welcome, and should hope that they would like as well to visit me, as they would in a more splendid situation. My darling Parke is as anxious, and so sanguine, that she casts all difficulties behind her, in her calculations, if I do not effect my plan, it shall not be my fault, be assured, and hope sometimes whispers me, that I shall be gratified in this first wish of my heart (at least, *next*, to that of my childrens health & happiness). Is it possible in any way to secure slaves in carrying them from this State to Penn[sylvani]a. I have a sempstress, and nurse who are very valuable to me, and I should not like to risk losing them by a removal. There is no certainty of retaining them by wages, if they fancy they could be happier elsewhere.

I see, in the account of your brilliant illuminations for Peace,

---

7. Deborah Grelaud, a French widow, opened an exclusive girls' school in Philadelphia in 1806. Several members of the Custis/Calvert family boarded there besides Parke Lewis, including Eliza Law and Caroline and Julia Calvert. PCD 1806; Lucy Leigh Bowie, "Madame Grelaud's French School," *Maryland Historical Magazine* 39 (1944): 141–48.

that a House in Union St was adorned with a Dove & olive branch, was it yours my Friend, or Mr Smiths?[8] I supposed it to be one of the two. Will you be so good as to make Parke play on the Piano when next you see her, & inform me how she performs, also sound her a little on the subject of her French. I have, some attempts in drawing & painting which I think are promising. Always re[mind] her to open her chest, & hold her neck well, she says that she stoops less than when I left her, I fear her breast may be injured if she stoops or contracts her chest—and tell her, to be careful that the bleak March winds, and April showers do not injure her health, advise her not to give up her pelisse [great-coat] & fur cape too soon, I trouble you with this charge, because she is so young, she will forget the advice in my letters perhaps, but when you repeat it to her, it will remind her of my anxiety, & make her more cautious.

Have I not wearied you my Friend by this long and wretched scrawl, I may say now with truth, that "With thee conversing, I forget all time" for the enemy reminds me that it is nearly half past one in the morng. All eyes, save mine, are closed in sleep, but I am ever awake I trust to *friendship* & *gratitude*, and these are your due My Well Beloved. If you have lately heard of Madame de Freire be so good as to inform [me] of her address, & all about her. Present me affectionately to the charming Mrs Derby,[9] *she charmed* me too much to be forgotten. I remember well our Beau Mr Sullivan.

My best and most affecte. respect to your Beloved Mother, tell her that "if prayers of the wicked may prevail"—mine will plead for her at the throne of Grace, they are offer'd daily and nightly for her health & happiness. Love and thanks to yr amiable Nieces & Mrs Mifflin for their kind attentions to Parke. Dear Elizabeth Ross has always a place in my affections.

For you My Beloved all the love which I ever felt and which can never diminish

E P L

8. A general illumination in honor of peace took place in Philadelphia on February 15. Bridges, public buildings, and private homes were decorated and lit up for the occasion. J. Thomas Scharf and Thompson Westcott, *History of Phila-delphia, 1609–1884*, 3 vols. (Philadelphia, 1884), 1:578–79.
9. Louisa Sophia Bumford Derby (d. 1864), daughter of Col. George Bumford, was married to Richard C. Derby (c. 1780–1854) of Newport and Phila-delphia. Newport *Mercury*, Apr. 8, 1854, Apr. 30, 1864.

[Woodlawn] 3rd Oct [1815]

I have taken the liberty of forwarding to my *Well Beloved* a bundle for My Beloved Child. Judge Washington[10] is so good as to take charge of it. Will you inform My Child by the Germantown Stage of its arrival, that she may go or send for it. It contains that indispensible article for cold weather, viz. *Flannel*. I hope that my Child will soon be near our *Pneumanee*, and I shall then hear of your health & your dear Mothers. I hope to visit Phi[ladelphi]a in Novr. but it is not certain, Mr L has not positively promised although my heart is set on it. The 27th of Novr. is my Childs 16th Birthday & I wish much to be with her—particularly as I shall be so long away from her afterwards. I wrote you a letter soon after My Child left me in August. Did you receive it?

I was mortified & hurt that Mr Lewis did not pay his respects to you when in Phi[ladelphi]a. He says that he had no one to introduce him & was unwell, or he certainly should have done so. Present me with affectionate respect to your Beloved Mother, & accept for yourself my unvaried affection.

Yrs ever
E P Lewis

I beg you play & sing in your best manner for my attentive and worthy friend Judge Washington. He is devoted to music.

———————————— ❦ ————————————

Woodlawn July 4th 1817

My Well Beloved,

My answer to your affecte & most welcome letter of April 20th was delay'd some time by company & other circumstances

---

10. Bushrod Washington (1762–1829), Washington's nephew, inherited Mount Vernon and took possession on Martha Washington's death in 1802. He was appointed to the United States Supreme Court in 1798, where he continued to serve until his death. Justices were required to serve as judges of the U.S. Circuit Courts; from 1803 until 1829 Washington presided over the Third Circuit (Pennsylvania and New Jersey), which entailed frequent journeys to Philadelphia. G. Edward White, *The Marshall Court and Cultural Change, 1815–35*, vol. 3–4 of *History of the Supreme Court of the United States* (New York, 1988), 161; Albert P. Blaustein and Roy M. Mersky, "Bushrod Washington," in *The Justices of the United States Supreme Court, 1789–1969*, vol. 1, ed. Leon Friedman and Fred L. Israel (New York, 1969), 248.

until the time approached which was to witness the change from E Bordley to E Gibson; I then postponed writing until I could offer my congratulations on this change, & again, the arrival of company interposed to prevent the accomplishment of my wishes & my *duty*.[11] My Darling Parke informed me last week that you had returned to town, *Mrs Gibson*; but I have not yet learnt *where*, or *when*, you were married. Accept, my well Beloved, of my warmest wishes for your happiness, may "Succeeding years, as ceaseless round a joining world they roll, still find you happy." Present my regards & congratulations to Mr Gibson, may you always be united in heart, mind, & pursuits, may health & every blessing attend you through your earthly pilgrimage, & after a long life of happiness may you enjoy eternal felicity in "another & a better world."

I am impatient to hear when I shall be so happy as to have you at Woodlawn, do not limit your time. It is not a Virginia fashion to pay *short* visits, & I shall be very averse to parting with you. Come then my Dearest *E G*, as soon as possible, and permit me to do all in my power to make you happy in my House. We will visit Mount Vernon & talk over all the scenes of our former happy life. Although not now my *E Bordley*, we will never forget that "such things were, & that they were most precious."

I am much gratified by your account of my Beloved Child, & Mr Gibson's approbation of her. I trust she will ever merit your friendship & esteem. I shall feel richer than you can yet imagine when she returns to me. In Octr. or Novr. she will leave Phi[ladelphi]a, but not without regret I am certain. She has met with such affecte. attention there, that her gratitude & mine, must ever be due. In two years perhaps, I shall place another darling Daughter with Madme. Grelaud. Although I think her unequalled as a maternal Instructress, yet it is a severe trial to part with my children. My happiness depends on them & to have more than a hundred miles between us is almost too much for my fortitude.

Although you will not have an opportunity to cultivate the *fine arts abroad*, yet you will not I hope neglect your talents at home. You will not give up music & painting, for pickling, preserving, & *puddings* although I have done so in great measure.

---

11. Elizabeth Bordley married James Gibson (1769–1856), a Philadelphia attorney, in 1817.

Eliza[12] is very happily situated, her husbands friends are devoted to her, she talks much about pickling & preserving, & no doubt will be very notable. Will you tell me something of your future plans, will you continue to reside in Union Street?

Parke says that poor Mrs Manigault has lost her youngest daughter,[13] I sincerely regret this event, Mrs M is so admirable a woman & was so good a Mother. Will you present my respects & condolence on the afflicting [dis]pensation & my affecte. remembrance to Mrs. [Deas].[14] I hope she will visit me when she returns to Carolina. Judge Tilghman[15] is much to be pitied, it is said that his Grand child will not survive. Who has the care of that unfortunate infant? My friend Patty Hare[16] is thought to be in a decline. She appear'd to be in perfect health when I was in Phi[ladelphi]a. How does our venerable friend Mrs Powel?

I hope to hear from you soon, & often, I beg you to present my affecte. & grateful acknowledgements to your sister Mifflin & her amiable Daughters; & to the friendly Mrs Camac[17] with whom I am very anxious to be acquainted. My love to Miss Ross & her Sisters, I shall be happy to see your neices with you. Regards to Mr G's sisters & to our old friend H[arriet] McCall. Believe me now & ever with sincere & unchanging affection

Yr Friend

E P Lewis

---

12. On April 5, 1817, Eliza Law married Lloyd Nicholas Rogers (c.1787–1860), a wealthy Baltimore lawyer. The couple lived outside Baltimore at the Rogers family estate, Druid Hill. Moore, 112; Edith R. Bevan, "Druid Hill, Country Seat of the Rogers and Buchanan Families," *Maryland Historical Magazine* 44 (Sept. 1949): 194–98.
13. Caroline Manigault (1803–1817). Low, "The Youth of 1812," 175.
14. Anne Izard Deas (1779–1863) was the sister of Margaret Izard Manigault. Langdon Cheves, "Izard of South Carolina," *South Carolina Historical and Genealogical Magazine*, 2 (1901): 217.
15. William Tilghman (1756–1827), a member of the wealthy Maryland family, was Chief Justice of the Supreme Court of Pennsylvania. His only daughter, Elizabeth Margaret Tilghman, had married Benjamin Chew in 1816. She died June 16, 1817, in childbirth. Her infant son died soon afterward. Leach, "The Philadelphia of Our Ancestors," s.v. "Tilghman."
16. Martha Hare (1779–1852) was the sister of Charles Willing Hare. Leach, "The Philadelphia of Our Ancestors," s.v. "Hare."
17. Sarah Masters (1758–1825), the daughter of a very wealthy English landowner, married Turner Camac (1751–1830), an Irish military officer. They came to Philadelphia in 1806 to manage her extensive Pennsylvania estates. Leach, "Philadelphia Families," 35, 72; Leach "The Philadelphia of Our Ancestors," s.v. "Camac."

Woodlawn Novr. 24th [1817]

My Well Beloved,

Your affectionate letter of Octr 18th which I received by the hand of my Beloved Child, has remained much longer unanswer'd than I could have wish'd; I have not valued it the less on that account, but being in duty bound to stay sometime with my Aunt, Sister, & Brother, on our way home, we have only been here four days, & this is my first moment of leisure. Accept my grateful acknowledgements, my dear Elizabeth, for your uniform kindness to our Daughter; she feels all she owes to her Philadelphia friends, as I could wish her to do, we are equally attached to that scene of our useful & happy days, & nothing but the impossibility of going there, will prevent our future visits. It is certainly gratifying to have my child again under my own care, but I am sensible of all the sacrifices she has made to return to us; she is ambitious to excel in the different branches of her education, & it would have been of infinite advantage to her to have devoted the *mornings* of this winter to her different instructors—& at the same time she would have enjoy'd the most improving society. She is endeavouring to make amends by her own exertions at home, but I cannot expect so young a girl to remain in retirement the whole winter, & if she goes from home she gives up her studies, of course.

I do not think *yet* of a change for life, indeed I should resign her to, almost any man, with *fear & trembling*—so uncertain are the ways of this world. But this, I *will* venture to say—that no *Virginian* shall receive her with my approbation. No *Southern* or *Western* youth, I trust, will be her portion. I know, too well, the evils attending the *slave* property, not to wish that my children may never encounter them. There is another evil too, attendant on a residence in the Southern & Western States. Education is very little attended to, to have our children *well* educated we must send them from home, & to me, the society of my darling Children, the power of watching over their opening prospects—of nursing them when sick, & working for them when well, is the most important ingredient in happiness. I feel as if deprived of my *limbs* when my children are away. Are not these reasonable objections to a *Virginia Son*? Am I not looking far into *futurity* when I think of the education of my *Grandchildren*?

We regret much that you cannot be with us this season, but

hope that the middle, or last of April, will see you here. Woodlawn is then in its *best dress*, & I should like you to view it to the most advantage. I hope that Mr Gibson will accord with our wishes on this subject. Will you not bring your amiable nieces with you? They have been so very kind to Parke, that I anxiously wish to have an opportunity of shewing the grateful sense we entertain of their goodness. You & Mrs Mifflin have been equally kind, & we think & speak of you, and our other Philadelphia friends with affection & gratitude unceasing. We hope to see Miss Gibson with you.[18] Present me most affectionately to *all* our friends. Regards to Mr G in which Mr L unites. Ever yours sincerely

E P Lewis

New York 21st June 1820

My Dearest Elizabeth,

I received your friendly letter a few days since, & should have answer'd it immediately but was prevented by company. We will accept your kind offer with the utmost pleasure. We cannot feel otherwise than happy under your roof, & I sincerely thank you & Mr Gibson for the friendly proposal. You will be surprised at our absence so much beyond the time appointed. The fact is, New York is enchanting, & the hospitality of its inhabitants inexhaustible. Since our first arrival here, the Douglas family[19] have devoted themselves to our service in the kindest manner, the most minute attention to our comfort—& my friends & the friends of my Departed Parents have rallied round us, & it will be difficult to part with them again.

We must however make the effort, on Wednesday next we will

---

18. James Gibson had two unmarried sisters, Eliza and Louisa Gibson. *Brief of Title to Several Tracts of Land* (Philadelphia, 1863), 6.
19. Margaret Corne Douglas was the widow a wealthy New York merchant, George Douglas, whom she had married in 1784; she and their children lived at 55 Broadway. Berry B. Tracy, *Federal Furniture and Decorative Arts at Boscobel* (New York, 1981), 11–19; Joseph A. Scoville, *The Old Merchants of New York City*, vols. 1, 3 (New York, 1889), 1:159; William M. MacBean, *Biographical Register of Saint Andrew's Society of the State of New York*, 2 vols. (New York, 1922), 1:162.

go to Elizabeth Town to see Mrs Niemcewitz,[20] & on Thursday to Bristol to stay a day with Mrs Lenox, & then to Phi[ladelphi]a. We have been to Mrs Dyckmans[21] on the North river & to West Point, & found the entrance to the Highlands[22] as charming as it was described. We are constantly engaged with morning visitors & invitations to dinner & tea. We had actually four invitations for the same day. The parties are very social, & made particularly for us. I never was in a more hospitable City. We have had several invitations to take up our abode in different families & the most earnest solicitations to prolong our stay until after the 4th of July. Mrs Read[23] from Georgia is here with two charming Daughters. We go this evening to Governor's Island to a party given us by Colonel House.[24] Tomorrow we dine with my old friend Thomas Morris,[25] & drink tea with Mrs. Vanbrugh Livingston.[26] On Saturday we breakfast with Mrs Varick[27] at Paulus Hook & drink tea with Mrs Floyd[28] in the City. On Monday at Morrisview & on Tuesday at Mr Peter Jays.[29]

You will think me quite dissipated but I cannot refuse those who so kindly urge our visits. Parke is charmed with New York.

20. Susan Livingston Kean married Julian Niemcewicz in 1800. In 1807 he returned permanently to Europe, but they remained on good terms; when she died in 1833, she left him an annuity. Niemcewicz, xxvii, xxix.
21. Elizabeth Corne Dyckman (1776–1823), Margaret Corne Douglas's niece, lived at Boscobel, a manor on the Hudson River. Tracy, 11–19.
22. The Highlands are a picturesque area along the Hudson River where the mountains come close to the river's edge.
23. Perhaps Catherine Van Horne Read, daughter of a New York merchant and widow of Jacob Read (1752–1816). Though he lived primarily in South Carolina, Read had inherited large estates in Georgia.
24. Lt. Col. James House of Connecticut was serving with the corps of artillery at this time.
25. Maria Morris's brother Thomas (1771–1849) had moved to New York and become a lawyer and politician. He served for many years as U.S. Marshall for the eastern district of New York. Leach, "The Philadelphia of Our Ancestors," s.v. "Morris."
26. Probably Maria Houston Livingston, the wife of Peter Van Brugh Livingston. Jerome B. Holgate, American Genealogy (Albany, [N.Y.], 1848), 170; Florence van Rensselaer, Livingston Family in America and Its Scottish Origins (New York, 1949), 119.
27. Maria Roosevelt Varick (1763–1841) was the wife of Richard Varick (1753–1831), attorney and prominent politician; he had been one of Washington's secretaries during the Revolution.
28. Probably Joanna Strong Floyd (1747–1826), the wife of William Floyd (1734–1821), who had signed the Declaration of Independence, served in the Revolution, and was active in New York politics.
29. Peter Augustus Jay (1776–1843), John Jay's son, had a lucrative law practice in New York. Frank Monaghan, John Jay (New York, 1935), 79, 428, 431.

Be so good as to inform my dearest America[30] of our health &
well doing. Agnes retires from the crowd, seldom goes out, &
never to a large party. Her favorite residence is a *large armchair*
in our chamber. Mrs Douglas although very young in appearance,
is always at home & extremely attentive to us. Present our united
affecte. remembrance to our good friends in Phi[ladelphi]a whom
we shall never forget. Best love to Mr Gibson & yourself & Believe me ever my Dearest Elizabeth

Yr affecte. & faithful friend
Eleanor P Lewis

Do excuse this wretched scrawl

———————————❧———————————

[Philadelphia October 1820][31]

My Dear Friend

We thank you & Mr G most sincerely for your kind attention
& the fine lemons. Dr C[hapman][32] thought it advisable to give
my darling Girl [Agnes] 10 dps. of Laudamun[33] last night in a
saline to check the operation of the bowels. She slept very well
[the] great part of the night, then had one bilious operation. I
gave by the Dr advice 5 drops more in a dose of bark[34] & she has
slept ever since except being occasionally awake a few minutes.
The Laudamun affects her head but she feels otherwise rather
better, her cough is very troublesome. The Drs Chapman & Parish[35] will give her calomel & gum arabic today, & quassia as a
bitter.[36] I believe the old french nurse will come if I want her but

---

30. America Pinckney Peter (1803–1842), the daughter of Thomas and Martha
    Peter, was at school in Philadelphia. Mrs. Walter Peter, "Peter Family Genea-
    logical Notes," Mount Vernon Library.
31. Nelly's daughter Agnes, a boarder at Madame Grelaud's school, became
    seriously ill in the fall of 1820. After some delay, Nelly was summoned to
    nurse her.
32. Dr. Nathaniel Chapman (1780–1853), a professor at the University of Penn-
    sylvania medical school, was one of the most respected doctors in the East.
    Charles Morris, ed., *Makers of Philadelphia* (Philadelphia, 1894), 37.
33. Laudanum was an opium solution.
34. Cinchona bark, the source of quinine, was a specific for malaria; because of
    its efficacy in treating that disease, doctors prescribed bark for a range of
    other diseases which it had no power to cure.
35. Dr. Joseph Parrish (1779–1840), a distinguished Philadelphia physician, was
    on the staff of the Pennsylvania Hospital.
36. Respectively a carthartic, demulcent, and bitter tonic.

she only does what the girl here can do. I cannot give up nursing her myself I should suffer more from anxiety than fatigue, I trust that Providence will enable me to do all that is necessary for my darlings recovery. Our united loves & every good wish for you & Mr G.

Yrs ever

E P L

If you can lend me a watch that *keeps time* you will confer a favour, I must give the powders every half hour.

————————————— ❦ —————————————

[Philadelphia October 1820]

My dear Elizabeth,

My Darling says she is better. She has no sickness or pain this morning, but sleeps uneasily from the 10 dps laudamun I gave at 7 oclock, & looks very badly. She had seven evacuations last night the Dr says not so bilious as those before. He directs me to give her every hour a little wine & tincture of cloves with animal broth. You will oblige me much by making the essence of Beef & sending sometime today another bottle of your fine old wine. She will like the broth best without seasoning except a little salt. She dislikes spice. The [mustard] plaster was of some service I believe. She sleeps very uneasily at present. I trust she will be better, but this day is against her. Our united loves & thanks & send my old gown. I hope the man will be expeditious as I am much in want of it.

Yrs ever affectely

E P Lewis

Her cough is still troublesome.

————————————— ❦ —————————————

[Philadelphia October 1820]

My Dear Friend

The Drs are to be here at 1 oclock. My Child is anxious to drink wine & water & if they permit it—I should like her to drink such as you sent me first with the nut taste because she likes it so much. Excuse me for imposing on your goodness so much, but my child will not survive many hours I fear.

Yrs ever
E P L

———————————— ❦ ————————————

[Philadelphia October 28, 1820]

My Dear Friend,

I rejoice to hear that my darling Parke is composed & better. I trust she will sleep well tonight & be quite refreshed in the morning. Tell her that her Angel Sister looks as calm & composed as a Saint & that I have cut off a great deal of her precious hair.[37] I had rather she should not come here again, because it would renew the remembrance of her grief & her Sisters sufferings. Tell [her] that I pray God to bless & comfort her now & ever. I gave the list to Miss Smith to add any that she knew had called. Mrs. Claypoole[38] I do not wish omitted or the others as they all called. Dr White[39] will admit My Angel into his family vault. That is a great comfort to me. I will do all I can to preserve my health & I hope my child will do her part to give comfort by preserving her own health. God bless you My dear Friend for all your goodness.

Yrs ever
E P Lewis

Mr & Mrs G[ibson], Mrs. Deas, Mr Carlo, Mrs Grelaud, Mr [illegible], Mrs McPherson,[40] Mrs Fisher,[41] Mrs Gardiner, Mr & Mrs Camac, Mr Mrs & Mr Brinton,[42] Mrs [Mary White] Morris, Mrs [illegible]

---

37. In a note to Parke, Nelly wrote: "Your Angel sister went off like an infant asleep. I stood by her the whole time. . . I beg you for Gods sake to cease to grieve, to go to Bed & endeavour to be well—for my comfort." Eleanor Parke Custis Lewis to Frances Parke Lewis, [28 Oct. 1820], Mount Vernon Library.

38. Elizabeth Ashburn Claypoole (1725–1836) was the wife of John Claypoole. *Genealogies of Pennsylvania Families from the Pennsylvania Genealogical Magazine*, 3 vols. (Baltimore, 1982), 3:906.

39. William White (1748–1836), presiding bishop of the Episcopal Church in the United States, was a civic and religious leader; he was Mary White Morris's brother.

40. Elizabeth White McPherson (1776–1831) was the widowed daughter of Bishop White. Leach, "The Philadelphia of Our Ancestors," s.v. "White."

41. Elizabeth Powel Francis Fisher was the widow of a wealthy Quaker merchant, Joshua Fisher.

42. John Hill Brinton (1772–1827) and Sarah Steinmetz (1769–1843) married in

[Philadelphia October 1820]

My Dear Betsey

I hope my Child [Parke] is much better today. I must go to the Church today but Parke had better not know it. I hope your niece [Elizabeth Mifflin] will stay with her & H[etty] McP[herson].[43] I send my Bonnet if it can be made decent I prefer it, as I wish to have my leghorn dyed & dress'd with crape. They say my Child [Agnes] has not changed yet, if so I cannot have her put into her coffin unless certain proofs of her being past recovery appear.[44] God bless you dearest Friend

Yrs ever

──────────── ❦ ────────────

[Woodlawn November 20, 1820][45]

My Dearest Elizabeth,

Parke has told you all about her journey & arrival at home except about my precious Ped [Angela Lewis], who is fatter than when I left her & as affectionate as ever. My darling Boy looks thin & low spirited, he has had the Influenza lately, & feels the loss of his Angel sister severely, so indeed must all that knew her. I feel her loss more than ever, this home which her affection & dutiful attention made so happy to me, is a blank without her. Wherever I go, & every thing I see makes me feel the desolation of her loss. I do not repine my dear Friend, I endeavour to be reconciled, & to think that it is for the best, but when I think of her sufferings, her anxiety to be at home, of the persecutions I was obliged to afflict her with, it makes me miserable. I fear that I

1795; their son was John Steinmetz Brinton (1798–1825). *Genealogies of Pennsylvania Families from The Pennsylvania Genealogical Magazine*, 3:473–74.

43. Esther McPherson (b. 1804) was Bishop White's granddaughter. Leach, "The Philadelphia of Our Ancestors," s.v. "White."

44. Mistaking a coma or trance for death and burying the living was a common fear in the nineteenth century. Relatives waited until the body had passed through rigor mortis, softened, and begun to give the first signs of decay before burial. Some arranged bells and other devices leading to the coffin so that the victim of a mistaken burial could be saved from asphyxiation.

45. Postscript to a letter from Frances Parke Lewis to Elizabeth Bordley Gibson.

injured her in some way although I cannot tell how, & I cannot forbear thinking that if she had been permitted to come home she would now have been with me. I have not told Mr L anything that would affect him. He never witnessed her sufferings, & is perfectly reconciled. She is ever before me, in health & in her last illness, but I do not wish to forget her ever.

I wished much to have gone to C[hrist] Church yard to see the spot which has concealed her forever. If it will not incommode you my friend will you go there & tell me how it is cover'd up. The kindness & sympathy you & Mr G have shewn to us has bound us all to you both forever. Remember us with affection & gratitude to your Sisters, nieces, & all, who have been kind to us.
May the Almighty bless you all now & forever.

Yrs most affectely & faithfully
E P Lewis

Woodlawn Novr. 22nd 1820

My Dearest Elizabeth,

Parke wrote you a long letter a few days since to which I added a postscript; I write now to make another request to you, relying on your goodness to excuse all the trouble I give you. In the summer I gave you a profile of my departed Angel, I then had several taken & distributed to some of her friends, & I have now only one, & my children have neither of them a copy. Will you be so good as to see if the one you have can be copied exactly at the Museum,[46] & if it can be will you have a doz. cut for me & send them by the Judge, & he will pay for them. He talks of returning the last of this month or the first of December. I hope the locket &c will be ready to come by him.

I hope we shall soon have a good opportunity of sending your pelisse, which was a of great use to my darling Parke. If you can get the music of the 16th Funeral Psalm it will much oblige me. Do write how the good Bishop & family are & all our kind friends. I did not write to Mrs Bayard[47] & I regret much that I have ap-

---

46. Probably the Washington Museum and Gallery of Paintings located in a large brick building on Market Street in Philadelphia. Started by Jesse Sharpless in 1807, it advertised the taking of profiles. Scharf and Westcott, 2:950–51.
47. Possibly Ann Bassett Bayard (d. 1851), wife of James Asheton Bayard (1767–1815), important Federalist politician, lawyer, and businessman.

peared to neglect her so much. Do my friend apologize for me & assure her of my affecte & grateful sense of her friendly offers of service.

I hope you explain'd to Patty Hare that we were not so heavily laden with obligations as she supposed, to Madme. G[relaud]. I shall always do her justice, as far as I really think her due, & I will never say anything that can injure her as a Governess, or lessen her scholars, but the lasting regret which her neglect of my earnest requests has caused me, & the uneasiness occasion'd to my suffering Angel by obstinacy & Aurora [Grelaud]'s want of thought & proper feeling—I cannot soon forget. Never will another of my children live under their care. Never shall another sufferer beg me, in vain, to take them from that hated house. Every scene is continually before me, & I try in vain to be reconciled. I do not murmur at the will of the almighty, but I regret most bitterly that my child was far from me when timely & proper attention & medical advice might perhaps have saved her—& is not Madme. G the cause of that, & although I am grateful for every kind act she did perform, yet in employing [nurses?] & not giving me timely advice she injured me past reparation. I believe she meant well but a desire to show her supremacy & a total forgetfulness of my rights as a Mother were the cause of her proceedings. The *effects* I shall feel in my heart as long as I live.

Pardon me my dear friend if I cause you uneasiness. It would be a poor return for all your kindness.

Our united loves & prayers for you Mr G & our other kind friends.

Yrs ever most faithfully
Eleanor P Lewis

Woodlawn
1820–1823

"[The woodbine] is in its glory, the last of April, here, the flower is a bright yellow bell flower—and has the odour of violets. The pillars of our portico are completely surrounded with the multiflora rose."

Woodlawn 27th Novr. 1820

My Dearest Elizabeth,

This is my darling Parkes birthday, may she live long & happily. It was also my Father's Birthday. We sent your pelisse today in the care of Major Vandeventer,[1] he has promised to have it forwarded by a safe hand. He inquired particularly about you & Mr Gibson. I enclose you $5 my dear friend. Be so good as to send me by Judge W the handsomest purse clasp, best gilt, that can be found in Phi[ladelphi]a, 2 neat gilt frames, not so large as your smallest plates or a saucer, they are for small engraved likenesses, & the balance in best gold thread, not Mrs *Pratts*, for she sells too small a quantity for the price.[2] Parke finds that her spools are very large & have very little on them. One purse required nearly 3 spools.

We are very anxious to hear from you, America mention'd that she had spent the day with you. I thank you my dear E for your friendly attention to that amiable girl, shall I impose upon you by asking you to extend your favour to Eugenia.[3] I love her very much, she was always an affecte. friend of my departed darling. I dreamed last night that I was in a new Catholic Chapel, & saw there a monument to my child, on the Altar, which was of

---

1. Christopher Van De Venter (d. 1838) was a West Point graduate who became a major in the quartermaster's corps before resigning in 1816; at this time he served as chief clerk of the War Department.
2. J. B. Pratt had a fancy goods store on Third Street. PCD 1820.
3. Rosalie Eugenia Calvert (1806–1845) was the daughter of Nelly's uncle, George Calvert; she later married Charles Henry Carter, nephew of Robert E. Lee. *Maryland Genealogies*, 1:161–62.

marble as white as snow—& that I heard a most eloquent &
affecting prayer from a Priest in white robes. How are all my
good friends. Tell me of your own household, & of them, when you
write. Mr Lewis & my little one have the Influenza. It is not however very violent. Columbia Peter is on a visit to us & Mary
Custis & her child will come this week. Washington left us yesterday.[4] My poor Parke has been obliged to take medicine, she is now
pretty well again but complains of being too weak to walk much
without fatigue. My dear Boy is in Alex[andri]a. I beg you to present our united & most affecte regards to Mr G—to your sisters,
Mrs & Miss Mifflins & all my other friends & accept the same for
yourself. When will dear Elizabeth write?[5]

> Believe me ever most affectely & faithfully yours
> *Eleanor P Lewis.*

My good Pastor Mr Wilmer[6] dined with us on Saturday. If
you knew him as well as I do, I am sure you would love & respect
him. I wish that you did know him. I told him that I would live in
Phi[ladelphi]a if I could, some day, & that I should then insist on
moving him too. He would be a great acquisition to you.

————————— ❦ —————————

Woodlawn Decr. 4th 1820

My Dearest friend,

The hand of affliction is again laid upon us, & I am obliged to
confess that my murmurings were unreasonable because my darling was not at home. *I was with her.* My poor Sister Peter today
lost her eldest child—my dearest Columbia, & she had not the
consolation of receiving her last sigh. My sister was 20 miles
above George Town, my poor niece came here yesterday week to
spend a week with me. She was in very fine spirits but looked

---

4. Martha Peter's son, George Washington Peter (1801–1877).
5. Elizabeth Mifflin (1797–1885), the daughter of John Fishbourne and Clementina Mifflin, was particularly close to her aunt, Elizabeth Bordley Gibson; she
   was also Parke Lewis's friend. Merrill, 56.
6. William Holland Wilmer (1782–1827) was an outstanding Episcopal clegy-
   man who served as rector of St. Paul's, Alexandria; in 1826 he was appointed
   president of the College of William and Mary.

badly I thought, on Thursday night she was seized with a violent colic, I never saw any one suffer so much as she did. Dr Henry[7] was fortunately here and attended her constantly until today. I sent for her Parents [Martha and Thomas Peter] & Dr Sim.[8] He only arrived today & pronounced immediately that she could not recover. I sent to hurry my poor sister but she arrived only two hours after the mournful event. I had the melancholy satisfaction of nursing my poor niece day & night, of reading to & preparing her mind for the aweful change, she was perfectly resigned & pray'd as long as she could speak. Her only care was for her Parents & sisters & brothers, she begged me *never to desert Mec* [America Peter]. Never shall I cease to feel for Mec particularly & for all of them as my own, she blessed her Parents, I kissed her for them & told her I was sure she had their blessing at that moment. She was an excellent most dutiful & devoted child. She begged me to give her love to them all & to bless them. She often rejoiced that she was here & only wished to have her Parents & family.

My dearest Elizabeth to you Mr G & the excellent E Mifflin I consign the task of breaking this to my Darling Mec. Her poor Mother bears it extremely well with great fortitude & resignation. She begs that Mec will not be unhappy, & that she will go to see her as soon as possible—the very moment she can will go to Phi[ladelphi]a. My poor sister thanks you most gratefully for your affection to her child & says she shall be most grateful for your kindness on this occasion. I know my friend, however painful this duty, you will take pleasure in soothing that amiable child, tell her that the affection & sympathy of all here are hers, her angel sister will be carried to Effingham the day after tomorrow to be buried near my Mother. May the Almighty now accept our contrition & preserve to us our remaining comforts, those that are gone we trust are in his mansions of eternal bliss. Our united loves & every good wish. Yrs ever most truly

E P Lewis

---

7. Henry P. Daingerfield (c.1782–1844), an Alexandria physician, was a long-time friend of the Lewises. Alexandria *Gazette*, Jan. 4, 1844.
8. Dr. Thomas Sim was a fashionable Washington physician. Anna Marie Thornton, "Diary of Mrs. William Thornton, 1800–1863," Columbia Historical Society *Record* 10 (1907): 145.

Woodlawn Decr. 29th 1820

My Dearest Elizabeth,

Your two favours of the 20th & 29th arrived in due time, the last came to hand yesterday afternoon. I thank you sincerely for them, & regret that your health is not so good as when I left you. This, is a snowy day, but I hope the sun will shine upon us tomorrow, & that you may enjoy it in perfection. I was much surprised to hear, that the letter of which Mr T[ucker][9] was to have been the bearer, has already reached you, we heard that it was lost. I gave it to Mr T last Monday week when he left us for Washington, he arrived there only in time to attend his duty in the House, & Sir William [Douglas][10] gave the letter & a magazine to a servant to carry into Mr T's room; on Saturday last when about to commence his journey, he found the letter gone, & thought it was lost. He requested Sir William to ask me for another letter as he did not like to relinquish the hope of your & Mr G's acquaintance. Several circumstances have prevented my compliance, & I rejoice that the first reached you, because I hope that Major Van will introduce him to you & my ever valued friend Mr G. I am certain you will like Mr T, particularly if you think him, as I do, like Lloyd Rogers.—& he can require nothing else, I am certain, but to be indulged with the society of Mr G & *his dear Rib*. I think you will be mutually pleased.

If you will visit us (as I hope sincerely you may, in the Spring) I will treat you like a Sister too, & that will prove that we were perfectly satisfied & happy under your hospitable roof. I never was ceremonious myself, or wished to be treated with ceremony. I like always to feel *at home*, under no restraint, to know that I am welcome to what is set before me, & then I care not how plain the fare may be. With you I had nothing to excuse, because the fare was always most excellent, & my *Host & Hostess* were the kindest

---

9. George Tucker (1775–1861), a Virginia lawyer married to Lawrence Lewis's niece Maria Ball Carter (1784–1823), was at this time a congressman. He later became a professor of moral philosophy at the University of Virginia and a well-known author in several fields.

10. The Douglases—William, George, Harriet, and Betsy Mary—were the children of George and Margaret Corne Douglas. George (d. c.1888) became a very successful merchant with a large East India commission business. Harriet married a lawyer, Henry Nicholas Cruger (b. 1800). Scoville, 1:38–39; Margherita A. Hamm, *Famous Families of New York*, 2 vols. (New York, 1902), 1:73.

& most attentive of friends. *The forlorn wig*[11] has not yet appeared, but when Major Van returns he will *fish it* out wherever it may be *ensconced*, & bring I hope the clasp, frames, & some gold thread, & the Harp strings if Parkes letter arrived in due time. My poor Sister has written you a letter of grateful acknowledgement. I hope you received it. I shall enclose the stone cutters epistle. Will Mr G have the goodness to inquire the price of the patent leather health preservers, (vests & drawers) & send me the price with the name & *number* of the *vender*. I beg you will give me timely notice when I impose of your goodness by the number of my commissions. I rejoice to hear that Dear Mrs Powel is so well, I will certainly write to her. Do my Dear always tell me about all my kind friends in P. & assure them of our grateful affection, & be always sure of it yourself. In regard to the gift for Mrs G[relaud] Parke thinks a silver cake basket will be best as they have work boxes & writing desks already. Have D G on it as handsome as $30 will procure—for Mr. Rober[jot][12] as handsome a seal as 20 dollars will procure with I H R very handsomely cut by Thibault,[13] Parke says that he cuts seals very well. On the paper which encloses the seal, be so good as to write a memorial of E[leanor] A[gnes] F[reire] Lewis to her friend Mr Roberj[ot]. Present the basket in Parkes name if you please to Mrs G.

Parke looks much better, & the dear H & B M D [Harriet and Betsy Mary Douglas] are better than cordials for her nerves, these affecte girls are as happy here as if in a gay City, & are very agreeable companions, good Sir W says he is quite happy, & we *hope* that George & perhaps *Charley*[14] may travel South soon. I

11. Lawrence Lewis had lost most of his hair following an illness the previous summer so Parke had ordered a gray wig for him. Frances Parke Lewis to Elizabeth Bordley Gibson, 20 Nov. 1820, Mount Vernon Library.
12. In 1794 John Henry Roberjot, an immigrant from Saint-Domingue, became the bookkeeper of Stephen Girard, one of Philadelphia's wealthiest entrepreneurs. He soon advanced to the role of private secretary and confidential aide, a position which he held until his death. Though apparently they were not related, he was very close to the Grelaud family: at one time he lived with them; the Grelaud sons were supercargoes on Girard's ships; and when Roberjot died in 1828, he was buried from the Grelaud house. John B. McMaster, *The Life and Times of Stephen Girard*, vol. 1 (Philadelphia, 1918), 287; Harry E. Wildes, *Lonely Midas: The Story of Stephen Girard* (New York, 1944), 96, 330; PCD 1813; "Flitcraft, Harley, Meiligh, Roberjot, and Wheatcraft Families," Historical Society of Pennsylvania, 24–33.
13. Francis, Frederick, and Felix Thibault were fashionable Philadelphia jewelers. Westcott, *History*, 5:1289.
14. Perhaps Charles Ludlow Livingston (c. 1800–1873), son of Peter Van Brugh Livingston and Maria Houston Livingston. Rensselaer, 119.

shall really regret if E Carroll takes W B from E Jackson.[15] Not that I think him a great prize, but it would do better for his Cousin than any other. How is my favorite W Camac?[16] Does he pay his devoirs [respects] to anyone yet, & the traveller what is he about? Col. Corbin's[17] Mother was a Miss Beverley—a fine woman I have heard. His Father was the famous travelled Frank Corbin, they live some miles from Fredericksburg. He is a Col. of militia, I know nothing about him & never saw him since he was a child. I should think Miss Sims would not be satisfied in the lower part of this State and with a moderate fortune, splendid as they have always been. It is a great risk for a Phi[ladelphi]a Belle.

Send the best Harp strings dear E & a good supply & I will enclose the cash as soon as I know how much. Mrs Cigoigne[18] is the best judge of strings I *guess*. How are Mrs L & Ann?[19]

If a seal sufficiently handsome can be had for less than 20 dollars, then get a key also if you please. Our united loves, to you, Mr G Mrs & Miss M's. The Bishops family, all friends in 6th Street the Camacs & Smiths & indeed all & every one of our friends.

---

15. Elizabeth Carroll was the daughter of Charles Carroll of Homewood and Harriet Chew Carroll; the Carrolls had separated in 1816, and she had returned to Philadelphia. Elizabeth Jackson was the daughter of Capt. William and Elizabeth Willing Jackson. The cousin in question was probably William Bingham, the son of William and Anne Willing Bingham. Leach, "The Philadelphia of Our Ancestors," s.v. "Chew"; Theodore A. Bingham, *The Bingham Family in the United States*, 3 vols. (Easton, Pa., 1927–30), 3:804–10.

16. William Masters Camac (d. 1842), the son of very wealthy Philadelphians, became a doctor but did not practice medicine; he was the first president of the Philadelphia Zoological Society. Sidney G. Fisher, *A Philadelphia Perspective: The Diary of Sidney George Fisher*, ed. Nicholas B. Wainwright (Philadelphia, 1967), 133; Nathaniel Burt, *The Perennial Philadelphians* (New York, 1975), 99–100.

17. Richard Randolph Corbin (1801–1853) later moved to Mississippi where he became a prominent planter. "Genealogy: The Corbin Family," *Virginia Magazine of History and Biography*, 31 (1923): 83.

18. Anne-Marie-Aimée Condemine Sigoigne, whose husband was a planter in Saint-Domingue, arrived in Philadelphia in 1799. For many years she and her daughter Adèle kept a girls' school in their house at 7 Washington Square. Talented musicians, the Sigoignes were on social terms with many of Philadelphia's leading families. Information courtesy Francis James Dallett, Mt. Taconic, Connecticut; Sidney Fisher, 67; PCD 1819–51.

19. Anne Hill Carter (1773–1829) of Shirley was the second wife of General Henry "Light-Horse Harry" Lee and the mother of Robert E. Lee. Widowed, she lived in Alexandria with her younger children. Her daughter, Ann Kinloch Lee (1800–1864), was in ill health, and they frequently traveled to Philadelphia for medical treatment; reportedly the muscles of Ann's arm had been accidentally damaged by her brother Robert. Edmund J. Lee, ed., *Lee of Virginia* (Baltimore, 1974), 341–42; Douglas S. Freeman, *R. E. Lee: A Biography*, 4 vols. (New York, 1934), 1:33.

Woodlawn Janry. 11th. 1821

My Dearest Elizabeth,

I have not *laughed* at your letter because I was in company when I received it, & they might have asked "Why do you laugh?—but I certainly did *smile*, & shall smile again whenever I think of its contents.[20] Is it poor *Sir William* who is so much to be feared, for only he will come here. George will not show his face in despite of all my invitations. Fear not, my kind & anxious Friend, Parke is just as safe from G & W D [George and William Douglas]—as from the *man in the moon*. If they possessed all that lies between Indus & the Pole, she never would love them, or could I wish that she should. I shall always be attach'd to & interested in their welfare, because I know them to be sincerely attached to us all, but I trust Parke will never dispense with *mind, manner*, & many other etcetera's that they never can possess. I know perfectly well that it is the first wish of every member of the D[ouglas] family to have Parke of their number, Mrs D always has said that any member of my family will be received with transport, and I firmly believe that Lorenzo might choose from her daughters (if he was old enough for them,) or Parke from her Sons—but the Mother, Daughters, & Sons, know perfectly well that Parke will never be one of them. I always say that I give Parke three to choose from—*Charley* [Livingston?] first & then William Camac, then John Brinton. The two latter you know, & I am sure approve of, Charley has even superior attractions, if he can give any good reason for not appearing here. Harriet D thinks that he is certainly attached to Parke. She often makes inquiries in her letters about him, but not one word has ever reached us yet. I really love William Camac & should give Parke to him with pleasure if Charley proves less than I think him now. My reason for placing him first, is, that my Angel Agnes always said she wished Charley to be her Brother, & because Parke admires him most. John Brinton has much to recommend him, but he does not (you know) possess *the graces*. I wish Parke to be happily married because I think she will be happier than if single. I hope she will live in Ph[ladelph]ia or N York because I know she will be more healthy & happy than in Vir[gini]a. But I think marriage too important a step to be *lightly taken*, &

---

20. Elizabeth had written to Nelly 8 January 1821 warning that the Douglases were social climbers who were attempting to lure Parke into marriage with one of their brothers. Mount Vernon Library.

never should wealth be my object, although I trust my Son will be *rich in pocket*, as well as in moral & religious principles, & mental endowments.

George D goes to Europe in the Spring & probably William too. Their Cousin William a very excellent & accomplish'd young man, is in wretched health, & the rich old Uncles wish the two only male representatives of their family to be with them. George will always remain they expect. William will perhaps return in four years. Their property (particularly G's) will be much encreased, but that will be no temptation to us. They have no hesitation in saying that Parke might take her choice—but they are well assured that she never will take either. William is one of the best & most unexceptionable young men I ever saw but you know that *Cupid* is not at his command—& Parke knows G's eccentricities too well, & the defects of his temper, to be endanger'd were he even handsome, which he certainly is not. William stays a good deal here but not constantly. They wish him to go home that G may come, but W does not wish to go, & I know not whether G can come. I like both very much as friends, but never never do I wish to have them as Sons. Do not fear my dear Friend on their account any longer, & be assured when Parke makes her choice you shall be the first to know it, I owe this to your unwearied kindness. Should the Almighty take me before she marries, I will hope that he will direct her mind always for the best, & rely on the kind friends I leave behind.

In regard to the Douglas family my dear Elizabeth, you are misinformed. Their father was a very respectable merchant. So were their Uncles, they made handsome fortunes & Mrs D who was an excellent manager has ever cared [for] her children very much. I assure you that no people in New York are in a higher rank than the Douglas! Col & Mrs Varick (Grandmamma's old friends) are their visitors, the Livingstones, Vanhorns, Loudlows, Verplanks, Edgars, McEvers, all those considered most respectable in New York are on the most sociable terms—that, I was *myself* an eyewitness of—& never heard one word to their disadvantage. My old friends all visit them—the Coldens, Jays, Van Ransalaers, Bensons.[21] I know no family better received in New York than the Douglas & I never saw a more hospitable noble hearted family. The girls are very amiable—they work, read, sing, play battledoor,[22] & converse about their travels, are per-

21. All these families were old friends and acquaintances of the Washingtons; many of them were Federalists.
22. Battledore and shuttlecock was a popular game that evolved into badminton.

fectly happy with us, & stay so long at our earnest entreaty. They submit to me in every thing & are as anxious to avoid the slightest appearance of evil as any girls can be. I have seen a great deal of them & I must believe from my own experience of their worth & estimation in society—that all you have heard is most *false* & *malicious*. You think that they would be anxious to induce a connexion between our families, because it would elevate them in society. You are very much mistaken, for I assure you they think themselves on just as good a footing as any of their acquaintance; they are just as well satisfied with their *name, arms, & crest* as any one you will meet with. Mrs. Hamilton & Mrs Varick with many others of *undoubted* rank in society are their visitors. Col Varick was a friend of their Father. They went with me by invitation to his house. If they are not well received, then I must doubt the sincerity of all my friends & the friends of my Grandparents in N.Y.—for to own knowledge they were received as old acquaintances when I was there. How then can any one lament *my degradation* from being a guest in that house! I cannot comprehend it.

I have, thank heaven, a heart which will ever be grateful for kindness & friendly attentions, although I shall not think it necessary *to give one of my children* in return for it. It is not at all likely that I should ever be dazzled by the glare of wealth or pageantry of greatness, I have had the good fortune to know, in the persons of my adopted Parents, what *real greatness* consists in, & I should think myself as much entitled to respect & attention in Phi[ladelphi]a, N York & every where else, if I was by misfortune reduced to work for my subsistence, as, when I was the adopted child of the first President & of the most perfect of women. With these feelings & sentiments, you need not fear that *I, or mine*, will ever be governed by interested motives, or that any man will be consider'd as a match for my daughter, who has not mind, manners, & every recommendation most desirable in a matrimonial connexion. I never saw but three young men who were at all objects of my anxiety as Sons—& should they all fail, I should be very apt to think that every thing happens for the best. They are C L. W C. & J B. If I could remove to Phi[ladelphi]a myself I should not care whether she ever married at all. There is no Virginian that I know of that I would like at all.

I know nothing of Captn. Cooper, except, that he is handsome, pleasing, genteel, a delightful musician, a poet, & recites extremely well. He is the Brother of Major Vandeventer's second wife, a Captn in the Army & attached to the Adjutant Genls department, he is devoted to music, & comes to accompany Parke on the Harp, but has no *sinister* designs. Major Van says the Captn thinks that a soldier of fortune ought not to marry. Parke cannot afford to "pack up her tatters & follow the drum".

I must recur again my dear Friend to the subject of your letter. Maria Tucker (Mr T's wife) lived in the same house with them in Washington & visited with them constantly. She assured me that they were very much attended to & Mr. Politica[23] as well as Mr. T. told me that Baron Stackelberg[24] was very much in love with BMD & several other gentn. The nephew of Mr Monroe (Genl Scotts aid)[25] is now her admirer, & the family very anxious that he should be accepted. Genl & Mrs S[cott][26] were very attentive to them. The American Officers at Sacketts Harbour & the best society of Montreal & Kingston, gave them parties last summer. The Brother of Walter Scott the Poet,[27] & his family, were constantly with them & they expect them in New York in the Spring. If they are so universally disliked, how does it happen that they get along so well where ever they go? Judge W was much pleased with them. I should like to know who are their accusers. I shall never hint a word of your letters to any of them, no one but Parke knows of them at all. I shall never doubt your friendly motives or those of Mr G, & I hope you will banish all fears of our weakness or compliance with any thing not consistent with our principles & self respect.

Do tell me what your plaster is for frosted [whitened, roughened] heels. I like to have recipes for all occasions. Mr W[ilmer]'s Sermon was most eloquent & affecting, I hope to get a copy of it, & when you come here, as, I hope you will this spring, I will shew it you. It is very long. I wish you would write frequently. Remember me most particularly to all my friends. How are Mrs Morris &

23. Pierre de Poletica, Russian minister, was an experienced diplomat who had previously served in the United States; his opinions had then been favorable to the Federalists. Samuel F. Bemis, *John Quincy Adams and the Foundations of American Foreign Policy* (Westport, Conn., 1981), 272; John Quincy Adams, *Memoirs*, ed. Charles Francis Adams, 12 vols. (New York, 1970), 2:406.
24. Berndt Robert Gustav, Baron de Stackelberg, was charge d'affaires of Sweden and Norway from 1819 until 1832. Bemis, *Adams*, 273.
25. Lt. James Monroe was the son of the president's brother, Joseph Jones Monroe. Harry Ammon, *James Monroe* (New York, 1971), 438.
26. General Winfield Scott (1786–1866) was at this time commanding the eastern department of the United States Army; his wife was Maria De Hart Mayo (1789–1862) of Richmond.
27. Thomas Scott (1774–1823) was Walter Scott's younger brother. James C. Corson, *Notes and Index to Sir Herbert Grierson's Edition of the Letters of Sir Walter Scott* (Oxford, 1979), 625.

her daughter & family. My best respects to the good old Lady & the Bishop & love to all who remember us affectely. Mr. R carried the wig to exchange it for one smaller & more grey.

Accept for yourself & Mr G every sentiment of grateful affection.

Yrs ever
E P Lewis

The wig was too large. The strings do well.
Shall I show yr letter to Parke. No one has seen it but myself.

Woodlawn March 22nd. 1821

My Dearest Elizabeth,

I have now two of your affecte and welcome letters to thank you for, & that would not have been the case, so long, had I not waited to ascertain whether a letter of the Genls could be procured for Mrs Derby.[28] I have applied to Judge W, & refreshed his memory, two or three times, & he always promised to send me one if he could find such as were proper to part with. I had, four, or five, from the Genl to myself, but they were not such as I could have parted with, as they related entirely to private concerns. I have, however, to oblige many of his ardent admirers, cut out sentences from them, & the remnants remain for my children. I hope to procure one for you, in a short time, & it will give me great pleasure to do so, or any thing else that will be agreeable to my friends, Mr G, & yourself.

I admired Mrs Derby's beauty, & unaffected simple manners, at Mt Vn, & although her beauty, is said to have departed, she was much admired in W[ashingto]n for her grace & propriety, but, my Dear Elizabeth, her Husband is the object of universal contempt & ridicule.[29] I never hear but one opinion about him, his folly, his impertinence, are the constant theme of all who see him. How can such a woman as Mrs Derby be happy with such a man! You know that a woman's consequence depends so much on the

---

28. Martha Washington had freely distributed keepsakes of George Washington to friends and acquaintances; Nelly followed her lead.
29. Sidney Fisher shared this opinion of Richard Derby. He referred to him as "a great fool," and commented on the couple: "He is horrible, but she is well looking, animated & sociable . . . ." Sidney Fisher, 110, 122.

respectability of her Husband. He has done so many mean things in Wash[ingto]n, that every one is astonish'd at Mrs D's choice. Mr Canning[30] was very much offended, because the managers of the Birth night Ball appointed him to lead Mrs Derby to supper. He said "She was not a Lady of any distinction" (he could only have objected on D's account.) Maria Tucker became acquainted with Mrs Derby, & was much pleased with her manners, & her taste in dress. I hope to become better acquainted with her, some-day, when I can see *her, often*, & her spouse *very seldom*.

I regret much My dear Friend that you have been so much indisposed, & sincerely hope that the Spring will renew your health & strength. We have had very fickle weather lately—last week, we were sitting with the windows open, in the morning, & at night there was a storm of snow & sleet. The fruit is injured but not destroy'd. I sent, a fortnight since, to Alex[andri]a to be forwarded by water, a box of woodbine for you, & one for Mr Roberjot. I thought it had been on its way long since, but heard yesterday that they were still in Alex[andri]a but expected to go soon. I hope they will arrive safely. When you get the box, have the earth & roots divided through the middle across the box with a spade, break away the sides & bottom of the box, then plant the two blocks of earth &c near a wall, or frame, put woods earth, or wood pile manure below & around your plants. This will make you two very fine vines, let one of them grow by Mr G's office, that he may have a woodbine bower to refresh him after his dry studies of law cases; & plant the other in a warm situation to please yourself, particularly, if you think that the heat is not too intense from the wall of your back building, that will do. It re-quires a warm situation, but not too hot. Water them in dry sea-sons, & particularly for sometime after they are planted—& in winter cover the roots with long litter. It is the most lovely vine, when in bloom, that I ever saw. It is an evergreen here.

Judge Washington takes charge of a small box, in it you will find a pair of card racks made by your Daughter for you. A watch bag and a pincushion by your friend—the pincushion is an old relick of past happy times. The silver tissue was a part of Grand-mama's wedding petticoat when she married the Genl—the lin-ing was a part of the dress she wore to the last Birth night in Phi[ladelphi]a. There are 4 pr of cambrick cuffs, which I hope you

30. Stratford Canning (1786–1880) served as British ambassador to the United States from 1820 until 1823.

will wear, as the[y] were made for you expressly. I hope they will fit well. The purse directed to my kind & dear Betsey Fisher, I will thank you to send her. The nankin crape I wish to have dyed & pressed in the best manner, & sent by the first good opportunity. I do not hesitate to ask favours of you my dear friend, because I know your kind heart. When you think I *impose*, you must tell me so—& whenever I can do anything for you rely upon it, I shall be more pleased to execute, than you to request.

I thank you much for the trouble you have taken about my commissions & am perfectly satisfied. My good Uncle proposes being in Phi[l]a[delphi]a. the 1st of April, & will take charge of the wig &c. I heard yesterday from Riversdale, the family bear their loss as well as could possibly be expected. Poor Uncle suffer'd excessively at first, & will, no doubt, long feel this irreparable loss, such a wife[31] is not easily found. He will carry dear Caroline & Julia[32] with him to Phi[ladelphi]a. & stay a short time. I heard, only a week before she died, that my kind Aunt was almost well; I had been prevented going to see her, by the roads, & the necessity of someone being with Mr L who could assist him if suddenly attacked, & anticipated going to R, as soon as Dr Henry came to stay with Mr L. On Monday, I heard that she had relapsed, but did not credit it because I had no news from her family, & on Wednesday night, Patty wrote me, that she died on Tuesday at 1 o'clock.

It will appear strange to you, but I really am ignorant what her disease was; my poor sister, to whom I wrote for information, was too much occupied with her own sad reflections to remember my request. You recollect that she was lame from a swelled knee. I believe that an imposthume was formed just above it, but I am not certain. Some persons thought it was a cancer in the kidnies, others, Scrophula [tuberculosis of the lymph glands]. She had seven Physicians, & no two of them agreed in opinion. Patty says, that my poor Aunt's sufferings exceeded all she has ever witnessed. She bore her illness with great fortitude, & died with perfect resignation. She said that she no longer wished to live, she had made her peace & was resigned to the will of her Maker &

---

31. Rosalie Eugenia Stier (1778–1821) married George Calvert in 1799. GWD, 6:353.
32. Besides Eugenia, who was at school in Philadelphia, the Calverts' daughters were Caroline Maria (1800–1842), who married Thomas Willing Morris in 1823, and Julia (1814–1888), who married Dr. Richard Henry Stuart in 1833. *Maryland Genealogies*, 1:161–62.

Redeemer; perhaps should she live, she should be drawn away by worldly pleasures & not be so well prepared at another time. I loved her as much as any connection I possessed. She was the most hospitable kind & generous of friends, & I shall long feel her loss. Her dear children are worthy of her. I wrote to my Uncle begging him to leave them with me whenever he left home, (he will not part with them altogether) & assured him I would be a mother to them. I will always endeavour to prove my love to her by affection for them.

During the last thirteen months I have lost six of my nearest relations. I feel like a shipwreck'd mariner on a rock in the midst of the Ocean, wave after wave breaks over me, & I remain there, fearing the approach of others. Do you remember, my darling Agnes, two nights before her death, in her delirium, she begged me "to go to the window, that her sister said there were so many coffins there, & she was frighten'd at hearing of so many"— prophetic were her words. *Three* have already been filled. May the Father of mercies shield us now, or enable us to meet his will with perfect resignation. I think of my darling constantly, & pray that she may be eternally bless'd, & that we may meet her hereafter.

My Darling Son will go this spring to Yale College. May he be preserved as a blessing to us, & an ornament to his Country. My darling Girls do not look very well, but I hope they will improve in health & good looks as the spring advances. We have only heard that Charley talks of us, & of coming here, he is a close student of Law. Mrs Camac writes Parke that "her old Beau", William, is much admired, & that they all wish Parke could have been there on the 21st. I shall always love William. I shall write to Dear Caroline today & mention your kind message. Parke wishes to have strings of the different sizes enclosed for her Harp. Will you be so good as to ask Mrs. Cigoigne to choose them for her—of the best quality, 3 *hanks*, or *rolls* of each size & color. Will you write me the cost of them & of the dying, & I will enclose a Bill of the U.S. Bank for them, the wig &c. Parke wants also, 2 of the largest sized silver strings, & two of the second size silver strings.

I wish you could visit us this spring when the woodbine is in bloom, you, Mr G & dear E Mifflin. Present us most affectely & gratefully to all friends in Phi[ladelphi]a—& always tell me of them. The good Bishop & his amiable family, Mrs Powel & her connexions, Mrs Morris & hers—Mrs & Miss Mifflins, Mrs Camac & the Brintons. We owe much to them all.

Poor Mrs Lee & the innocent sweet Ann. Major H Lee (the half brother of Carter) has seduced his sister in law, Miss McCarty, defrauded her of great part of her property, & they would have gone to South America together after deserting his wife, had not Miss McC's unexpected confinement disclosed the nefarious business. He is justly detested, & she is miserable—has returned to her poor Grandmother who must think that she has lived too long.[33] What is death to the innocent, compared with this irreparable disgrace. I am sorry to hear that Carter is travelling about with his vile Brother. They are both *Deists*. May the Almighty change Carters heart for the sake of his amiable Mother & Sister. If you go there again present me most affectely to them & to Mr C. Our united loves & prayers for you & Mr G—My dearest Mec & Eugenia.

> Ever most truly yours
> *E P Lewis*

Woodlawn April 23rd. 1821

My Dear Friend,

Your long wished for letter to me of the 18th. ult. arrived today, & I hasten to thank you for it; & first, I will write the recipe

---

33. Major Henry Lee (1787–1837), the son of General Henry Lee by his first marriage, was the master of Stratford Hall. In 1817 he married a neighbor, Ann Robinson McCarty (1798–1840). She and her sister Elizabeth (1800–1879) were extremely wealthy orphans. Elizabeth came to live with the Lees: Henry Lee became her guardian, and subsequently, her lover. When she had a stillborn child, the affair became a public scandal. In disgrace, Elizabeth went back to her family—her grandmother, Margaret Robinson Rose of Mount Rose Plantation and her stepfather, Richard Stuart. Lee was also disgraced, not just for seducing his ward, but for mishandling her fortune. Though he repented (apparently sincerely), paid back most of the money, and was forgiven by his wife (who never again communicated with her sister), the world did not forgive him. He lost Stratford, and his attempts to reestablish himself through politics were blocked by his enemies. Throughout his troubles, Charles Carter Lee (1798–1871), Anne Carter Lee's second son, stood by his half-brother and was one of his firmest supporters. Henry and Ann Robinson Lee spent their last years abroad and died impoverished. Elizabeth McCarty, ironically, married Henry Storke, the new owner of Stratford Hall and inherited the estate from him; she is buried in the garden. Clara S. McCarty, *McCartys of Virginia* (Richmond, 1972), 24; Ethel Armes, *Stratford Hall: The Great House of the Lees* (Richmond, 1936), 366–410; Lee, 404.

for "Horehound Syrup" as it will be the most *useful ingredient* in my answer. Take of fresh horehound, *as much* as you please, say a double handful, wash it in several waters, & pick off all dead leaves. Then put the good part into a tin saucepan, pour on it as much vinegar as will cover it well. Stew them until the vinegar is very bitter, take out the leaves, add a desert spoonful of fresh butter, & as much brown sugar, or fine honey, (the latter is the best) as will make it a rich syrup, or candy, if you like it best, boil it as much, or more, than any other syrup, or boil it to candy height. It will keep any time and is the best remedy for a cough that I ever knew tried. I regret much that you & Mr G suffer with colds, & hope that they will soon be entirely removed.

We have had very fickle weather lately, a *thunder* storm at night, & a *snow* storm the next morning. Ice that would bear a Horse & yet the trees uninjured by the frost—except the Apricots, & they died with the early frost. It is astonishing that anything escaped, a violent wind, & a cloudy sky, saved the fruit it is supposed. Yesterday & today the weather has been delightful, & next week, if this weather continues, my woodbine will bloom. I wish you could be here to see it.

My *good, honest, faithful* & *zealous* friend, Major Vandeventer, brought the canton crape perfectly well. Nothing ever suffers in his hands believe me. I assure you that he is one of the most amiable men I ever saw—perfectly honorable, & to be depended on always, I know no gentleman that I would sooner ask a service of, because I know that it would be conferring a favour on *him**. We persuaded Parke to walk when he was last here, his friend Captn. Smith & the gallant Major attended us. He has furnished her with dumb bells & battledores, & is much & most kindly interested in her health. He calls me "Mother" & Parke "Daughter", & fills the filial & parental characters admirably. We see him very frequently. Mr Monroe and Captn. Cooper also came with the Major & Captn. Smith, Genl Gaines,[34] his aid & other military Beaux will be here soon.

My Dear Friend, I do not believe that Charley is on his way here, Major Van was very anxious to bring him along, they lodged in the same Home at Phi[lladelphi]a. He told Charley that he had seen nothing of *Spring* in N.Y & Phi[ladelphi]a—& he had better

*I think so too Mamma *F P L.*

---

34. General Edmund Pendleton Gaines (1777–1849) alternated command of the eastern and western divisions of the army with Winfield Scott.

come with him to W[ashingto]n. If they failed to find it there, they would proceed to Virg[ini]a. Charley replied that "he would like to come to Washington, but business would recall him to N.Y. I fear my dear E. that he is not to be relied on. I wish much to know exactly *what* he means, or if he means anything—he shall not trifle here however charming he may be—*that is poz.* He call'd at the Ds in N.Y. to make most particular inquiries, spoke in the highest terms of Parke, & regretted that business prevented his visits to Wash[ingto]n in the winter, & of course to Woodlawn. It cannot be *business*, you know, when *pleasure* keeps him in Phi[ladelphi]a. I only wish *to be certain* of his views & intentions, & many reasons as I have to be interested for him, & *first of all*, that my departed Angel wished him to be her Brother— yet if he does not feel the worth of my dear child, we shall, neither of us regret him, I shall think, as usual, that all is for the best. If he has no intention to address her, he does not act as honorably as a gentleman ought. If he does, it is high time he should decide, I think. She knows too well what is due to herself to fall in love with anyone who does not really love her—& if he trifles any longer—he will come in vain if he does come.

Her health is very delicate, & she does not take as much exercise, by a great deal, as she ought. I have been very uneasy about a bleeding at the nose which she has had a good deal of lately. It has however relieved her headach very much, but it makes her pale. Dr Henry D says that he hopes it will be salutary. I wish Mr L would go, & take us with him, to Ballston this summer, a pleasant tour would be of infinite service to him & to my dear Parke—& my little Angela too. My dear Boy will go to College this spring perhaps next month. It is a great trial for me to part with him, to be so far from him. This is the misfortune of living on a Virg[ini]a Farm. It has cost me more in parting with my darlings, than it is worth by many many degrees.

We have not yet received the articles or the letter by Dear Mec. Major Van told us she had arrived, he will bring them next Saturday, when he intends to introduce little Eugene to his *Grandmother*. Ped intends to give the little man a tea party, with *miniature* biscuits &c. She is certainly intended for a City Lady she is so fond of giving parties. I am very happy to find that you like the articles forwarded. I knew that you would take the "Will for the Deed." I also rejoice that you have been so gay—& I am sure it will benefit your health. I have not danced for twenty two years, & nothing can ever move me to that again, I am convinced.

I once enjoyed that amusement above all others, but I lost all taste for it after I was married. Parke has just finished a beautiful head in crayon, to replace one that was not well finished, she shaded it in ten days, she was too impatient in drawing the outline, & did not catch the gay expression of the countenance exactly, but it is very neatly shaded, & far better than one that required more than two months at School.

Let me hear from you as frequently as you can, nothing gives me so much pleasure as hearing from my friends when I cannot see them. Do my dear E make inquiries about *Charley's goings on* in P—& learn as much of his character & conduct as possible. It will be of service that we should know *what he is*, let the affair go as it may. Mrs Camac will see him, no doubt, & if he says any thing of Parke, she will probably hear it from Captn. Ricketts.[35] How is the amiable William, & what figure does he make in society? You know how deep an interest I shall always feel in his welfare. How is *the modest traveller*? has he cast an eye of favour on anyone yet. Did you receive the $10 by Major Van, & how much do I owe you. Add to the debt, if you please, 2 handsome gilt purse clasps, & one dozen best white silk corset laces. Poor Mrs Lee! I fear she will not have much comfort in her Sons. One is fond of low company & dissipated, & Carter is too much with his worthless Brother Henry, & too blind to his faults to escape pollution, I fear.

How do my venerable friends, the good Bishop, Mrs Powel, & Mrs Morris? They, & you & *yours*, & my other kind friends, always live in my heart, & are visible to *my mind's eye*. Assure *all*, of our kindest remembrances. Parke is happy to receive Mr G's *love, always*, & returns it with interest. It must have been a joyful meeting with your Brother. How long will he remain on Shore? I hope dear E M's brother has also returned to his family in safety. When you see E Ross I beg to be affectely remember'd & so does Parke. Will not A Allen[36] then return to England? I thought he had determined to do so. I should like to meet with him again. I hope his health is restored. Do tell me how poor Charles Hare

---

35. Philip Livingston Ricketts (1798–1859) married Mary Masters Camac, the daughter of Turner and Sarah Masters Camac. Leach, "The Philadelphia of Our Ancestors," s.v. "Camac."

36. The Allens were one of the most prominent families of Philadelphia. Andrew Allen (d. 1850), the brother of Nelly's girlhood friend Elizabeth Allen, had been one of her youthful admirers. His father was a Tory who spent the Revolution in England, and the family frequently returned there. The younger Allen had served as British consul at Boston (1805–1812). Delancey, 208–11.

[is].[37] What is his present situation & [where] he is? I shall always wish him health, peace, & prosperity. Mr L's strength returns very slowly, he still suffers with flying gout & cannot do without an opium pill every night.

Our united & most affecte. regards to you, Mr G & our friends, in and about Phi[ladelphi]a. May health & every happiness attend you all, prays your faithful & sincerely attach'd friend

Eleanor P Lewis

Woodlawn Octr 1st. 1821

My Dear Friend,

It is a long time since I wrote you or heard from you, I supposed you were absent, & we have all been ill. My darling Parke is in very low health, she was seized with a bilious fever & has never been well since, & Dr H[enry] D[aingerfield] fears she is in a decline. She is very nervous & low spirited, & Mr L has consented that we shall go where she always likes best to be, to Phi[ladelphi]a. We expect to go in eight or ten days. Do you think Mrs Carver's the best boarding house.[38] My child prefers that. Will you engage two good lodging rooms, opening into each other would be best—or rather will you engage them conditionally.

I have just recover'd from a bilious attack, & my little one too who will go with me. I trust change of air & scene will benefit my Child, & that it is only a low nervous complaint, although she is thinner & weaker than you ever saw her, & her complexion is as sallow as possible. Eliza Rogers was sick here lately, but she is quite well & gone home. My sister is still confined here but will soon be well I hope. Our united loves & every good wish for you & Mr Gibson & our other kind friends.

May health & every blessing attend you now & ever prays

Yr affecte & faithful friend
Eleanor P Lewis

---

37. Charles Hare became insane and was confined in the Pennsylvania Hospital. Sidney Fisher, 486–87.
38. Sarah Carver kept a boarding house on Fourth Street. PCD 1821.

Mr Lewis says that he cannot stay more than a night or two. Therefore one pleasant cheerful room on the second story will be all that is necessary. We contemplate staying four or five weeks.

————————— ❦ —————————

Woodlawn 7th. Octr [1821]

My Dearest Elizabeth,

Your very friendly letter I received last night—& thank you sincerely for the kind interest you express; since I last wrote My Child has rode out every day & is certainly better. Her spirits are much improved by the thought of being at Philadelphia—& she begs you to get us into Mrs Carvers at all events. The bustle is the very thing she depends on for her rapid recovery. The large room on the second story with two Beds in it will suit us exactly. We sleep on mattrasses over Beds all the year round, & shall prefer them if convenient. Fire in our room of course.

We hope to be there on Sunday or Monday next. If the weather permits we shall go to Arlington on Wednesday. Our journey must be slow as my child is too weak to be hurried. We go to Baltimore in a hack or the mail stage. From then in the Boat to french town, from thence across to Chester in a coach, & take the Boat again. I rely on the air of Phi[ladelphi]a on the pleasure my child feels from the prospect of being there for her recovery if the will of God permits. I keep up her spirits as far as I can although my own will sink frequently when I think of my situation last Octr, & when I see my remaining companion & friends as I fear, going in the same & that I sometimes think will be the Destiny of all my children—& my own at the last. It is hereditary on both sides. However my child is stronger, looks better, & I will hope for the best. She offers most affecte love & thanks to you for your kind interest in her health. I have not seen America since I parted with her in your house. Our united loves to you Mr G & his Sisters to all our friends in Phi[ladelphi]a.

In great haste Most faithfully yrs
E P Lewis.

————————— ❦ —————————

Arlington Novr. 6th. 1821

My Dearest Elizabeth,

After a long silence I again address you—& most sincerely do I regret to tell you that our journey to Phi[ladelphi]a is set aside for this season. My long illness—the indisposition of my Darling Daughters—of my maid—then a slight indisposition of Mr L—& lastly very bad weather. This is the third or fourth day of constant rain, since we were well enough to begin our journey. The season is so far advanced that Mr L thinks it would be hazardous to venture. Perhaps better fortune will attend us in the Spring.

My Darling Parke is much better, but still thin, pale, & occasionally nervous. Our fears of *decline* have been dissipated, she has recover'd her strength very much by changing the air. She will spend a few days with her Friend Miss Vanness,[39] in Washington, & we shall pay Caroline [Calvert] a visit before we go home. I must do all I can to enliven her this winter. If possible I will spend a fortnight in W[ashingto]n in the gayest part of the season. Her health is so dependent on her spirits, that company is essential to her. She does not like retirement at all. We have a very agreeable circle of military Beaux who are always very willing to exchange the City for the Country for a *day*, once a fortnight, & sometimes more frequently. With their Books & musical instruments, in addition to their agreeable conversation, they enliven us very much. We shall have some celebrated members of Congress this winter, to whom our friend Mr Watts[40] has given letters of introduction. But after all, my Friend, no place, no climate suits Parke half so well as Phi[ladelphi]a; & although I am not at all anxious for Parke to marry—yet as *I* am tied down to Vir[gini]a, I often wish you had some lad there who loved her as she deserves to be loved, & who was her *congenial soul*. To ensure her health & happiness, I would even consent to part with her forever.

---

39. Ann Elbertina Van Ness (d. 1822) was the daughter of General John Peter Van Ness (1770–1847), civic and social leader, and Marcia Brown Van Ness (1782–1832), an heiress and important philanthropist in Washington, D.C. On December 27, 1821, Ann Van Ness married Arthur Middleton (1795–1853), son of Henry Middleton of Niewport plantation, South Carolina. Langdon Cheves, "Middleton of South Carolina," *South Carolina Historical and Genealogical Magazine*, 1 (1900): 247; Moore, 182.

40. Beaufort T. Watts was secretary of state for South Carolina; he later served as a diplomat in Colombia and Russia. Lanman.

I have not been so ill for seven years as I was lately. I was ill at home for a fortnight. The day after my arrival here I relapsed, & was extremely ill. I never was so near derangement in my life. For three nights I was so restless, my forehead so tight & painful, that I could not lie down & was tempted every moment to quit my Bed, & run out of the house. I thought the night air alone could relieve me. I was excessively bilious & very weak. My spirits very much depressed, & no appetite at all. Afterwards I had a rheumatic headach, which was relieved by binding to my head the leaves of the American poplar. They produce violent perspiration & caution must be used in taking them off lest it should be checked too suddenly. I am now nearly as well as ever. My little Ped is well. But we are never secure from relapses in the diseases of this autumn. I never left home in such low spirits in my life, I could not account for it. I felt as if taking a last farewell of every object. No doubt it was the first approach of the illness which so soon attack'd me. My children had the ague & fever. I rejoice that you & Mr G have enjoy'd such health. My darling Son is well, he has enter'd College & is much pleased with his situation. I hope he may leave it with honor, & with an unblemish'd character. How is John Brinton. I never hear anything of him, he was an ornament to Yale College. But my poor Boy has not *his* devotion to study.

Mec is at home, I have not seen her yet. Was she much admired. Is William C much of a Beau, & how are his good Parents & Sister? Does Eugenia improve in her studies & appearance? I feel sincere gratitude to my friends in Phi[ladelphi]a for the kind interest they evince by calling to inquire about us, & to my respected & Beloved friend Mrs Powel for her attention. Present my love & every good wish to them, & assure them, that the *Sunny* moments of My Life are those which I have the good fortune to pass in Phi[ladelphi]a & that my fervent prayer is to pass the last years of my life with them, & to be buried in Christ Church yard. I hope that the good Bishop & family are well, my respected & dear friends Mrs Morris & Mrs Nixon.

Alexandria & George Town have been afflicted with the yellow fever this summer. The cold weather has removed it, I believe, but this Country has been universally afflicted with the most obstinate fevers. Our servants, our neighbours—every part of my family except Sister Peters have suffer'd severely. Her sons were sick but not ill. They are now perfectly well. Mr P's Mother, a very old Lady, died suddenly a few days since.

Will you be so good, my friend, as to inform me what we owe

Mrs Carver for her preparations on our account. You will confer a
favour by procuring me some shoes from Desplat.[41] My No. is
12½. My instep is high, those of that No. which are loose in the
instep are best—across the foot, & the toe, my foot is narrow. I got
some last fall which fit very well except being a little tight just
across the instep. Will you have them of the best prunelle [heavy
woolen fabric]—& french morocco—6 pr black morocco—4 pr
best black prunelle—2 pr thick spotted silk black. Some of his
shoes fray out at the sides before they are worn out, from not having enough turned in; & one pr of my morocco shoes broke out
from the sole for more than an inch before they were half worn.
However, those shoes were (like Pindars razors, *made to sell*.) One
pr of morocco I was obliged to cut in the instep before I could wear
them. He must not make them wider in any part except the instep
& that not much wider. Parke wishes to have some shoes made by
Krafts[42]—but will send you a shoe by the first opportunity. Will
you ascertain the price of my shoes, & I will forward the money to
you immediately. I should like to receive them by Judge Washington if ready in time for him. Are chinchilly caps & trimmings
worn & what is the price of them? Parke would like to have a cap
this winter if fashionable.

Will you not come in April to see us—or in March or May as
you like best, as you are employ'd at home for the winter. When
will dear E Mifflin visit us, nothing would delight us more than
to have her at Woodlawn. The frosts have check'd disease, & I
trust we shall have no more of it. You have not sent me a pattern
of a Baby's frock yet. Ah! forgetful of the wants of *little ones*. I
wish you had *one* to remind you in future. Do write to me frequently—& tell me of all that interests you, & my other friends.
Next to being in Phi[ladelphi]a is to hear from it. How is poor C
Hare? What is said of Ann Lee's hand. Car[ter] expected to go for
her this fall.

I have written you a long letter, My dearest Friend, & I fear
you will think that I have made a vow against ever writing de-
cently. I always determine to be a *neat scribe*, but my incorrigible
carelessness defeats my good intentions. Excuse all my errors of
every sort, in consideration of the sincere love I bear you. My sister Mary C offers you her love. Mr L's respects to you & his friend

---

41. Stephen Desplat was a ladies' shoemaker with a shop on Fourth Street. PCD
1819.
42. Henry Kraft was a shoemaker with a shop on Walnut Street. PCD 1821.

Mr G. Parke, Ped, & I offer our sincere affection to you & Mr Gibson.

> Love to all friends. Yrs ever most faithfully
> *E P Lewis*

———————————————❦———————————————

Riversdale Decr. 3rd. 1821

My Dearest Elizabeth,

The amiable Major brought the shoes, & your kind letter to Parke, in safety to us a week since. Parke's shoes fit very well, but the white satins did not arrive. I am sorry to say that a pair of mine are too large. Indeed they are all too large, but I can wear four pair. The man made a mistake & made them too wide across the foot. They are rather too long. I believe No. 12 would do better—but have them just across the instep, the size of those I return. The four pair of prunelle, 2 pr of spotted silk & 2 pr of black morocco—which are all too wide across the foot, & rather too long. I am very sorry to give you so much trouble, my Dear Friend, but you know shoes stretch so much that if too large at first, they are soon very uncomfortable. Will you be so good as to have them of the best prunelle, & blackest silk.

Parke passed two weeks in Washington with Miss Van Ness very pleasantly although the Citizens said it was very dull. Washington is now full of the great men of the Nation, but we expect tomorrow, to *turn our backs* on them & go home. Parke will probably come up again during the winter, I wish her to do so. I know not if *I* can. Her health is so much restored now that she will not be in danger of requiring my care, I hope. I passed a very pleasant week with Mrs Vanness, she is a very amiable woman, & they were extremely kind to us.

By the way, I will tell you a secret. *Keep it to yourself*—my dear. A certain Judge Johnson,[43] Senator from Louisiana, formerly of Tennessee—admires Parke, but fears that "she is too fastidious to be easily won". He is much like a *monkey, I* think, & *murders English & Grammar*. Of course, *wont do*. I hope he will

43. Henry Johnson (1783–1864) entered the U.S. Senate in 1817; later elected governor of Louisiana (1824), he continued to be active in state politics until 1850.

take the advice of his friends, & keep *á la distance.* I told them plainly that *he* was not the *plan.* I shall inform you, if any other *great men* cast an eye at our Daughter. It appears to be the general opinion that Parke is too *difficult* to be pleased—& that she will remain always single. If she can find a *congenial soul* & *wishes* to marry, I hope she will, but for my own part, I think she is happier as a single woman.

I have not received your kind letter by the Judge. Indeed I know not if he has arrived yet. I have been from home, eight weeks—& it is time I should return to prepare my household for the winter. I am much recovered, but not quite well yet. My little darling has a bad cold yet. My darling Son is doing well, I hope, at College; he says, he studies very constantly. Dear Caroline looks well, I think, I have been here almost a fortnight, & Parke, a week.

The weather is very unsettled. I hope we shall return home before we have a snow storm. The Majors account of the anxiety of our friends to us, is very gratifying. Be assured, *we* are *nothing loth.* I am glad that you like him so well, he deserves all the good you can think of him. He is my prime favorite, my adopted son. He always calls me *Mother*—and used to call Parke *Daughter,* but he considers her now as his *Sister*—which is more applicable as he is my Son. Be assured you will never have cause to think less well of him. He has a sweet little Daughter, & niece, at Madme. G's. Colo. Gadsden[44] is a most amiable & agreeable man. His heart & temper resemble Major Vans—& they are congenial spirits, of the same age. He is thin & does not look at all robust in person, but his mind is highly improved, & his manners very pleasing. We shall have them with several others frequently, I hope, this winter. Soldiers care not whether the roads are good, or the weather. They always come when they say so. I hope soon to receive your valued letter, which I shall reply to as soon as received. I hope frequently to hear from you my Friend. And we unite in wishing you, Mr G & our other kind friends ever happiness here & hereafter.

Most affectely yrs
E P Lewis

---

44. Col. James Gadsden (1788–1858) of South Carolina, at this time serving in the army, later became a railroad promoter and minister to Mexico who negotiated the Gadsden Purchase in 1853.

Woodlawn 3rd. Janry 1822

Your affecte letter of Decb 30th my Dearest Elizabeth, arrived this evening. The one by Judge W, has remained so long unanswer'd that I am really ashamed of it; & more particularly, as Mrs Carvers moderate charge was not attended to as soon as it ought to have been. I enclose you $15. Be so good as to pay her, & the balance due for the shoes. Desplat has cause to complain, but I am *not to blame*, nevertheless, because I had not a shoe with me that *did* fit well, & none could be got at in my absence. If he makes them by my last directions, No. 12—the *instep* not too tight, they will do. At all events, if made in the best manner, & of the best materials *he shall never see them again*. I suppose he may make Parkes white satin, as Krafts is delinquent. Be so good as to have 2 pr made for her—No. 11—that was her No. I believe.

She is well, gay, & *very happy*, she writes me. I carried her to Genl V[an] N[ess]'s on the 24th & returned home the next day, taking church in my way. They had a splendid wedding, & all *look'd their best*, P says. Seven Bridesmaids & Groomsmen—all *charming people*. On Friday & Saturday all the attendants dined at Genl V's. On Monday & Tuesday the Bride received company. Tonight they have a Grand Ball—on Monday another—& on Tuesday Mrs [John C.] Calhoun[45] gives a Ball to the party. P does not wish to come home yet, & she may stay as long as she pleases. She will probably visit her Aunt P. I know not whether they have come to George Town yet. They stay much at Oakland, 20 miles from Town, a very dismal place, but the Boys are *Farmers*. Mec dislikes it cordially. She look'd very well when I saw her, She never writes to me, & I know not their plans for the winter.

Mr L, Angela & myself are here, & since P went away have only had company twice—but we are not lonely. My little one is all life & spirits, & devoted to me. I know that you would love her, she is so gentle, so smart, & so observant of every thing that will give her Parents pleasure. She watches my looks, & if I appear sad, she says, smile Mother, I do not like to see you melancholy. I am sure she kisses me fifty times a day—my eyes, mouth, neck— & her great delight is to sit in my lap, between dark & candle

---

45. Floride Bonneau Colhoun Calhoun (1792–1866) was the wife of John C. Calhoun, James Monroe's secretary of war; a South Carolina belle, Mrs. Calhoun was known for her entertaining. A. S. Salley, Jr., "The Calhoun Family of South Carolina," *South Carolina Historical and Genealogical Magazine* 7 (1906): 154, 159.

light. She has a fine voice, & is now learning to sing a *french* song, the "Beau Dunois". She pronounces very well. I wish that I lived where she could have every advantage of education, she would improve rapidly.

But I can never send another darling to a Boarding School. I feel too severely the sufferings of my lost blessing—than whom, no child ever deserved more the devoted affection of a Parent. I thank you, my dear & kind friend, for your tender remembrance of her. I feel her loss as much as ever. I recall continually every act of her life, every incident of her illness, & lament every harsh word I ever gave, & every instance of denial to her requests. I never can speak of her to anyone without tears. I never venture to look at the profiles, or the sketch of her, but she is ever before me, in sickness, & in health; I visit constantly the Groves that she was so fond of, where I marked her name the day before I left home to nurse her. I have planted flowers, & shrubs that she best liked, there. I kiss her name, pray that she may be eternally blessed & rewarded, & that we may be reunited to her in the mansions of eternal bliss. My thoughts often rest upon that spot where I saw her laid, & much do I wish that I could visit it. I enclose you some verses that I wrote on the 8th of Decr. I always wish'd to write, but I never could until then, I have not done her justice. But I *feel* much more than my pen could express, of her excellence. As a *child*, she had no superior, indeed in every relation she was fault-less. She was too gentle, too innocent for this world, I trust she is in the Bosom of her Savior & her God.

A faint tribute from a devoted Mother to the memory of a dutiful, affecte & faultless Child.

> E A F Lewis died Octr 28th 1820, aged 15 years.
> "Why then do you grieve for me Mother"! she cried,
> (As I painted the joys of the Blest)
> "Why then do you grieve" Dearest Child, I replied,
> Thou will go to a haven of rest.
> For Thee, my lost Angel, even "Death had no Sting,"
> And no terrors the cold silent grave;
> Though thy Maker recall'd thee in life's early Spring
> He resum'd but the blessing *He* gave.
> Thy end was so peaceful, so pure was thy life,
> Could a *wish* now restore thee again;
> 'Twere a *Sin* to expose thee to sorrow & strife,
> To a world of temptation and pain.
> But I ever must mourn, (though I will not repine)

That those eyes are now shrouded in Death;
Which bent with the fondest affection on mine,
'Till my Darling resigned her last breath,
Yes! thy virtues my memory e'er will retrace,
Thou wert all a fond Parent desir'd;
Thy temper so mild, & so lovely thy Face,
But thy *heart*, more than all, I admir'd.
Not one selfish feeling inhabited there,
For *others*, alone, thou didst plead;
The oppress'd & afflicted were ever thy care,
Unoffending in *thought, word & deed.*
"To adore thy Creator in spirit and truth,"
And submissively bow to his will;
To the close of thy life, from thy earliest youth,
Thou didst strictly thy duties fulfill.
To the spot thou most loved do I often repair,
And with kisses embalm thy Dear Name,
"To meet Thee in Heaven" is ever my prayer,
And my last sigh shall murmur the same.

Decr 8th. 1821.

Most sincerely do I sympathise with my friends, Major and Mrs Jackson,[46] in their great affliction. Elizabeth you know was *my* favorite—& look'd as likely to live as any girl I ever saw. But so it is my friend. Those who appear destined for long life, are cut off in a moment almost, & those who tremble on the brink of the grave—linger on, year after year. I trust Ann will remain to comfort her amiable parents. I beg you to present me most affectionately to them, & to assure them of my sincere condolence, & prayers for their future happiness & the preservation of their remaining Darlings.

Love & every good wish to each of my Phi[ladelphi]a friends. I rejoice in good Mr Camacs recovery. I never heard that he was ill. I confess that the "amiable William" ever has been, & will be, the object of *my wishes* as a son in law, until Parke has chosen her *spouse*—& then perhaps, I shall still *covet him*, for Angela. We

---

46. Major William Jackson (1759–1828) was an Englishman, reared in South Carolina, who served in the Revolution. During the constitutional convention, he was one of George Washington's secretaries. He was secretary of the Society of the Cincinnati for twenty-eight years. He and his wife, Elizabeth Willing (1768–1858), Eliza Powel's niece, were favorites of the Washingtons. Their daughter, Elizabeth Willing Jackson (b. 1803), died December 21, 1821. GWD, 5:156, 162; McCall, 25.

heard that the family would certainly be in W[ashingto]n this winter. I am told that Parke looks *charmingly* now. I wish William were there, *who knows what might happen.* There is no one in W[ashingto]n that would suit *half so well—members of both houses* not excepted. How old is William. Parke is 22. *I* should not stand on *trifles.* I have not seen Eugenia yet. Is she pretty. If Ann Lee is at home, I have not heard of it. I seldom go to Alex[andri]a never indeed in the winter, unless on my way to W[ashingto]n.

I have just received a most dutiful affecte letter from my Darling Son. He wishes we were near enough to visit him sometimes—& begs me to come next Summer. I will, if I can, certainly. These are my great drawbacks to comfort, being separated from some of my darling children always. If they were always well & happy, I should not regard it. But to fear they suffer from the absence of my cares & exertions for them, is very painful. You know not these feelings my dear Friend. My amiable *adopted Son* (not *son in law*) the gallant Major will visit his mother in a day or two, & I will ask him to appoint a trusty *receiver* of my shoes. I hope Desplat will make the 8 pair, they shall not be *returned again.* I only heard that W. Bingham was engaged—the *fine woman* must be *mad*, I think, to choose such a *scamp.* Our united & most affecte love, and prayers that every year may find you & Mr G in health & happiness for many many returns—ever

Your affecte & faithful friend
E P Lewis

Shall we not hope to see you & Mr G soon. Be so good as to send me 6 of the very small brushes used for velvet painting—for veining leaves & doing the outlines. They are short stiff hair bristles I believe fasten'd with copper or brass. I am teaching myself for variety.

Woodlawn Febry. 10th. 1822

My Dear Elizabeth,

I received my shoes last night from the good little Major, & am happy to say they fit very well. I hope Desplat will remember the size, No. 12—& can promise to employ him as long as we both live, if he works well & faithfully. These are very neat shoes, & I thank you much for having them made for me. As I go to W[ash-ingto]n this week, they are in the very *nick* of *time*. Be so good as to procure me six veining velvet brushes. They are of horse hair, very short & brought to a point—& confined with a broad band of copper or brass. A person who teaches velvet painting has them for sale—and gold bordering such as I enclosed you patterns of in my letter of last week. Be so good as to send these articles by the first opportunity.

Now my dear friend I will give you the *whole truth* in a few lines. The gentn does not hesitate to acknowledge it, & has authorised me to do so always. The Major has been a devoted lover of *your* & my Daughter, has been positively rejected long since—& is now the suitor of another Lady. I am his *confidant* as well as his adopted Mother. I gave him my entire consent to gain Parke if he could. Although his situation, children, & widowhood, were serious objections, yet his heart, his principles & his disposition were so unexceptionable that I consented most willingly to receive him as my *Son in law* if P could love him. She could not, & he has wisely changed his feelings. I think he will now succeed, & marry his *present* Love, who is a very fine woman. He will always be my adopted Son & the object of maternal affection. He pays me always filial respect, deference, & affection, & has the most gentle temper I ever knew. It is impossible to know him & not to be his friend. My darling Parke is in *tip top* spirits, enjoying herself much at the City parties, she has made many pleasant new acquaintances.

We shall return home in two or three weeks. Present me most affectely & respectfully to the good Bishop & family, & to all my other kind friends. Accept for yourself & Mr G our united affection & believe me ever most sincerely & affectely yours

E P L.

———————————❦———————————

Arlington March 4th. 1822

My Dearest Elizabeth,

I received your affecte letter & the brushes & binding in G Town. I thank you sincerely for them, & am induced to ask another favour of you, as Captn Cooper will be in Phi[ladelphi]a in a few days, & that will give you an opportunity to send the following articles. A sheet of handsomest morocco paper of scarlet—a sheet of dark purple or mazarine blue morocco paper—A sheet of handsomest green in waves—and the balance in the prettiest gold bordering—some broad & some narrow. Will you also procure for me two pair of the handsomest screen handles, & send them with the paper by Captn Cooper, & inform me of the price. I leave the choice to you.

I came from G Town yesterday to stay a few days here with my excellent Sister, & left Parke with her maternal friend Mrs Van Ness, who has really watched over her & cherish'd her with a mothers care & kindness. Mrs Van N is lonely since her charming daughter left her, & I could not refuse Parke to her when she assured me it would be a gratification. I shall go for her on Thursday or Friday, & on Monday next we go home.

Yes, I have conversed with Mr Poinset,[47] & admire him extremely, he has the keenest eye, the most knowing countenance I ever saw. Every one admires him. He is coming to Woodlawn, & offer'd to teach me Spanish, & to lend P Spanish Books. He is perfectly acquainted with every modern language. I really envy him his acquisitions. I have seen too, Wolfe Tone,[48] Son of the Irish Patriot. He is the most diffident, awkward, & singular looking mortal I ever saw, but remarkably intelligent, well informed, & interesting in conversation. Mr Keating[49] I saw several times, I like him because I believe you & Mr G like him, & for his own sake too. Do you know Mr Gray[50] of Boston—a very elegant, handsome, genteel man, a Lawyer & son of the rich Gray of Salem. Captn Finch[51] is a fine martial looking figure & face. I think him a little like what my good friend Major Jackson was, formerly, though certainly much handsomer. Report makes him a Beau of Miss Tayloes.[52] It is not generally credited.

---

47. Joel Roberts Poinsett (1779–1851) was a South Carolina congressman, who later served a controversial term as American minister to Mexico.
48. William Theobald Wolfe Tone (1791–1828) was the son of Wolfe Tone (1763–1798), a famous Irish revolutionary and founder of the United Irish Society. A supporter of Napoleon, the younger Tone settled in New York in 1816. At this time he was serving as a lieutenant of artillery.
49. Either John Keating, Jr. (c.1798–1824), or William Hippolyte Keating (c.1799–1840); both were attorneys who dealt with James Gibson. John H. Martin, *Martin's Bench and Bar of Philadelphia* (Philadelphia, 1883).
50. Francis C. Gray (1790–1865) was a wealthy Bostonian who devoted himself to public affairs and literary pursuits.
51. Probably Captain William B. Finch who had joined the navy in 1806 and had commanded the *Prometheus* from 1814 through 1819.
52. Catherine Carter Tayloe (b. 1801), daughter of John Tayloe III and Anne Ogle Tayloe of the Octagon, Washington, D.C. George McCue, *The Octagon* (Washington, D.C., 1971), 95.

I went to a drawing room, the first I have been at since The Genl was President. I had few acquaintances, & really felt *alone in a crowd*. The *royal family*[53] were as attentive & gracious as I could have wished. I attended one of Madme. de Neuvilles[54] evenings. She is so amiable & friendly that every one is at ease & happy under her roof. There was an immense crowd, I had many friendly greetings & enjoyed myself extremely. The Indians[55] were all there & much amused with the dancing. They were charmed with Mrs Greenleaf[56] who was painted *up to the eyes*, They called her a *squaw* & one Indian remarked that although he had *sixteen wives at home*, he should like to add that squaw to the number. I never saw the ravages of time & (an unquiet conscience if you will permit me to say so) so apparent as in her. Her *countenance*, even, is totally changed. Its expression is really horrible. I was very much afraid she would scrape acquaintance with me. Anne Morris I met several times, & regretted that it was not in my power to pay her more attention. I never have the command of a carriage in G Town, & Mrs Brown[57] (with whom she staid) lives at a great distance from Tudor place.[58] I wish'd much to have seen her at Woodlawn.

The weather was bad, [a] great part of the time, & the walking impassable for Ladies. Moreover my military Beaux were tied

---

53. President James Monroe and his family were considered unusually ceremonious and pretentious. Accused of aping royalty, they were frequently ridiculed.
54. Anne-Marguerite-Henriette Rouillé de Marigny (c.1779–1849) married Jean-Guillaume, baron Hyde de Neuville (1776–1857) in 1794. Royalists, they were in exile in the United States from 1807 until 1814. With the Restoration, Hyde de Neuville was appointed French minister to the United States in 1816 and served until 1822; the couple's elegant style of entertaining was a source of much comment. Mme. de Neuville was a talented watercolorist who executed many landscapes during her two American sojourns.
55. During the early nineteenth century delegations of Indians frequently visited Washington and were entertained by the president. In 1822 Pawnee chieftains made an official visit; on their departure they staged an elaborate farewell ceremony in front of the White House. Ammon, 405.
56. Ann Penn Allen Greenleaf (1769–1851) was the extremely beautiful cousin of Nelly's girlhood friend, Elizabeth Allen. In 1800 she married James Greenleaf, an early Georgetown property owner and associate of Thomas Law. This marriage no doubt incurred Nelly's disapproval: Greenleaf had been divorced by his first wife for desertion. Delancey, 202–11; GWD 6:338–39; Allen C. Clark, "James Greenleaf," Columbia Historical Society *Record* 5 (1902): 233.
57. Perhaps Pamelia Williams Brown, the wife of General Jacob Brown (1775–1828), commander of the United States Army.
58. Tudor Place was the Georgetown mansion of the Peter family, designed by William Thornton, and built 1805–1815. GWD 6: 305–6.

to their offices almost entirely. This is a very busy time with them—& Tudor Place is not a good station for acquiring *recruits* of that description. Mec sometimes says that she anticipates only a life of *single blessedness*, from *necessity*. She is very social naturally, but her Parents & Brothers do not indulge her taste for society. She is much admired when she is permitted to appear abroad. Your daughter has her share of admiration, & attention. She is much better than she was in Decr. but does not look quite so well as when I first came to W[ashingto]n. She has had a bad cold. My little one has had returns of her chills, but is again free from them. I am sometimes far from well, but if I can only journey to, & beyond, your dear joy giving City, this Summer, I shall resuscitate I am certain. If I do not I know not how I shall fare, for I shall be liable to the same attack that almost destroy'd me last Autumn. My darling Boy is well, & wishes much that we should visit him.

Miss Mallon[59] is with America, she is pretty, & seems good temper'd, but I should judge, *not at all* intelligent, she is very quiet, but very insipid. She is much more secluded, I suspect, in this *great world*, than she was in Phi[ladelphi]a. She has not the easy manner of one accustom'd to the best society, & appears almost afraid to *breathe* sometimes, lest she should give offence. Her voice is a good deal like her Mothers *silver tones*.

Phi[ladelphi]a is very gay I hear, how are all those I love & admire, for whom I cherish grateful feelings which can never die whilst I have life? I wish that I could prove this to them by more than *words*. Cannot you & Mr G come this Spring. I know not when or of whom your Daughter will make choice—but, if she ever does, will you not "come at our bidding, with haste to her wedding." Do not wait however for this *uncertain event*. Has your woodbine lived through the winter? I hope it will flourish finely.

Will you be so good as to inquire of Caldcleugh[60] (the man at the corner of Walnut & third Streets) if he will sell the saucers of carmine in his boxes of velvet colours seperately, & what will be the price. They are beautiful & I have nearly used mine. My Sisters beg to be particularly remember'd to you & Mr G. Parke & Mec, & little Ped, & her Mother, send you love & kisses, & every

59. America Peter was a student of Catherine Mallon (c. 1773–1824), a widow who kept a girls' school on Walnut Street; Mallon's daughter was her friend. Biography file, Historical Society of Pennsylvania.
60. Robert A. Caldcleugh began as a stationer and became a manufacturer of paper hangings, copying European patterns. Westcott, *History*, 5:1247.

good wish for you, Mr G, & E Mifflin. Our united loves to all we love & respect.

Your affecte & faithful friend
Eleanor P. Lewis

Be so good as to ask Caldcleugh to put the paper & binding very carefully that it may not be injured.

————————— ❦ —————————

Woodlawn June 13th. 1822

My Dearest Elizabeth,

I wrote you a short letter on Thursday morning, and committed it, (with $10 enclosed,) to Judge Johnson of Louisiana, a Senator, and a *Col* into the bargain; & though "his blushing honors are thick upon him", yet he is a modest, amiable, unassuming man, &, sorely against *his* consent, an old Bachelor. He intends to pass the summer in the North, as the Session was protracted so much, he could not return home conveniently. I omitted to request you to send me 4 handsome Purse clasps, gilt, in addition to the other articles, with a cake of Prussian Blue, a cake of light Prussian Blue, and one of best Carmine. Should my cash not be sufficient to cover all these little *items*, be so good as to charge me the balance, & it shall be forwarded in the shortest possible time.

Mr L is not at home yet, & our travels are uncertain, I hope we shall go, I have this morning been obliged to administer a dose of calomel to my little one, to prevent the return of fever & bilious symptoms, she look'd so badly, & complained so much yesterday, & our neighbours are becoming unhealthy. We regret much that you & Mr G were prevented journeying South, but I trust you will come in the Autumn, & bring E Mifflin with you. I recollect Mr Sullivan perfectly, & always liked him very much. He was one of my partners, at the last Birth night I attended, in Phi[ladelphi]a. He would not be apt to recognise "Nelly Custis's *little light figure*," now, I think.

A[ndrew] Allen must ever be the polish'd entertaining gentleman—with him, it is innate. I should delight in a days confab. with him, of all things. I know no one with a *neater wit* than his— keen as the razors edge, & as polished. I had heard of H Ms engagement, & sincerely hope it will be for her happiness. I love, admire, & respect the good Bishop & Mrs Morris, & feel an affecte interest in the welfare of their families. I know no one who appears to fulfill all her duties more perfectly than M[aria] Nixon. Assure them all, & every other of my kind Phi[ladelphi]a friends of my sincere & grateful affection, & for you, & Mr G, remember that you are always at the *head of my list.*

My poor Sister, E[liza] P Custis, suffers severely from a liver affection. Her Physician fears that she can never recover entirely. Her state is very precarious. She is in Maryland, with a friend, & has never been able to come to us, or to go to her child. Our best & favorite friend & Physician, Dr. Henry Daingerfield, has constantly attended her. E[liza Law] Rogers & her family are perfectly well. My Sister M Custis & her Daughter have gone to Frederick County. They have been very sick with chills & fevers, I trust the change of air will restore them.

I regret much that your head & eyes are so painful, I have experienced immediate relief in headach from Marshalls Seidlitz powders [effervescing salts], & common poplar leaves bound to the head produce violent perspiration & relieve almost immediately, particularly in rheumatic headach. Weak cologne & water, is an excellent application for the eyes—& the pith of Sassafras twigs, in rose water, is a very cool & pleasant remedy.

I would gladly send you blossoms of the woodbine, but it has been long out of bloom. It is in its glory, the last of April, here, the flower is a bright 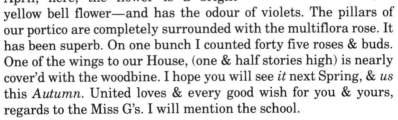 yellow bell flower—and has the odour of violets. The pillars of our portico are completely surrounded with the multiflora rose. It has been superb. On one bunch I counted forty five roses & buds. One of the wings to our House, (one & half stories high) is nearly cover'd with the woodbine. I hope you will see *it* next Spring, & *us* this *Autumn.* United loves & every good wish for you & yours, regards to the Miss G's. I will mention the school.

Ever yours most truly
E P Lewis

Woodlawn Oct 14th. 1822

My Dearest Elizabeth,

I promised to write you, soon after our arrival, & this is the first leisure moment. On Tuesday we reached Druid Hill.[61] My poor sister is better than when I left her in July, but still far from well—& although she bears her irreparable affliction better than her friends thought possible, yet it is a fatal blow to her peace. The sweet little Babes alone, attach her to life, I trust they will enable her to exert herself & to overcome ill health & painful unavailing regrets. Mr R[ogers] is cheerful, but I frequently saw tears in his eyes. It is a sweet spot, but every object reminds you that its brightest ornament is removed forever. We remained a week there and parted with difficulty, my poor Sister was very averse to our leaving her, but we could not delay longer, and Mrs Murray, Mr R's sister was expected daily.[62]

We staid, part of Wednesday, & Thursday at Arlington. Mary Custis has recover'd considerably but is very delicate yet. She inquired particularly for you & Mr Gs sisters, & offers her friendly regards. My niece Mary has grown very much. I did not see Sister Peter & her family. Mec was at a wedding out of Town. They are all well. We returned here on Friday & I have been very busy as you may suppose, I have still much to do, to make us comfortable. My friends tell me that I have gained no accession of health by my tour. I fear so, for my *glass* tells me I never look'd less healthy. A longer absence on the North river & in dear Phi[ladelphi]a might have done much; perhaps a hard frost may suffice. Let me hear from you, my dear Friend, as frequently as you can. Tell me how you & yours are, & all my other good and dear friends.

Will you, in your walks, inquire the price of large thick hair-mattrasses—& dimity bed curtains. *Cultivate the idea* of paying me a visit next Spring, & beg Mr G to regulate his business so as to effect this desired object. I have a box of woodbine for you, I will send it as early in the Spring as possible, that it may have the fairest chance. It blooms the last of April. Several of my neigh-

---

61. Druid Hill, an estate close to Baltimore, was the home of Lloyd Rogers. His wife, Eliza Law Rogers, died August 10 and was buried on the estate. Moore, 112.
62. Harriet Rogers (b. c. 1789) married John Robert Murray (1774–1851) in 1807; they spent most of their lives in New York. Bevan, 194–95.

bours have died since I left home & two of my half sisters are in very delicate health. In less than thirty months, eight of my nearest connexions have died. We did not stop at Riversdale, but I had the pleasure to hear that Caroline is well. You will see her in Phi[ladelphi]a this month I suppose. Present me most respectfully to the good Bishop, Mrs Morris & Mrs Powel—most affectely to their families, Mrs Jackson—and Mrs Mifflins family. How are poor Mr & Mrs Lowndes?[63] I feel sincere interest in their welfare. Tell her that I have placed Genl Cotesworth Pinckney between the Genl & Grandmama. Poor old Major Garden[64] gave the engraving to me & I value it highly. He has promised me Genl T Pinckney[65] also.

Present us always most affectely to Mr & Mrs Camac & Mrs Ricketts. Our united & most affecte love for you & Mr G. May health & every blessing attend you prays your sincere & faithful friend

E P Lewis

Woodlawn Janry 15th 1823

My Dear Elizabeth, I received last night your affecte letter, which relieved me from my fears in some measure, but causes regret for the nervous affection which gives you so much pain, & deprives me of so much pleasure. Cannot you find some remedy, will not cupping, or blistering the back of the neck, prove radical cures? Seidlitz powders, & poplar leaves give me relief. The leaves bound to the head (of the American poplar) produces violent perspiration & consequent relief. I have been on the point, several times, of writing to you, but something has occur'd to prevent it. I have

---

63. William Lowndes (1782–1822), South Carolina congressman, was married to Elizabeth Pinckney (c.1781–1857), daughter of Thomas Pinckney. Lowndes had resigned from Congress in 1822 because of ill health. Hoping to recuperate by travel, he sailed for Europe but died October 27 on board ship and was buried at sea.

64. Major Alexander Garden (1757–1829), a South Carolina planter who fought in the Revolution, published in 1822 *Anecdotes of the Revolutionary War in America*, which he dedicated to the Pinckney family. George C. Rogers, *Charleston in the Age of the Pinckneys* (Norman, Okla., 1969), 151.

65. General Thomas Pinckney (1750–1828), brother of Charles Cotesworth Pinckney, was a soldier, Federalist statesman, and diplomat.

felt very lazy this winter, averse to moving at all, for three months I was not out of this yard, & seldom out of the house.

Last Monday week I carried my Beloved Child to poor Mrs Van Ness, who expressed a wish to have her society, & although unwilling to part with her, I could not refuse one who under happier circumstances had been so kind. They were all very much affected when we met, but Mrs V N, is a model of piety, resignation & every Christian virtue, no young girl could be in better hands than hers. You would love, admire & respect her, my dear Elizabeth. She has a Heavenly mind indeed. I staid until Wednesday, & then returned home, Parke will remain four weeks, she will not attend parties while there; when she goes to Tudor she will visit probably with Mec. Mrs V N rides out with her, & her friends call on her there, so that her time passes pleasantly, & she has the gratification of feeling herself a source of consolation to that bereaved Parent. Poor Ann [Van Ness] Middleton suffer'd more than I can describe, but faith and the hope of Salvation smoothed the bed of Death. She was perfectly resigned—her last words were, "God tempers the wind to the shorn Lamb." Arthur[66] looks very miserable, poor young man! His loss is severely felt. He left us this morning on his way to Charleston, where business will detain him until the Spring. It is affecting to witness the affection between the Mother & Son in Law. She told me that while he was near her, she had still a part of her child. They had been engaged two years, & married with the happiest prospects.

I am happy to hear that Mrs Humphries[67] approves of our daughter. Mrs H is a charming woman—a fine looking & elegant woman, I think. I am very partial to her, & she paid us the most marked & friendly attention. Her Husband was a long time in our family, & a favorite of the Genls. I first saw Mrs H. twenty one years ago.

Since I wrote you, Mr Francis C Gray of Boston has paid us two visits. He was on business at Wash[ingto]n, & will return there again, I believe, this month. I was much pleased with him. He is sensible, highly cultivated, perfectly unaffected & unassuming—very pleasing & amiable in disposition & manners. I

---

66. Arthur Middleton (1795–1853) became a lawyer and planter; he lived much abroad and served as secretary of the American legation in Madrid. In 1841 he remarried. Cheves, "Middleton," 247.

67. Ann Frances Bulkeley Humphreys was the widow of David Humphreys (1752–1818), one of GW's favored aides and secretaries, later a diplomat and businessman.

hope to see him again when he comes to Wash[ingto]n. I think you would like him very much. Messrs Poinsett & McDuffie[68] are expected it is said. Mr Watts will be in Wash[ingto]n today.

Mec is very pretty this winter, & much admired I hear, she is as amiable as ever, she goes more into company than the last winter—& Sister P intends giving a Ball I hear. I know not whether I shall go there at all this winter, except to bring P home. I feel an unaccountable listlessness, I am almost a vegetable. My painting even has been neglected. I have read "Bengers life of Ann Boleyn—Chalmer's of Mary, Aikins of James 1st & now the voice from St Helena" By the way, how well Bona[parte] understood the art of puffing himself. I think, though, with all his faults, his fate was very hard in that horrid Longwood.[69] Mr L is well as usual, Lorenzo with a slight cold, but ready to dance & sing at any time. He went to Wash[ingto]n yesterday. Parke looks as when you saw her. My precious Ped, generally well except the toothache, & always at hand to cheer me by her affection. I hoped that dear Caroline was well. I fear that hers will prove a *consumption*, she has long been delicate. Her spirits are very even, she does not wish her Father to marry, if he marries *prudently*, I should think it advantageous to his children. He is so rapid & *rough* even in his movements, although a most affecte indulgent Father.

George is a fine young man & very amiable. Washington is gay, but not as much so as last winter. I called on Mrs Genl Lee on my way to the City. She looks well, & spoke very affectely of her Philadelphia friends. Sweet Ann looks like a Saint, her hand is I believe in the same state—it is tied up as when you saw it. My poor sister was better when I heard last—her grandchildren well. We have had a wedding in our neighbourhood, a young Lady of 16, to a Gentn. of 38, at least, with four children. She says, that,

---

68. George McDuffie (1790–1851) was a South Carolina lawyer who served in Congress 1821–34; he was subsequently the state's governor and U.S. senator.

69. *Memoirs of the Life of Anne Boleyn, Queen of Henry VIII* by Elizabeth Ogilvy Benger was published in England in 1821, in Philadelphia in 1822; *Life of Mary Queen of Scots* by George Chalmers was published in England in 1818, in Philadelphia in 1822; *Memoirs of the Court of King James the First* by Lucy Aikin was published in England and Boston in 1822. Barry Edward O'Meara's sympathetic portrayal of Napoleon and his views, *Napoleon in Exile; or, A Voice from St. Helena*, was based on personal acquaintance; it was published in England and Philadelphia in 1822. Napoleon died at Longwood, his residence during his exile (1815–21) to St. Helena, an island off the coast of Africa.

"respect & esteem she feels for Mr M & they are sufficient." How are dear old Mrs Powel, Mrs Morris & the Bishop, our best respects to them. Our loves to all our friends, to you & Mr G most particularly.

May health & peace be yours my dearest Elizabeth, on earth, & eternal blessings in a better world.

Ever yours most affectely
E P Lewis

———————————— ❦ ————————————

Woodlawn March 20th. 1823

My Dear Elizabeth,

I wrote you a long letter lately, which I hope you received in due time; The good Judges departure for Philadelphia gives me an opportunity to trouble you with a commission. I enclose $10 of one of the D[istric]t Banks, which is in high repute here. If it should be objected to, I have no doubt the Judge will exchange it most willingly for you. I send a shoe also, Be so good, my Dear Friend, to have me six pair made by Desplat, of the very best materials, & in his best manner—3 pair finest & best black prunelle strong and well sewed—1 pr handsomest lead color'd prunelle, & 2 pr best black danish satin exactly the length of the shoe sent, but not quite so wide in the prunelle vamp. The 6 pr will cost $9.

Now you will think me a goose, perhaps, in the use to which I wish to apply the *odd* dollar. Do you remember the Jewellers shop we went into where I wished I had gone first to buy America's earrings, & tried, in vain, to exchange them? He had a number of pretty little articles in mother of pearl—one a monkey holding a gilt glass. I believe it is a seal, or an ornament for a watch. Be so good as to send me that *monkey*—with the shoes. He had Bears & divers Brutes, & some fish—but the *monkey* is my preferable choice. Who would not prefer a monkey to a *Bear*? Should the monkey cost more than a dollar, you will oblige me by substituting a bundle of handsomest gold binding for it. This pattern will be preferred.

Mr L has been very sick, with a violent cold, he is much better except an inflamed eye. My children are well. My dear P. at home again. I shall send tomorrow a box of woodbine to Alexandria to be forwarded to you. I hope [it] will live. Break the box & put it all together into a hole with light earth, water it always in dry weather, & particularly when first planted. Do, my dear Friend, take up Mr G by main force, (if fair means fail,) & bring him here the last of April, that I may crown you both with woodbine. Bring E Mifflin also. Our best loves to *you* & *yours*, & to our other dear & good friends.

Ever most affectely yours
E P Lewis

❦

[Woodlawn] April 29th 1823

My Dear Friend,

Since my very long letter I have written twice, but not one line in answer have I received. Judge W carried one letter with a shoe & 10 dollars & one was sent by post to inform you that the Betsey had on board two boxes of woodbine. I hope all have been received in due time, & in good order. You requested last spring (when too late) blossoms of woodbine, as it is now in its glory, I send you a small bunch. I fear its beauty & fragrance will be gone before you receive it. You cannot imagine a more luxuriant beautiful vine than it is now, & it is an evergreen—never loses its leaves although the bloom does not continue for more than two weeks.

I have sometimes indulged a hope that you & Mr G were coming here, & therefore did not write. Never until last night have I been able to procure the paper containing the visit to Mt Vn. It is (like most travelling stories) a little *ornamented*. John Allison (the *planter* as he is very erroneously styled) was once, one of the Gen'ls overseers. *Mt Vn* consisted of 8000 acres divided in to four Farms. Each had an overseer, they attended to the negroes & were subject themselves to the supervision of a Manager who overlooked the whole. This Manager kept a weekly account of every occurrence on the different Farms. The overseers were accountable to the Manager for every thing—were completely under his direction & this Manager render'd an account of his stewardship to the Gen'l himself. Allison was a common overseer, is a very common labouring man, who can just read & write sufficiently to be understood. He made some money by overseeing, raising Horses & fishing, has bought a few acres of land & has perhaps a few negro children & one or two grown negroes. He lives on the road between Mt V & Alex[andri]a—is a very common poor man—whose family are knowing in horse flesh & very apt to *romance* or *quiz*, or *tell fibs*—when occasion serves.[70]

The Gen'l never called his negroes *his children*, I know for a certainty. He was a generous & noble master & they feared & loved him. He would have blush'd to find such trifles fame, (as giving *fish* to the poor)—frequently 100000 herrings, and sometimes more are caught [in] one draught. Many were an[nually] fed & clothed from his and Grandmama's hands, besides the charity almost daily bestowed on wayfaring persons. But it was their aim to conceal from the *left* hand, what the *right* performed, & accident only discover'd their good deeds. I never heard of his talents as a *sermonizer*, I have no doubt however that he said & *did* all that the occasion required. *Toddy* is a virginia beverage much in vogue, but few use *whiskey* who can afford to buy West India rum. The Genl rode every day to his Farms & returned at 2 o clock generally—dressed & dined at 3 every day, except Sunday—2 oclock was the hour on that day, to accommodate his servants with a long afternoon. Before the Genl was Pres[iden]t—all the linen & woolen cloth, & stockgs worn by the negroes were made at Mt Vn—spun, woven & made up—towels too. Grand Mama wore h[um]ble cotton homespun when we went to N.Y. Grandmama made all my stock[in]gs & Wash[in]g[to]ns herself until we went to N.Y. Mr L is perfectly well, we are so so. Parke, Ped, & I very anxious to breathe *northe·n* air this summer. Best love to all our friends, to you & Mr G particularly. Mec's love. Ever most faithfully yours

E P. Lewis

Excuse haste.

———————————————— ❧ ————————————————

70. George Washington's correspondence bears out this view of John Allison. In a series of letters to his manager, William Pearce, Washington expressed doubts about Allison's fitness, writing in 1794, for example, "I hope, and wish Allison may turn out well . . . it is a family of very little respectability." Washington, *Writings*, 34:58, 135, 152, 343.

Woodlawn May 7th. 1823

My Dear Elizabeth,

The very day on which I last wrote & enclosed the Jessamine to you, your affecte answer to three other epistles came to hand. I rejoiced to see it, for I had many fears, some for your health & the rest for their non arrival in Phi[ladelphi]a. I wish you would try Seidlitz powders & poplar leaves for your distressing headachs. I awoke today with an intolerable headach, & Seidlitz have removed it. This is always the case with me. I knew that the vine was the Bonabide—Carolina Jessamine, but I also have heard it called Woodbine. The latter name I prefer'd, particularly as there are two other kinds of yellow Jessamine—one a green or hot house plant. Our largest vine covers the gable end of a house higher than Mr G's office, & is the most luxuriant & beautiful evergreen I ever saw. It hangs now in rich wreaths, attaches itself to every projection, & insinuates itself into every crevice. It may be classed with parasite plants. We all regret that you cannot come with Mr G to enjoy its sweets. The multiflora will bloom the last of this month.

My dear Friend, Mr L & I are very anxious to give our dear son some useful employment—to detach him from the idle life which he necessarily leads here & in Alex[andri]a. & we have thought a residence in Phi[ladelphi]a might do more for him than any other plan we can devise. Does Mr G take students of Law, & will it be agreeable to him that Lorenzo should enter as a student with him. If you approve this, will you tell me all that is to be done. Where Mr G would advise him to board—all necessary expences—in short all that this matter requires. We think that Mr G's example & advice as to Law, & reading, & morals, & conduct, will be of lasting advantage. The society of yourself & my other female friends will gratify his fondness for refined female society, & make him emulous to improve that he may be a more agreeable companion. I really do not believe that he has any vices. My friends in Alex[andri]a assure me that his time is all passed in the society of Ladies. He is idle—but I trust he will overcome this evil habit. We want him to study french, to attend the lectures at the Academy, & to do all that you & Mr G think right & proper. I had rather part with him to live in Phi[ladelphi]a than any other place. The destiny I would ask for all my children would be a Northern residence, but this spot will be my sons when he is

23, he will be 20 in Novr., & I wish him to improve the previous years.

I wish Parke, Ped, & I, may have the comfort of breathing your air this summer. We are very doubtful yet. Mr L goes certainly to Kenahwa [western Virginia], & if we do not go part of that rout, I know not what we shall do. I wish only to go to Phi[ladelphi]a & beyond. We are going tomorrow for a few days to visit my half sister Mrs Robinson,[71] who is, I fear, in a deep decline. Our united loves & every good wish for you Mr G & all our friends in Phi[ladelphi]a.

Yours in true affection
E. P. Lewis

———————————— ❦ ————————————

Woodlawn Oct. 25th. 1823

My Dear Elizabeth,

Your very kind letter arrived two days since & I return you my most sincere thanks for your prompt & friendly attention to my commissions. Will you be so good as to procure & forward as soon as possible, either the set 86 pieces at $30, or the *very large* set at $32 whichever you think best worth having. I prefer the broad gold border below the gold edge to the flower'd border. I enclose $30—one 20 & one 10 of the U.S. Bank. Should you like that at 32 best, I will forward the balance immediately. I hope this cash will arrive safely as I am extremely anxious to bestow the China, soon as possible, on the best of physicians & most disinterested of friends, Dr. H. P. Daingerfield. He risk'd his health, neglected his Farm (his sole dependance) to devote his time & attention to us, day & night, without fee or reward. He saved our lives (under Providence) by his unwearied care & attention. I do not imagine that any pecuniary reward can repay such obligations, but I love him as a Brother & Benefactor, & it is a gratification to me to give him what I know he admires, & what his finances do not admit of his indulging in. He is so disinterested & modest that I can only serve him by stealth. Will you be so good as

---

71. Ann (Nancy) Stuart (b.1784) married William Robinson of Westmoreland County in 1806. Alice C. Torbert, *Eleanor Calvert and Her Cirlce* (New York, 1950), 48, 119–22.

The Washington Family by Edward Savage and David Edwin after Edward Savage, 1798. The National Portrait Gallery, Smithsonian Institution, Washington, D.C.

Eleanor Parke Custis by Robert Edge Pine, 1785. The Mount Vernon Ladies' Association of the Union, Mount Vernon, Virginia.

George Washington Parke Custis by Robert Edge Pine, 1785. Washington/Custis/
Lee Collection, Washington and Lee University, Lexington, Virginia.

Eleanor Custis Lewis, attributed to James Sharples, c. 1799–1800. Woodlawn Plantation, a Property of the National Trust for Historic Preservation.

Elizabeth Bordley, attributed to Andrew Wallace, c. 1820, after Gilbert Stuart, c. 1796. Woodlawn Plantation, a Property of the National Trust for Historic Preservation.

East Front, Woodlawn Plantation. Woodlawn Plantation, a Property of the National Trust for Historic Preservation.

Eleanor Custis Lewis by John Beale Bordley, 1841. Kenmore Association, Fredericksburg, Virginia.

Lawrence Lewis by John Beale Bordley, 1841, after John Beale Bordley, 1832. Kenmore Association, Fredericksburg, Virginia.

to have the box directed to "Dr Henry P. Daingerfield, care of W Fowle & Co. Merchants, Alexandria, D.C.—& very carefully packed, enclose me, if you please, the Bill of lading, his nephew is one of the firm, he will convey it, & the surprise will render it acceptable to Dr Henry.

When I can collect more cash (not an easy matter with me at present) I will trouble you for other articles on the list. I never lament my slender finances so much as when I receive obligations, & cannot make such returns as my gratitude & inclination would prompt. We Virg[ini]a wives must be satisfied with such small sums as our improvident Farmer Husbands can venture to spare. *They* always anticipate *squally* weather, & are very moderate indeed in their disbursements.

I am sorry to say that my Darlings are still Prisoners in their rooms. My poor Boy has had chills & fevers, violent perspiration at night, & is thin as possible, pale & weak. He has [missed?] the chills & is now left depressed in spirits. Bark in powder gave him convulsions, Quinine occasioned excessive nausea & vomitting. He has been cured by bitters (water infusion). Poor Parke is thin, pale, & feeble, she cannot take Bark or bitters, horehound Tea & Porter are her remedies, of course her convalescence is very tedious. She is satisfied with her books, & is so disappointed in being deprived of her visit to the North, that she is careless about leaving her room. Today, however, she has told me that confinement is becoming irksome. I rejoice that she thinks so. Our late illness has deranged us both in a very essential particular, & until *regularity* can be restored, we cannot be entirely well. Her inactive life is very injurious in that particular. I take exercise enough, but at my age I cannot expect to fare as well as I trust she will. Mr L has had the gout in his stomach lately, but is now relieved. My little one fattens on Bark, she is the only member of the family who can take it in any shape. I take aqua fortis & hard cider alternately—sometimes one, & the day following the other—to keep the bile in subjection & am almost worn out with anxiety. We have so long been afflicted.

My dear & revered Friend Mrs Powel has sent me a beautiful silver Inkstand—but lovely as it is, the inscrip. is the most charming part of it. "A testimony of cherished affection from E[liz-abe]th Powel to her favorite Eleanor P. Lewis. Have I not cause to be proud of it? I trust she will continue well this winter, & that I may be so fortunate as to see her next June. If we live I trust we shall then certainly visit the North.

Will you choose me two saucers of the palest & prettiest carmine, for the dollar now in your hands, & send them by Judge Washington. I have only part of one saucer which is a pretty color, the rest are very dark red, & spoil velvet painting. When my poor children are well again, I shall paint for them some keepsakes. Assure my dear E Fisher of my affecte remembrance. I hope her son is well, & makes her happy. How is poor C Hare & old Mrs Izard,[72] & Nancy Deas & all the Carolina row,[73] are they well? Assure every kind friend of my affecte & grateful recollections. Our united loves & prayers for you & Mr G. Mr L & L's best respects. Lorenzo is very anxious to be with Mr G. God bless you both now & ever.

Yr affecte E P Lewis

————————— ❦ —————————

Woodlawn Decr. 2nd. 1823

My Dear Elizabeth,

We returned home yesterday from Arlington, where we left my dear Sister Mary, as well as usual, but her constitution is extremely delicate. She begs to be affectely remember'd to you. Her precious Daughter has chills & fevers yet, although she looks fat & well generally. You would love this sweet modest girl, so humble & gentle with all her classical attainments. She has wit & satire too, when they are required. I love her most affectely, she was the favorite Cousin of my darling Agnes & is devoted to her memory. My Brother has recover'd, & exposes himself to the changes of weather as much as ever. My Darling Parke had chills & fevers at Arlington, she is now happily freed from them & looks a little better, but has a bad cold yet.

---

72. Alice DeLancy Izard (1745–1832) was the widow of Washington's friend and supporter, Senator Ralph Izard (1724–1804) of South Carolina.
73. In nineteenth-century Philadelphia, rows of town houses were extremely fashionable. Carolina Row on Spruce Street between Ninth and Tenth was built sometime between 1811 and 1813. Margaret Manigault's winter home on the corner of Ninth Street was part of this row; other members of the Izard-Manigault-Deas family of South Carolina lived in small houses along the row. Low, "The Youth of 1812," 174; Kenneth Ames, "Robert Mills and the Philadelphia Row House," *Journal of the Society of Architectural Historians* 27 (1968): 140–42.

My dear Boy is much improved in health & strength, although he has a cold still. He is very anxious to go to Phi[ladelphi]a & if his health admits of it will go in a fortnight, weather permitting. Do you think that he can get a comfortable room, with a carpet, & a fire in it, at the boarding house you recommended near you. I feel very anxious about him, & should wish to have him in a room well aired & carpeted. My little one is well, Mr L much better & I improving except a cold & some rheumatic pains occasionally. Mec is perfectly well, she comes to G Town a few days before Christmas. My little grand nieces & nephew are nearly well of the measles. By the way, my darling Boy has never had that disease, & Dr Henry is very anxious that he should not take it this winter. I hope it is not in Phi[ladelphi]a.

The china has arrived safely and is much approved of by my good friend. The shoes too, came safely. Mine fit very well. I wish the morocco of that size, as they always draw my feet—& the 2 pr American kid—No. 12. The fur shoes are too large, but will do to wear over Parke's. Judge W this day sent the pink saucers. Major Van (who has a handsome & amiable wife) told me that Captn Tone will leave Phi[ladelphi]a soon, & that he will direct him to ca[re] for my other shoes. Many thanks my dear Friend for your kind attention to my commissions.

When my dear Boy goes to Phi[ladelphi]a I will beg of you to write me as often as you can, how he is, & to give him advice to be careful of taking cold, or any other advice that you think he requires. I have lost five of my eight Darlings, & was very near losing him & my little Ped this summer, you may imagine how anxious I must be when parting with him.

I received, on Saturday, a letter of eleven pages from my dear Mrs Humphreys, with a charming little book for Angela—"The Toilet."[74] Have you ever met with it? Mrs H speaks very highly of Mr Ritchie to whom Miss Otis[75] is to be married. He is 40 years old, however, & his property $300,000, I have heard. There is a perfect rage for marrying this year, I think, I never take up the papers that I do not see several announced. I rejoice in dear Mrs

---

74. *The Toilet. Ugly-Girl Papers; or Hints for the Toilet* by Stacey Grimaldi was published in London in 1821.
75. Sophia Harrison Otis (1799–1874) was the daughter of Harrison Gray Otis (1765–1848), one of Washington's supporters who became a very successful Boston lawyer. She married Andrew Ritchie in 1823. William A. Otis, *A Genealogical and Historical Memoir of the Otis Family in America* (Chicago, 1924), 202.

Powels good health & spirits—long may they continue. My children unite with me in affection for you & Mr G. Mr Ls respects.

Ever yours most truly
E P Lewis.

Best regards to all my Phi[ladelphi]a friends in which my family unite.

Chapter Five

Love and Marriage
1823–1827

" . . . marriage is too important a step to be *lightly taken . . .* "

[Woodlawn] Decr. 22nd. 1823

My Dear Elizabeth,

I received your very friendly letter the day after my dear Boy left Wash[ingto]n. I regretted extremely that he left us before it came to hand, as I should have done all in my power to detain him at home until all danger was over. I have been miserable about him, & Dr H & I immediately advised him to return as soon as he received our letters. I heard tonight from him, the letter was written after passing the evening with you. He says that his cold is better, & that he has taken a room at 331 Market Street. Do tell me where & what the house is, I am much disappointed that he has not gone to the house you recommended, & have written tonight to beg him to consult you about changing—which is the most likely to be healthy and a proper residence for him. He had not received my letter advising him to come home, & therefore I know not what he will do. If he was not in danger, I should prefer his being in Phi[ladelphi]a, properly situated, to remaining here, but as it is, I feel extremely anxious & uncomfortable. I must rely on the goodness of my friends to have him properly taken care of, & to send for me as soon as he is ill.

Lieut. Butler[1] (aide to Gen'l Gaines, a most amiable young man—the grandson, son, & nephew of brave soldiers, & protegee of Genl Jackson,) will leave with you a Box for my dearest Son, & a bundle containing the following articles—13 yds black gros de

---

1. Edward George Washington Butler (1800–1888), son of one of the five fighting Butler brothers of Revolutionary war fame, lived with Andrew and Rachel Jackson after his father's death in 1803. He graduated from West Point in 1820; at first assigned to topographical duty, he became General Gaines's aide-de-camp December 8, 1823.

Naples, 12 yds figur'd lustring—2½ black satin, some broad &
narrow lace, a crape dress, & a dirty merino shawl. Will you have
the goodness my dear Friend to have 2 handsome dresses made
for me in the best manner. Madme. Peto[2] is my favorite, she is so
neat & fits so well. The crape dress is exactly the proper size &
length. I wish the two silk dresses to fit as that does. I wish a tuck
just above the hem because the edge wears out very soon & requires hemming anew. The broadest lace is to be put on the skirt
of the gros de Naples in a wave—the narrow is to trim the sleeves
&c. The figur'd lustring may be trimmed like the crape or in any
way that may be prettier, I like the half sleeves very much of the
crape. If the dress is trimmed with figur'd gauze they may be
made in that way—or in any way that is thought best. Will you
my dearest Elizabeth have them done in the best manner & as
soon as possible for the first safe opportunity. They had best come
in a cheap trunk just large enough to hold them, or in a strong
band box of the proper size & sewed up in baize or carpeting. I
would not give you this trouble could I get my gowns made tolerably here. I gave $5 for a dress last summer & could not wear it, I
gave it to P who luckily fits herself very well & has made a body
[bodice] to it. If my darling Boy is well, I have promised to visit
Washington this winter with P, & the crape is the only decent
dress I have, & I wear only black. Will you inform me soon as possible of the cost of this commission, & I will forward the money to
you immediately with many thanks. The shawl I will thank you
to have well washed, it is too much soiled to wear, we have no one
here who understands washing merino shawls.

I hope to see my friend Mrs Elwyn[3] here, if not in Wash[ing-
to]n. Emily is a very fine girl I think. I thank you my dear friend
for your kind sympathy. You know not indeed how many heartachs a mother is heir to—how tedious time is when she is anxious
about an absent child, & one so lately rescued from the grave. I
think of my poor Boy constantly—tell me candidly what *you*
think of his health & looks at present. We are getting over our
sallow look very slowly. My poor P looks still very badly. Mr L is
much recruited but constantly subject to flying gout. I beg you to
offer our thanks to Mrs Derby for her kind inquiries. Will Mrs
Ritchie be in Wash[ingto]n this winter. Mrs Humphreys speaks

2. Elizabeth Peto was listed as a corset maker on Fourth Street. PCD 1819.
3. Elizabeth Langdon Elwyn (1777–1860) was a member of a prominent Rhode
   Island family; she and her husband Thomas Elwyn, an Englishmen, lived in
   Philadelphia. Scharf and Westcott, 2:1462.

very highly of Mr Ritchie. Mr B will leave Wash[into]n next Thursday. Did you receive a letter lately enclosing $20. Captn S promises to send a military messenger to you soon as possible, all our loves & best wishes for you Mr G & all friends.

Yrs ever
E P Lewis

Do not wait for a *military* messenger if a careful civil one offers.

[Woodlawn] Wednesday [January] 14th 1824

Many thanks my dear Elizabeth for your most welcome letter just received tonight. Your kind consideration for my anxieties gives me *great* comfort in being so far from my child, "*Our* darling Boy". I rejoice in his improved & improving health, & that Mr G is satisfied with his diligence. Most devoutly I always pray that he may be virtuous & useful, as well as healthy & happy. He wrote to Ped who is much charmed to receive letters, & is very fond of her Brother & Sister. She often speaks affectely of Mrs Gibson. She blush'd deeply when I read what you said about her looks & Lieut B. I am happy to find you much pleased with G. W. Butler. He was born on the 22nd Febry., the Grandson, Son, Nephew, & Cousin of brave Soldiers, He will not be spoilt I dare affirm. He has been much in the world, is a favorite wherever he is seen & known, & possesses, without exception, the most guileless heart & temper I have ever known in one of his sex.—a very affecte & grateful heart. He told Julia Livingston[4] that he "admired Mrs Gibson excessively",—He wrote me a beautiful letter the day before he left Wash[ingto]n & said that the thought of leaving his old Father (Gen'l Jackson,) & his kind friends at Woodlawn, made him regret leaving the neighbourhood very much. When he is here he is contented to sit all day & converse with Parke & myself— & we feel perfectly at home with him. Any one might think themselves happy in such a Son. I doubt whether he would wait for my Ped although he appears not prone to fall in

----

4. Julia Livingston (1801–1882) was the daughter of Judge Maturin Livingston and Margaret Lewis Livingston of Staatsburg, New York; she married Major Joseph Delafield in 1833. Hamm, 1:82.

love. It was reported & believed in NY. that he was engaged to Julia Livingston, but there is no truth in it. All the family prize him very highly, he is much with them but no love in the case.[5] My dear Parke is pale & thin, tho' better. Next month we will try what Wash[ingto]n will do—& in the Spring, I trust, see Phi[la-delphi]a & my darling Boy & all those I love & prize so much. Many thanks my dear friend for the commissions [done?]. I am glad you have paid yourself. Will you send P a large Box of hand-somest sealing wax *parfumée*, & Ped a small one at 75 cents. Moss has them, large at $1.25/100—small 75/100 the balance in pretty seals—one of them the "eye" & "may it watch over you"—the other—cupid climbing a ladder & the motto "Rein sans peine"—for P. & P. I will write to Captn Smith about my trunk &c. I have not yet seen or heard of my shoes. I will write to G Town to inquire. Lloyd has returned to Baltimore. Should any of our friends come down before my *civil* messenger goes there, I will thank you much to send my articles with due caution to make them *inside* passengers &c. Our loves & blessings to my darling Son. I shall write to him in a day or two. I wrote two days since, & inclosed to you, Our united affecte & grateful remembrances for you, Mr G,

I am ever yours most truly
E P Lewis

Excuse haste & a vile pen &c.

———————— ❦ ————————

Woodlawn Febry 2nd 1824

My Dear Elizabeth,

I have postponed writing since the receipt of your last kind letter, in order to inform you of the safe arrival of my trunk. Our intimate & most excellent friend, Captn Smith, has just informed me of that fact, & I have sent to G Town for it. Again I offer my sincere thanks to you for the trouble you have taken. I have no

---

5. Although they were not engaged, the relationship between Edward Butler and Julia Livingston was warmer than he led the Lewises to believe. E. G. W. Butler to Anthony Wayne Butler, 22 July 1822, Anthony Wayne Butler to E. G. W. Butler, 26 February 1823, Butler Family Papers, The Historic New Orleans Collection.

doubt I shall be perfectly well pleased with the articles. Will you be so good as to expend the $1.25/100 in two seals & the rest in handsome gold binding. Did my dear Boy ask you to inquire for a white imitation scarf, with lead or claret color'd border at $20— largest & handsomest. One of my Sisters wishes to get such at that price, I doubt much her success. But she pressed me to inquire, & I hope you will excuse the additional trouble. I hope your pains are removed & that you are the better for this bracing weather. The last two days have been very cold, & the winter has set in now in good earnest. I trust this clear cold air will remove the varioloid [form of smallpox] from Phi[ladelphi]a. What contradictory accounts we hear of it! My trunk has arrived, all safe & the trimmings sleeves &c very tasteful & pretty indeed. I fear the thin silk is too slight to retain its beauty long—but that is my fault & not Madme. Pitaux. They certainly excel all others in neat sewing. The trimmings—P admires very much.

I am happy to assure you my dear Friend that Gen'l [Andrew] Jackson is not the wretch he is represented.[6] Mr Tucker has conversed with several persons of great respectability & well acquainted with every circumstance, within the last week. He left us this morning, & this is declared to be the real state of the case. Miss Donaldson [Rachel Donelson] ran away with, and married, her first husband at 14 years old. Genl J had lived a long time with her Parents & was under obligations to them. He did not see the Daughter for two years after her marriage during which time she endured the most cruel treatment from her husband, he frequently beat her severely, & forced her to fly for refuge to a neighbours house. She was persuaded to return several times & was obliged to leave him as often, at last Gen'l J happen'd to witness this conduct & was called on, as her Parents friend, for protection. He interfered, & threaten'd to chastise the husband if he was ever guilty again. He still persisted, & she was obliged to sue for a divorce. A considerable time elapsed after this before she married Gen'l Jackson. Her first Husband was never a soldier under J—& has been dead many years. Mr T adds, that the circumstances of this case gained Jackson the esteem & approbation of the whole neighbourhood in which they occur'd. Col Gadsden always speaks of Mrs J as an excellent woman & he is devoted to

---

6. In the course of the presidential campaign of 1824, scandalous stories were circulated about the circumstances of Andrew Jackson's marriage to the previously married Rachel Donelson.

Gen'l Jackson. Col Hayne[7] assured me that no man was ever more vilely calumniated than Jackson—& these are most honorable & very correct evidences. I shall like him or Mr Calhoun. I think them the most honest & pure patriots. Write to me my dear friend whenever you can do so without inconvenience. I shall be very happy to see Mrs & Miss E—& much obliged by Mr Ps kind attention to my darling son. All our loves & every good wish for you & Mr G.

Yrs ever affectely
E P L

———————————— ❦ ————————————

[Woodlawn] 15th April 1824

My Dearest Elizabeth,

Your kind letter of the 7th I received yesterday & most gratefully do I thank you for your watchful care of my Darling Boy. I know no one, my dear Friend, who has so uniformly befriended my Beloved children as you have—and I beg you will ever speak to him with as little reserve as if he were your own nephew. I am sure he will be most grateful for the friendly interest which such conduct manifests. Poor fellow he is so *susceptible*, that he is continually in love with some one. At *17¹/₂* he was actually *engaged* to be *married*. He was independent in great measure of his Father & myself, & the damsel (Mrs Judge W's niece) 3 years older & resolved to marry him. We sent him to N E—& when he reflected how painful it was to us, he wrote to her & they released each other. He has since been in love more than *twice*. I have heard several times this winter that he was in love with *Esther Maria Coxe*,[8] but as I also heard she was very amiable & correct, & as her Mother was one of my old friends, I did not interfere at all in the matter. He wrote me lately to know how I would like a Philadelphia lady for a *Daughter in* law, I supposed that he meant

7. Senator Robert Young Hayne (1791–1839) was a South Carolina Democrat who later became known for his leadership in the nullification movement.
8. Esther Maria Coxe (1804–1885) was the daughter of John Redman Coxe (1773–1864), a distinguished Philadelphia physician, author, and professor, and Sarah Cox Coxe. *Descendants of Colonel Daniel Coxe of New Jersey*, Historical Society of Pennsylvania.

Esther Coxe, & replied to him that I could certainly love E. M. C. if she was all I had heard she was, although I should prefer Mary Custis, or Eugenia Calvert—but if they loved each other & could be happy together here, I would certainly not object. He has since written "not so fast, my Dear Mother, I am not over head & ears in love yet, although I admire the young Lady very much". I trust he has not implicated himself too far to retreat honorably. There is indeed a *solemn* objection to the Lady in question. Poor Theodosia Sayre! I knew very well, & heard of her derangement, but supposed her dead. How can a child or a Parent be happy with one so near & dear in a situation so much worse than death. It would be a dreadful risk, & I trust he will not think of forming such a connexion. I shall write to him tonight, I will not give him the slightest hint of *your* letter—he may suppose that I have had the report from other sources. I wish to write at once, because "we know not what a *day* may bring forth"—& I shall only mention the report, & remind him of the dreadful situation in which he has seen the wife of one of his cousins. My Dear friend, you know not how many anxieties you escape by not being a mother. I wish to make my children happy in every respect, but there are so many chances against it. My dear Parke [is] much better than when in Wash[ingto]n (there she was *thin* & *sallow* & *sick*, indeed,) but not so well as I could wish. My little Ped has had a slight chill & fever today, & is bilious. I shall give her calomel tonight which I trust, with the aid of Bark, will make her well again. I did not see half so much of Mrs & Miss E as we wished, she expected to be in Phi[ladelphi]a tonight. Our united loves & every good wish for you & Mr G & our other kind friends. God bless you both, now & ever prays yr affecte

E P Lewis

Cannot you & Mr G be persuaded to come to *us* now for a *change*, or as a *bounden duty*. The spring is later than usual, but the week after next, the woodbine &c will be in full bloom, I think. Do my Dear be persuaded.

Yrs ever *E. P. L.*

I received a farewell letter from poor Rogers last night. His lovely children were well when I heard, a week since, from my Sister. Mec will bring my knick knacks, my dear friend. Do not trouble yourself about the shawl. It is of no consequence at all.

[Woodlawn] May 2nd. 1824

My Dearest Elizabeth,

I thank you most sincerely for your kind visit to my darling Boy, & your friendly letter received today. It was indeed a great consideration to hear from some kind friend, as well as from him. Do my dear Friend write as soon as you receive this, & tell me how long he has been sick, & all the particulars—& how he is at the time of writing. I cannot avoid being very anxious about him. He was so ill last Summer, & every one has been indisposed this Spring that was so last Summer. Has he been confined to his bed at all. Does the Quinine agree with him? Last Autumn the Bark in powder gave him convulsions—& the Quinine disagreed with his stomach. Will you be so good my dear & kind friend, to state to me all about his indisposition, & always to inform me of his health. I suffer'd very severely last Monday with a rheumatic nervous & bilious headach all united. I was really fearful of the loss of my senses, but 4 seidlitz doses, covering my forehead & temples with poplar leaves & binding over my head a silk handkerchief & over that flannel, made me quite well. The next day I took two Seidlitz & have had no occasion to take any other remedies. Ped is well & still takes Bark. Parke has a headach tonight, she is still bilious & will take blue pills [laxative] which agree better with her than any other medicine. We hope to leave home the first of June, but if my darling Son requires me, I will go at a moments warning. I shall be very anxious until I hear again.

We have made a most agreeable acquaintance the last week, Mr. Joseph Coolidge of Boston.[9] I think him the finest young man I have ever known. He had several letters of introduction to us, all speaking of him in the highest terms—and he deserves all that can be said in his praise, I am certain. He is highly improved by Books & travel—his conversation is the most agreeable possible, free from affectation, parade or pedantry. He is modest, frank, unassuming, & speaks of his mother with such devoted affection

---

9. Joseph Coolidge (1798–1879), Harvard graduate and inheritor of a handsome fortune made in the China trade, had traveled extensively in Europe. The following year he married Thomas Jefferson's granddaughter. Edwin M. Betts and James A. Bear, Jr., *The Family Letters of Thomas Jefferson* (Columbia, Mo. 1966), 457.

that I am certain she is most amiable—very genteel in his appearance, elegant in his manners, a very sweet voice & smile. In short I have not, in these degenerate days seen any one to compare with him. He staid five days with us, & has promised to return again when he has visited some places of note in this State. He reminds me of *you*, his profile *I* think resembles yours in some respects & his smile when he speaks is like yours—so that I have these additional reasons for admiring this elegant & accomplish'd young man. He is not 26 yet—has been 4 years in Europe & returned with Mr Ritchie, of whom he speaks in the most exalted terms. I enclose you a bunch of woodbine. I wish to send a box of it to my dear Boy, but I cannot hear of any one going immediately to Phi[ladelphi]a. I sent a box of roots to dear E M. by the Sally & Esther sometime since, did it arrive. I will thank you to send the seal "2 hearts bound" by J W. How does your woodbine succeed now. Our united loves & every good wish for you Mr G & all our dear friends in Philadelphia, tell Mrs E I wish she could see Woodlawn now, it never look'd so well. Our loves & blessings to my darling Son.

Ever yours most truly & affectionately
E P Lewis

[Woodlawn] Monday night [May 1824]

My dear Friend,

　　I have this moment received your two kind letters. Mr L will make arrangements tomorrow for me to go immediately to my darling Son, I trust I shall hear tomorrow night more favorable accounts. I am indeed extremely anxious about him. I prefer much being in the same house with him. Assure him my dear Friend of my devoted love & that I will come as soon as possible. I write to Dr D[aingerfield] to beg him to go with me immediately.
　　God bless you & guard & restore my darling Son.

Ever yours
E P Lewis

Woodlawn May 13th. 1824

My Dear kind Friend,

Most gratefully I thank you for your goodness in writing me so particularly about my darling Son, it has removed a weight from my mind. If he does not fatigue himself too soon, he will I trust be better during the summer than he would otherwise have been. The bile of last season took such entire possession of the system, that it appears almost impossible to dislodge it. I am frequently obliged to take Seidlitz powders, & have hitherto escaped chills, I shall be very particular that we may be able to leave home early in June. I trust we shall stay some weeks at Nahant,[10] that is the most reviving air I ever breathed, & Mr L has almost consented that we shall go. My dear daughters complain occasionally, but I trust I shall preserve them from any serious indisposition, & if we once turn our backs on the South, I shall anticipate only health, & the gratification of seeing all our good friends North & East. I wish you could go with us to Nahant, & no doubt Mrs Derby will use all her influence to prevail with you.

Mr Tucker, Judge Johnson & Mr Watts have promised to find Mr Coulson & pay him every attention as soon as he arrives in Wash[ingto]n. Mr Tucker wrote me that he had sent to the different boarding houses to inquire for him, but he was not then in W. I begged them to shew him the way here, I hope to have an opportunity to pay him attention for your sake. I have never yet heard of your nephew[11] my dear friend, I applied to several influential men in Wash[ingto]n & they assured me there was not a vacancy in the Marine Corps for a Lieutenancy.

I was very much shocked at Mrs M[anigault]'s death. She is indeed a general as well as an individual loss. How much she has suffer'd poor woman! from such repeated losses of her children.[12]

---

10. Nahant is a summer resort in Massachusetts, located on a narrow peninsula extending south from Lynn into Massachusetts Bay.
11. John Beale Bordley (1800–1882), the son of Elizabeth's half-brother Matthias Bordley, was at this time attempting to secure a military appointment. Unsuccessful in his military ambitions and later at law, Bordley became a highly regarded portrait painter; most of his career was spent in Maryland.
12. Margaret Manigault had twelve children, only three of whom survived her. During her years in Philadelphia, five of her children died, including her eldest daughter, Elizabeth Morris, who was killed with her young son in an 1822 hurricane. Low, "The Youth of 1812," 175; Betty-Bright P. Low, "Of Muslins and Merveilleuses: Excerpts from the Letters of Josephine du Pont and Margaret Manigault," *Winterthur Portfolio* 9 (1974): 42.

I fervently hope that she has gone to a bright & glorious reward. Will you offer my respectful affection & condolence to Mrs Izard. My love to Mrs Deas. Have Mr & Mrs Ralph Izard come to Phi[la-delphi]a yet.[13] I intend making keepsakes for Mrs D & Mrs R Izard to carry with me, such as I sent to you & my other friends. I wish you would tell me what I can make for you that would give you pleasure; it would add much to mine to do it as well as I could. All our loves & most grateful acknowledgements for you & Mr G.

Ever yours
E. P. L.

———————————— ℰ ————————————

Staatsburgh 10th. August [1824]

My Dearest Friend,

I received a letter from E. Coxe[14] today, saying, that you were going to Schooleys Mt today, & that the best way to catch you with a letter was to write to Phi[ladelphi]a I should not have postponed writing so many weeks my dearest Elizabeth had I known where to direct my letters, We had a disagreeable journey to this place, & my darling Boy was so thin & feeble that I was almost in despair about him, happily the air of this pleasant place & the kindness of its charming inhabitants have restored him very much. He went to Saratoga, eight days since, very much improved in health & appearance. I hope to see him in a day or two. My dear daughters are well, except that poor little Ped has the toothach continually & I have repented fifty times at least that I had not resolution enough to make her submit to having them extracted. I know not when I can have it done now as it will be sometimes before I see dear Phi[ladelphi]a again, & I do not like to trust a common country dentist. There is one near this. I fear my wished for visit to Boston will not take place this Summer. Mr L finds a difficulty in furnishing the *funds*. It is a grievous disappointment to us all. We have been here, four weeks

---

13. Ralph Izard (1785–1824) was Margaret Manigault's youngest brother. GWD, 5:501.
14. Edmund Sidney Coxe (1800–1861), the son of Tench and Rebecca Coxe, was an attorney who practiced in Philadelphia. *Descendants of Colonel Daniel Coxe.*

last Sunday, & I shall not be here, probably, more than two weeks longer, we think of going to Schooleys Mountain for some weeks if we cannot go to Boston, & perhaps to the sea shore. Tell me, my dear friend, what you think of the latter scheme. The accommodations, expences &c at Schooleys & the Shore—how long you will remain & where you go afterwards.

The M. LaFayette is expected in N.Y.[15] & if I can, I will go there to meet him. What a splendid reception he will have! How gratifying to us all to see it & to be in Boston when he is there. You may suppose how gratifying it would be to your *children*, & I should have the additional pleasure of seeing one who almost idolised The Gen'l & Grandmama, & the friend & Brother of my happy days—George.

Mr L is in Jefferson C[it]y, Virg[ini]a in perfect health, he does not mention coming to us yet. This is a very gay & happy neighbourhood. We go to tea parties (six miles *out* & six miles home again)—to dinners *12 miles* out & back again. There will be a tea party here tomorrow. I went to one at William Allens,[16] (And[re]ws Cousin) last Friday. He has grown very old, his wife & daughters are handsome & pleasing. We have splendid views of the river & mountains. I passed a day & night with the widow of Gen'l Montgomery[17]—a wonderful woman of 81—faculties & memory perfect—& Mrs Garretson[18] a lady of 72, a charming amiable woman & affecte friend of Grandmamas—both sisters of Mr Lewis.[19] The family here are very kind & affecte & the neighbours very attentive. We go to a pretty little Church on Sundays & hear very good sermons. Parke & I have learned to make very neat *shoes*, & it is a very simple business. Your favorite Lt Butler came with us & will go away on Thursday. He is as amiable as

15. During 1824–25, Lafayette spent over a year traveling through the United States: his visit became a national celebration as states, cities, and individuals vied to entertain him.

16. William Allen was the son of John Allen (d. 1778) and Mary Johnston Allen. Delancey, 207.

17. Janet Livingston Montgomery (1743–1828), a sister of Chancellor Robert Livingston and the widow of General Richard Montgomery, had been a close friend of Martha Washington. GWD, 5:511.

18. Catharine Livingston Garretson (1752–1849) was Mrs. Montgomery's sister. George Dangerfield, *Chancellor Robert R. Livingston of New York, 1746–1813* (New York, 1960), genealogical chart.

19. Another of the Livingston sisters, Gertrude (1857–1833), had married General Morgan Lewis (1754–1844), Revolutionary War soldier, politician, and onetime governor of New York, who was known for charitable and community service. Dangerfield, genealogical chart.

ever, but his mind is not *first* rate, he has had very *moderate* improvement I think. I never was so long with him before. He is not fond of reading. I wonder often that he is not tired to death of doing *nothing*.

Signor Guiseppe was with us in Phi[lladelphi]a & N.Y. *no symptoms* on either side of what I wished. He was not *himself* at all & acknowledged that he was not *well* or *happy*. His father lost his Spanish claim & he intends to enter into business as a merchant. He is tired of a life of elegant ease, & thinks he ought to comply with his Grand Fathers wish that he should be a merchant. His own predilection was for Theology before he went to Europe. He is as much *my* favorite as ever & I earnestly wish to know why he is not "well or happy."

Write to me soon, direct to the care of Gen'l M Lewis, Staatsburgh N.Y. Tell me about the Yellow Sprgs.[20] Our united best loves for you & Mr G.

Ever most truly yr affecte friend
E P Lewis

Tell me about your visit to Andrew.

———————————— ❧ ————————————

Woodlawn Oct 22nd. 1824

My Dearest Elizabeth,

After a weary journey we arrived safely yesterday morning. We had a very crowded Boat and Stage, tho' very civil companions & charming weather—some very cross children & improvident Mothers. Ped lost a large bag of her commodities on the road, but it came tonight with two stray dressing boxes. Mr L has been very sick since Sunday with the gout in his breast, but is doing well again, & very glad to see us back home. Our good Dr was here & inquired particularly about you & Mr G. My Dearest E, I left my scarf for you to have washed for me, & forgot to leave you any cash. I now enclose $10 & hope you will receive it safely. Be so good as to select for me two of those stone stewing stoves bound with Iron—one as large as your preserving *furnace* (I believe *they* are *furnaces* rather than *stoves*) & one rather smaller. If you think

---

20. Yellow Springs was a resort in Chester County, Pennsylvania.

a larger size better, then send me the larger & one the size of yours. Ask Mr G to give them into the care of some good Captain who will deliver them safely to Cazenove in Alexandria. I send too a pattern of nymphian gauze. Mrs Woolsey Rogers[21] in New York will procure for me, I am sure, 3 yds like it, of Aaron Fountain, in Broadway. I got it from him at a dollar per yd. It is the *low* store, & nearest to St Pauls Church of the two stores.

The fair *W[right]s*[22] did not go to Mt Vn with the Gen'l [Lafayette] or to *York* with him, or Alexandria, nor did I hear of them at Washington. Tho' they *are there* at Mrs Freemans boarding house. Camilla was at Mt Vn with the Douglas after the Gen'l left it, but returned the same day to Washington. *Entre nous,* dearest Bet, do I not deserve well of my country for this good deed, cost what it may to *myself,* I shall always rejoice that I have *served him, so far.* I have not yet received the promised letter, but I will *live* on *hope* ['ere?] I die [of] despair. I know that, [but] for [me], they would have now been tarnishing his glory by their presence. They were resolved to go, & he could not *say no,* until I taught him how to set his mouth & pen to a *negative* position. *This is only for you & I, my dear.*

My Dearest Bet you & Mr G must come in the Spring, I will not allow *you* to say *no,* remember. All our loves & ever our grateful acknowledgements for you & Mr G. Excuse haste write to me often, love me always, & believe me ever yr faithful affecte

E P Lewis

My Dearest E. I, by mistake brought from Mrs Olmsteds[23] "Pray papa" & LaFayettes welcome by Tappan, the words, tune by Fest—Welcome warrior, it begins. Will you buy those two & replace them & inquire for my "Absence"—I left there.

---

21. Catharine Cecilia Elwyn (d. 1833), the daughter of Thomas and Elizabeth Elwyn of Philadelphia, was the second wife of Benjamin Woolsey Rogers, an importer in the hardware trade. William Dunlap, *Diary of William Dunlap, 1766–1834,* ed. Dorothy C. Barck, 3 vols. (New York, 1930), 3:667; Joseph A. Scoville, *The Old Merchants of New York City,* vol. 2 (New York, 1863), 320.
22. British writer and reformer Frances Wright, Lafayette's great friend, wished to join his official party on their American journey. Because she was rumored to be his mistress, his family objected so strongly to the plan that Wright and her sister Camilla traveled to America independently, but joined Lafayette frequently. See Celia M. Eckhardt, *Fanny Wright: Rebel in America* (Cambridge, Mass., 1984).
23. Mrs. S. Olmstead kept a boarding house on Fourth Street. PCD 1824.

[Woodlawn] Novr. 22nd. 1824

My Dear Elizabeth,

I received your kind letter of the 3rd, & should have answer'd it sooner, but supposed you would be absent in Trenton. Mr Lewis has consented to Lolen's return to Phi[ladelphi]a, & I hope he will go in a few days—& be very attentive to his studies. He promises that he will do so, & I trust, as he is now *21*, he will be sensible of the great importance of his time, & not waste it any more. He appears now in very good health, &, if prudent, will continue so I trust. I shall feel anxious, but I am sure he will do better in Phi[ladelphi]a than here, & he is so anxious to be there that I could not reconcile to my self to detain him. I received a dear little letter from the good Gen'l, and as you wish to hear of him, I will copy it verbatim.

Monticello 7th. Novr.

My Dear Nelly, I have depended upon your Brother, & let me add upon your own heart to do justice to my feelings for you in the several circumstances, one above all, which have followed our separation, It is Brother George [Lafayette] I mean, & I know your Brother Custis will also have express'd my affectionate remembrance of you & dependance on your sympathising filial sentiments, now, my Dear Friend, I should have many things to say, & so many that I had better wait until we meet. We shall be near you by the end of the month. Present my affectionate regards & good wishes to Mr Lewis, to your children, & believe me forever your paternal tender friend

Lafayette

It is sealed with an excellent profile of *his* adopted Father, & *my Father* [Washington], & I value it most highly. Today my dear George arrived, he left his Father in Fred[ricks]b[urg] & came to stay until tomorrow, then he must meet his Father in Wash[ington]n & they will be here, I hope, the last of this week, or the first of the next. On the 20th. Decr. they must go to the South, & will be gone until the 20th of Janry. Then in March they go to New Orleans, & will go from thence to Boston.

They will be here again before they quit us *forever*. How much I lament that I shall see so little of them, I hoped to have had my good friend George here, [a] great part of the winter—& the roads and weather are so bad for his excellent Father—exposure to cold will be apt to make him liable to the gout. They ought to have mercy on him. They have been much gratified with all they have seen in Virginia, & have met with devoted enthusiasm. I have committed to the care of George—the order of the Cincinnati in a little box of my manufacture—Blue & Buff—cushions of Grandmama's dress to protect it in travelling, & a cipher of WLF [Washington LaFayette]. W. LF very well made & closely entwined in a wreath of Laurel—the border is of "Forget me nots" on dark blue *starred* paper, the lining Buff. I hope he will like it—& the letter which accompanies it. The W[right]'s did not travel with him. They were at Norfolk & at Mr Jeffersons, but left him there & went to the Natural Bridge[24]—altho' invited to Mr Madisons. I hope they will go to N.Y—& not follow him farther. I know not where they are at present. The Douglas' travelled with them, but did not go to the N.B. They are gone to Wash[ington]n on their way to N.Y.

My furnaces have arrived & I like them much & thank you very much for them. Mrs Elwyn will procure the nymphian gauze from her daughter, perhaps, tell me if I owe you more than the $10, my dear Friend, & I will enclose the balance. I received the letter you sent. How is the good Bishop & will you assure his amiable family how sincerely I sympathised with them on his late accident. I trust he has recover'd entirely & has returned to them. Offer our united affecte remembrances to all our good friends. *Guiseppe* was at Mr Jeffersons *courting* Ellen Randolph,[25] George says, & not in good spirits, he suspects, not successful. I shall cut him out of my books for not calling to see me on his way. He sent his *profound* respects. Our loves to Mr G & yourself.

Ever yours
E P Lewis

No news lately from Lt B. *all safe* I hope. [S]he is better & more composed.

————————————— ❦ —————————————

24. The Natural Bridge, located in central Virginia, spans Cedar Creek; it is 215 feet high with a ninety-foot span.
25. Ellen Wayles Randolph (1796–1876), the daughter of Martha Jefferson and Thomas Mann Randolph, was Thomas Jefferson's granddaughter. Betts and Bear, 4, 15.

[Woodlawn] Novr. 24th. 1824.

My Dear Elizabeth,

I enclose you a part of a sleeve button containing the General & Grandmama's hair, of which I am very anxious to have a handsome breast pin made, for George: will you, my dear E have it done by Thibaut soon as possible. The Gen'l goes to Carolina &c the 20th Decr., & I wish to have the pin to give to my kind and faithful Brother & friend before he commences his long journey, he has none of their hair, & I know that he will value it more than anything I can give him. If you could only have it done to send me by Mr Bordley, what a favour you would confer, I should like to have it here by the 15 of Decr. if possible. The chrystal appears very good & perhaps it would be better to put that chrystal with the hair just as it is in the new gold socket—set with good pearls in the best manner. The gold foot I intended should represent the *fasces* because that is a symbol of *Union* I believe, & the little *heart* is the cover [of] the fastening of the pin which must be strong & neat. On the back of the socket I wish to have engraved GMW (George & Martha Washington) to GWLF. to George W LaFayette. I enclose $5 & will give my Lolen 2, in silver; if it costs more than seven, I will send the balance—& be very much indebted to you. Will you set Thibault about it immediately, & beg him to hurry that it may be ready in time, & be well done. I have one for Lolen, which I will have set as soon as I have *funds*, & he wishes for it. It will be as well not to say, perhaps to Thibault *whose* hair is in it, as it is now so *scarce* an article. The Gen'ls hair was cut off in 76. a part of what is in the button. Will you be so good as to copy the directions, & give them with the button that he may not mistake them.

I thank you for your kind letter & rejoice that you & Mr G are so well. We shall be very happy to see Mr Bordley, & hope he will come, with, or without a guide. I will certainly do all I can to aid him in his appointment, but I fear, my dear friend, he thinks more of my influence than I can prove. My *will* he can never judge too sanguinely of, but my *power* is very limited indeed. I will endeavour to interest my friends to use their exertions for him, & will apply to Old Hickory, himself, as soon as he comes to Washington. I intend to pay my *dévoirs* to Madame Hickory, promptly.

I wrote you a few days since about our dear good General, & about the Wrights. They did not travel with him at all, tho' *excessively* anxious to do so. They came to Mr J's, after him, & left it several days before he did, for the Natural Bridge. "A few days in Athens"[26] I have read, it is *printed*, & a very pretty thing. I read it last winter. The Gen'l & George have gone to Baltimore, & will be here I hope early next week, I am very anxious to see him again, he sent me word that he would come to *my door*, & if I would not admit him, he would force his way a little, to gain admittance, I can safely promise to receive him with *open arms*. I have a fine saddle of Venison for him. I wish I could detain him here, until I was tired of him. My good Brother George left us yesterday. I do not believe that Uncle objected to receive the Gen'l, because he loves the notice of all who are high in repute. He would not admit the travelling committee, & they had the presumption to prevent the Gen'ls going. I trust they will not follow him *here*. Dr C was mistaken, I told him that I *fear'd* I should not be so happy as to visit Phi[ladelphi]a next summer, you know that I did not *wish* to be away *now*, because the time is so short that I can have an opportunity to see the Gen'l & George.

I rejoice in the worthy Bishops recovery, & hope he will escape any pain & inconvenience from the accident. Excuse my wretched scrawl, my dearest E. accept for Mr G & yourself our warmest affection. Offer love to all friends, & Believe me ever most affectely yrs

E P L

———————————————❦———————————————

[Woodlawn] Wednesday night [December] 22nd. [1824]

I have just received your kind letter My Dear Elizabeth, & this night your good nephew is probably in Wash[ingto]n. I shall send to Mr Tucker tomorrow to request him to bring Mr Bordley here with him on Christmas day. I hope he will come & spend his Christmas with us. I have employ'd two or three friends to plead for Mr B's Lieutenantcy, & I sincerely hope he will succeed. I shall not go to W[ashingto]n until after Gen'l Lafayettes visit here, in

---

26. *A Few Days in Athens*, published in 1822, was Wright's vindication in fictional form of the epicurean philosophy which she followed.

Jan'ry, but I requested Captn Smith Gen'l Macomb,[27] & Captn Chase,[28] to request Gen'l J[ackson], in my name, to use his influence. I wish that *I* did, indeed possess influence, but I fear not. Poor Major Jackson was disappointed, & I have not yet heard if Mrs Palmers Sons have any prospect of success. However, I will not fail from *supineness* or *neglect*—& if I can *do* nothing, at least my friends will give me credit for a sincere desire to serve them.

I shall write to Mr Tucker to deliver the breast pin to my dear friend George. I thank you very much for your kind attention, & I know he will value it above all his worldly goods. I have received a most affecte answer from his dear Father—he was delighted with the Order &c, & with a splendid pair of card racks I have made for him. I am completing, now, a beautiful Box for George, & have a pair of [fire] screens to paint for the Gen'l. He was so much pleased with Parkes, that I promised him a pair. We have had the happiness to receive him here. He came to dinner on Saturday the 11th & remained until Tuesday. He dined at Mt Vn on Sunday, & returned to us at night. We had a large company for him on Monday. He was very happy here & [most] paternally affecte. I love him most devotedly. I felt as if my *own great* adopted Father was in my house, it was the first time I had ever received one in *that* character under my roof. It was a *feast* for me while he staid, & I was weeping for three days after he left us. He kissed P, Ped & myself every morning & repeatedly the day he left us. Poor George told me he had never been so perfectly happy since he came to the U.S. & thanked me a thousand times for preserving my friendship for him. No one can deserve my regard more than this faithful friend who has loved me so many years, in spite of time, distance, & the changes & chances of life. They will stay much longer with us when they come in Janry. I know not how I shall bear to part with them *for ever*—as I must, I fear, next summer.

The dear old man, spoke to me of the W's—& I said, "I hope they do not go *South*", he said, no. They go to N.Y. when I go South. I trust [the] *link* is *much weaker* than when they left. Mr Lee of Bord[?] goes about beating up for *visitors* to them, as sev-

---

27. Alexander Macomb (1782–1841), at this time head of the corps of engineers, became commanding general of the U.S. Army in 1828, the position he held until his death.
28. Perhaps William Henry Chase of Massachusetts who served in the corps of engineers.

eral gentn have told me. They were so *coldly* received at *Monticello*, that they left it sooner than the Gen'l. I did not mention them until the Gen'l spoke, & I shall not visit, or invite them here. They *are not* universally visited in Wash[ingto]n. Lorenzo will pay you the dollar due, my dear Elizabeth, I am very glad you procured the little case for the pin, I am sure I shall like it, & I will have another made by Thibault as soon as I can furnish the *cash* necessary. I do not care about the gauze at present. The first work I do after the *La Grange* [Lafayette's estate] keepsakes, will be for you, my dear & ever kind friend. The Gen'l goes to Charleston, Savannah, N. Orleans—Niagara &c to Boston, by the 15th June—*not* I believe to Sp America. He will be in Balt[i]m[ore] on the 27th Decr. then for a day at Fredk.town, certainly to Phi[la-delphi]a before he leaves us altogether. They will come here next summer before they quit us forever.

I hope Mr B[ordley] will be much with us, & that we may make his time pleasant. Love to you & Mr G from all here. Our loves to all friends.

Yrs ever truly
E P Lewis

Guiseppe is a scrub. He sent me many kind messages but did not come himself. I have scratched him out of my Books.

———————— ❦ ————————

[Woodlawn] Janry 26th. 1825

My Dear Elizabeth,

I have just received your affectionate & welcome letter, & hasten to thank you for it. For the last week I have been asking myself *whose* was the fault, that we did not exchange letters as usual, & had almost settled the question *against* my self, when yours made its appearance. My Dear Friend, you are much too *modest*—not even the *La Fayette's*, dear & precious as they will ever be to my heart, can set aside, as *old a friend*, to *myself*, & the *best friend*, except Dr Henry, that my dear children know.

I should not have waited for your letter, busy as I have been, night, & day, but that I hoped to hear from Old Hickory some cheering news for your good nephew. He has not yet written to me, however, I suppose he hopes to succeed, or he would not have neglected a Lady's *love letter*. I wish it was in my power to serve you & yours. I am sure you have a right to every exertion & act of kindness in my power. Some one told me the other day that Mr B would return soon to Washington, He promised me to consider this as one of his homes, & offer'd to be my protégé & I accepted the office of *Guardian* with great pleasure. We were all very much pleased with him. If he should succeed, I hope to see him here very frequently. My dearest E, you & Mr G must visit us the middle of April, & then you can see all the paintings in Washington, & how prettily *nature* paints Woodlawn at that season—& to Mount Vernon. We will go wherever you please. I will be entirely at your disposal.

The dear Gen'l has written me two or three letters, & one to Parke. He has not been able to come again, but my dear George passed three days here just before they left Wash[ingto]n for Richmond. I am very anxious about them now, because I have not seen their arrival in R announced, & this day they expected to be in Baltimore again, on their way to Harrisburg. I have not yet received a letter from Richmond, & I think, if all is well, that George has certainly written. They will be in Wash[ingto]n the 3rd. or 4th. of Feby & I go there to be with them, as they commence their long journey after the 22nd. which is to be in the Rotunda of the Capitol. I will write you all about it. George has had a beautiful engraving of his Father, a proof copy of the fine painting, framed for me in Washington. I shall bring it home soon. Only two were sent from France, the Gen'l had promised one to Commodore Rodgers,[29] & this, George was resolved no one but me should have, & that no one but himself should present it. You may judge how precious it will be to [me]. The more I know of his family, [the] more attached I feel to them all. [Parke] & Ped love George dearly, indeed no one could see him, & listen to him, as we do here, & not love, esteem & respect him. The world are unacquainted with half his excellent & estimable qualities of heart & head. Did I tell you that I had received charming letters from his wife & Sisters?

Parke is in Alex[andri]a on a visit—well. My little Ped is not very well. I hope change of air will restore her. I am at work day & night, like *Penelope* half the time. We have not been to Wash[ingto]n yet. I have been but once out of the yard since I came home,

---

29. Commodore John Rodgers (1773–1838) was a naval hero and senior officer of the U.S. Navy.

but am pretty well. The City is full of strangers & very gay. It appears *most probable* that Old Hickory will gain the day, but it is not certain. *Madme. H.* [Rachel Jackson] is an excellent plain *motherly* woman, but by no means elegant. I intend to teach her the *graces*, what think you of it. Will it entitle me to rank with *Hercules of old*. I am very happy to hear that my dear Boy is more studious. I trust he will not neglect the advantages in his way. I do not believe that he has any idea of forming an engagement. Our united love & respects for you & Mr G. Love to all friends.

Yrs ever most sincerely & affectionately
E P L.

Poor Mr [Robert Goodloe] Harper's was a very sudden & afflicting loss. It must have been apoplexy. I suppose. I congratulate you on the improvements in yr village.[30]

———————————————❦———————————————

[Georgetown] Febry 15th 1825

My Dear Elizabeth,

Your kind letter was brought to me this morning by Mr Derby, who looks uncommonly well, & I really like him, he is always so friendly in his manner & so very *odd*. I shall call on Mrs Derby tomorrow morning certainly, & will pay her every attention in my power. Perhaps we may meet this evening at Mrs [Salazars?]. I am invited, but Parke is not quite well & the day is very damp. A friend of mine has been employ'd to procure an invitation for them. I shall converse with much pleasure about you, & my other dear friends, with Mrs D, who cannot have a stronger recommendation in my eyes, than she possesses in your affection for her.

Your good nephew is not here, I believe, I have not seen him, I fear he has no success. Gen'l J[ackson] told me he had called twice on the Secretary's of War & the Navy, & was assured that no vacancies existed, & no hopes could be given of success. I know

---

30. For the past five years, extensive public works projects—digging canals and building a dam—had been under way; the work was reaching completion, providing water to Philadelphia and water power for manufacturing. Scharf and Westcott, 1:596, 610–11.

that Old Hickory has exerted himself as far as possible. The papers will tell you of our disappointment, & I hope also, that we have more cause to be proud of Andrew Jackson defeated, than the Adams party have of their *Clay* Pres[iden]t.[31] The most shameful intrigues have given him the Presidency, & I suspect his *reign* will not be an enviable one.

We came here on Saturday week & called on the dear old Gen'l [Lafayette] on our way to deliver my keepsakes. He was delighted with them & received his *dear Nelly*, as he always does, with the greatest affeçtion. My dear & good George brought me in the evening—the fine engraving of his Father which I prize most highly. On Sunday they came to tea here. On Monday we paid visits, but Mrs Hickory was sick & we did not see her until Friday. She is very plain, but has an honest excellent heart, & was delighted to see us. She said we were very great favorites of Gen'l Jackson.

On Wednesday my dear George attended Parke & I to the drawing room. His Father went with LaVasseur.[32] We were graciously received & had the pleasure to see our candidate greater in defeat, even, than when his prospects were most flattering. We have not been out since. P has had a bad cold. When Jackson congratulated Adams, the latter blushed to the *top of* his *head*, as well he might. Poor George has been in great affliction since Saturday. His mother in law—the most excellent & charming woman in France,[33] died suddenly, & her loss has thrown her family into the deepest affliction. Poor George is most painfully situated as he cannot leave his Father, & is so far from a wife whom he adores. He has the best heart in the world. He comes every day to us, & I much prefer exerting myself to console him as far as it is possible for *friendship* to accomplish, to any party that I could attend. He does not go to parties, but will attend the Birth night from respect to the memory of his adopted Father. Last evening

---

31. In the 1824 presidential election, no candidate gained a majority in the electoral college though Andrew Jackson received a heavy plurality of the popular vote. The election was thus thrown into the House of Representatives, which chose John Quincy Adams as the sixth president. Henry Clay, Speaker of the House, was instrumental in Adams's selection; when Adams appointed Clay Secretary of State, it was widely believed that a corrupt bargain had been made.
32. Auguste Levasseur, Lafayette's secretary, accompanied him on the American journey. He kept a nightly journal which was published as *Lafayette en Amérique, en 1824 et 1825, ou, Journal d'un voyage aux Etats-Unis*, 2 vols. (Paris, 1829).
33. Comtesse Destutt de Tracy.

he came to us, & as P was not well enough to go, I prefer'd staying at home. Mr & Mrs Derby had an invitation, & I suppose went to Mrs [Salazars?]. Sister P gives a party on Friday where I hope to see them. I go this morning to call on her.

The W[right]s leave Wash[ingto]n on Friday for Mr Madisons. I would not go to see them, & have not met them. They are not in such repute here as they have hoped & tried to be. They cannot induce any one to receive them as a part of the Gen'ls family, altho' they stop at no mean attempts to secure it. They will not go to Charleston where they would not be received—but intend going to N. Orleans, as they have some property there it seems— & think of going to Pittsburg & thence to Phi[ladelphi]a. Miss W has read her Tragedy[34] several times to small circles. Some persons like it very much. On Wednesday or Thursday next, I must part with those whom I love most dearly as a Father & Brother— & we may never meet again. I have sometimes thought it unfortunate to be susceptible of very strong attachments. When we are so apt to be sever'd by death or distance.

My love & blessing to my darling Boy. Our united loves & every good wish for you & Mr G & our other friends. Believe me unchangeably your affecte

E. P. Lewis

Altho you could not come now, my dearest E. *you must come* in April to Woodlawn, I have not been *once* to Congress yet. The drawing room was crowded to excess. There will be another on the 3rd March. I shall not visit Mrs Adams at all. I do not respect her Husband & I despise his Father.

———————— ❧ ————————

Woodlawn April 5th. 1825.

My dearest Elizabeth—

It is a long time since I wrote you from Washington, but I have not yet heard from you. I hope indisposition is not the cause of your silence. I came home with Ped, ten days since. Today, Parke arrived with her Aunt Peter & family, & with them, *Mr Butler*. He is the choice of my dear Child, after mature delibera-

---

34. Fanny Wright's play *Altorf*, first produced and published in 1819, dramatized the Swiss struggle for independence.

tion she says. They are engaged, She is willing to be a Soldiers wife, to follow his fortunes. He is Aide to Gen'l Gaines, who will be station'd to the west, after Decr. next, for two years, & then they go North again. She is convinced she says that this roving life will make her more healthy & happy. His income is only $1400—& Mr L from the situation of his property cannot give them any addition at present, I shall give her half of the only property in my power 600 acres of Kenahwa Land—not of much value at this time, if ever. I suppose they will be married in the fall. I have told you how unexceptionable his character & disposition are. He is honorable, correct, dignified—with a most amiable & affecte disposition, but he is not such a *mind* as I thought Parke would have selected. He is 3 months younger than herself, was born on the 22nd. Feby., & bears the name of G Washington.

You cannot imagine, my dear friend, how anxious & unsettled I feel. I cannot object to Mr B—& he is my child's choice—the only preference she ever acknowledged, or felt, I believe, & yet I tremble at the thought of the difficulties, the privations she will endure, the almost impossibility of my going so far to her, in time, if she is sick. If she ever becomes a *Mother* I would be with her if I could get there alive—& I know that I should then suffer much more than I ever did myself. I hope it is not a *crime* to hope that she never may be in that situation. Indeed I would *pray* that she may not. My dear Elizth. you know not how much pain you escape by your exemption from maternal feelings. It is not corporeal suffering, but *mental* that I regard. May the Father of All, watch over, bless & protect them, here & hereafter. I hope you & Mr G will come to us the last week in April or *week after next*. The woodbine will bloom early—& I wish so much to have you here. Will you be so good as to inform my dear & respected friend Mrs Powel of my child's engagement. She is interested in all that interests me. Our united loves & every good wish for you & Mr G. Love to all friends.

Yrs ever most truly
E P. L

Woodlawn Octr. 2nd. 1825

My Dear Friend,

I wrote you a letter before your departure from Phi[ladel-phi]a, but I have never received a line from you, altho' I am very happy to hear that you are in good health. Lorenzo tells me that you look remarkably well. I sent by Mrs Van Ness, (who left it at Bishop White's, or at least was requested to do so,) a work bag of velvet painting, which I hope you will like. I tried to make it worth your acceptance but it did not please me altogether. I hope you will use it & like it. Do tell me if you received a package sent by Mr Bennett,[35] scarffs & a veil of Parke's to be washed. Mr B left it, I believe, with Mr G as you were not in Phi[ladelphi]a. Will you send it by the first safe opportunity, & will you write me what I owe you. I am very anxious to hear from you.

We have escaped bilious fever this Summer, by taking aqua fortis, as our good Dr Henry directed. I was certain that I should be ill, & I should have been, had I not followed his advice. I have several times been tormented with a most disagreeable sensation in my head, a *ringing* which deprives me of hearing entirely, & makes me very dull & stupid; yesterday, I was obliged to take 4 doses of Seidlitz powders before I was relieved, & today the erysipelas has appeared a little on my face. I dread so much de-rangement or water on the brain, that when I have those unac-countable sensations, I am uneasy until they pass away. Without Seidlitz, I could not live I believe, but I never take them unless my head is affected—& they always relieve me. My dear Daughters are as well as usual.

Poor Butler went away for six *weeks*, & has been detained as many months. I wish I could show you his letters, you would be much pleased with them. He hopes to be with us this month. The wedding day is uncertain, but my son in law has my entire appro-bation. I wish his *pecuniary* recommendations were greater, but I could not ask a more noble heart & disposition, & they are most important.

I have parted with my Beloved *Father* & *Brother*, I miss them very much, but this week they will be happy *at home*, I hope, & then I shall be reconciled. George regretted much that he could not see you in Phi[ladelphi]a. I had the com[fort] to see them, & to embrace them, just before they enter'd the steamboat. & the day before, the Gen'l shewed me the picture of his wife, which he wears in his bosom, & permitted me to kiss it. It is a favour that his own children never enjoy'd but once, & George said to me "I

---

35. Charles Bennett (d. 1839) was a very successful Alexandria merchant. Eth-elyn Cox, *Historic Alexandria Virginia, Street by Street: A Survey of Existing Early Buildings* (Alexandria, 1976), 11.

am happy to think that you have received from my Father, the most tender proof of affection in his power to bestow." I prize it as it deserves. Madme. L[a] F[ayette] has a most heavenly & saint like countenance. Would you believe that *Miss* W[right] asserted in N. Y. that *she* had the refusal of Gen'l La Fayette's *hand*. It is *sacrilege*. He said to George "People little know the many ties I have, The devotion I feel for your Mother's memory, or they would not circulate such reports."

I shall remain at home all the winter & devote myself to my precious Angela. I wish of all things to board with her in Phi[la-delphi]a to send her to a day school (she sleeps in my bosom al-ways) but Mr L thinks he cannot permit it yet, & I must do all in my power for her. Our united affection for you & Mr G & all friends.

Ever yrs most truly
E P Lewis

———————— ❦ ————————

[Woodlawn] Octr. 7th. 1825

My Dear Friend,

By a mistake of the Alex[andri]a post master, I did not re-ceive yours of the 28th & 30th, until last night. Accept my sincere thanks for this long affectionate letter which has relieved me from great anxiety. I could not account for your silence, I did not attribute it to neglect, but I knew not what to think about it, as my dear Lolen & Edd. Coxe wrote me that you look'd remarkably well. I rejoice very much that you have had so pleasant a tour, & have derived so much benefit from it & am very much gratified by your kind reception of my work.

I am now very busy for my children, & if I have *good luck*, this Autumn & Winter, I will do *innumerable* things, make keep-sakes of every variety. I delight in this kind of work, and as I attend also, when required, to the usefuls, my conscience acquits me of a misapplication of time. I shall not leave home again, unless my friends in G Town are ill, until next Summer, I cannot attend to my little Darling when I am in G Town, & she is too old to be neglected. I wish much to go with her to Phi[ladelphi]a to board at Mrs Olmsteds—make her a day scholar & have her with me every night. I cannot part with her at all, her constitution is too delicate. Mr. L has not consented yet, but I hope he may before it is too late. In the interim I am doing all in my power for her myself—but, interrupted continually by domestic duties, company &c, she is necessarily too much neglected, & has not steadiness enough to go on well unless I am near her. I cannot procure a teacher of music here, & she has a fine ear. Neither Parke or myself are competent to instruct her in that science.

I wrote to you early this week, I hope the letter has gone more *directly* to you, than yours came to me. The scarffs &c I am happy to hear are in your hands. I hope a safe opportunity will offer to forward them. Will you be so good as to say how much they cost for making clean & *neat* again.

I gave you an account, I believe, of the dear Gen'ls departure, & how much my dear George regretted that he could not see you again, how kindly both spoke of you. They are now, I hope, safe & happy at home. This day four weeks they went to Sea, I received a letter by the pilot. In 4 or 5 weeks I shall hear from them, I am extremely anxious for those letters, to know how they are, & how received. It appears now like a pleasant *dream*, that they have been here. They will certainly come again, the Gen'l assured me of it—& George says he thinks nothing of such a voyage.

You must have had a very pleasant visit to [our] old Friend Andrew [Allen]. He could not [be] otherwise than *most agreeable*, & the change in his character, was all that he ever required to make him every thing his friends could wish for him. My impressions have never been in Mrs A's favour but when I knew her, she was not a *congenial* spirit or mind with Andrew. Now, she has doubtless improved. Edmund speaks very highly of her. We were sincerely sorry to hear of the severe visitation on the poor Brintons & Mrs B—& thank Heaven that they have found consolation, where it is only to be found in such affliction. Dear kind Mrs Camac, my dear Son tells me she is dead of a fever—& her fears were prophetic, she did not live to welcome her darling home! How are poor Mr C & Mary R[icketts]. I beg you to offer our affecte condolence. I regret that P did not write to Mrs C after her engagement, I pressed her to do so, as every attention was due to Mrs C's kindness to her always.

Our united & most affectionate love for you. Our respects & regards for Mr G. Mr L's for both. Write soon to yr ever faithful

E P Lewis.

The thermometer has been above 80 several days. Love to all kind friends, I rejoice in the good Bishops health. Affecte respects for him, Mrs M & Mrs Powel.

———————— ❦ ————————

[Woodlawn] Decr. 10th 1825

My Dear Friend,

Your kind letter arrived in due time, & the shoes we received from Washington last week. We are very much pleased with them, & much indebted to you for your kindness in procuring them. I hope they will give my poor Parke exercise, without *drawing* her feet, as morocco is so apt to do.

Mr B[utler] arrived eight days since, he is thin, & was not very well for a few days, but looks much better now, & I hope will not be again indisposed. The fatigue, exposure to a sickly climate, & constant rain in journeying were enough to try a stronger constitution than his. He goes to the West, this winter, with Gen'l Gaines, & Parke will not leave me since I have been ill. B is very anxious to be married in the Spring, but if Parke will consent, I am well disposed to retain her with me until his tour of duty brings him again to the North. I dread her going to the West, the distance, the difficulties in travelling, her delicate & indulged habits, poor B's limited resources, all make me dread her going so far out of my sphere of action. He has no certain provision for his wife & himself except his limited pay. I know not when Mr L can assist them, & you know how delicate & *Lady like* are her habits. B ought to have some land near Pittsburg, but his duties as a Soldier have prevented any attention to the business, & it is very probable that it has been sold for taxes. I am sure that he is not calculated to accumulate property. He cares too little about it, & is very sanguine but I know so well how many trials await them, how little she is calculated to bear up under them, with all his affection, that I am very anxious indeed about her future fate.

We are all well at present. I am very happy to hear that my dear Son is so well beloved, I hope he will always be most grateful, & exert himself to deserve the good opinion of his friends. I hope he will be more studious in future, I will not mention your intelligence, be assured, & I am much indebted to you for it. Have you a good dyer of black cloth in your City. I have a beautiful shawl which requires dying, & I should like to have it done in the best manner. What do they charge to dye & dress kerseymere? I hope you have entirely recover'd your health my dear Elizabeth, & that this fine weather will be favorable to a continuance. Parke & Angela take long walks with Mr B. Poor Mrs Camac I most sincerely regret her death, & shall ever retain the most grateful recollection of her kindness to my dear Parke. It must have been a dreadful shock to William & her niece. Will you my dear Elizabeth, assure her family of our most friendly & grateful recollection. I hope the intelligence of poor Mr Camacs failure is not correct.

I have this moment received letters from my dear George, his wife, & sisters, They are all well, the dear old Gen'l remarkably well. Matilda Lafayette suffers from cutting her wisdom teeth, they occasion the most distressing headachs. The family are most happy, & their reception the most cordial. They deserve all the pure & perfect happiness of which mortals are capable, never were hearts more pure & noble than theirs. They all express the kindest sentiments for me, & the most cordial invitation to La Grange. George says "My Father loves you with all his heart, & desires me to tell you so." I love him with *all my heart* I am sure, but I never anticipate the happiness of being with them again, in this world.

P[arke] will be in Wash[ingto]n sometime this winter, I expect, but I shall remain at home & try to improve my little Ped. She is very attentive now, she has learnt 6 tunes by herself (by note) on the Harpsichord, I hope to procure a good teacher for her. I taught her one tune—& she acquired the rest herself. Dear little Ped, she is a blessing to me, & capable of every acquirement, with a contented happy, & most disinterested temper. Her health is generally good, & she grows fast.

I hope soon to hear from you. Will you assure my dear Mrs Powel, & all my good friends, of my affection & continued grateful recollection. Our united loves & every good wish for you & Mr G.

Believe me ever most faithfully your affecte & obliged
E P Lewis

[Woodlawn] Janry 17th. 1826

My Dear Elizabeth,

I was much pleased with the receipt of your kind letter which I had so anxiously looked for. I cannot excuse your disinclination to *writing* since it augurs so unfavorably for my future gratification. I rejoice in the good health of yourself & Mr G, & in the good account you give me of my dear Son. My dear friend, when you feel disposed to neglect epistolary correspondence, only reflect on the deprivation to your old friend, *exiled* as I am from the society I love so much, & you will be too *charitable* to persevere in your *indolent* propensities.

My dear Parke & Butler went on Saturday to Arlington. Gen'l G expects to go soon. Mr. B will not leave us so soon, but probably will not remain long after him. They appear to have decided on being married in the Spring, & of course, I must submit, altho' it will be a severe trial. If I could only be *certain* that she would not require my care I would not murmur at the separation, since it is her wish. She is very much attached to him, & he is devoted to her; I think of him as I always have done, except, that his *inferiority* in talents to herself, is more conspicuous, the more they are seen together. He writes elegantly, but his conversation, save on military subjects, is very *boyish*, & every one is forcibly struck with his inferiority, & surprised at her choice (with her high notions of intellectual superiority,) altho' he is a favorite from his steady habits, his excellent principles. She says he has a great deal of common sense. I trust they will always be attached & happy. He is the only one she ever loved, & if she is satisfied, we must be content. He is prudent & honorable—& she must learn & practice economy.

My little Ped attends to her studies & had she a *better* teacher, & one with fewer interruptions, she would progress most rapidly—she has a very fine & apt genius. Her music master still disappoints her, but she has acquired nine tunes without him. We cannot procure tutors here. My Dear E, all I have said of B. is *for you alone.*

I enclose five dollars, will you be so good as to procure for me 1¹/₂ or 2 yds best white cotton velvet—*very thick* & *fine nap* on the *right side* & *very fine* & *closely woven* on the *wrong side*, very white & unsoiled—also 3 or 4 sheets of the black paper used in tracing "Theorems" for velvet painting—& a sheet of best gold paper like the pattern. If any cash remains, the rest in finest stiff velvet brushes for common painting—the articles to be very carefully put up, that the black paper does not interfere with the velvet or the gold—& sent by the first safe opportunity. Excuse me this trouble, my dear friend, as I have no one to depend upon so kind as yourself in executing my commissions.

I have just received letters from France. Clementina (George's third daughter,) has been at the point of death with the scarlet fever. She was out of danger but not yet recovering on the 27th. Novr.—& the eldest Son of poor Mr Frestel, had lost three fingers of his left hand by the brushing of his Gun. The dear Gen'l, & the rest, were well. I have received charming letters from his daughters—& the most paternal messages from him.

I should be very happy to see my old friend Andrew again, & to hear his amusing conversation, but my unlucky stars always keep him from Phi[ladelphi]a when I am there. I should like to be so happily situated as Mrs Elwyn is, altho I should not give so many parties, I am sure. My side is occasionally painful, but I hope I shall escape salivation. Dr D recommends a long journey to me, but if Mr L consents, how can I go one way, when my poor Parke is gone a different one. This is a sad life, my dear friend, we are ever in pursuit of happiness, but it has so many drawbacks, so much alloy in the very best situations, that it eludes our grasp.

I was much pleased with Mr & Mrs N Amory[36] at Boston, they are very excellent & most hospitable people. I passed two evenings at their charming country seat. How is my venerable friend Mrs Powel, I have written twice to her this winter, but know not whether my letters have been received. Will you be so good as to present us particularly to *her*, to all my respected & dear friends & most affectionately to my dear *Mr & Mrs Gibson*, & believe [me] ever most faithfully yours

E P Lewis

Excuse blots & haste.

———————————❧———————————

36. Nathaniel Amory (1777–1842), a wealthy Boston merchant, owned Belmont, a waterfront estate; his wife was Mary Preble Amory (1786–1865). Justin Winsor, ed., *The Memorial History of Boston*, 4 vols. (Boston, 1881), 4:633.

[Woodlawn] Febry 12th. 1826

My Dear Elizabeth,

Many thanks for your kind letter which I received last evening—& for your attention to my commissions. I hope Moss has secured the gold paper from the possibility of being rubbed. I am very happy to hear that you have recover'd from the Influenza & that Mr G had escaped entirely. Mr L & Mr B have been very much indisposed with it. Poor B spit blood two or three days, but flaxseed tea, & since, milk punch, have restored him, altho' he is yet pale & thin. He took Calomel & other medicine, at first, as it is here accompanied with bilious symptoms. Angela was quite sick but no longer suffers from it, & Mr L's cold will soon disappear I hope. P & I have had it very slightly.

I thank you my ever kind & faithful friend for your *reproofs* & consolation, but permit me to say, that *maternal* fears & anxieties, can only be appreciated by a *Mother*. My love is perfectly free *from selfishness*. I prefer much that she should never regret me, or *feel* my loss, when separated by necessity—& were I *certain* that *she* would never be a *Mother*, at all events, *not*, while so far from me, I would be tranquil. Indeed, I know that we are all in the hands of a most just & merciful Providence, I have never murmured even when most *fatally* bereft of what I most loved & doted on, & I will do all in my power to divest myself of painful anticipations, & *hope* for the best.

I am naturally elastic in disposition, & prove to find some good in every event of life, but at the same time I have very anxious feelings occasionally. So I had, my dear friend, when youngest & gayest—& after marriage, I prefer'd a *room* in my Beloved Grandmama's house, to a Palace away from her. I was never so happy as when with her—never so *safe*, so secure from misfortune, as when under her maternal eye. I never felt any love so powerful as that which I entertained for the best & most Beloved of Parents—not even for my children have I ever felt so much as for her. Gratitude, the best feeling of our nature, was the foundation of that affection, & therefore it was more powerful than any other.

I did not confess my dear Lolen's *secret*, because I thought it would be best to come from him. You had a *right* from your goodness to him, to *expect* his confidence. I entirely approve of his choice, & will be to his sweet Bride, as kind & indulgent a Mother

as she could wish to have. Mrs Coxe may rest satisfied that I shall
consider it a sacred & a pleasing duty to be, as far as in my power,
a friend & parent to her child—as I wish my own daughter to find
friends in the Sisters of her Husband, so will I be to the [daughter] of [one] who is willing to [entrust] her *treasure* to my son. I
hope [he] will ever be worthy of it, & I rejoice that I can without
hesitation, adopt his choice as my Beloved daughter.

We shall be very happy to see Mr Bordley again, & I will certainly do all in my power to ensure his success, I do not know Mr
Southard, & I fear he will not succeed, because it is recommended
to appoint Cadets from West point. I have, alas, *no interest* at
court, but be assured he shall not fail if *I* can do him service, I will
employ those who will endeavour to assist his views. The fear of
refusal will never deter me from attempting to serve my friends, I
have no idea of that kind of pride. We must risk something, before
we can be certain of success in anything.

I rejoice to hear that my friends are all well. Will you ask my
dear Mrs Powel if she has received two letters from me, I would
write with pleasure whenever I had any thing to say, but I am not
certain that she gets them—unless my good friend Patty will
write for her. Present me affectely to all friends, most respectfully to the good Bishop, Mrs P, & Mrs M. Our united affection for
you & Mr G & believe me ever most truly yours

E P L.

Our kind regards to your nephews. Be so good as to wrap the
velvet so securely from the black paper that it cannot get the
slightest *dust*. It soils very easily.

———————————————— ❦ ————————————————

[Woodlawn] March 19th. 1826

My dear Elizabeth,

I received your kind letter on Friday; I wrote immediately to
Mrs Van Ness who will look out for my package. I thank you very
much for it, & above all for your kind interest in my Beloved
child. She will be married on the 4th of April, & must commence
her journey to Cincinnati on, or before, the 15th. The time approaches rapidly, & I cannot avoid being extremely anxious about

her. I would willingly go, to see her safe, if in my power. I hope the Father of Mercies will enable me to bear it with fortitude, to rely on his goodness—above all, that he will shelter her under the shadow of his wings—be her shield, & preserve her from all evils. She has a very bad cold now, the rapid change from Summer heat to this cold raw weather, is the cause of it—she is very susceptible of the variations in our climate. I shall write to you as soon as she is married. They would be very happy to visit Phi[lladelphi]a to see all our good friends there, but it would be much out of their way—from hence to Wheeling is the shortest, best, & most direct rout for them. They will not return until 18 months hence—when Gen'l G[aines] changes his head quarters to N.Y.

If I can provide the *needful*, I will go to them, the Summer after this, & return with my Beloved child. If she can only escape being a *Mother* during this long absence, I will bless Heaven for this best of mercies. My dear Friend, you cannot conceive the anxiety I feel on that subject. I was always prone to looking forward to probable consequences, & trying to make provision for them— but *this* prospect has ever filled me with dread. She is naturally nervous & low spirited, & that situation is peculiarly calculated to excite depression & nervous feelings—that even *I*, have shudder'd to anticipate in my *own* case, fortunate as I generally was, when the crisis arrived. I try indeed to say "Thy will be done O! Lord." I know her to be in the hands of an All Wise, & All Merciful God, but we cannot always control our feelings, & I know not why, death has ever been more terrible to me in *that* shape than in any other. Mrs Gaines[37] & the Gen'l are most excellent people & have assured [me] of their kindest regard & service. Old Hickory speaks of her as of a daughter. B's sisters would be most affecte friends, but they are far from Cincinnati, but in such circumstances, I would be more to her than all the rest. I have nursed her so many years.

I wish I possessed Mr B[ordley]'s charming talent. When does he come to W[ashington]. I have written to my friends about the appointment, but have not yet heard from them. When he comes down, I hope we shall see him here. My dear Lolen appears very happy. I hope God will bless him & his lovely Esther. If my children are well & happy, I will never complain of any other circum-

---

37. Barbara Blount Gaines (d. 1836) was the daughter of William and Mary Granger Blount of Tennessee.

stance. Our united & most sincere affection for you & Mr G. Love to all our kind friends. May you & yours ever enjoy every blessing prays your faithful & affecte

E P L

———————————— ❦ ————————————

[Woodlawn] April 23rd 1826

My Dear Elizabeth,

Your affecte & kind letter to my Beloved Child, she received last Tuesday, & requested me to assure you & Mr G of her most affectionate love, & grateful acknowledgements for your kind wishes, & for all your goodness to her. She will write to you from Cincinnati, where I hope she will be, in safety, next Wednesday or Thursday.

She left me on Wednesday last, & I had a letter from Baltimore, She had a very pleasant journey so far, & anticipated a very prosperous journey throughout—as she was assured, by all who had travelled that road, that it is excellent, & the accommodations admirable. Butler took a stage to himself, which makes it more easy for my darling Parke, as she will not ride before breakfast, or after sunset & will get to Wheeling in 5 days, travelling 50 miles a day, with changes of Horses. The Steam boat will take them to Cincinnati in 2 days. When I hear she is safe there, well & happy, I shall not repine at our separation; since it is her choice to be there, & Gen'l & Mrs Gaines will be a Father & Mother to her. I am sure that Butler will do all in his power for her comfort & happiness, & she is sincerely devoted to him. I cannot avoid being anxious, but I will rely upon the Mercy of Providence to restore her to me in safety.

We had a merry wedding. My child was so nervous & so much agitated that we exerted ourselves to make her gay. Mrs Mason of Alex[andri]a her old school mate a charming woman, assisted us very much. We had only her single Aunt & Cousins, B's Brother officers, & Gen'l J[ackson]'s friend Mr Eaton[38]—our good Dr Henry, our near neighbour Mr Foote,[39] my Lolen & his friend Mr

---

38. John Henry Eaton (1790–1856), a lawyer, politician, and senator from Tennessee, was one of Andrew Jackson's chief supporters and advisors.

39. William Hayward Foote was a connection by marriage of the Washington family. GWD 6:259.

Knox. Our house would not accommodate more. My married Sisters I could not invite. We had the ceremony performed by Dr Wilmer, it was very solemn & impressive. We had dinner company two days & her young friends staid until Monday. On Wednesday we went to Arlington, on Thursday to Washington & G Town, where she remained until Wednesday last. She expected to have gone much sooner, & therefore did not go prepared to accept invitations.

My darling Boy leaves me on Tuesday, & I shall then devote all my time & cares to my precious Angela. If we can be healthy here, I shall not leave home at all until I go to my Son's wedding, & next summer, I hope to visit my poor Parke at Cincinnati, & pay my respects to Old Hickory. I have had a letter from our good Gen'l [Lafayette] & George lately. They are all well & happy, & still anticipate a visit to us before a long time.

My dear friend, next week will be our prettiest time here, I cannot offer you the same inducements that I had when my dear child [was] here, but if Mr G & yourself would [make] such an excursion, you know, I hope [how] happy we should be to see you here. This has been a very cold unfavorable Spring. The frost has destroy'd our chance for fruit I fear. Perhaps it may contribute to our health, & if so, I shall be contented.

I can scarcely realize that my dear Parke is married & gone so far. Poor Mec will be united, in June, to Mr Williams,[40] they will come here two days after, I expect. She is in very delicate health, & much changed in her appearance. He is a genteel young man, has an affecte grateful heart, but not at all remarkable I think for talents. He will attend Gen'l Bernard[41] in Octr & she will probably stay with her friends the two months of his absence. I hope it may turn out better than her friends anticipate.

My Son tells me that my venerable friends Mrs Powel & Mrs Morris have lost their memories very much, particularly the former, I fear that I shall never see her again. I shall write to her by

---

40. William George Williams (c. 1801–1846) of South Carolina was a West Point graduate and career military officer.
41. Simon Bernard (1779–1839), an outstanding military engineer, had served Napoleon as aide-de-camp. After Waterloo, he came to the United States and, on Lafayette's recommendation, he was employed by the army corps of engineers. With the courtesy title of brigadier general, he was virtually in command of military planning and construction of a complete system of defense, including forts, roads, and canals. He returned to France in 1830 to serve Louis Philippe.

Lorenzo. Esther wrote me a sweet letter by Lolen. Her picture is extremely well painted, but not quite so pretty as she is.

Our united loves & every good wish for you & Mr G. Love to all friends. Ever your affecte & obliged

E P Lewis

———————————— ❦ ————————————

[Woodlawn] June 21st 1826

I was much pleased, my dear Elizabeth, to see your hand writing, & lost no time in complying with your wishes; but Judge W[ashington] informed me, that he had already given his vote to Mr Wm Herbert,[42] of Alex[andri]a—a most excellent man, with a large family & very confined circumstances, & had recommended him as much as possible to his Brethren of the Bar. Otherwise, he would have had much pleasure in complying with Mr Gibsons request & Mr Condy's[43] wishes. I hope you will never doubt my willingness to gratify every wish you can form, that it is possible for me to effect. I wish *I had influence*, that I might exert it for those I have so much cause to love & be indebted to.

I thank Heaven, that all my darling P's letters speak most favorably of her health & happiness, she is charmed with Cincinnati & every thing about it, & I trust will continue healthy & happy. Mrs Gaines supplies my place in the most exemplary manner. She is blessed indeed in such a kind maternal friend. Butler is very happy & very kind in anticipating her wishes. Therefore I feel perfectly satisfied with her lot—and if she has no more *serious anticipations*, I shall wait with patience the time for our reunion. If I can, I will go there next summer.

In the meantime, my darling Boy is well & happy, & I have only to watch over my little one, to educate her, to employ myself, & to *endeavour* to *escape* a bilious fever this Summer. I have taken frequent doses of my favorite Seidlitz, & am very prudent, but I own that I do not expect to escape. Every year that I am here, I am ill, & Mr L thinks he cannot afford to send me to the north or

---

42. William Herbert, an attorney, was the son of William Herbert (1743–1818), second president of the Bank of Alexandria and twice mayor of the city. Brockett, 116.
43. Jonathan W. Condy (c.1769–1828) was a Philadelphia attorney and associate of James Gibson. Martin.

West, & in no other direction will I go, as I could gain nothing by travelling in Virg[ini]a.

I am much interested now in studying Spanish. I began without a teacher, while P was at school, but I was not satisfied with myself & declined. Lately a Spanish Patriot, the friend of Riego,[44] came to see me, He is devoted to Gen'l LaFayette, & owes to him obligations which fill his whole heart. I never saw one more devoted & more grateful than he is. I read a little Spanish to him, he told me I had a pure castilian accent, he gave me an admirable Dictionary, & has taught me to sing in Spanish the Hymn of Riego—of Miranda & a fine constitutional song of his own composition. I have translated them all, & have learnt more in about five or six transient visits here & in Alex[andri]a than all my lonely studies gave me. I am in raptures with it, & resolved to persevere until I am a good Spanish scholar. If I could only take regular lessons 3 months, I would work so hard that I would be perfect in it. But Mr L will not permit it, he cares for no language but English, & thinks it nonsense for me to learn; but it is certainly an innocent gratification, & I will learn by myself. I hope to be able to teach Ped some day. She learns french as well as I could expect—& of her own accord, translated a Fable the other day— very well indeed for one with her limited advantages.

I feel much interested for poor Mr Carrasco, he was the friend & aide of Riego—had Parents, friends fortune & independence. His Parents & Brothers were murder'd with Riego—his estate confiscated. Gen'l L F released him from a french prison, he is a banished man, depending on his talents, as a Teacher, for support. He is a devoted Patriot, devoted to the memory of Riego, of Washington, & ready to die for Gen'l La Fayette. You will not then be surprised that I feel so anxious for his success. He is very honest, has lost every thing for conscience sake & is now doomed to bear the scoffs of many *mushrooms* [upstarts] of the day, who see in him only a "poor tutor". I am making diligent inquiries for a place where he can get scholars enough to support him. Genl La Fayette gave him a letter of recommendation, & proposed him as teacher of foreign languages at West Point. Perhaps next session it may be acted upon—but in the meantime the poor man must be

---

44. Major Rafael del Riego y Nuñez (1785–1823) was the leader of the 1820 constitutional revolt against Ferdinand VII. Overthrown by French troops of the Holy Alliance, he was hanged. His aide, an officer named Miranda, wrote a hymn in his honor which became a symbol of Spanish liberty. Salvador de Madariaga, *Spain* (New York, 1930), 90–92.

provided for. He has only six scholars now in Alex[andri]a. I have
written to know what chance he would have in Cincinnati, & Dr
Mason has written to Richmond, but I know not how it will be, &
in 2 or 3 weeks he is without employment in Alex[andri]a.

He has a valuable Book, a History of the most interesting
period in modern Spanish warfare. This Book would be most valuable to the public, & most lucrative for him, but alas! he has no
money. Few care whether he *lives* or *dies*, & I, who would aid him
with all my heart, have not the means. If some kind friend could
whisper to the rich and liberal, Mr Girard,[45] the circumstances in
which this faithful friend, & banished Patriot, is placed, by ad-
herence to principle & consistency, then he would perhaps bestow
the means of present support & for publishing his Book. Gen'l La
Fayette gave him 100 dollars when he parted with him on board
the Brandywine, but he says "you know I was obliged to support
myself before I could get any scholars." In the district so few care
for such acquirements. As I am a favorite of La Fayette & speak a
little Castilian, the poor man tells me all his difficulties, & I
believe all he tells me, he is small, homely, & odd, but intelligent,
enthusiastic, most grateful & honest hearted. He was educated at
the Academy at Madrid, & composes fine Spanish verses, patriotic, he told me he would write me a song of 20 *verses* if I chose. My
dear friend I wish devoutly that some one could interest Mr
Girard for him. I never lament not having Fortunatus' *purse* so
much, as when I see such sad reverses of fortune. A *stranger* too,
without interest & without employment, how happy I should be to
think that I had been instrumental in procuring him some support, & how acceptable it would be to my Beloved Father La
Fayette. I hope soon to hear from him & from George. Senor Carrasco has lent me the Tragedy of Riego, I shall translate it, &
when I am so happy as to see you again, I will show you all my
translations, & sing you my Spanish songs.

E Mifflin will laugh I think to hear of my *studies* at 47—but
so she did when I *said* that I would learn *velvet painting*. I will
make her *enjoy* patriotic Spanish songs as I do. Riego's motto was
"vencer o morir", as *mine* was 28 years ago—"Conquer or die"—&
so it shall be with regard to the Spanish language. It is so noble
and so sweet. But I shall enjoy it much more, if my poor *Tutor* is

---

45. Stephen Girard (1750–1831), a French-born financier, was known for his
charities, eventually leaving a large part of his fortune to the city of Philadelphia for the purpose of education.

made independent & happy. He attended the funeral of Madme. Riego, who knew not, he says, of her Husbands death, she thought him still a prisoner. They were most generous and benevolent both.

Pardon me my dearest Elizabeth that I have written so much without speaking of your dear Father's letters. I mentioned them to Judge W & he promised to search. I should have been very happy to see my dear Augusta Palm[er.][46] I loved her very much formerly—& should have enjoy'd myself extremely in your happy circle. I lament very much that I could not have been with my venerated & Beloved Friend when she found pleasure from my society, even now, to be near her, to assist in amusing or interesting her would be most gratifying to me. Do tell me, from time to time, how she is, & if she remembers me, always assure her of my grateful affection & respect.

We have *no* fruit this season & scarcely any vegetables. A fine rain on Sunday gives us a *ray* of hope for the future. Our most sincere love to you & Mr G—my dear Boy, & our other best friends & believe me ever, Dearest Elizabeth

Yr grateful & devoted
E P Lewis

———————————— ❦ ————————————

[Woodlawn] August 3rd. [postmarked Sept. 5] 1826

My Dear Elizabeth,

I should *scold* you, instead of thanking you, for your affecte. & welcome letter. I think, since you apoligise for having *no* amusements, no pastimes to describe, do you not know *well*, that I value my dear old friends in Phi[ladelphi]a, more than any other recommendation in that, always to *me*, delightful City. I have long anxiously wished to hear from you, of you & yours, & my other good friends, but I could not tell whether you were at *home*, or at Trenton. Lolens epistles are not very frequent, & never

---

46. Augusta Temple Palmer (b. c. 1784) was the daughter of Sir John Temple, the British Consul General during Washington's first term. While New York was the nation's capital, the families lived near each other on Broadway and the girls were friendly. Anne H. Wharton, *Salons Colonial and Republican* (Philadelphia, 1900), 49–51.

long—& *Esther* is the prevailing theme. This is all natural & right for him, I suppose, but I am not the less anxious about all that concerns my other friends. The excellent Bishop! pity he should *ever* decline, altho' I am certain no one is more certain of eternal felicity. I wish that my worthy and distinguished Pastor Dr Wilmer, could be his assistant, altho he would be a great loss to his congregation here. Cannot you *electioneer* for *him*, my dear E. The more you know of Dr Wilmer, the more you will respect & love him.

I wish most earnestly to be in Phi[ladelphi]a again, to see all my dear & good friends, particularly Mrs Powel & Mrs Morris. Those venerable friends of my deceased Parents, have my most sincere love, & filial respect. *I* cannot avoid envying Betsy Campbell, *altho' not for her juvenile Spouse*, believe me. My love to her, to Mrs MacP—& all who love & recollect me kindly. I wish you could be induced from Mrs Jones description, to *tarry here many days*. I was very sorry to part with them so soon. My love to her.

My Beloved Parke is much improved in health & strength, but (*entrenous*) I fear she will have more cares than she anticipated. She hopes not, but Mrs Gaines thinks, *that in 5 months.* I have entreated her to come here the last of Octr. If she cannot, then I must go to her in Decr.—& this will be most inconvenient in every respect as I shall not be able to carry my precious Ped, & to leave her, or *not* to be with my poor child on such a trying occasion, will make me very unhappy. Butler & herself are much attached & very happy—altho' not over burthen'd with cash. My dear Mec & Williams are devoted to each other—her Parents are reconciled & she appears perfectly contented. He is very affecte & generous to excess for his limited income.

My little one has been much interrupted this summer, by company, dancing school & latterly by occasional headachs. She had a large party, for a week, eleven girls, & 3 Boys, & they were very merry *wise*, except that no lessons were learnt in the [time]. Mr L has been in Fred[eric]k County for several weeks. We have escaped sickness here, altho many of our neighbours have been very unhealthy. We expect to go in 8 days on a visit to G Town, for a change, as Dr H advises, but I had rather stay at home, unless I could go to Phi[ladelphi]a or Cincinnati.

I have attended as much to my Spanish as I could, & am much pleased & interested in the study, altho I had only 8 lessons. My unfortunate protegé has gone to Albany, in the hope of better times. Poor man! He had a host of enemies, they raised the most horrid stories of him, which I do not believe one word of & there is a very respectable Lawyer in Washington who offer'd him to sue them for defamation, but he has no money to fee Lawyers. *I* think of him as highly as ever.

Our Beloved Gen'l & dear George were well on the 29th. May, I hope soon to hear again. Pray can you tell me where are now the *Wrights*? My Ped & I offer respects love & best wishes for you Mr G & all our friends in Phi[ladelphi]a & believe me ever most faithfully & affectely yours,

E P Lewis.

Love & Blessing to my dear Lolen & his lovely Esther.

------------------------------ ❦ ------------------------------

Arlington 28th. Octr 1826

My Dear Elizabeth,

It is a very long time since I heard from you, I hope you have had good health. I have been sick for the last seven weeks—& still have regular returns of the Quartan ague [malarial chills and fever]. Fortunately it comes at night but I fear it will be long before I am well, it is so obstinate, & I cannot take Bark in any form. My darling Ped has had chills but fortunately they are checked, & she looks much better. I look as thin & badly as you can imagine & frequent pains in the side remind me that my liver is not right. I have suffer'd salivation lately, but it has not relieved me.

I am very anxious to go to Cincinnati this winter to stay with my darling Parke. She expects to become a Mother in Jan'ry or Febry, & you cannot imagine how anxious I feel for her safety, & how much I wish to be with her at that trying time. She has been so far fortunate. She has never had an hours sickness, is stronger & fatter than she ever was in her life, is very active, in fine spirits, takes more exercise than she ever did & is comfortable & surrounded by very kind friends. I know that every thing will be done for her, but it would be so much better for us both if I could be there—if I am well enough. Mr L has not said whether I shall go or not. I must go the last of Novr. if I do go, & cannot return until April.

I sent to you, my dear friend, 2 shawls, Edith Cook promised to leave them with Lorenzo. The one which has the whitest border is Angela's, it is stained by lying in a store, she wishes to have it cleaned & whiten'd. The other with the yellow & dark border I wish to have dyed of the best black, & so well dressed that it will not rub off on my clothes, as home dying generally does. Will you be so good, my dear Friend, as to have them done in the best manner, as soon as possible & inform me of the cost—& send them by the first good opportunity.

My best love to you, Mr G. Mrs. Powel & all other good friends, in which my Ped unites. Believe me ever most affectely yrs

E P Lewis

————————————❦————————————

[Woodlawn] Decr. 24th. 1826

My Dear Elizabeth,

Your kind letter of congratulation arrived two or three days since, & I return you my most sincere thanks for it. I was surprised, at first, that you should have heard the news so soon, but Butler is so enchanted with his Son, that I suppose he has written *circulars* to every City in the Union. I have had four letters from him, & all written in the most perfect happiness. My Darling Parke fatigued herself in packing & lifting Trunks, & very unexpectedly the little darling made his appearance—without causing much pain to his dear Mother, & altho' born at *seven months*, & without *toe nails*—he was fat & healthy, & has continued to grow & improve beyond all *former experience*, his delighted Parents think. Indeed they are almost crazy with delight. My dear Child has never had the slightest indisposition—no fever, eight days after, she sat up nearly the whole day, fixing her Babes caps. She is most happily situated, an excellent nurse, the kindest most attentive Husband, & many friends ready to do every thing she requires for her comfort. I thought it a dream, that it was too great happiness to be lasting, I felt humbled & thought myself undeserving of the Almighty's goodness. Dr Silman[47] says that,

---

47. John Sellman (1763–1828) was born in Maryland and served as an army surgeon under General Anthony Wayne. Stationed in Cincinnati in 1793, he resigned from the army the following year and set up a private practice there.

had the Babe been born at *nine* months, it would have been so large as to have caused an unusual degree of suffering to my darling child. Thus the goodness of the Almighty has made even her *imprudence* the source of good to us all.

You will readily suppose that my Grandchild is the object of my devoted affection. The *Child* of *My Child*, it excites even more interest than I should perhaps feel for my own, at its present age. My Beloved & revered grandmama declared that she had never loved any child so much as she did Parke, her *great* grandchild. It is certain that the title of *Grandmother* is most dear to me & excites the most anxious & affecte feelings. I know that you will rejoice in the happiness of my Beloved Child & the Husband *you* always admired & esteemed—indeed he deserves esteem & affection. He possesses the noblest heart, & the purest principles, & Parke appreciates them properly. She sent a message to her Father which I will transcribe for you. "Tell Father that I told his Grandson that I dedic[ated] him to God & his Country, he [lay?] back his head, & looking me full in the face, *smiled* his determination to redeem the Pledge"—& this at *6 days old*, is he not a wonderful Boy. His name is George Washington, & P says he is exactly like Butler. I am most anxious to see them, & I hope it may be in my power to visit them next summer.

Ped & I have missed our chills. Quinine has cured us both. I take the Pills, & Ped the liquid. We return our best thanks for the articles sent, we have not seen them yet, but have no doubt they will please. Dear Mrs Powel I rejoice in her health & good spirits, assure her, & Mrs M, & the good Bishop, & all kind friends of my affecte & grateful recollection. Our united & best love & kindest wishes for you & Mr G. Write to me when agreeable to you my dear friend, & believe me ever most faithfully yours

E P Lewis

Ped is almost crazy to see her dear little nephew.

A founder of the Cincinnati Medical Association and one of the city's prominent physicians, he continued to treat the military throughout his career. Charles T. Greve, *Centennial History of Cincinnati*, vol. 1 (Chicago, 1904), 294; Otto Juettner, *Daniel Drake and His Followers* (Cincinnati, 1909), 30; Records of Spring Grove Cemetery, Cincinnati.

[Woodlawn] April 5th. 1827

My Dear Elizabeth,

I received your kind letter on Tuesday night, & thank you sincerely for your attention to my darling Son, & to myself in informing me of his situation, altho' when I saw your hand, at first, and not his, (as I had not received a letter for some time) the blood ran cold to my heart; I knew at once that he must be sick, & I fear'd almost to read your letter. I agree with you in thinking that he could not be more favourably situated. I have ever feared the measles for him, & rejoice that the evil is now over, & so well over. I had it, exactly at his age, & my life was in danger, I did not recover from the effects for several months—& lost an Angel child with it. I am sure that Mrs C has done all that any Mother could do, & dear Esther's sweet countenance & conversation would make a more serious indisposition, light. I hope they will ever feel for each other as they do now, & have as few of the trials of this life, as is consistent with our mortal probation.

You are the *delinquent*, my dear friend, & I often wish to see your hand & superscription. I know you too well to doubt an affection which you have so often proved by your maternal kindness to my Beloved children, but I wish that your *eyes* & your *head* would permit me to hear more frequently from you.

My darling Parke has been very sick this Spring, she fatigued herself too much with her dear Babe, she is the most anxious & devoted Mother, & has been very costive [constipated] ever since her confinement. This affected her strength & appetite, & she was languid & feverish. She has had every kind attention, that she could require, & was much better when I last heard. Her lovely bright black eyed Boy, is the Idol of his Parents. They think "the Sun never shone on his equal"—& I have no doubt of it—indeed I am almost crazy to be with them. I think it unkind & cruel to stay from her when I know she would be better were I with her. My darling Boy wishes me to attend his wedding, & I should rejoice to do so, but the time is so uncertain, my poor Parke is so far from me & her health not good. I cannot postpone going to her later than June; if Mr L permits me to go, as I hope he will. I [love] my dear children equally, but [I] think it my duty to attend the [one] whose situation is least advantageous. I would do both, if possible.

My darling Ped grows very much, I have devoted myself to

her improvement this winter, when I was well enough to do anything. My health is not entirely restored. I am trying to prevail on Mr L to permit me to board at Mrs Olmsteds, that Angela may be a day scholar at Mrs G's, I would go with her in the morning, & call for her in the evening, & she would sleep with me at night. In this way she would have every advantage of education, & would still be under my care. I cannot part with her, & her constitution is delicate, her disposition too affecte, to permit me to do so. She is now 14 & is very anxious to be at school, if she could be with me at night. I should like to have two rooms upstairs, one for a parlour, & would have a maid servant who would sleep in my room. Will you inquire (not as from me) what the terms would be, for Ped, a maid, & myself. When Mr L came to see us (he would not live there) he could have a Bed in the parlour, it could be put into my room in the morning.

Mec has a Daughter & they are both well, she will reside in G Town. Ped & I unite in love & respects for you & Mr G & all kind friends. Ever most truly & affectely yours

E P L

Will you draw me a pattern of a pretty body & sleeves such as worn now. I am making frocks for Ped.

How are Mrs P & the good Bishop. I wish much to see you all.

———————— ❦ ————————

[Woodlawn] April 27th. 1827

My Dear Elizabeth,

I return you many thanks for your kind letter & the patterns which we are much pleased with, particularly No 1. but our mantua maker [dressmaker] does not understand exactly how it should be cut in the body. Will you be so good as to *cut* me a pattern of the body (it is full before & a little full in the back, the one you recommended for Angela,) & the row of scollops for the neck. She does not fit it well under the arm which arises from her ignorance of the proper manner of shaping it, & I am too stupid to assist her. If you can cut the pattern & enclose it by the next post you will render us a great service as we shall then know how to proceed with certainty. I thank you sincerely, dear friend, for all the trouble you take in my behalf.

I think Mrs Os terms *high*. I cannot tell whether Mr L will consent to Ped's wish & mine yet, I would do anything to be with her always & give her at the same time the advantages of education in Phi[ladelphi]a. She is too delicate for me to be easy away from her, & too affecte to be happy herself away from me, anxious as she is to be at school. Mr L does not like the expence, but if he will consent to my having only a bed room at Mrs O's I would be content—altho' I should prefer a private parlour, to being in a crowd of strangers.

I shall not say anything of it to Mrs C[oxe]. I should think her unreasonable to wish me to sacrifice the interests of my Ped, to remain with Esther, when there are so many friends who would do every thing to make her happy, in their power. I will love & care for her as *my own* always, but the child who *really* requires my care the most, must have the preference of course. My Beloved Parke is better & I trust improving rapidly—she has been very weak & thin, & almost destroy'd herself by nursing. She is now more prudent, & has the loveliest & sweetest of Babes—you may imagine how anxious I am to see them.

I am happy to hear of the good Bishop's health, & wish I could have heard his lectures. Poor C[harles Hare] his life has been *worse* than *death* for many years. May he now enjoy eternal happiness. Did he know his family & was he sensible of his dying state. There never was a better or a truer heart than his.

My dear Mec has chills & fever & has lost her milk, Her Babe is fat & healthy & eats altogether I believe. I have heard that a blood vessel broke in her breast, & nothing flowed from it but blood which induced her Mother to take the child from the breast. I never heard of such an accident. She is with her Mother. What would I not give to have had the care of my poor dear child—but I was not well enough to go to her. I hope she will never go to the *West* any more.

I hope your face is well, I have found *raw cotton* to the face, & a silk handkerchief on the head, best for that tormenting pain. Our loves respects & best wishes for you & Mr G. Kind regards to your good nephew. Kind remembrance to all friends, love to my darling Son & his love.

Ever yours truly & affectely
E P L.

[Woodlawn] May 4th. 1827

My dear friend, I have just received your kind letter & its en-
closures, for which I thank you sincerely. It is for the wedding of
my dear Boy that my Ped is preparing, & also to carry new fashions to my darling Parke, I was anxious to get them. Thank
Heaven she is now getting well rapidly I believe, & her dear Babe
is not fatiguing to her now. She sleeps & eats well & of course
gains health, strength & spirits. The darling is the *sum* & substance of all perfection—I live in the hope of seeing them this
Summer. I regret very much that you will be absent when I go to
Phi[ladelphi]a altho' if it gives you health & happiness I ought
not to regret it.

If we live until next April I hope you will come here. You will
have all your adopted children to welcome you. This place will be
in its prettiest trim, & it is the long Session of Congress—so that
you may accomplish many things. Mec & her blue eyed girl, too,
will rejoice to see you—she is to keep house in G Town. Judge
T's[48] death must affect our venerable & dear friend Mrs Powel—
they had been friends & neighbours many years. How is my kind
old friend—should you see her, will you tell her that I hope soon
to see her.

Can you tell me anything of a young gentle of modest &
pleasing appearance who was in W[ashingto]n last winter, & a
good deal in Virg[ini]a this Spring. His name is Mr J D Coleman,
his Parents &c are all dead—he has an Uncle, a merchant Benedict Dorsey[49]—he appears to be of a Quaker family. I wish to
know of his family fortune, character & standing in Society—he
lives or intends to live at 132 N[or]th 2nd. St. If you have not leisure to write will you ask that favor for me of Mr Gibson, as (for
particular reasons, I am anxious to know all about him as soon as
possible. Is he the son of the rich *Iron* man—& is the pretty Sister
[who] was in Phi[ladelphi]a when I was [last] there dead. I am
anxious to know as soon as possible all about J D Coleman.

You have our loves & our fervent prayers for a pleasant &
safe journey & happy return to your home & friends. Our loves &

---

48. For many years William Tilghman and Eliza Powel were next-door neighbors
   on Chestnut Street; Judge Tilghman died April 30. Westcott, 5:1290.
49. Benedict Dorsey was a china merchant with a store on Second Street. PCD
   1828.

respects to Mr G, kind regards to your nephews. Ever my dear E your affecte & most faithful friend

E P L.

Excuse this wretched scrawl, it is very late & I am in haste, as the letter will go to the post tomorrow.

Ever yours
E P L.

———————————— ❦ ————————————

Woodlawn June 24th. 1827

My dear Friend,

I was very happy to see your affecte letter of the 10th & to hear that your dear niece is better. May The Almighty restore her to you & her other dear friends is my fervent prayer. We left Phi[ladelphi]a last Friday week, of course your letter was forwarded to this place. We came here on Monday, Ped & I, & Esther & Lolen on Tuesday. I fear she does not find her future residence so pleasant as she anticipated. I feared she would form higher expectations of its comforts & beauties than experience would realize, from the rather extravagant description given by some of our friends—but she is so amiable & so much attached to her Husband, that I trust peace & contentment may be hers, here. She behaved admirably on every occasion, & looked lovely & interesting. Dr & Mrs C are expected next Thursday & I hope they will be pleased with the home of their child. I yet keep the keys to assist E until she feels *at home*, but I consider her as the mistress of the House now, & myself only as a visitor. She is a great favorite with all who have seen her, & will make friends wherever she is known. My dear Boy is very active & industrious, & much pleased with his wife & his farming & housekeeping. He does not like leaving home so soon again, but I believe it is best for them not to be here late in the Summer.

I missed you very much in Phi[ladelphi]a. I had the pleasure of seeing Mr G & E Mifflin sometimes, & hearing of you. I should have left it with more regret had I not been so anxious to visit my darling Parke. Lolen offers to go with me as soon as he conveys his wife to Phi[ladelphi]a—about the middle of July. If I can find a proper escort, I will go before that time, I am so very anxious to see my darling P & her precious Babe. I had a letter from her last night in which she expatiates on the merits of our darling, I feel as she does in regard to him, & am most anxious to be with them. I dread lest something should again occur to prevent my going, & that she may be sick in the Summer. I shall rejoice to be once more with her & we will not part soon again if I can avoid it. Butler & P will be very happy to see your amiable nephew I am certain—& to receive your letter. Do tell me what Mr B thinks of *our charmer*.

Dear Euge[ni]a looks very well, she is at her fathers with Caroline, & George.[50] Caroline is very thin—Her little girls very pretty. Dear Mec is very delicate, she has a sweet good Babe, but she is a helpless Mother, she cannot suckle it, & knows very little about the care of children. I hope you will see *my* little treasure next autumn, & his *devoted* Mother. I never knew one more devoted than my darling P.

Poor Eliza's eldest daughter was in Phi[ladelphi]a when I was there, a few days, I wish you could have seen her—she is a lovely intelligent [girl]. Rogers means well, but he certainly knows nothing about the care necessary for girls. I wish he had a good & kind hearted wife. My Sister Mary C always makes kind inquiries about you & expresses sincere regard. They are all well, her charming daughter still unattached. There are few worthy of her I think. I saw Mrs Elwyn, she was not at all well.

I shall not say anything about boarding in Phi[ladelphi]a until the Autumn. My darling Angela is much grown, & every day makes me wish more & more to see her at a proper school. She goes with me to the west & if we remain long in Cincinnati I shall send her to school there, that her time may not all be lost. She is awkward in large company, but I hope some day to see her equal to any girl of her age. My first wish is to give her every advantage, without being separated. I would submit to any arrangement to accomplish that object.

My children unite with me in best love & kindest wishes for you & Mr G—in affection & good wishes for your Sister & nieces. God bless & protect you, my dear & excellent friend prays ever your faithful & affecte

E P Lewis

Excuse this scrawl—my script & pen are most wretchedly bad.

---

50. George Henry Calvert (1803–1889) had recently returned from study in Germany.

Chapter Six

The Louisiana Years
1828–1840

"Would to Heaven that my darling children could leave Louisiana forever, we could be far more healthy & happy in Virg[ini]a or dear Phi[ladelphi]a."

[Woodlawn] April 13th. 1828

My dearest Elizabeth,

I sent you a message by Mrs Coxe, that I would write you a letter as soon as my Beloved Child returned. I hoped she would have been with me ere this—but to my sorrow & astonishment she has been confined with *twins* in Louisiana, & I cannot hope now to see her until the last of this month. She would not inform me that she was pregnant lest I should be anxious & unhappy about her, & I cannot be sufficiently grateful to the Father of Mercies, that she was relieved from her situation where it occur'd; with her Husbands excellent Sister, from whom, & her whole household, she has met with the most devoted affection & care. My child was only 3 months advanced, & had only known it six weeks, her health was uncommonly good, & she was very active.

They would have commenced their journey the week previous, but were disappointed of the Boat. How dreadful & dangerous would her lot have been, had she been taken on board the boat, or on the road; that rough road she could never have encounter'd with safety. She had the best assistance & after some pain for six or eight hours, she gave birth to two little girls; the first had been lifeless two or three days, the other, the image of our departed Angel.[1] The afterbirth grew to her side & was partly

---

1. Their first child, Edward George Washington Butler, Jr., lived less than a year; he died in 1827 while Nelly and Angela were visiting the Butlers in Cincinnati. Butler Family Papers, Historic New Orleans Collection.

decay'd. On the fifth day she wrote me a long letter, she was then sitting up at work, & was doing uncommonly well, & surrounded by the most kind & excellent nurses. Poor Ed suffer'd much while she was ill, & was as careful as possible of her.

His Sister writes me that my child is adored by all around her, & indeed, my dear friend, I know that you will rejoice with me, that *my* darling child & *your adopted* [daughter], will leave none but friends, admirers & grateful hearts, when she leaves Louisiana & the West. She is the most exemplary wife, was the most devoted Mother, & has been the most generous benefactress to the poor & destitute. You may imagine how lost I feel without her, & how much happiness I lose when she is far from me. Indeed I have felt *tired of life* frequently this winter, when I reflected on the distance between us. A letter is a month in coming to me—& how anxious I am on every account for her—& I fear the necessity of making better provision for a young family than his pay, & his health too suffering by such constant confinement to his desk as his duties require, will force them to reside in Louisiana at the risk of their lives—& if it should be so—I too must go [there]. My poor little Ped—I cannot bear such a separation. Would to Heaven they were independent & could reside where they chose.

My darling Ped grows very much, & improves, I hope, altho' she has no instructor but her old Mom as she calls me. She is as devoted to me as ever, & very fond of her Sister Esther, who loves her. We all love & admire my dearest Esther, she is most amiable affectionate & everything we could desire, lovely & unaffected notable attentive & contented, & Lorenzo is very happy in his choice & very industrious & bustling. I trust they will have many happy years together. But much as I love Esther she cannot fill Parkes place—no child can replace the one far away from me. I will write again when my darling is restored to me, & be assured I shall never forget all I owe to your affection & kindness, or love you less than I have done for 30 years & more.

Will you be so good as to get from Desplat as many prs of best french soft morocco thick soled walking shoes No. 12¼ (12½ are too long, 12 too short for morocco) as $10 will buy, & send them by Mrs Coxe. Our united love & best wishes for you & Mr G—to my venerable friends Dr White & Mrs Powel & to my other dear & kind friends in Phi[ladelphi]a. I enclose $10. Direct best [of] french morocco.

[Woodlawn] Janry 23rd. 1829

My Dearest Elizabeth,

It is a very long time since I have written to you or received a letter from you. Be assured it is not from any diminution of affection towards one of my oldest, best, & always most Beloved friends; but from a dislike to writing & the knowledge that it was painful to you to write frequently, as you have always complained of your eyes. I cannot, however, permit my darling Boy to go away without writing a few lines, to assure you of my most grateful & faithful affection for you, & I hope to hear sometimes from you, when not inconvenient. We are all very anxious about my dear Esther, but I hope that she will be rewarded for her tedious confinement & indisposition by the possession of a *little treasure.* My dear Son is very anxious to be a Father.

My darling Parke too expects to be confined in May—poor thing she looks forward with great pleasure & anxiety to the Birth of a Boy exactly like her first. It has cheered her spirits very much. You knew, I believe, that she lost twin girls last winter. I feel constant anxiety & dread about her, she has been so unfortunate. She will remain with us until after her confinement—this is a comfort to me. But indeed had she not wished so earnestly for another Son, I should have been very happy that she should not encounter again what she suffer'd before. The life of a *Mother* my dear friend is always anxious.

My darling Ped has grown & improved very much, she is very attentive to her studies & I try to do all I can. Her talents are excellent, & could I *risk* parting with her, she would excel, but whenever I think of it, the fate of my angel Agnes is before me. Had not Parke been pregnant we intended passing some time in Wash[ingto]n with my Sister to procure teachers but now it must be postponed.

It would make [us] all very happy to see you & our good friend Mr G here. Cannot we hope for it. The carriage is ready for my Son & I must conclude with our best loves & best prayers for you & Mr G, Mrs M & her daughters. P would rejoice to see dear Elizabeth. God bless you my ever dear friend now & ever yours most affectionately

E P L

[Woodlawn] July 6th. 1829

My Dearest Elizabeth,

You have thought me remiss I fear, in being so long silent, when my darling Parke *your daughter* too, & her *Babe* might have been my subjects. The fact is, my dear Friend, that I have been so constantly occupied in attending to them, & since Lorenzo & Esther came home, in caressing their precious Boy, I have scarcely written at all, or done anything except nursing & fondling my little treasures. I assure you that no one is more blessed in *Grandsons* than I am. Lolen's is the sweetest, best & loveliest Boy I ever saw. Parkes lovely, intelligent, but *too violent* in temper at present; He is, however, a sweet Boy, grows finely, & is already very fond of lying on his Grandmothers Bosom & kissing her.

My poor Parke is very well, thro' her confinement, has been uncommonly fortunate, but is so anxious & dotingly fond of her little darling, that I fear she will make herself always miserable about him. She calls on me continually to examine her Babe, she is certain he is very sick, or has hurt his back, his arms, or a pin sticks him, altho' he only uses *one* pin, & that is as secure as possible. She is uneasy at the idea of going to visit old Hickory, because I am not willing to stay at the Palace with Angela.[2] She is too young to be ever in company, & I have no taste for any company but that of my family & particular friends. I shall be near, at my Sisters, & ready to nurse him day or night if she requires it.

In Octr my poor Children & their Babe will go to Cincinnati, & I fear I shall not see them for a long long time. Lolen goes sometime this summer to Audley, Fred[eric]k C[ount]y—& I shall be deprived of both darling Boys. I shall miss them extremely, for altho' I do not love them *better*, I love them quite as dearly as my own. I shall be continually anxious and uneasy about my poor Parke, the loss of her first dear babe; makes her so constantly miserable about this. Dear Esther looks delicate, but she has not been sick, & is in fine spirits, & Lolen & herself dote on their Boy—indeed he is a little Angel. My darling Ped is devoted to her nephews—she has grown very ta[ll] but we have both been sick this summer with chills & fevers, my child is thin & pale. The weather has been so rainy & uncomfortable, when not extremely

---

2. Elected president in 1828, Andrew Jackson was now resident in the White House.

hot, that she cannot take proper exercise. Mr L is very well, at present in Fred[eric]k.

How are you my dearest friend, & Mr G. I hope well, & that I shall soon hear from you. I wish that we could have you here before my poor Parke goes to Cincinnati. It will not be in her power to visit Phi[ladelphi]a I expect. Ed has gone to Gen'l Gaines in N. York. He intended, if possible, to call on you.

Our united & most affecte love to you my dearest & ever kind friend, with fervent prayers for your health & happiness. Assure Mr G. of our regards & best wishes. Believe me ever most truly yours

E P L

Love to all kind inquiring friends.

———————————— ❦ ————————————

[Woodlawn] Decr. 9th. 1829

My dear Elizabeth,

I was much gratified to see your writing again, & hope, my dear Friend, that nothing will occur, in future, to deprive me of the satisfaction of hearing from one I have loved so long & so well. I was extremely sorry that Mr L could not call on you & Mr Gibson. His stay was so short, & he was so much engaged, that he was obliged to omit what was his *duty*, & would have been his *pleasure*, calling on you & on my venerable friend Mrs Powel. His going to Phi[ladelphi]a was not anticipated when he left home. He went to Balt[imor]e to get a Piano for my darling Angela, & hearing there of the poor Judge's [Bushrod Washington's] illness, he hurried on to see him, but was too late. Our good neighbour is indeed a great loss to us all, he was friendly & affecte. His nephew, John Augustine Washington, is an excellent man, & his wife is a very fine woman. They will reside half the year at Mt Vn. John is very fond of improving grounds, & it is in good hands. It was a merciful dispensation to poor Mrs Washington, & to her friends that she, so soon followed the Judge, life had nothing for her after his decease.

I wish, my dear E that I was certain of going to Phi[ladelphi]a. When my darling Parke expected to be in N.Y. I hoped to persuade Mr L to permit me to go with her, & procure tutors for my dear Angela. But alas, there is no certainty in army arrangements. *Our* old friend Gen'l Gaines, has unluckily changed his mind again, & prefers the Western department. The station is now to be *permanent,* & if Ed remains with Gen'l G, my poor Child must reside at the West. I fear they will go from me in the Spring. I would give much that Ed was independent of the Army. It is so inconvenient to depend on the caprice of these generals. I hoped to retain my poor child near me until they went to Louisiana to reside, but now that hope is destroy'd, & I have no hope of having her until Ed leaves the Army. It is her choice to reside in Louisiana, but she would have been much pleased to remain near me until Ed commenced the life of a Planter. My darling little Boy, I shall miss him so much, & my poor child is weak & thin & far from well. She has been very ill this autumn, & has not recover'd yet. She is much *surprised* that you should speak of *her* Son's *empty* knowledge Box. We beg to assure you that he is a little *Solomon.* Indeed he is remarkably intelligent, sweet & saucy.

We miss very much, my darling Son, dear Esther, & sweetest Washington. L & E write to us frequently. My precious Babe has suffer'd a good deal with his eye teeth, & E says, evidently misses his Grandmother, & Aunt Angela. I felt so rich & happy with my darling Boys, both of them [all] that a Parent could wish for. [They] looked like twins, & were so fond of me & of each other— & now, I fear soon to be deprived of this precious darling—& to go so far & for so long an absence.

My darling Ped & I are trying to improve our time until I can go somewhere for her benefit. I have often told you, my dear friend, that *Parents* have many more pains & anxieties than those who never had children. At the best, they are as Mrs Powel says, "careful comforts". All mine have been ill last summer.

I saw Mrs A's death announced & regretted it for her Husbands sake, poor Theodosia & Ed Coxe's,[3] to whom she was an affecte friend. What has become of Edmund Coxe—he has entirely forgotten his "indulgent [?]" as he called me, but my memory is more *tenacious.* Will you present my friendly recollections to A Allen, & request him to recall me to the recollection of his Sisters.

I wrote lately to E Mifflin. It will give us pleasure to pay

---

3. Probably either Dr. Edward Jenner Coxe (1801–1862), a brother of Esther Coxe Lewis, or Edward D. Coxe (1793–1819), a son of John D. and Mary Footman Coxe. *Descendants of Colonel Daniel Coxe.*

every attention to your nephew, I wish that I could further his views in the Navy, but I have failed in every application, except one & it is in vain for me to apply for any one. My letters are unanswer'd. Our best love & kindest wishes for you & E Mifflin & respects for Mr G. Ever your faithful & affecte friend

E P L.

————————————————❦————————————————

[Woodlawn] March 19th. 1832

My Dear Elizabeth,

Your kind & friendly letter, so much like our *good old times*, gave me great pleasure as I should sooner have demonstrated, had I not waited to hear from Mrs. Turner. I have just received her letter, & hasten to copy the part relating to the Governess. "I am ashamed to trouble you & your friend yet farther, but you will oblige me by inquiring, if the young Lady mentioned in Mr Waleb's paper who had lately arrived from Dublin, would come to Virginia. Her age is certainly an objection, but as I cannot obtain what I wish, I must accommodate myself to what offers. The salary is the same that the Miss Wydown's received, & as much as we can afford to give. But you will be so good as to inquire what this young Lady's terms are, & when she would come on. I am most anxious to obtain an Instructress for my children, & if within my ability, *must* do it." Mrs Turner is a very fine woman, & an excellent Mother; she is also a most fortunate one, she has a very large family, 2 sons in the Navy, very fine young men, others pursuing different avocations, one at West Point, & all *exemplary* young men. Her Daughters charming, amiable, & well brought up. Mrs T was a Randolph, a first cousin of my Sister Mary Custis. Mr T is a most worthy man, but not so energetic & efficient as his wife. Thomas (T E's friend) is an *oddity* but very correct & gentlemanly, it is very pleasing to see his attention to his Sisters. I knew of poor T E's death, indeed I anticipated it when he was here. I am sorry to lose Mrs E's message, present my love & kind wishes to her, & family, if you please.

I regret that I cannot say we have seen your amiable niece. Mr L has been ill all winter with Influenza & gout, & is still confined to his room. The roads from this to Alex[andri]a are, & have been, so dreadful, that our carriage has not been over it since the 21st. Decr. E & Angela have been confined here all winter, & I

know not when they can get to Wash[ingto]n. We have had an
unexampled winter. On Saturday last a snow storm, violent wind,
& the creek frozen. Every day or two we have rain. I have inquired at Alex[andri]a, but have not heard of Miss B[ordley]
there. I wrote to my niece Mary Lee,[4] & her mother intended
going over to look for Miss B, at W[ashingto]n but my Sister has
been confined to her room, & bed, & still much indisposed, &
Mary her self sick. I hope however that we shall be so fortunate
yet as to induce her to visit us, as soon as the road is safe. We shall
be very happy to make her acquaintance. I hope her Brother succeeds well as a Painter.

I was much gratified indeed with the account of the Centennial celebration [of Washington's birth] in Philad[elphi]a & regretted sincerely that we could not have witnessed it. Phi[ladel-
phi]a has never been backward in showing honor to his memory,
altho they have not built a *monument* yet. I am ashamed of Virginia, she is too pompous, too parading, too full of *words* rather
than *deeds*—she demands that the "remains" should not be
removed from the State, & denies *anything* like a *shelter* or
security for them. They have tried to induce insurrection by their
stupid inflamatory speech only made for *effect* to the *north* &
[*East*] & decry anything to advance colonization, & the *real* interests of those *dark* torments of our lives. *Our* native State *Maryland*, built a *monument*—debated with *closed doors*, sought not
applause from a distance, & subscribed *200,000 dollars* for colonization. Their motto is, *deeds* not *words*. I was *not* one of the *Pe-
titioners*, my dear Elizabeth, & do not approve of acts which *sound
loudly*, but only encrease the evils which menace us. To do good,
we must proceed *cautiously*, & *noiselessly*. Emancipation *must* be
gradual—& all this uproar creates discontent, & induces insurrection & murder. Those ideols, T. J. Randolph, & Faulkener, &
some others actually *invite* murder & outrage, by telling these
ignorant people that we fear them & are at their mercy.[5] The
"Liberator"[6] has done less harm, than the speeches of our delegates.

---

4. Washington and Mary Custis's daughter, Mary Anna Randolph Custis (1808–
   1873), married Robert E. Lee (1807–1870) in 1831. Moore, 183–91.
5. Thomas Jefferson Randolph (1792–1875), Jefferson's favorite grandson, was
   a member of the Virginia House of Delegates, as was lawyer Charles James
   Faulkner (1806–1884). In 1832 there was a great slavery debate in the Virginia house; both men spoke in favor of gradual abolition.
6. Abolitionist William Lloyd Garrison (1805–1879) founded the militantly
   antislavery *Liberator* in 1831.

The coach you mention was Govr. Penn's, & was presented by the State to Grandmama. It was left in Phi[ladelphi]a & I do not recollect what became of it. Those were our *happiest* days—& I like to recall them altho' it saddens me. The affection I then felt for you my long tried friend, has been encreased by your kindness to my darling children, it will never decay, I hope to hear frequently from you. My darling Parke has two lovely children—a daughter on the 7th. Feby. The children are exactly alike & resemble their Father & myself. P was very anxious to show you her Son.

Our most affectionate love & best wishes for you, & respects for Mr G & best wishes, in which Mr L & Lolen unite. Believe me ever most truly your affecte friend

E P L

Kind love to Mrs & Miss M, Elizabeth & all friends. There is now a safe & good vault at Mt Vn.—*not ornamental.*

———————————— ❦ ————————————

Audley Augt. 24th. [1832]

My Dearest Elizabeth,

Without knowing whether you will ever receive this, as you may leave the Sweet Springs before it arrives there, I cannot deny myself the pleasure of conversing with you "à la distance" in the hope that we may soon be *hand in hand.* Your first kind letter, from the Warm Springs, I received at *Bath*, where we passed a pleasant fortnight. The second, I had the pleasure to find at the Battle Town post office, where we stopped on Wednesday 22nd on our way here. I had one from Mr L at the same time, saying that you were in much better health, & confirming your statement of his own improvement. We rejoice in these good effects from your tedious journeys, & hope soon to witness them ourselves. The measles being at Old Point, deterred us from going there, & we came here; Bath being recommended for Loren's ancle, & E's health we packed up & went there. The place is much improved since my visit, *20 years* since, it was crowded & our accommodations not very good, but the fare was excellent, & my Son's foot much benefitted, E's health improved too, but Ped & I were not so fortunate. She looks very pale, & weak but we go next Monday to the Sulphur Spring near Winchester, & think that water will do us both good.

I had the great pleasure to see at Bath, our friends Mrs [Catharine Elwyn] Rogers, & Mr Poinsett, & your very amiable & agreeable friend Miss Barron.[7] They were at Bath when we arrived, but did not remain long as the damp air was injurious to Mrs R. Miss B & I talked of you a great deal, I found her intimately acquainted too with all my Carolina friends, & regretted extremely their early departure. Mr P was, as he always is, a charming companion. Miss B & I made ourselves very merry with him, he called himself "A Lamb" in our hands, but we declared that he was a Wolf in Sheep's clothing. Mrs R was lovely & interesting as ever. Her son is a very fine Boy & very like, (altho' much handsomer) poor Thomas Elwyn.[8] They were going to York & Lancaster in Penn[sylvani]a. Mr P immediately to Carolina. The Nullifiers[9] vex him very much, & well they may. They are mad to all intents & purposes, & ought to be supplied with straight waistcoats.

Mrs Lenox, Miss Kean, & Miss Prowall were at Bath, in the opposite house to ours. Poor Miss P, will never recover I fear. Mrs L is *very* old & infirm, & Miss K has lost much of her beauty—but *none* of her spirit if her fellow boarders speak truth. She inquired particularly about you—Your health & where you were. Mrs Paca & family were with us. She is a very amiable woman, we often talk[ed of] you, her daughter came there very sick, but was much improved by tepid bathing. Mr P was so unwell from the water disagreeing with him, they left the day we did.

Susan Taylor[10] we met on her way there, to stay a week. She is very glad to hear of your intended visit here, & hopes to see you at her house. I hope you will certainly come this way, & that I shall enjoy your society again. I felt in a *dream* when you left

7. Perhaps Isabel Barron of Charleston, South Carolina.
8. Catharine Rogers's brother, Thomas Octavius Elwyn. Scharf and Westcott, 2:1462.
9. Several southern states took exception to the tariff of 1831, which put high tariffs on manufactures and low ones on agricultural products, to their disadvantage. South Carolina politicians, such as John C. Calhoun, led the nullification movement; they declared that each state had the right to "nullify" or veto federal legislation, and if necessary to carry the point, to secede. Poinsett was a leader of unionist forces in South Carolina. Eventually President Jackson's threat to call up troops brought an end to the nullification controversy in 1833.
10. Susan Randolph had married Bennett Taylor of Avon Hill. "Taylor of Southampton &c.," *Virginia Magazine of History and Biography*, 24 (1916): 213.

Woodlawn, but I hope *often* to find you *there in reality*, & *here* too. How did Mrs Iredell[11] get along—travelling over rough roads was so new to her. I should have liked much to see Patty [Hare], her Brother & family, they are among my favorites in Phi[ladelphi]a & have ever been kind & attentive to me. The bathing at Bath is the best in the U.S. & has done infinite good to Lolen's ancle. I am surprised that Mrs Hare did not try it, as hers, I believe, was a sprain.

Our united loves & every good wish for you & Mr G & hoping soon to see you & that you may be able to read this letter, I am ever most truly & affectionately yours

E P Lewis.

Mrs Skinner[12] of Balt[imor]e was the *Belle* of Bath this season.

——————————— ❦ ———————————

Audley Oct 30th. 1832

My Dearest Elizabeth,

Your affecte letter of the 14th. arrived in due time, & we are much gratified by your cordial & most kind assurance of welcome at your new house. I *hope* Ped & I may *find ourselves there*, but I have *many fears*. Lolen is so busy that it will be late probably before he can go to Phi[ladelphi]a, & Mr L may think it too late for us to go & return, we could not stay all winter & he will not be willing for us to go before Lorenzo so that it is uncertain.

As to Mr L himself, he is much obliged & gratified by your invitation but he never leaves Woodlawn in the winter. My poor Parke will be disappointed of her promised visit from her Father. Unless Dr H would go & *insist* upon his going Mr L will never reach Louisiana altho' he believes it is the best place for him, & unluckily our good Dr cannot leave his Farm this winter. My poor Parke is very anxious we should all go, but it is impossible. Were it not for Angela, I would go most willingly & gladly to spend the winter with my poor child, & her precious Babes. They are all

---

11. Probably Hannah Johnston Iredell, widow of Supreme Court Justice James Iredell (1751–1794), one of Washington's Federalist appointees.
12. Perhaps Elizabeth Davis Skinner, wife of John Stuart Skinner (1788–1851), postmaster of Baltimore and publisher of the *American Farmer.*

well, but she feels our absence as the greatest drawback to her happiness as her distance from me will ever be to mine. Mrs Coxe feels so much Esthers being here, what would she do if Lolen had taken her to Louisiana. I hope they may have a happy winter together. I suppose they will go the last of Novr. or first of Decr. Mr L, Ped, & I, go home next week I expect. We are all well— except the remains of a bad cold my darling Angela has had lately.

The weather is growing *wintry* here, I hope bad weather will not commence so early as it did last winter. The day I received your kind letter, your nephew arrived here from Leesburg—in very good health & spirits, he is still with us & very busy. He was so much pleased with Neagles[13] picture of darling Wassy that he has copied it, very well indeed. Moreover he has almost completed a *speaking* likeness of Mr L for Lorenzo, & tomorrow I sit for mine for Loren. We are all much pleased with Mr L's likeness, it is most admirable. I hope he will have some other portraits in the neighbourhood, & have some engagements for next summer as he goes to the South this winter. I am sure if Mrs Taylor was at home she would have her children taken. Her Son is recovering rapidly, but she will not return this winter, I expect. If she can leave John she will go to Richmond. Mrs Hares recovery was indeed miraculous. I rejoice that they are all well. I met Miss Abby Nelson,[14] Patty's cousin, at Mr Burwell's[15] yesterday, & she mentioned Patty's visit to Pagebrook.[16] I wish she could have been here to see us. All her friends at Pagebrook are well.

This is the best country neighbourhood I have ever known, It is rather far from this for our rough roads, but I hope now the *Ice is broken*, that Esther will find very agreeable society hereafter. I used to like them very much when I was in this county some years since.

---

13. John Neagle (1796–1865) was a very well-known Philadelphia portrait painter.
14. Probably Abby Byrd Nelson (1792–1868) of Clarke County. The Hares, through the Willings, were related to the Byrds, Pages, Nelsons, and Burwells of Virginia. Leach, "Philadelphia of Our Ancestors," s.v. "Willing."
15. Nathaniel Burwell, Jr. (1819–1896), was the owner of Carter's Hall, a plantation in the neighborhood of Audley; his wife was a Page. J. E. Norris, *History of the Lower Shenandoah Valley* (Chicago, 1890), 649.
16. Pagebrooke in Clarke County was the plantation of John Page (1760–1838) and Maria Byrd Page (b. 1761), whose mother was a Willing of Philadelphia. Descendants of Charles Willing, Willing Collection, Helen N. Worst Collection, Historical Society of Pennsylvania.

How is dear E Mifflin, I hope she enjoyed herself at the gay wedding. Do ask her how my adopted *Edmund* deported himself on the occasion. He calls himself "[the] last of the Mohicans, the last Signer of the declaration of Independence" since his Brother's marriage. He wrote me a very affecte & amusing letter lately.

My love to Mr G & tell him that I fear his friend Cushing[17] the Boston Nabob is guilty of turning Joe Coolidge's head. Only think of his going off to China to seek his fortune, leaving his fine family for a year or two. If his schemes prosper he returns for them to reside there ten or twelve years. Is it not madness to risk health & happiness for the chance of more wealth, when he has already so much. I suspect he has neither Mr Cushing's constitution or his *energy* of character.

My dear Friend I fear you will scarcely be able to read this scrawl. My pen & ink are bad, it is late, I write on my knee to avoid incommoding my poor Ped by the light, it is late, & I am cold. I thank you sincerely for being ready to call on me as a *Sister* & shall be most happy if I can be there to assist and so will *our Ped*. How is Mrs Iredell. I hope she was as much pleased with her visit to Virginia at last, as at first, & that she will come with you next spring.

Mr Bordley sends you & Mr G his love & respects. He will soon write. Accept for yourself, Mr G & E M our affectionate regards & every kind wish. Good night, God bless you, ever yours most truly

E P L

————————————— ❦ —————————————

[Woodlawn] Jan'ry 29th. 1833

My Dearest Elizabeth,

I thank you most sincerely for your affectionate & welcome letter of the 25th. It is like yourself, my dear & ever kind friend, to anticipate my wishes. I feel very much gratified by your & Mr

---

17. John Perkins Cushing (1787–1862), spent several years in Canton, eventually becoming a partner in Perkins & Company, China traders. He returned to Boston in 1831. Grafton D. Cushing, "Typescript of Cushing family genealogy, especially the family of John Perkins Cushing (1787–1862)," Massachusetts Historical Society.

G's kind approbation of my darling child. She wrote me that she "was surrounded by every comfort that your kindness could devise, or she require."—& I was very certain of that when she was under your roof. You have ever been the kindest of maternal friends to all my darling children, & I could not have my precious child any where more happily situated. She wants nothing to make her happy but to see her Parents, & that gratification you did *your best* to procure for her, by your most friendly invitation. I am certain she will never find a moment of ennui with you. She has an affectionate & grateful heart, is a *reasonable* & happy disposition, & indeed she has everything to make her happy with such kind friends as Mr G & yourself.

I am always with her in thought & constantly wish I could see her. I thank you very much for your description of her dress & appearance. My Sister & I thought we could *see her*. Her dress must have been beautiful & becoming. I do not think any one will ever say of her, as my dear & lamented Friend, Mrs Powell, used to say of *me*—"You look as if your clothes were thrown on with a Pitchfork." My Tiffin [Angela] is always neat. I was always too restless to take time & pains in dressing. If *cover'd modestly*, & *clean*, I cared for nothing else.

My Darling has always conducted herself with great propriety, & modest dignity, & I trust you will not permit *her head to be turned* in your delightful city. Phi[ladelphi]a has always been to me exhilarating gas, & I think it will never lose that effect upon my spirits. I am extremely curious to know *where* the party was last *Thursday*. Angela spoke of it twice, you, in your letter, but neither of you say at *whose house* it was. Had she worn her *pearls* I should have had cause to *suspect* a *wedding* to *surprise* me—but the *cameos*, & *gold chains*, reassured me. Do tell me, my dear Friend, whose party it was.

I had many fears & regrets in parting with my youngest darling, my *last prop*, but I rejoice that I encouraged her to go with Lolen & Esther. She has entered the world under so much more agreeable circumstances than she would have done in Wash[ington]n particularly this winter. The Phi[ladelphi]ans have been so uniformly kind & indulgent to me & mine. I always consider'd Phi[ladelphi]a as my strong hold. When she does return, I trust the Almighty will restore her to me in health & safety, & then I shall be richly rewarded for all my anxiety. Mr L is very much gratified to hear that she is so great a favorite & very willing to part with her for her own gratification. He is very well this winter. We are both rejoiced that her society is so pleasing to you & Mr G. I hope my darling will be able to go to the opera, she would enjoy it so much, but unless *invited*, I should not like her to go into any Lady's box. My dearest E, I do not like her to walk entirely alone, I always feel anxious *here* unless she has some one with her, I read of so many accidents, mad dogs—drunken people &c, that I cannot avoid feeling anxious. She is more precious to me than life, & therefore you will excuse my fears.

Did you receive a letter from me some weeks since. I hope you will write as often as you can do so without inconvenience. Mr L unites with me in kindest regards to you & Mr G. My love to you & to all our good friends. God bless you dearest E, ever gratefully & truly yours

E P L

Maria Palmer is one of my great favorites, I rejoice that her daughter & mine will be always attached friends.

———————————— ❦ ————————————

[Woodlawn] Feby 5th. 1833

My dearest Elizabeth,

My Darling Child wished to have written to you today, but as she had two other letters to write, & I wished to thank you for your two kind letters by her, & all your & Mr G's parental kindness & attention during her happy tho' short residence with you, she has postponed complying with her promise for a few days. She feels most gratefully your constant efforts for her comfort & happiness, & was quite as happy and contented as if you had given her a party every evening. She would have been most happy to have staid longer in Phi[ladelphi]a with you, had not her dear Brother been obliged to return. The fear of our being sick, & her being unable to come to us & anxiety to see us, alone induced her to return. She was perfectly happy there & feels most gratefully every mark of regard & kindness. Anxious as I was to have her again, I did not wish her to return so soon, she had so many gratifications, but she appears as happy as possible & as fond of her home as ever. You may suppose that she has interested & amused us all by the adventures she met with at the different pleasant parties she attended.

They had a wet unpleasant day, but came along with perfect

safety. They arrived in G Town on Thursday, evening & were persuaded by my Sister to remain until Saturday morning, & they all attended a crowded dance at Genl Macomb's, except my Son. W[ashington] Peter, my nephew, attended his Sisters & cousin to Gen'l Mac's, & spent a very happy evening. She met many of her acquaintance & they appear'd very much pleased to see her. Her dress, hastily selected, was the claret silk, her amethysts, & fashionable curls. She was in fine spirits, & look'd well. All remarked how much she had improved by her visit to Phi[ladelphi]a. Her dress fits beautifully.

On Saturday she came home with her Brother, & I had the happiness to see them safe & well. I had often felt so anxious before she came, that I began to fear I never should be so happy as to see her again. One night I thought I was dying & felt unhappy knowing how great a shock it would be to my darling affectionate child. Thank Heaven my fears & anxieties are at an end. I should have been willing to spare her, had she been anxious to remain.

Be assured dearest Friend, that I would most gladly take up my abode in Phi[ladelphi]a for some months at least, for her sake as well as my own, that she might take lessons in Music, & french, & painting. I cannot but *hope* for such a happiness, but when she has opportunity & is willing to leave me for Phi[ladelphi]a I shall certainly consent even if obliged to remain behind her. She was too happy not to wish to be again in Phi[ladelphi]a altho just now, *Home* is so delightful to her. She brought your kind gifts, & Mr G's with her in perfect order, & has put them carefully away. I often thought I could see you *petting* her, & it gave me the greatest pleasure to learn that she was of so much service to you & Mr G in cheering your retirement. I wish I was near enough to admit of sending her to pass the day with you frequently.

I hope you will come to us again this Spring or Summer. We shall be very much delighted to have you & Mr G with us again. I hope you receiv'd my letter. Angela received one of mine returned yesterday, there is another also, sent from Alex[andri]a on Friday. My darling Parke & her treasures are well, Ella will be a year old on the 7th & she says, Mama Baby, Mama *Titty*, "how dare you" when any one offends her. I think it is uncommonly early. Darling Son is well. Mr B's sister is very ill, but, they hope, not dangerously. I direct always to "Mrs E G W Butler Iberville, Parish of Iberville, Louisiana via New Orleans."

We have the pleasure to hear that dear Esther is every day improved in health & strength. My darling Son misses her & his

Son very much. He unites with his Mother in best regards, respects & thanks to you & to Mr G, mine & Angela's to Mr G—&
our love & gratitude for you my dearest E & prayers for your continued health & happiness. Ever your affecte & faithful friend

E P L

Love to dear E Mifflin. Excuse this wretched scrawl.

———————————— ❦ ————————————

[Woodlawn] March 10th. 1833

I had no idea, my Dearest Elizabeth, that I was so great a
delinquent, until this moment, when looking on the date of your
long kind letter I find it as Feby 14th. I waited from week, to
week, in order to tell you something of *our* Darling Angela's
movements at Washington. I went up with her some days after
the receipt of your letter, staid one day at my sister Peter's, &
returned to take care of my dear niece America, & her sick children. Mr Williams was sent to Alabama & Florida, on a survey,
by the Topographical department, & as Mec was obliged to shut
up her house, she came to spend some weeks at her Birthplace.
Her children had most severe colds, & as our good Doctor H was
detained at home by unavoidable business, I could not leave them,
& Mr L, without any *medical* friend. Mec is again poor thing in a
progressive state, & is often very complaining. Mr L has been
quite well all winter.

The first ten days were very dull, as to parties, only one at
Mrs Mead's,[18] which bad weather & a dark night deprived them
of. However, Angela is happy any where & any how, & she was
perfectly contented. The very interesting debate between Mr Calhoun & Mr Webster,[19] she was deprived of by a violent snow
storm & the House being crowded to suffocation. Mr [Francis C.]
Gray wrote me, that "Calhoun was much excited, but did not
bring forward a single *argument* to support his cause; W's argu-
ments were most powerful & convincing, but he was not suffi-

---

18. Perhaps Margaret Butler Meade (d. 1851), the widow of Richard Worsam
    Meade (1778–1828), a Philadelphia merchant who had moved to Washington,
    D.C.
19. To oppose South Carolina's assertion of the power to nullify federal laws, a
    Force Bill authorizing the president to use armed force to collect tariff duties
    was proposed. In February 1833 Daniel Webster and John C. Calhoun debated
    the issue in the Senate.

ciently excited, his victory was *too* easy." Angela was one day in the Senate, but only heard that savage of the Miss[issipp]i *Poindexter*,[20] speak.

She attended the drawing room with her Aunt & Cousins, & was very much pleased, & very politely attended to. She wore the white satin, with her amethysts. The next night she was at the French Ministers, in her book muslin, a bow & ends of beautiful coquelicot [poppy red] gauze ribbon at the skirt, & a bunch of white flowers, small bows on the shoulders—cameo's, gold chain across her forehead, a small wreath of natural geraniums & arborvitae on her head, with hair *à la Kemble*,[21] which she says is *very becoming*. She danced with Mr Gray, Allan Deas,[22] & W Palmer Fanny's Brother—she says he is very much of a gentleman. I hope he will visit us, & I wish Fanny could be with him. She has been to parties at Gen'l & Mrs [?] Mason's.[23] Last Thursday a very pleasant party at her Aunts, where she again danced with W Palmer. She expects a party from Col House, & some others.

She has made many acquaintances among the Beaux, but she is *entirely heart whole*, & never will choose a *Nully* [supporter of nullification], rely upon it. I think the *Nully's* are hiding their *diminished heads*. Mr P[oinsett] sends me all his speeches, they are most excellent. You are, indeed, my dear friend fortunate in never having been a *Mother*. It is a state of incessant [care] & anxiety; all the comforts & the blessings derived from dutiful & excellent children, cannot make amends for their loss, or the anxious anticipation of their future lot. I have never seen a young man to whom I would be willing to confide this blessing, I have *heard* of *but one*. To you alone I will confess it—*H Binney*.[24] From

---

20. George Poindexter (1779–1853) was a Mississippi lawyer and politician; at this time serving in the Senate, he strongly opposed Jackson and his policies.
21. Fanny Kemble, a popular actress, apparently set the style, fashionable during the 1820s and 1830s, of wearing bandeaux of pearls or other jewelry to confine masses of hair dressed high in a topknot. Dorothie Bobbé, *Fanny Kemble* (New York, 1931), 35; Richard Corson, *Fashions in Hair* (London, 1984), 466–67.
22. Probably Fitz Allen Deas, son of William Allen Deas (b. 1764) and Anne Izard Deas. *South Carolina Historical and Genealogical Magazine*, 2 (1901):217.
23. Probably John Mason (1766–1849) and Anna Maria Murray Mason. General Mason was the son of George Mason of Gunston Hall, and Mrs. Mason was the sister-in-law of Edward Lloyd, a prominent Maryland politician. They frequently gave lavish parties at their Georgetown residence. Pamela C. Copeland and Richard K. Macmaster, *The Five George Masons* (Charlottesville, 1975), 100, 257–60.
24. Horace Binney, Jr. (1809–1870), the son of one of the nation's most brilliant lawyers, was a businessman and later a member of Philadelphia's Common Council. Charles C. Binney, *The Life of Horace Binney* (Philadelphia, 1903), 6, 248, 412.

all I have heard, & from her own opinion from the short & very few opportunities she had of judging, I think he would make her happy, & might win her heart if he sincerely loved her. She has received no evidence of his approbation farther than politeness when they met; his mother & sister showed her great affection, & interest in her happiness, & she is much pleased with them. He combines (if report is just) all the requisites for her happiness, but how seldom do events the most desired occur. I have at present *no hope* of this & many fears that it may *never* be realized. This is for *you alone*, dearest E, from your kindness I never wish to conceal anything.

I thank you much for your statement relative to poor Mrs R. I *could not* doubt her perfect innocence, or Mr P's honor & it astonishes me that even the most correct men appear to feel *pleasure* in the *supposed* degradation of *our sex*. It is from this base propensity that so many slanders arise. How is poor Mrs R. May she find that happiness in eternity denied by an unforgiving mother & a merciless world.[25]

Our united love & best wishes for you & Mr G in which my dear Mec begs to unite. Ever gratefully & affectionately

Yours E P L

Love to all our kind friends. The Spring is coming on, begin now to think, at least, of coming here. We shall be most happy to see you.

———————————— ❧ ————————————

Dunboyne[26] *Decr. 5th. 1833*

My Dearest Friend,

You were so kind as to wish I would inform you of our safe arrival here & of the welfare of my Darling Children. After a fatiguing journey of 3 weeks we were so fortunate as to arrive here in health & safety, last Sunday morning. My Darling Parke

---

25. Catharine Elwyn Rogers died of tuberculosis March 14, 1833. Apparently gossip had linked her with Joel Roberts Poinsett. Dunlap, 3:667.
26. Dunboyne was the Butler plantation in Iberville Parish, Louisiana, approximately two miles above Bayou Goula on the west bank of the Mississippi River. *Detail Map of the Lower Mississippi River* ([Washington, D.C.?], 1894), chart 68.

has a cold & cough & does not look so well as I hoped to have seen her, but she is not confined & I hope will soon be well. Her blessed Babes are well & very lovely & engaging. My Sonny has grown very much, & is very like what he was two years since, my little Grand Daughter has the most lovely eyes & eye lashes & the most perfect little figure. She is remarkably smart for one so young, & has the sweetest voice, speaks very distinctly. Mr L was rather indisposed with a cold on board the Boat, but he is doing well. My darling Angela is very well and delighted to be again with her Sister and the precious children who are already extremely fond of her.

After a separation of two years, I am most happy to be with my poor child again, & she is so happy to see us that I should be satisfied with her home were it in the most disagreeable part of the world. She has a small house, indeed quite a cottage, but she has made it as neat as a band box, & we have very comfortable rooms. We expect to pay a visit of two or three weeks, to New Orleans, during the winter, & until we set out on our return I wish not to leave my darling at all. Unfortunately my children cannot leave home next summer, & I must again part with my child & her precious Babes. I never can feel reconciled to being so far from them, so much I wish that I could see her happy & comfortable in the North or East—or in our own State. It is so far, & it is so great an undertaking to come to her, or for her to visit me. She likes this climate, and has been hitherto well, but there is always a risk in so damp and so warm a climate. Since we arrived we have frequently been obliged to have all the windows open, & at night the dew is like rain. They have had several frosts in Novr. which injured the cane very much & the uncommon long drought too has been a great disadvantage. My Son hoped to have made 300 Hogsheads of sugar with a great quantity of molasses but he will scarcely make [?].

The Ohio is a very beautiful win[ding] river with innumberable Islands. The Mississippi more winding & a noble river, but it is as muddy as possible, the banks continually falling in, alternately an immense Sand bank or whole acres undermined— Canes, trees &c slipping in the banks. The [——oss?] is very melancholy at this season, for the trees look dead, mistletoe in bunches on them like leaves. There are some splendid live oaks on this place. It spreads very far & produces a most delightful shade. The Pride of China abounds here but it is not in leaf at present. In Feby the spring commences and my Darling Parke says that everything is then beautiful. At present we have warm weather & naked Trees, except the evergreens, & I confess that a bracing air, & snow & Ice are more congenial to my taste in Decr. The frosts in Novr. killed the roses & they are not yet budding out again.

How happy I should be if my darling Parke were in your delightful City. Indeed my friend she is buried alive here. Her fine mind, her attainments are all thrown away. Hers is a life of domestic toil far from every one of congenial tastes & habits. Poor thing she can scarcely express her happiness in having us with her, & altho' I had rather be with her even on the top of the rocky mountain, than even in Phi[ladelphi]a without her, yet I cannot feel joyful. I must leave her in May to the same risks, the same toils & privations, & I know not when I may hope to have her at Woodlawn. Ed appears wedded to this State and he has I fear a life of toil in prospect. He is always sanguine, always hoping to make great crops & always as yet disappointed. I would not for the whole State, that Angela too should be settled here, & I shall always hope & pray that my Darling Parke may at some future day, remove to a home more congenial to her taste, more favorable to the improvement of her children.

Your last kind letter has been long unanswer'd, I was too much engaged before I left home to write. My Darling Son & his family were well, but I am very anxious now to hear from them. My darling Angela is well & happy, she is to take lessons on the Harp & in French next week if her Sister is at leisure. We are happier at home together than we could be anywhere in the State.

I hope to hear from you my dearest friend. My children unite in love & best wishes for you & Mr G—Mrs & Miss Mifflins. Parke charges me to *do justice* to her Daughter & Son, but how can I give you an adequate idea of *such Babes*. Mr L's & Ed offer best respects. May you and Mr G enjoy health & every blessing prays your most affectionate friend

E P Lewis.

Excuse this scrawl.

———————————— ❦ ————————————

[Dunboyne] Feby 9th 1834

Your affectionate letters, my dearest Elizabeth, of the 10th. Jany, arrived last Tuesday. We were delighted to hear from you &

to find you in better health than we fear'd from the wet winter & your rheumatism. Angela is most grateful to you for your tender recollection & has a lively & affectionate remembrance of your kindness & her delightful visit to Phi[ladelphi]a last winter. She hopes to renew it sometime hence—& we shall be in Phi[ladel-phi]a I trust on our return home by the Lakes & Niagara. I think I can assure you that Louisiana contains nothing sufficiently attractive in a *matrimonial* view, to induce her to cast anchor here. She is very much pleased with all she has seen, so new & so different from all she has hitherto seen, & expects to be very much pleased with New Orleans. She would be very sorry not to revisit this State, but it would never be her choice as a *Home.*

I hoped my Darling Parke & her blessed Babes would be able to return with us, but I despair almost of that happiness. She thinks it her duty to remain as Ed made so poor a crop this Season. It saddens my present pleasure my Dear Friend, when I look forward to a separation in May. It is so very far, our reunion is so uncertain & depends on so many contingencies. The risks to her health in staying here—she & her blessed Babes have suffer'd so much for the two last summers from prickly heat—for two months they were cover'd from head to foot with it & it almost made them crazy. Although the heat is not so oppressive out of the sun as sometimes with us, because they have the sea breezes, yet it is more lasting & weakening & more apt to produce fever or prickly heat. We have had 2 months of almost incessant rains & dense fogs—very sudden & great changes in the temperature, & have had violent colds & coughs. My darling Parke, Ed, & my blessed boy have yet very troublesome coughs & Parke is extremely thin. I feel constantly anxious about her.

We have had delightful weather for the last week, the grass is very green, hyacinths, jonquils & narcissus have been in bloom since Decr. & wild violets. The yard is full of mocking birds, red birds, & others. The river has risen 2 feet since we came here & is still rising. Innumerable steamboats, most of them very large & splendid, *ships* & *brigs* lached to small steam boats ply up & down between Natchez & New Orleans. [Rafts?], flat boats, sloops, *acres* of driftwood ever vary the scene. The public road passes by the Gate, just beyond is the Levee, & near it flows the majestic Father of waters. It is very pleasant to walk on the Levee & see the waves dashing along.

We have an excellent neighbour Mrs Thompson[27] formerly

---

27. J. R. Thompson (b. c. 1794) was a native of New Jersey who owned land in

Miss Montgomery of Jersey. Mr & Mrs T have been the kindest & most attentive friends to my Child. She is a cousin of Mrs Coxe's neighbour Mrs Astley[28] and is a very sweet woman. They have a very pleasant place nine miles off—& the river bends so much that it is almost exactly opposite to this house, I never saw so winding a river. We have several gentlemen visitors here, intelligent & very agreeable. Dr Page of Boston, a friend of your lamented Mrs Derby is very amiable & literary—he is a great friend of Parke's & often lends her Books. He lived 3 or 4 years with Henry McCall[29] the brother of my old friend Harriet, who is 14 miles lower than this, but will remove very soon to Mr Thompson's & practice medicine in this neighbourhood. Mr & Mrs T & Dr P dined here on Friday, my sweet Ella's Birthday & the Dr who is very fond of children brought her a beautiful Doll, some candy & oranges. She says when I ask who she loves "Dr Page." He is consumptive & looks wretchedly.

My sweet Granddaughter who is just two years old is a perfect curiosity, she is so small, her form is so perfect, so ladylike, she is so graceful, so engaging, & so very intelligent. She speaks so well, is so acute, so fearless & flies along like a Bird. She is so fearless & independent that we dare not leave her a moment alone. She flew out of the house today, across the yard, opened the Gate & was off up the public road before her brother missed her. She is very sweet, soft & engaging, but has a *determined* spirit, altho very affectionate. If you ask her for sugar, she points her little finger to her *mouth*, & then offers her mouth to you to kiss. Her hands & feet are remarkably small & soft & beautiful. I know not how to leave her when I am obliged to go.

My darling boy is beautiful & smart & has a very affectionate & generous disposition. I teach him his lessons every day. For their sakes as well as my darling Parke's I wish they could all go with me for 2 years. There are no schools, no churches here for many miles. Sunday among the French & Creoles & indeed

Iberville Parish valued at $200,000 in 1850; his wife (b. c. 1795) was also from New Jersey. United States Census for the State of Louisiana, 1850 (Washington, D.C., microfilm), roll 231.

28. Thomas Astley was a Philadelphia merchant. The Astleys lived at the southwest corner of Ninth and Walnut streets; the Coxes at the northwest corner. PCD 1834.

29. Henry McCall (1788–1859) of Philadelphia had come to Louisiana early in the nineteenth century. He lived on a large plantation, later known as Evan Hall, above Donaldsonville. McCall, 39–40.

among the Americans too is like any other day. Pedlars go about, cake sellers, & they really appear to have no idea beyond this world & its enjoyments. We do not visit or receive visits on Sunday, but it is a gala day here generally.

We have some splendid Trees here, immense live oaks & magnolias. I took a walk of 3 miles yesterday with Mr L to the woods to see a live oak 21½ feet in circumference at 3 feet from the ground. I secur'd you a small piece of moss from the bark & a wild violet gather'd there. There are a number of Indians living a few miles off, They are a remnant of the Natchez Tribe, & Choctaws—poor dirty humble & grateful creatures. Parke has been very kind to them & they often come, the women with baskets to sell & always present some to her & the children. They make very curious & pretty baskets sometimes. The men sometimes come & bring venison. They are almost naked & appear to be almost insensible to cold. This has been the coldest & most uncomfortable winter that has been known for many years in Louisiana. We had Ice & Icicles two or three days & hail like snow it was so thick.

The Harp was silent almost two months but the fine weather last week has enabled Ped to string it & she has learned two songs. She reads a great deal of English, some french, works, walks, plays with the Babes & is as happy as if in the midst of gaiety, altho she enjoys that so much. She is soon to ride on horseback. The road is very level, & soon will be in fine order. The gentlemen say that nothing can be more delightful than riding by moonlight here. The nights are so very bright and in summer so very pleasant. She is always benefitted by riding on horseback, They have delightful Spanish saddles in this country which must be better I think than ours.

Mr L rides & walks constantly & is delighted with the country. He has had some gout pains, but very slight. Spring will burst upon us at once now. The Planters are burning off the cane tops & we have all along the coast on both sides the most brilliant & beautiful fires at night. The Houses are so near each other on the river that it looks like a village on each side. The long moss is pretty when near it, but has a very gloomy appearance at a distance.

I hope soon to hear again from you my dear Friend & I will in return give you an account of our New Orleans trip. Parke would be most happy to see Phi[ladelphi]a & to shew her babes to you &

our friends. Our best love & wishes ever attend you & Mr G—Mrs & the Miss M's & all our friends. May we meet in health & happiness this summer. Ever most truly & affectely yours

E P L

Where is Edmund Coxe, & how.

———————⚜———————

[White Sulphur Springs] July 4th. 1834

My dearest Elizabeth,

You will be surprised to see the date of this letter. We are here on our way home. My health was so bad before I left Louisiana from an old tendency to Dropsey which had reappeared, & from liver disease to which I have long been subjected, that the Physicians advised Mr L to bring me here & I took a violent cold in New Orleans & had the worst cold & cough I ever experienced anywhere. I neglected it to go to parties with my darling Angela, as I could not bear to mar her pleasure or to slight the kindness of our generous & hospitable friends there. A violent dysentery ensued, & total loss of appetite, & the dysentery, or rather constant discharges of acrid bile from the liver, continued until I arrived at Guyandotte. The land travelling in a hard going hack affected a cure I believe.

We have been here a week & the water operates beneficially. I shall remain ten days longer & then go to the Sweet Springs to try the water ten days before we return home. My limbs & body were much swelled in Louisiana, but it had disappear'd before I reached Guyandotte, altho' the weather was excessively hot all the way up the river & the Boat was very crowded. We left my darling Parke's in a Boat of the first class, but the water was so low we were obliged to change our boat four times. No accident occur'd, & we had a very pleasant party.

I left my darling & her family with great regret & nothing but the low state of the River & having engaged our Berths in New Orleans would have reconciled me to come away. From great imprudence Ed was really very ill & had to take nearly 100 grs of Calomel before we left him. My poor Parke expects to be confined in August & was helpless in great measure & apparently bilious. Ed has recover'd since we left him but my darling child has been sick from fatigue & anxiety & I feel miserable & most anxious to hear how she is. I hope on from day to day to hear good news. My blessed Babes were well when I left them but it was almost a month ago.

This separation my dear friend is the most dreadful evil to a Parent. I have not heard from my darling Lolen since the birth of his Twin Sons. Mr Wikoff[30] who left us at Guyandotte told me they were all well when he heard of them & that Mrs Coxe was there. I hope Lolen will be here soon as I have written for them. I am all impatient to see him & his family. 8 months we have been from home & we long to see Woodlawn again.

We had a most cordial & warm hearted reception in New Orleans. Angela was quite a Belle and had *three acknowledged* captives in her train. They gave her a most splendid party at Lake Ponchartrain & were ever in attendance on her movements. One in particular was her perfect shadow & devoted himself so entirely that he at last gained a *victory*. He came up the coast to see her several times & at last she consented to engage herself to him—& has made up her mind to be resident in future in New Orleans—for all the months when it is safe & pleasant to be there. Her choice is the finest young man in Louisiana—the most popular in New Orleans. Even his rivals retired when they found his whole heart & soul devoted to her. I never saw any one so entirely wrapped up in another as he is.

Charles Magill Conrad is his name, he is 27,[31] handsome, remarkably genteel & refined in his appearance—a very bright intelligent countenance, fine talents, highly improved—most noble heart [&] sentiments, irreproachable character from his earliest youth, & the most affectionate disposition—remarkable for his sincerity & veracity. He is the first young Lawyer in New Orleans, stands very high at the Bar & his practice is constantly encreasing. I never saw any young man so universally beloved & respected as he is by all classes in the State. Wherever he is known but one opinion of him prevails. He is literary, very industrious, devoted to his profession & speaks French & Spanish as well as he does English. In short he is just after *my own heart* &

---

30. Henry Wikoff (c.1813–1884), a wealthy Phildelphian, studied law but didn't practice. In 1834 he went to Europe, becoming known as a dilettante, traveler, and writer; his best-known book was *My Courtship and Its Consequences* (1855).

31. Family records and the *Dictionary of American Biography* give Conrad's date of birth as 1804.

will be a great hit of yours when you know him as I hope you will some day.

The only drawback is his residence. There he must remain for some years at least, he is a Virginian by Birth, his Father removed when he was 3 years old. He has 4 Sisters & 3 Brothers, all excellent & intelligent & all most anxious to make him & his choice happy. She will never be in New Orleans after the middle of May. If she does not leave the State she will go to some pleasant & safe residence until Novr. It is sad to be obliged to fly her *home* & to have a home in such a climate, but he is worthy she thinks of the sacrifice, it is a sacrifice, but I trust the Almighty will preserve my darling Child and make her happy. Conrad is her *first* choice, the only one she ever thought she could marry, his disposition & tastes are very congenial, & I feel the most perfect confidence in his character & disposition. I love him very much already. I shall go with my darling Child & her home will be mine. I would very much prefer Phi[ladelphi]a or Boston or Virginia, but I do not know so fine a young man or one who suits us so entirely as Conrad, and therefore we cannot hesitate as her heart has decided for him. No other man in the State could have tempted her to go so far from Woodlawn.

He is very anxious to be married in Oct. He will be with us in August, but she says she must stay one more winter at Woodlawn & go to Phi[ladelphi]a if possible. He is obliged to return to New Orleans in Novr. & can not come again until next July. He dreads very much leaving her again before he is married & says he shall have the most gloomy anticipations. He will never neglect his duty but he is indeed never happy out of her sight. It would be very inconvenient for me to go soon again, but I shall leave it entirely to them to decide. Mr L expects to go again this winter, he was so much healthier the last winter. Conrad depends on his profession for support, but if his life & health are preserved & he has been hitherto remarkably healthy, he will have an ample support & I hope in a few years may have it in his power to remove. If he ever does, he will prefer Phi[ladelphi]a. In two or three years he will not be confined to the City after May. It is disagreeable to be obliged to leave home every Summer for health, but the greater part of the Ladies do so.

They intend conveying water all over the City in pipes for the horses & to water & wash the Streets. That will do much to improve the health. At present or at least the 15th. of June, the City was perfectly healthy altho' the heat & dust were very oppressive. I trust it will leave our country entirely this Asiatic Cholera,[32] it has done much mischief the two last seasons. I was very ill two hours the day I left Louisville but a mixture made by a druggist in New Orleans of camphorated alcohol & peppermint I believe, relieved me and a dose of Seidlitz made me as well as I had been before the attack.

We have found every where the kindest friends & much they lamented our departure altho' they anticipated our return this Autumn. Dr. Page, Mrs. Derby's friend, is very much our friend. He is a most beautiful poet & writes a beautiful letter. He is a very literary man & has given us some of his beautiful verses. I prize them highly.

I gather'd some oak leaves for you & send the two largest live oak leaves I ever saw. They have changed color. Sickness & occupation prevented my writing sooner but I would not neglect your request. I wish you were here this season my dearest E for much I wish to see you. If we do not go South in Novr. I hope to see you again. My darling Angela has suffered much with nervous pain in her face. I trust that the Sweet Springs & the journey will do her as much good as they did you.

We have some few very agreeable people here. C. [Sla—zar?] is here & I am sorry to say is a very great vagabond. I do not notice or speak to him, he is not received in any genteel home in N. Orleans. He kept a gambling house last winter. My E loves the worthless more than the worthy child it appears. God bless you dearest friend. All our love to you & write

Ever

E P L

———————————❦———————————

[Woodlawn] Janry 18th. 1835

My Dearest Elizabeth,

We all unite in wishing you & Mr Gibson many happy returns of the New Year. We hope that all causes of anxiety may be forever removed, & that your life may glide on as smoothly &

---

32. Asiatic cholera became a worldwide epidemic in the 1820s. It reached the United States in the summer of 1832 and created havoc for the next two years.

happily as mortality permits, until the Almighty summons you to receive the reward of a well spent life. My best thanks for your affectionate & most friendly letter. You have indeed ever been my "faithful friend"—& I wish it had so happen'd that our latter years had been passed near each other. Your letters give me always the greatest pleasure, but when you do not write I attribute your silence to indisposition & never to neglect.

I have waited longer than I should have done in order to announce the arrival of the lovely Twins. They came on Friday last, safe & well, altho' they crossed the Shenandoah on the *Ice*, in arms. Think of such *young* Travellers encountering such hardships & being uninjured! They have grown very much, & improved in engaging & intelligent ways. John the youngest, has two teeth, Lawrence, one, & another just through the Gum. I really think they know me, they always hold their sweet mouths up to be kissed, & their arms out to come to me. They are most sweet & lovely, & very good Babes. My darling Wassy was very anxious to be here with us—he is well & very lively.

If I had my darlings from Louisiana what a lovely set of grandchildren I could exhibit. Parke says that her youngest daughter, Caroline, is a *perfect Beauty* & a *model* for goodness. She was born in August. She is small but very healthy, intelligent & as wild as possible. Her elder children are very lovely. They are well except Ed (Mr B) who is far from well. P thinks he has dyspepsia to a great degree. Their crop has been good, but their difficulties cannot be removed unless they have equal, if not superior crops for next year. What a bar to comfort & independence & happiness is a narrow income, & how little do those know the value of a few thousands, who have more than they know what to do with. When I see my dear children anxious & uneasy, & with so many difficulties from which a few thousands would relieve them I cannot but feel unhappy that it is not in my power to relieve them.

My darling Angela is very happy to be with us this winter, altho' she regrets her absent Love. He is an excellent correspondent & *every week* they exchange letters. He is very much engaged with Law business but finds time to write regularly. She is not reconciled to absence or the distance which separates them, & says Time is much too slow in his progress. He can not yet ascertain when we may expect his return. He has had a cold lately.

Angela has made you a pair of screens, they are transfer'd, she hopes you will be pleased with them, & they will be sent up as soon as I can hear of a safe opportunity. They are not so well varnished as we could wish, but it is difficult to make it very smooth without polishing & we have not strength for that part of the business. Angela offers her best love & thanks for your affectionate wishes & expressions. Parke always offers her best love to you & Dear E Mifflin & her respects for Mr G. Mr L has had some gout & sighs for the climate of Louisiana, but he has not been confined this winter. I was afraid during that severe weather that he would be laid up entirely. I am much as usual.

I should like to see Miss Martineau[33] from your description, altho' I do not admire her Tale "The Charmed Sea." Have you read many of her Tales?

I hope you have not suffer'd in health from the extreme cold lately. I never felt such weather. It has moderated very much. The snow was 21 inches here. Be so good as to present me affectely to all my old friends in P. Accept for yourself & Mr G our most affecte & respectful regards & believe me ever yours truly & faithfully

E P L

Excuse a bad pen & wretched scrawling, but it is very late & the servant goes early to the Office.

———————— ❦ ————————

[Woodlawn] March 23rd. 1835

My dearest Elizabeth,

Your affectionate & very welcome letter I received this evening, & you will see how much I prize it by the early reply to it. Many thanks, dear & true Friend, for your & Mr G's kind feelings & expressions towards me & mine. They are ever most cordially reciprocated. I wish I could promise myself the happiness of being near you with my darling children, but we are none of us *fortunes* favorites, as to wealth in possession, or the power of making it certainly & rapidly, & therefore we can only toil on where our

---

33. Harriet Martineau (1802–1876) was an English writer who became famous in 1832 when she began publishing a series of didactic stories, *Illustrations of Political Economy*. "The Charmed Sea," an explanation of monetary systems presented through the tale of Polish prisoners in Siberia, was published in 1833. Martineau traveled in the United States from 1834 until 1836 and published her observations as *Society in America* (1837).

destinies lead us. *"Hope* comes to us," but *certainly* as regards residing in your charming City, never will I fear. Mr L & I cannot live more than a few years anywhere. He is too infirm, & my liver is too much diseased ever to be well again. I shall most probably have a return too of dropsical symptoms this Summer as I have had for the two last.

Our Farm here, never very productive, is worse than ever. This has been a dreadful winter to us. The wheat appears to be entirely destroyed here & in Fred[eric]k our stock suffers very much & no grass yet to sustain them, corn to buy & negroes to feed who make nothing, this is a gloomy prospect, is it not? Mr L intends to buy a small place near our Dear Parke, and if he lives, to remove our negroes this fall & try to make cotton. That climate suits him best, & it is best to be near our darling children.

An earthly Paradise would be nothing to me separated from my darling Angela. I love my darling Son as dearly as I do my daughters. He deserves my love for his affection & duty, and it is most grievous to go so far from him & his precious Boys & dear Esther—but my daughters are far from all other friends & need my care more than he does.

In La. the latter part of the winter has been uncommonly severe. The Orange & Lemon Trees all killed, a great part, if not nearly all the plant cane killed. Poor Ed must try to make both ends meet by planting cotton with the cane that is not quite dead. This year he made the only tolerable crop he has had since he went there, & part of that was lost on its way to Richmond. My darling Parke has many trials & difficulties—she has had a severe cold & cough this winter. Her precious Babes are well & she writes me that her last daughter is a perfect model of beauty & sweetness of disposition. I have never seen her. The other two are remarkably intelligent & beautiful. Eds health is very much improved.

My dear *Charles* has been perfectly well this winter, & working he says like a galley slave. He has a great deal of business to attend to as a Lawyer, I trust he will always be successful. I certainly could not find one better calculated to make my child happy. The more we know of him, the more we are satisfied of that. He writes every week, excellent letters, & has not a thought I believe, that he does not impart to his Dear Angela. He is working incessantly to shorten the time of his separation, but he will not be released I expect until late in June or July. I wrote him of your remembrance, & he begged to be most respectfully presented to you & Mr G. He has a very affecte grateful heart. If he lives & retains his health he will have sufficient for comfort & independence, but he is too generous & cares too little for wealth ever to be wealthy, & therefore he must drudge on where he is best known. N. Orleans is improving astonishingly, & if we escape War with France it will continue to do so.[34]

The Coast too near Dunboyne (Eds) is improving by new American settlers from Miss. (removing for health) instead of the lazy Creoles—this will add much to Parke's comfort in every way. The Creoles are indolent & dirty, & places which will produce with scarcely any trouble, flower & everything beautiful are really disgusting under their management.

Lolen E & their 3 darling Boys have been here several weeks. The blessed Twins improve in size, beauty & intelligence. Precious Law[renc]e the smallest has been very sick teething he is better today. They have been a week at Arlington—Angela almost four weeks. Dear Mec is well & has another daughter. I wrote Angela all your kind expressions tonight. She will be as often with you as possible. Mrs. Coxe kindly insisted that the young couple should stay with her. I do sincerely hope my dearest friend that all may be as you & Mr G wish in regard to your affairs.

I am very busy working a cover for Angela's Piano on canvas & cloth in cruels. How is Com[modor]e James Biddle.[35] We were with him at the Wt. Sulphur. We like him very much. Our united most affectionate love to you & Mr G—to dear E M & C M. May God bless you now & ever prays your attached

E P L

Mr Bennett has your screen in his care for Phi[ladelphi]a.

---

34. American citzens claimed over $12,000,000 in damages from France, mostly resulting from the Napoleonic Wars. Negotiations over the claims dragged on for years, and in 1834 President Jackson called for a law authorizing reprisals on French property if the claims were not paid. The French government broke off diplomatic relations, and there were fears of war. The claims, however, were finally settled peacefully.

35. James Biddle (1783–1848), a Philadelphian, was a successful naval officer; in 1846 he negotiated the first treaty between the United States and China.

Dunboyne. Parish of Iberville Louisiana July 27th. 1836

My Dearest Elizabeth,

Most welcome indeed is your affectionate letter of the 7th. I received it on Tuesday, & hasten to answer it, I was then near N. Orleans on my way to this place, the home of my darling Parke & her precious Babes. To my *shame* it would be that I have not written to my earliest, my truest, & my dearest friend since I have been in La. I have been in such wretched health & spirits that I could scarcely exert myself to write to my children. I received your kind letter by Mr [Richard R.?] Corbin several months after date, some one gave it [to] Mr Conrad at his office. I did not see Mr Corbin at all, & I should have written, but I was at deaths door almost with the most violent cough, & most anxious about my darling Angela's situation, & my darling Parkes bad health.

You have never known, my dearest Elizabeth, the anxious mother's feelings, but they are overwhelming, particularly when you know that your child requires your aid, & feel entirely deprived of the power to be useful. When I landed at Mr Frederick Conrads 30 miles above this,[36] it was very early in the morning, there had been a great deal of rain, & in descending from the upper deck of the steamboat my foot slipped, I drew my arm from Charles because I feared to make him fall too, & fell from the upper to the lower deck striking my back against every step as I went down. I was so severely hurt that during the week I staid there, & for several weeks after I could scarcely sit up at all.

When I came here my poor Parke had a severe cold, chills & fevers, then came my darling Lolen very sick from his journey, I then went to N.O with Angela and two days after she was cover'd with the chicken pox, her house entirely unfurnished, the boxes all to unpack, Charles so engaged with important business that he was unable to assist me. At last we were comfortably established & my child well. Then she was worried with sick & refractory servants & then, without any exposure or imprudence came on my dreadful cough, this I really thought was my death warrant. At last I was released but left very thin & weak.

---

36. Charles Conrad's brother, Frederick, also a lawyer and politician, lived at The Cottage plantation, a few miles south of Baton Rouge. Rachel O'Connor, *Mistress of Evergreen Plantation: Rachel O'Connor's Legacy of Letters, 1823–1845*, ed. Allie B. W. Webb (Albany, N.Y., 1983), xvi.

Then my Angela was seized with the measles & on three days after was prematurely deliver'd of a little delicate Babe. The smallest I ever saw, no one thought it could live & I was afraid almost to dress & undress it. My poor child was confined several weeks from the debility produced by measles & the shock of so rapid a delivery. She is now happily in very fine health, & the blessed Babe is as fat, as fine a girl as any one of her age (4 months. She is christen'd "Angela Lewis" & is the darling of Mother Father & Grandmother. She is very like her father & he is devoted to her, he is her best nurse when business admits of his being with her. He is a most generous affectionate & indulgent Husband & a very fond Father. They are perfectly happy. Angela has nothing to regret [except] the distance between her & [?] dear friends. Her new Brothers & Sisters are all most kind & affecte. I suppose Lorenzo described her house &c.

Mr L had a fit of the gout but he is as partial as ever to a Louisi[an]a winter. He is worse in Virginia. I have been with Angela & Charles to two watering places on the Gulf of Mexico— the sea air & bathing were very beneficial to Angela. This summer climate has been as trying to me as the winter. My strength has been completely prostrated. I who would never lie down even at night when I could sit up, have [lain] almost all day on the bed, so weak that I could not sit up. I never felt so useless, so helpless in my life. I am very thin & so changed that all who see me are shocked at my appearance—but I feel better since I have all my darlings in this quarter around me, except my darling Grandson who is at school 30 miles off & very well situated; & here I expect to remain until late in Novr. We shall then return to N.O. & my darling Parke will pay us a long visit. I expect my poor child is far from well, excessively thin & weak.

I trust her husband will realize a fine crop this season, his prospects have been most flattering so far. It will relieve him from debt if he succeeds & my poor child from great anxiety & my child be enabled to visit her Sister and partake of society more congenial to her tastes. Here she is literally buried alive. Her health her spirits destroy'd by over exertion, no congenial mind or pursuits to compensate for domestic drudgery. I have often lamented that Ed left the Army. He has never yet made a good crop & Parke has endured fatigue & privations which I never anticipated for her. She is a very anxious Mother & she feels the absence of her precious Boy very much. She has 3 lovely children—two charming little daughters. They are enchanted with their little Cousin, & my poor child is cheered & benefitted by having us all with her again.

How little my friend can we anticipate the future fate of our beloved children. Parke by nature & education formed to adorn any society—now fixed where her talents are buried, her resources of no avail, for unfortunately she has not that elasticity of temperament which rises superior to all difficulties—which could people a desert & looking only thro the bright vista of hope finds enjoyment in any situation.

May the Almighty prosper their efforts for independence, & enable her to go North the next Summer. We all hope if we live to see Woodlawn & Audley next summer. My darling Son feels our absence severely. My darling dutiful affectionate child, & it is a severe privation to me to be so far from him, but I could not leave my poor daughters in a climate so much more trying than ours, & I cannot wish him to remove because I think his present situation far preferable to any here, altho the profits are less even in the best years there. Yet the expenses are far greater here, & I know that he could not live in this climate. Even in winter he suffer'd from the warmth of the weather. My precious Grandson & my dearest Esther are well.

I thank my dear Ann for her kind inquiries & I beg you to offer her my affectionate remembrances. My kindest wishes for her Daughters happiness. My dearest Elizabeth, you have ever been my truest my dearest friend. All my youthful attachments are as strong as ever. I have no idea of happiness beyond Phi[la-delphi]a & my earliest & best friends, & could I remove my darling children & grandchildren I would live & die near you. Perhaps we may never meet in this world again, but your affection for me & mine will only be forgotten when I cease to exist. My children love & honour you with filial respect & affection & their children will be taught to reverence you as their Parents. They beg me to offer you every thing affectionate & respectful in their heart, to assure you of grateful feelings for blessings to them & their little ones. The precious babes would be most happy to give you their sweetest smiles & kisses. They are indeed *Jewels* tho' sources of great anxiety. We all beg to be most affectionately & respectfully remember'd to Mr Gibson. May the evening of your life be as unclouded as you have ever *deserved* my dearest friend, I could not wish you a happier one.

I rejoice to hear of A[ndrew] Allen's happiness. He has fulfilled all that his fine talents gave promise of. Do assure him of my friendly recollection. I shall never forget our lamented friend & *her* friend & Andrews congenial wife must be indeed a fine woman. Excuse this crossed letter dearest friend & may the best blessings of Heaven ever be yours & Mr Gs & hereafter with prayer of your faithful and devoted friend

E P L

Charles retains a grateful recollection of your and Mr Gs kind attentions to him.

N.O. April 20th. 1837

My Dearest Elizabeth,

Most joyfully welcomed your affectionate letter of March 22nd. I had several times intended to write you, hoping to receive a letter in return & anxious to hear of my oldest & dearest friend & my other kind friends in Phi[ladelphi]a but I find it more diffi-cult to write now than formerly and postpone it from day to day. I had a theme last summer and winter which could give interest to my letters, my angel grandchild—my blessing—she was all I could ask of Heaven. The sweetest, the best, the loveliest, but she is no longer here to bless her Parents and her Grandmother. The almighty for wise & good ends for *her sake*, at least, has recalled her to himself.

I told you how very small & delicate she was at first & how anxious we were about her, change of air & exercise made an astonishing change. She became the finest the healthiest child I ever saw, her limbs were so firm so smooth, they were like pol-ished ivory. She had the finest chest, the most perfect form I ever saw, her features & expression were her fathers, her dimples & smile her mothers, she was remarkably intelligent, & a very observant & withall the most heavenly temper & most affection-ate disposition. I was always with her, she was my idol, she gave me health—consoled me for all I had left behind. Her Parents idolised her & she was devoted to them, admired by all who saw her & sweet & gentle to all.

In an evil hour she caught the whooping cough, & that dreadful disease with the irritation of teething was too much for her. Convulsions came on & after much suffering & every exertion to save her, she closed her innocent life on the 25th. of March. She was a year old on the 17th. I need not tell you what a blank she has left in our existence, how gloomy this house is now which she made so gay and happy. My darling child feels most deeply but she has borne the affliction with the resignation of a Christian. Her Father too feels it most acutely. She was his recreation after the toil of business. Time only, with the reflection that she is far happier than we could have made her, can console us.

My child looks thin & pale & I feel constant anxiety about her. I have suffer'd several weeks with the Influenza & my cough is still very troublesome. We are very anxious to go home this summer, but Charles is so much engaged that I fear we must resign all hope of it. We often sigh for our peaceful quiet Woodlawn, but A cannot leave her husband, & I cannot leave her & we must bend to circumstances.

Would to Heaven that my darling children could leave Louisiana forever, we could be far more healthy & happy in Virg[ini]a or dear Phi[ladelphi]a. This City is overwhelmed with commercial distress at present & all classes feel the pressure of the times.[37] The Planters lost by early frost considerably, & since by the fall of sugar & cotton. My darling Parke is *buried alive hoping* from day to day to overcome the spell which binds her to the soil of Louisiana & still she *hopes*, but I fear in vain. She has four fine children—2 sons & 2 daughters. Her last dear Babe I have not seen yet. We hope she will visit us next month, we left her the 1st of Decr. I hear from Mr L & my darling Son, they are all well & the last dear Boy is a very fine one I hear. I wish most ardently to be with them again—but I cannot leave Angela & my poor Parke.

We often talk of our happy days with you & Mr G & our other friends in Phi[ladelphi]a & wish they could be renewed. I thank dear Caroline for her affecte remembrance of us & beg you to assure her of our constant affecte. To all my kind friends I beg our affectionate love & best wishes. Perhaps we may never meet in this world, but I can never forget all their, & particularly *your* love & kindness for me & mine. If we ever visit Phi[ladelphi]a again I will live over again some happy days. My children unite with me in love & respects for you & Mr Gibson. My darling

---

37. The depression of 1837, which involved nationwide bank failures and bankruptcies of merchant houses, hit New Orleans very hard.

Parke would offer hers if she were with me. Write to me when it is not painful to you. May God bless you & yours my dearest friend. Ever most truly yours

E P L

Woodlawn Augst. 13th. 1839

My Dearest Elizabeth,

I am really ashamed to see the date of your last most kind & welcome letter, March 18th. The fact is, when I received that letter I was almost crazy with anxiety about my darling Angela, I had just heard that she expected to be confined in June, & she was so uneasy lest I should be sick if I went to the South at that season that she insisted on my not even thinking of it. The anxiety & my own swelled limbs, & the difficulty of going south at that time determined me to remain, but I was miserably anxious as you may suppose.

I determined to wait until I could announce to you her safety & the Birth of my *10th.* grandchild. She had miscalculated & was not confined until the 3rd of July. She always assured me that her health was uncommonly good, that she was remarkably active & entirely free from apprehension. Her kind indulgent Husband who gratifies every wish in his power, had exerted himself to obtain a most pleasant summer residence at Pass Christian, & there they fortunately were most comfortably established on the 23rd. of June with an excellent nurse & *all requisites*. On the 3d. C walked out early in the morning & when he returned in about an hour, he found Angela well & comfortable in Bed, & a fine Boy dressed & sleeping by her. On the 4th. day she wrote to me & has been so well all the time that she says she can scarcely believe that she had been confined. She has a fine flow of milk, her sweet Boy has never had an ache, & grows & fattens finely. They call him Lewis (his name is Lawr. Lewis) & he promises to be exactly like his lovely Brother *my own* sweet Charley. Charley is very fond of his little Brother & very often begs his mother to suckle him—& he kisses the little hands most tenderly.

Most sincerely do I wish that I could show you *all* my darling Babes. My darling Parke expects another in Octr. Dear Esther also. My darling Angela is most truly grateful to the Giver of all Good for his great mercy to her. I need not say how deeply I feel *all* his mercies to me & mine. Parkes letters are filled with the charms & intelligence of her little flock, particularly the youngest Lawrence. She has an arduous task having to teach her eldest Latin, french, & English, & her two little girls their lessons, besides making the greater part of their clothing & all her own. She is well and they are all healthy this summer so far. She is most anxious to return here & to see all her old friends again, but I know not when she will be so happy.

We have been detained here two or three months by the necessity of having a proper *shelter* made to protect the Sarcophagi at Mt Vn. Mr L has at last completed it, & I am told that it is a very great improvement to the Tomb, & will be a complete protection to the marble. I have never seen the Genls, It was only uncover'd since the work was completed. I hope to see them before I go to the South in Octr. Mr L left home today for Audley & I shall be there I hope next Saturday. My limbs swell occasionally & for the last few days I have been very lame with the rheumatism in my hip. I have a plaster on it which will enable me to travel on Saturday. Our most faithful excellent friend Dr Henry D[aingerfiel]d remained here to attend me to Audley where he has been long expected. He offers to you & Mr G his respects & best wishes.

I hope my dear friend that you & Mr G are now perfectly well. Have you remained all summer in Phi[ladelphi]a. If you visit any of our Springs cannot you take Audley in your way on your return. You will not, I hope, *doubt* our sincere pleasure in seeing you & Mr G there. I have been much engaged all Summer in making preserves for my darlings. They have very little of our fruits there & of some that we like best, none at all, I have done all in my power to supply the deficiency. I have worked 2 table covers & a seat for La. & as soon as I get to Audley I shall work a greek cap for my darling Lolen. What think you of the *eleven* seats yet to work, besides other things.

I hope dear Elizabeth & her Mama & Sister are well. Dear Maria Nixon & her family I hope her poor child has recover'd, I see C Bollman has gone to England. My love to all kind friends. Do write to me at Audley & tell me all about yourself Mr G & all our old friends. Believe me my dearest friend in all situations most truly most affectionately yours

E P L

Kindest regards to Mr G. My children always remember you & Mr G most respectfully most affectely.

———————————— ❦ ————————————

Audley Novr. 5th. 1839

My Beloved & ever kind friend,

Your affectionate letter of tender & sincere sympathy I duly received & have postponed thanking you for it sooner, as I supposed you would be absent from Phi[ladelphi]a until Novr. Let me now assure you of my grateful thanks for this, & all the many many kindnesses received from you & dear Mr Gibson by my darling children & myself. In more than 40 years, my truest kindest friend, you have rejoiced in my joy, & mourned with me in grief, & never have I found the slightest change in your heart since we first loved each other.

I have often told you, my dearest friend, that you were happier in being without those precious objects of devoted affection which bind our hearts to earth, & altho sources of happiness, are also sources of most heartrending anxiety & overwhelming affliction. Of eight precious children I have outlived six. But to all but this last beloved & most excellent child, I have been permitted, by the Almighty, to pay the last duties, to resign them myself into the hands of Him who giveth & taketh away—& that was a consolation in my bereavement. This blessed child had lived in my Bosom, had been the constant object of my anxious cares, we were scarcely ever separated, she was so devoted to me, she relied on me so entirely. It was a great trial when she was obliged to part with me. Her sad expression ever was before me even when I heard of her health & happiness.

When I heard that she expected to be confined I was anxious & miserable, it appear'd to me that I never should see her again if I did not go then. But she feared for my health & begged me not to go. Mr L was obliged to remain at Woodlawn to attend to the work at Mt Vn. & I staid. When I wrote to you I was full of hope & gratitude to the Almighty. After I came here I felt very anxious about my darling Parke, but quite secure in regard to my blessed Angela. She is gone from me & never can I forgive myself that I was not near her in those dreadful hours when congestion of the brain destroy'd her senses & her life. Her poor Husband [is] a perfect wreck. My precious Babes were well, & I hope to go to them on the 13th or 14th.

My darling Parke is deeply afflicted & is not yet confined. I dread almost to hear from her. My dear Esther is safe & well & the happy mother of a very fine Boy. Mr L is as usual & bears his loss with resignation. My darling Lolen & his dear Boys are well.

I hope to bring my precious babes & their poor Father with me next Summer. He gives them to me & is only anxious to do everything that his Angel wife wished, & to comfort us in our affliction. Poor fellow he is most truly & deeply afflicted. I do not murmur at the Almightys will but how can I be at peace with myself. Pray for me my Dearest friend, that I may be able to do my duty to my orphan Boys, & be worthy to rejoin my departed angels in a better world.

Our united love & prayers for you & Mr G. Ever most faithfully & affectionately your friend

E P L

———————————— ❦ ————————————

New Orleans Decr. 20th. 1840

Most sincerely do I thank you my Beloved friend for your long & most affecte & welcome letter, it is a *mine* of pleasure to me my truest & most beloved friend, & I should not have postponed writing so many weeks had I not been peculiarly situated. I received it a short time before I left my darling Parke & she had great pleasure in reading so kind a letter from her excellent friend whom she has ever most truly loved & respected. She was then sorrowing over my expected departure from her house to try again another winter voyage without friend, protector, or servant—& her feelings were embitter'd by the recollection that her Husbands unprovoked & gross insults had driven me from the home of my only remaining daughter.

Yes my dear friend, my darling child whose wishes were anticipated as far as possible in the home of her Parents, has suffered almost ten years of sorrow & privations of every kind, & for the last six years the most brutal treatment—except *striking* her which he knew every *man* on the coast gentn. & common creoles would have resented. She is everywhere respected admired & beloved. He is so arrogant, & on politics so violent, that his cousin

Judge Butler told him that nothing but his respect & affection for Parke induced him to enter his doors. He has all the violence of Gen'l J without his gentlemanly manner.

To strangers he is so soft & gentle you would think him the best temper'd person alive, the kindest husband & father, even to *me* before any one not of his family. He says "Mother" & is all attention, but he has hated me ever since my Darling married Conrad. His advice & consent were not required before her engagement, & he tried to prejudice Mr L against C & me because he thought I had influenced my darling & Mr L to consent, but much as I liked C, I did not, he was my childs own unbiased choice & is in everything very very far B's superior. As long as Mr L lived & he thought he might expect anything he carefully concealed from us his feeling towards my unfortunate child, & as far as he could his hatred of me, but now he has nothing except what I can give out of my annuity of $1000, I have nothing, & therefore he keeps no terms.

My child wished me to pass the winter with her, & I wished to stay as long as I could keep my precious orphans there, & he was resolved to prevent it. He came into her room while she & Darling Sonny were ill in bed & said, "he moved to La. to get as far from me as possible & he would be *damned* if he ever went where I was again, that my name was mentioned with ridicule & contempt throughout La. & even his poor wife suffer'd from its being known that I was her Mother. That I made my Husband miserable & shorten'd his days—& much more of the same. When I was coming away he said he was glad of it & hoped I would never come again. He cursed P & myself & said he cared neither for her feelings or mine. I told him that I prefer'd his censure to his praise that I felt such unutterable contempt for him, I should dislike myself if he liked me.

He treats his poor children often so cruelly that Sonny told his mother he felt tempted to throw himself into the river & nothing but love for her prevented. He is now at an excellent school 30 miles off. Little Caro only 6 years old, was playing about the room, he called out "You Damned little Imp of *Hell*, I have a great mind to box you all over the house." You can judge how totally unworthy so great a brute is of my excellent child. She has been a slave to him, she has been buried alive, only once for five weeks she was permitted to visit her precious Sister, & he has reproached her ever since with that indulgence. She has most excellent kind friends on the coast who would go through anything to serve her, but she will never be well or happy until she once more breathes her native air & meets those who have always loved & known how to appreciate her.

Nothing would have prevented my childs leaving him forever but the power he has over her poor children, she could not leave them to certain destruction, & until his outrageous conduct to me she concealed from me all he had done to make her miserable. He has the most selfish malignant mean disposition I ever knew, & I have never even read of any one like him except Daniel Quilp the Dwarf in "Master Humphreys clock".[38]

My dear friend you have regretted not having children, far better is it for you that you have none. I had eight such as any mother might be proud of, six are, I humbly hope & believe, blessed Angels in Heaven & that they were worthy to be so, I thank the Almighty. My only remaining daughter suffers a *living death* & cannot pray to be released because she is the only stay her poor children have, if *my* life could be spared they would not be given to my care, He is the worse possible example (except that he is *strictly honest & moral*), his Sisters are his counterparts, as mean as selfish, as little addicted to *truth* telling as he is.

I begged him not to charge *me* with the sin of inducing him to live in La. in fact his Sister & brother *Bell* sold the plantation to him, persuaded him to buy it for thrice as much as it was worth, that she might live in a large brick house, & he might remove from a neighbourhood where his dishonest dealings had made him despised, & as soon as B was *master* he pressed Mr L myself & my darling Angela to pass the winter with them, & tried to persuade Mr L to settle near him, so much for his veracity.

For the estimation in which he says I am held in La. I have found everywhere respect & kindness. Several of P's friends pressed me to stay with them this winter, but that I could not do. Since I came here my precious orphans have been so unwell that I could not bear to leave them & here I remain in C's house until May when he hopes to go with me & his darling Boys to Audley, & we have hopes of gaining B's consent to my darling P & her Babes going with us, I hope to collect of money due me $1000 & that my child shall have, perhaps that may induce his consent. Everyone declares that her life is at stake if she remains another summer

---

38. Daniel Quilp was a character in *The Old Curiosity Shop*, first published as a serial in Charles Dickens's short-lived periodical, *Master Humphrey's Clock*, 3 vols. (London, 1840–41).

here. She was extremely ill last year & this Summer darling Sonny very ill for two months, & the youngest, Lawrence, very ill for several weeks, I had chills & fevers but soon recover'd, & my little darlings escaped all summer, since the cold weather they have had violent colds & very sore mouths & ears, darling Charley has suffer'd very much but is now getting well & I trust will soon be entirely recover'd.

My sweet Lewis has the [most] splendid dark blue eyes, but in other respects is most like his Father, he has a very high spirit but a most affectionate disposition & engaging ways. My Charley is more gentle in countenance & disposition. They are lovely Boys & much admired, & I found that I could not leave them, I could not reconcile myself to leave them to those, who could not if they would, devote themselves entirely to them, & Charley always begged me not to leave them, I am nearer too to my darling Parke & she dreaded my going so far at this season, she is much better but not quite well & if she was ill & wished for me, I would go in spite of B's brutality.

I live only for my poor darlings & for their service, but I often recall with melancholy pleasure the happy days & dear kind friends I formerly knew. It gratifys me more than I can express to be so kindly remember'd by them in these days of gloom & absence from my own dear home, & my darlings at Audley. I hope to see you & my other kind friends before I "go hence to be no more seen." Your affection dearest E I never can cease to prize as it deserves. My poor child offers to you & Mr G her affecte respects to all her friends & mine. I beg you to offer our love & kindest wishes, I rejoice in their happiness & sympathize in their afflictions. C presents his best respects. May the Almighty ever bless you & Mr G & all my old & kind friends with every blessing temporal & eternal prays your devoted friend

E P Lewis

Chapter Seven

The Widow at Audley
1842–1851

"I work from breakfast until candlelight, & then read as long as I can keep my eyes open, rise before the Sun & read or work until breakfast."

[Audley] Janry 10th. 1842

My Dearest Elizabeth,

Accept the united wishes of your old friend, & her children & grandchildren, that you & Mr Gibson may be restored to health entirely, & yet live many happy years before you depart to receive the reward of a life well spent. Your welcome & affecte letter, my dear friend, has made a long journey since I received it. Knowing the gratification my darling Parke would receive from your kind remembrance of her, I enclosed your letter to her, & it returned to me only yesterday.

My child begs me to offer her most affecte respects & grateful acknowledgements to you for your kind sentiments & expressions of regard & approbation, & your pious wishes for her happiness. Accept mine, my friend, for the interest you feel in the welfare of my precious children & Grandchildren. You were a Mother to my dear children when in Phi[ladelphi]a, & I am certain that you would love equally, if you knew them, my precious orphan Boys & my dear Parkes four fine children. I have lately received letters from three of P's children, her eldest son, 12 years old, one daughter 8, the other 6 years old, beautifully written & expressed. They are all three good french scholars, The Son progressing too, rapidly, in English, & Latin studies. At his examination lately, his French & English speeches were much admired, & he passed his examination with great credit. He is the Pride of his Mothers heart, & he is more indebted to her for his improvement than to any other. The little girls are very neat sempstresses of plain work, & in worsted work & flower making. The youngest Son, 4 years & a half, is a fine Boy.

C & my own Babes had a very tedious passage to Louisiana. They landed at his Brother Fredk.'s on the 11th. Novr., & C went immediately to N.O where he was detained by law business & the legislature until the 17th. Decr. On the 19th. he brought them to my Darling Parke, & I have had 3 letters from her since, filled with their sayings & doings—all most precious to me. Until they came to her I heard nothing of them, except, that C *heard* they were well. You cannot conceive how anxious, how heartsick I was to know more of them. My child has made me feel happier than I have been since they left me. She says they are rosy with health, strong, active, & the sweetest best behaved Boys she ever saw. They kneel & say their prayers morning & night, & every thing they are told I would wish them to do they do at once, they are very polite, & obedient, & affectionate. They knew my picture at once & talk to it every day. Lewis says "Good morning Grandma. Why dont you speak to me, Norah (the white nurse) why will not Grandmama speak to me". This portrait Mr Bordley painted last Summer, Lolen sent mine & his Father's to Parke, & they are great comforts to her. She thinks them perfect likenesses.

My Charley, 4 years old last August, is more grave than his Brother (2 years last July) but equally affectionate & devoted to his little Brother. Going down the Ohio the Boat struck a rock which did no injury but created great alarm. Norah who is the most excellent & faithful girl I ever knew—took up Charley to put on his shoes & cloak, Lewis was asleep. Charley resisted & said "Norah take up Lewis first, would you let my little Brother sink, Grandma told me I was the eldest Boy that I must take care of my little Brother, I cannot leave him to sink," & when his Father came, who was the first gentleman in the cabin, & wished to take Charley, he insisted on his taking his little Brother, & he followed with his nurse. Charley says when he comes again to Uncle L's he will stay with me & never leave me again. Lewis told Parke, "Grandma said God bless my little Boys, & she cried so much & went in the rail car". Lewis is the astonishment of every one for his precocity, he speaks as well as Charley, he is a great critic. He says "Charley *littlest* is not the proper word, smallest is the proper word. They sleep in P's room, she told Lewis It is too soon to get up yet, it is not daylight yet. Lewis said "daylight is not the proper word, daybreak is the proper word". The first night Lewis did not like to cover his feet, P told him, Grandma will grieve if she hears that her Lewis will not cover his feet. He said immediately, "I will be cover'd, cover me then." He said one day,

"Oh how I wish to see my little sister," they asked him which is your sister, he replied "Charley says she is up in Heaven, I wish I could go to see her". They both speak often of their Angel Mother & wish to go to see her.

On board the Boat, Lewis hit Mrs Whites' little girl & his Father shut him up in the state room until he would beg her pardon. After a time he said "let me out Papa I will be good." as soon as he came out he clasped his little hands & said, "forgive me this time Papa I will not do so any more" & kissed him. He then went without being told kissed the little girl & begged her pardon. My Charley has written me two little letters his aunt holding his hand, & Lewis wrote a line in the same way—& says he writes like a *Boy* Parke says he acts like a *man*. He is the most fearless independent character—lovely & engaging. & my sweet Charley has his Mother's disposition, he is very thoughtful. He went into the room I used to occupy to look for me. My sweetest darling Boys, I love them & feel as proud of them as their Mother would have done. They are identified with her in my heart, & their motherless state makes them still more the objects of my devoted love. They are very happy with their Aunt, She & her children dote on them. Indeed all who see them love & admire them as every one did my Angel Angela who ever knew her. When they go to N.O I shall hear less of them. C is always engaged. No Father ever more doted on his children than he has ever done, but he only sees them at meals. His office is in a different street & he is much engaged. & his sister & nieces who will be with him this winter— altho fond of his children do not like writing & cannot conceive how anxious I am to know all they say & do.

If we live to meet again in the Spring, & my poor darling Parke & her precious children can come, I shall be happier than I have been for a long time; but I fear my poor child will be again disappointed. B's crop has failed this season from drought & early frost, & he will not I fear consent. I am as happy here with my darlings who are all affectionate & kind to me, as I can be away from my poor child, & my orphan Babes. But my poor Parkes fate, & my helpless Boys so young deprived of their dear Mother, are constant sources of unhappiness to me.

Cannot you & Mr G come here next Summer. There is a Sulphur Spring near which is excellent for Erisipelas, & I can then show you I hope, *some* if not *all* of my little treasures. They are well worth such a journey. I have written you a long letter, my dear friend, but I know that it will interest you. I rejoice in my dear E Fishers happiness & hope it may continue many years. My love to all kind friends & best wishes for them all. L & E offer to you & Mr G their respectful & affectionate remembrance. I heard from Mrs B Bordley on Saturday. Mr B had gone to Savannah for five or six months, Mrs B & her daughters were with her Mama at Mrs Loverings near Balt[imore]. They were well. Mrs B is a charming woman I think. I hope to hear soon again from you my dear friend, & of all our mutual friends. Where is dear Caroline [Calvert] Morris. My best regards to Mr G.

My love & kindest wishes for my dearest friend ever most truly & faithfully yours

E P Lewis

Audley April 5th. 1844

My Dearest Elizabeth,

Your kind affectionate & most welcome letter of March 28th. I received yesterday, & I hasten to thank you for it, & to give you some information relative to my dear afflicted niece. I received a letter from Martha—(poor Mecs eldest daughter) who, with her sisters & youngest Brother, reside with their Grandmother; the eldest Son is at school at Buffalo. Martha was with her poor Aunt on board the Princeton, & by her presence of mind saved her poor Aunts life, or *reason* by concealing her knowledge of the dreadful effect on Captn. K, until they returned to W[ashington]n & were sustained by poor Brits Mother & Brother.

Captn. K left them at one end of the ship where they were all sitting together, from a sense of duty as head of the Bureau of construction, to see the Gun fired off. When the explosion took place, she inquired for Captn. K, but had no idea that he had suffer'd, she was told that he was with Mr Upshur who was badly wounded.[1] She asked several of the officers to show her where

---

1. On February 28, 1844, a large party of dignitaries, including the president and members of the cabinet and Congress, visited the *Princeton*, the first steam-propeller-driven battleship; among its guns was the largest in the fleet. Fired in demonstration, the gun exploded: the dead and wounded littered the deck—"killed and shockingly mutilated." Among the casualties were Captain Beverly Kennon (1793–1844), chief of the Bureau of Construction and the husband of Martha Peter's daughter Britannia Wellington Peter (1815–1911), and Abel Parker Upshur (1791–1844), the secretary of state. Sidney Fisher, 159.

Captn. K was, & permit her to go to him—but they assured her that she could not see him. At last Miss Claiborne (Captn. K's sister in law, rushed in, exclaiming "Brit Captn K. is wounded". She was near fainting, & insisted on going to him. Martha pacified her & went to make inquiries. She heard an officer say "Captn. K never breathed." Captn. Shubrick[2] assured Brit that he was slightly wounded, & advised her to go home immediately & prepare to receive him—that he could not then leave Mr Upshur, & no one could be permitted to go where they were except the necessary attendants. This quieted her fears, & she returned to her house where her Mother was waiting with her infant. Brit said, "Mother they say that Captn. K is hurt, & I must fix his room to receive him" she went up stairs, & Martha then told my Sister "Poor Aunt Brit does not know it, but Uncle K is dead". Immediately they sent to G Town for Wash[ingto]n Peter who broke the dreadful intelligence as gently as he could. The effect on her was most distressing indeed, she kept her Bed several days & her grief was almost too much to bear. She insisted on knowing all the particulars, & Wash[ingto]n told her every thing. Captn. K's Brother arrived & her first interview with him was most affecting. She was most eloquent in her grief, & in doing justice to her devoted & noble hearted husband, & said she never would forget how tender & devoted to her was the expression of his countenance when he left her to see the gun fired, saying "he would return immediately". She is now with her fatherless Babe with her Mother, the dear Boys & Miss C have gone to Richmond with their Uncle Dr K who is their guardian.

Martha writes me yesterday "Poor Aunt Brit is pretty well, of course very much distressed, but I think bears her affliction very well. She is now comfortably fixed at home. The Baby is the most lovely child I ever saw, & very lively & intelligent. On the 28th. March, being the day *one month* on which its poor Father was killed, Aunt Brit wished to have it christen'd, Mr Butler[3] came up

---

2. William Branford Shubrick (1790–1874), a distinguished naval officer, was chief of the Bureau of Provisions and Clothing.
3. Clement Moore Butler (1810–1890) was at this time rector of St. John's Church, Georgetown; a distinguished Episcopal clergyman, he delivered obituary addresses on important occasions at the White House, the Senate, and the House of Representatives; he later served as rector of Trinity Church in Washington. Mary Mitchell, *A Short History of St. John's Church, Georgetown, from 1792 to 1968* (Washington, D.C., 1968), 4, 7–8; "Address Delivered by Rev. Clement M. Butler, at the President's mansion, on the occasion of the funeral of Abel P. Upshur . . . " (Washington, D.C., 1844); "The Road to Rome" (Alexandria, 1860).

in the eveng., & christen'd it "Martha Custis."[4] Aunt Brit was very much distressed. The Baby wore around her neck tied with a white ribbon, a small gold heart filled with its Fathers hair, it was a present from him a few days before his death." A happier family I never knew than they were—& in one moment how dreadful the reverse. I only knew Captn. K of the sufferers. I know not of Captn. Ss[5] intentions except from newspapers. I have just copied your kind condolence to them. They will appreciate it most truly.

My darlings are doing well. My girls in La. are most happy in having the Revd Mr Fay[6] & his wife (a daughter of Bishop Hopkins[7]) as their Instructors, & improve to the great joy of their Mother, astonishingly in all good, useful, & elegant acquirements. My Boys (*10*) are all doing well. Mr Conrad is well & writes me *very* interesting letters. He will return this Summer.

I am most happy to hear of so many dear & well remember'd friends—& wish I could see them all again. Can not you & Mr G visit us this Summer. We should rejoice to see you. My love & kindest wishes to all my friends. Our affecte regards & respects to you & my friend Mr G. Ever most truly your devoted friend

E P L

Excuse this hurried scrawl. The post will not go down again until next Tuesday & I did not wish to wait so long.

———————

Audley August [9?] 1844

My Dearest Elizabeth,

You have no doubt been surprised at not hearing from me at New Port, as I *promised* that you should, & will be still more sur-

---

4. Martha Custis Kennon (1843–1886) was to marry her cousin, Dr. Armistead Peter. Genealogical files, Tudor Place.
5. Captain Robert F. Stockton (1795–1866), the commander of the *Princeton*, was exonerated of blame for the accident by a court of inquiry. Later in his naval career, Stockton was a leader of the California independence movement.
6. Charles Fay came to the Bayou Goula area as an Episcopal missionary in 1844; by 1846 he was holding services in New Orleans. Hodding Carter and Betty Werlein Carter, *So Great a Good: A History of the Episcopal Church in Louisiana and of Christ Church Cathedral, 1805–1955* (Sewanee, Tenn., 1955), 62–63, 81.
7. John Henry Hopkins (1792–1868) was the first Episcopal bishop of Vermont.

prised to find me at Audley without having seen me in Phila[del-phia]. In fact, my time was so entirely occupied at New Port, & I was in so constant a bustle & confusion, that I had not time to write more than once to my Son. I promised to inform you about the company accommodations &c. We had good rooms & *moderate* fare, but I found a host of kind affectionate friends, & the air so fine & so bracing that I recover'd the *use of my limbs*, nearly lost before I went there, & I could walk more than a mile & go up to the 3rd. story of the Ocean House without feeling fatigued. We were four days in N.Y on our way to New Port. C had business to transact there, & I had four teeth drawn for my darling Charley, & a small pebble which had healed up in his forehead & caused an eruption on the skin, cut out by a Surgeon. My precious boy bore both operations remarkably well. As we returned through N.Y. he had two more teeth drawn, & two plugged. I fear his teeth will never be good, the first were so injured by acids when he was ill in La. that they decay almost as soon as they are well through the gums. The loss of his decay'd teeth, & the pebble have improved his health & appearance, & could he have staid longer at New Port he would have been still more robust. He bathed only three times, his Father was too unwell from a bad cold to admit of his bathing all the time—& C would not go in with any other. Lewis went in once, but it alarmed him very much, & cold bathing did not agree with him at all. I did not bathe but the *air* of New Port, the most bracing & delightful I ever felt, improved me very much. I wish we could have remained longer, but C was obliged to return to La., & I was too anxious about my darling Parke, & felt too responsible in regard to my orphan Boys, to remain without their Father.

It appears like a delightful dream my short residence at N.P. Years have past since I was so kindly cherished & loved as I found myself there. Mrs & Miss Grant, & Miss Perkins[8] of Boston, Mr, Mrs, & Miss Abbott Lawrence,[9] Mrs & Miss C Kuhn,[10] & Mrs Ann K Williams of Phi[ladelphi]a, Mrs Oliver & her family of Balt[imor]e & many before this visit, *strangers*, vied with each other in showing me affection & kindness. My friend & favorite,

---

8. Perhaps the daughter of Thomas H. Perkins (1764–1854), a wealthy merchant and philanthropist.
9. Abbott Lawrence (1792–1855), wealthy Boston merchant, manufacturer, diplomat, and philanthropist, was married to Katherine Bigelow; they had seven children, including two daughters.
10. The Kuhns were a prominent Philadelphia family.

Mr Frank Gray of Boston, came to see me & staid four days with me. G[eorge] Calvert his wife & her Sisters[11] Mr & Mrs Derby, the charming Mrs Middletons, Senior & Junior.[12] My poor friend Patty [Hare] walked to see me, it was sad to see her look so badly, but she is much better they say than she was. John Powell came several times, but I only saw his wife in the street.[13] She did not visit me, nor did Mrs Clark Hare.[14] I had hoped to have remained in Phi[ladelphi]a two or three days, but C was so much hurried we did not stop a moment from one steamboat to the other. We left N.Y. on Thursday & arrived here this day week. I found my Children & Grandchildren here, well, but I have not been well myself since I left N.Y.

Do write soon to me, present love & kind wishes to all my friends & accept for Mr G & yourself our best love & kindest wishes. Ever most truly & faithfully yr friend

E P Lewis

———————————— ❦ ————————————

[Audley] Decr. 10th. 1844

My Dearest Elizabeth,

As Esther expects sometime this week, to visit her Father at Philad[elphi]a I with pleasure take the opportunity to thank you for your most welcome & much valued letter of Novr. 18th. & to send you a specimen of my youngest Granddaughter's handy work, a Bag sent me after my return from N. Port. I wish it was in *colors*, but you will not value it the less that it is in black & lead color. She is only 10 years old & the work (except the balls & the

11. Nelly's cousin, George Henry Calvert, a well-known poet and essayist, had settled in Newport in 1843; his wife was Elizabeth Steuart (1802–1897); her sisters were Sophia Steuart Delprat (b. 1796) and Rebecca Steuart Thorndike (b. 1801). *Maryland Genealogies*, 1:161, 2:59.
12. Probably Mary Helen Hering Middleton, the wife of a wealthy South Carolina planter, Henry Middleton (1770–1846), and one of her daughters-in-law. Cheves, "Middleton," 245–46.
13. John Hare Powel (1786–1856) was the brother of Martha and Charles Willing Hare; he was adopted by his aunt Elizabeth Powel and her husband Samuel Powel and assumed their name. His wife was Julia DeVeaux of South Carolina.
14. Esther Binney Hare was the wife of John Innes Clark Hare (1816–1905), a Philadelphia judge.

making up which her Mother did) it is entirely her work, & you will acknowledge that she is a very neat needle woman. The eldest has made a pair of mats for you, for your table, of shades of blue, but Govr. Johnson has them in charge, & I fear I cannot get them in time to send by Esther, but if her Brother should return for her, I hope to have them to send by him. The youngest will work a watch case for Mr G when the days are longer.

At present they are at school to the Revnd. Mr Fay, & his excellent & most accomplished wife, (the Daughter of Bishop Hopkins of Vermont) & are so closely occupied in their various studies, English, French, Music, & drawing, that they have little time for fancy work. My Darling Child is most happy in seeing them improving so rapidly, & in the improvement of her youngest Son under her own care, & the eldest at the George Town College—& she blesses as I do, the Almighty hand which has temper'd her otherwise most painful lot in life, by these abundant mercies. Mr Fay is their Pastor, & after so many years without religious services, they have church now & the communion service, & an admirable school only two miles from them. If Mr Fay remains with them, I do not expect to see my darlings next Summer, but if they continue well, my Daughter will prefer keeping them a year or two longer with Mrs Fay, as they will then be near *her*, rather than bring them to Miss Mercers school,[15] in Virginia, which is a days journey from Audley. If she could be permitted herself to pass two years with her friends here, & visit all our dear friends at the North, it would renew her youth. I trust that I shall have it in my power to visit my dear friends in Phi[ladel-phi]a, to see you all once more, altho as well as most persons of my age, I cannot expect to live long, & I really *long* to see & converse again with all the dear & kind friends of my youth, & happiest years.

What a pleasure I should have in visiting all those places where my revered Grandparents were in winter quarters during

---

15. Margaret Mercer (1791–1846), daughter of John Francis Mercer, onetime governor of Maryland, reduced herself to relative poverty by freeing the family slaves on her father's death. She then began teaching school, eventually opening a girls' boarding school at Belmont, a farm near Leesburg, Virginia, which became known for its academic standards and religious and moral tone. Before her death of tuberculosis, she wrote two influential books on education, *Popular Lectures on Ethics or Moral Obligations for the Use of Schools* (1837) and *Studies for Bible Classes* (1840). Her sister-in-law took over the school after her death.

the Revolution. I have always wished to do so, & do you know that I would willingly cross the Ocean too, & even visit *India* if I could. What think you of a *Rover* of 65—with a disease of the heart, affection of the liver, & rheumatism, & *deaf too*, I assure you, in one ear. What say you to a voyage to *Palestine* by way of experiment. Were it not for my Motherless Boys & want of adequate *funds*, I really should be very much tempted to go forth upon my pilgrimage.

I do not expect to keep my darlings long. Their Father will probably take them from me next winter. Lolen & I could not avoid smiling at your idea of the "sweet tones of my young ones." If you had our *seven* Boys in your house, all trying which could make *most noise*, you would hear too much *without your tube* for your comfort.

I thank you much dearest friend for your affecte & *always* most interesting letters, they are ever most welcome. Our united loves & every kind wish for you & Mr G—dear E Mifflin & love & kind wishes to dear Patty my dear M Nixon & her family Mrs Jackson & all friends, & believe me as truly as sincerely affectely your friend as in our early & happiest years

Ever yrs
E P L

———————————————— ❦ ————————————————

Audley near Berryville Clarke C[ount]y

April 3rd. [1846]

My ever dear Elizabeth,

Your dear kind letter of March 18th. gave me very great pleasure, as all your letters have *ever done*, & *ever will* do. The only reason of my long silence was the fear of giving you trouble, you complained of headache from writing, & therefore I did not wish to cause you any ache that I could avoid. In truth, my Dear friend, you never wrote more beautifully than you do at present, either as regards composition or penmanship, & it is most refreshing to my old eyes to recognise the hand writing of a beloved friend of the *olden times*. I wish I could charm away those headaches entirely. I must recommend my infallible remedy, I am often attacked with headache, bilious, rheumatic, or nervous, & for all, my remedy is, a *double dose* of Seidlitz powders. It has never failed to relieve me, & I have used no other remedy for more than twenty years.

I intended writing to you on my 67th. Birthday, the 31st. of March, but I had determined, if possible, to finish a piece of worsted work for my Darling little Lewis Conrad on that day, & after working diligently until candlelight I failed to accomplish my object. I however did finish it on the 2nd. of April, just six weeks after I commenced it. I am now about commencing another piece, I have still nine to work if my life & my eyes admit of it. Do you ever indulge in that fascinating work. I work from breakfast until candlelight, & then read as long as I can keep my eyes open, rise before the Sun & read or work until breakfast. I have no time for *walking* & happily exercise is not *essential* to my existence— altho a long rough ride in the Stage every summer is certainly beneficial. A visit to my dear old friends makes me forget the lapse of time, & renews my youthful *feelings* at all events. I wish it may be in my power to see them this summer. Dear Patty I have often thought of her kindness in walking to see me at Newport, with her weak health. She ever has my kindest wishes for health & happiness, & my sincere love.

I trust, dear friend, that you & Mr G will have no return of indisposition. To dear Mrs Deas E Fisher & all our old intimates my best love & kindest wishes. I should like much to see Mrs Sullivan, she is a charming woman & was one of my kindest friends in Boston, & her excellent Husband. I had a great regard for Mrs Lloyd too, whom I have known since 1790. I was then *eleven*, & she was a young Lady in company, *at least 16*. Hannah Breck, but *Hannah* is now *Anna*—is it not strange to be ashamed of ones *age & name*.[16] She is a most amiable woman nevertheless, & I love her as I used to do. Dear Mrs Jackson, Maria Nixon, E Mifflin, the McCalls, & a host of other well remember'd & dear friends. My *heart* can never be *cold* to any of them, however frosty my "[bow?]" may be.

My Darling Parke & her family are well, & her dear children improving always. Her two Daughters lately sent me each a beautiful drawing in pencil. They improve fast in french & music, & in all useful & ornamental pursuits, & her eldest son stands well at

---

16. Hannah Breck Lloyd, the sister of wealthy Philadelphia merchant Samuel Breck, married James Lloyd, Boston merchant and U.S. senator from Massachusetts. Breck, 18.

the College in G Town. My Darling little Conrads are well & happy in New Orleans, learning french as well as English with an excellent Tutor. Mr C will bring them to me early this Summer, & I *hope* my Darling Parke & her children will be permitted to come again. She has been detained there 14 years. Mrs Williams is very kind in writing to me, she is one of the most amiable & happy tempers I have known. Sweet Susan Daingerfield is well, with her Father in Alex[andri]a. I have informed her of your kind inquiry.

Lolen & Esther expect to pay a visit to the D[istric]t next week. All are well here but E still looks delicate. She had a confinement of two months in the winter. And now Dearest E I will conclude with our united loves & respects for you & Mr G. May God bless & prolong your lives. Ever most truly & faithfully yours

E P L

———————————— ❦ ————————————

Audley March 28th. 1847

My Dearest Elizabeth,

Your kind & welcome letter of Decr. 30th., has been very long unanswer'd; I have had many sources of anxiety, & I always thought "when this is happily over, I will then write to my true & dear friend E B." But another & another care succeeded, & at last I have determined to delay no longer since I have *some* pleasant information to give you. My Darling Parke is well & has her youngest Son with her, 10 years old, very attentive to his studies, active, affecte, healthy, & a *great shot*. He killed 42 cedar Birds & a plover in one day. The eldest Son has arrived safely at the Carolina College & is studying hard, & hopes to do his Parents some credit. He left home with a bad cold & had a very fatiguing journey, but is now well & very much pleased with his situation at Columbia & has already acquired some very kind friends there. It is a very desirable situation for him, & therefore his devoted Mother is reconciled to his absence.

Our precious Granddaughters are well & perfectly happy & contented at Belmont, improving in all their studies; I am certain they could not be in better hands than Mrs Mercers & her assistants. They have had bad colds, & so has almost every one I believe, but have been most kindly & judiciously treated & are now well again. Sissy [Isabella Butler] is 15. My Darling child altho anxious & happy to have them at Belmont, cannot avoid feeling all a Mothers anxieties about them. She says "no words can tell how anxious I am"—so *I* felt for *her* when at school in Phi[ladelphi]a. I fear that my child will not be able to leave home this summer, B's crop did not turn out so well as he expected, & he dreads what he considers *unnecessary* expence, visiting young Daughters & a Mother 68 years old, besides other dear friends. [President James K.] Polk offer'd B a Colonelcy of Dragoons, but had previously promised him a Brigadiers command, & he has almost decided not to accept.[17]

My own darlings Charley & Lewis Conrad paid a visit of several weeks to their relatives in Attacapas, where they were most cordially welcomed as the "sweetest & finest Boys ever seen there," (as poor Norah writes me). I did not receive a letter for almost two months, & I was very very anxious & unhappy about them. N writes Feby. 21st. that they are perfectly well & happy & their Father very proud of them. They will come to us early I hope this summer. L, E & their Boys are well. Wassy (18) is at the Virg[ini]a Military Institute, at Lexington, well & doing well. His Parents expect to visit him this Summer. L E & 3 Boys will pay a visit soon to the Potomac for two or 3 weeks.

I am busily engaged in worsted work, a screen with 3 figures & very rich colours on canvas, in single or Tapestry stitch, for my granddaughter Caroline. It is very tedious but I shall not leave it until completed. I shall work a Piano cover for the eldest, Isabella. I had a dozen pieces to work, & the cover will be only the *sixth*. I never go abroad except to church. See the occupations of a *Grandmother* my dearest E.

Parke begs me to offer kindest love & respects to you & Mr G. Love to E Mifflin & Mrs P McCall.[18] My love & best wishes to all my dear & kind friends. L & E unite their affecte respects to you & Mr G. Dear Robt. [E. Lee] is with Gen'l [Winfield] Scott & I trust will escape all evil. Our fears & anxieties are all for the noble Genl [Zachary] Taylor & his brave little band. May the

17. Butler accepted the colonelcy and commanded the 3rd. Dragoons which saw action in the Rio Grande Valley during the Mexican War. Butler Family Papers, Historic New Orleans Collection.
18. Jane Mercer, the niece of schoolmistress Margaret Mercer, in 1846 married Peter McCall, a Philadelphia attorney who was the nephew of James Gibson. McCall, 36–39.

Almighty be their shield. A halter for Polk & a scourge for Scott if Taylor is not safe. With these *truly just* if not *christian* wishes I am ever yours most truly & affectely

E P L

------------------------------ ❦ ------------------------------

Audley Oct 3rd. 1847

My Dearest Elizabeth,

I have much to thank you for in your two most excellent, kind & welcome letters of the 13th. & 28th. of Septr. I have known your faithful friendship so many years, that even before I received your precious assurances of sympathy, I was certain of your participation in my grief, & kind Mr G's also.

I ought to have written immediately on the receipt of the first letter, but I was not quite well & very anxious about my Darling Parke. Her neighbourhood & negroes have been very sickly this summer, & even dear little Lawrence (the only child with her, in his eleventh year) had been slightly indisposed. Her last letter, altho sadden'd by the knowledge of her dear Brothers death, assured me of her own health, the convalescence of her valued neighbours, & that *all* were doing well around her. The yellow fever has been at two villages near her, but the cases easily managed did not excite any apprehension, & it never spreads in the country. I trust that *my only one* will be preserved in health for her dear childrens sakes. Her daughters are with Mrs Mercer where every care & kindness is extended to them, & I trust that their dear Mother will be with them next Summer. Their eldest Brother is doing well in South Carolina where Col Preston,[19] Pres[iden]t of Columbia College is a kind Paternal friend, & most attentive guardian. I hope he will do honor to his Parents & friends.

The death of my Darling Son after an illness of only two weeks, is a shock to all who knew him as well as to him immediate family, for he was universally respected & beloved by all classes in our community, & we have received many tributes to

---

19. William Campbell Preston (1794–1860), lawyer, classical scholar, and states-rights politician, was elected president of South Carolina College in 1845.

his exalted worth, very soothing to our wounded feelings. None was ever more patient, than he continued to be throughout his illness, painful as it was, & he submitted to every remedy without a murmur. He knew the importance of his life to his helpless family, his six sons, but he submitted to the will of his Almighty Father & was enabled to say "Thy will be done," & died as gently as an Infant sinks to rest—not a struggle, & his countenance after death, as calm as peaceful as in sleep. It is the *belief* of his eternal happiness, his reunion with my other Angels in Heaven, that reconciles me to his loss my Beloved Friend.

But anxious I must be for the dear children whose loss can *never* be repaired. The example of such a Father, at an age when he was *all important* to them, they are too young to appreciate, except the eldest, G W, who feels deeply *all he has lost*, but has the consoling recollection that his Father when leaving him at the Military Institute not four weeks before his death, said to him with tears "My Son you are all that I could wish you to be." We find it yet difficult to realize that one in apparently robust health in the midst of his usefulness should be so suddenly called from us, but it is His Will "who gave & hath taken away". E is well, & bears her loss with fortitude. My Sister & Niece (Mrs Lee) are with us at present.

Accept for yourself & Mr G our love & every kind wish. As ever yours most truly & affectely

E P L

I have enclosed your last kind letter to my dear Parke.

To Dear & much respected Mrs Bradford[20] & *all* my kind friends much love & kind wishes.

——————————— ❦ ———————————

Decr. 17th. 1848

My Dearest Elizabeth,

I was exceedingly rejoiced to see your dear hand writing. Your excellent affectionate letter of Novr 27th. most truly do I

---

20. Susan Vergereau Boudinot Bradford (d. 1855) was the daughter of Elias Boudinot of New Jersey and the widow of William Bradford (1755–1795), George Washington's attorney general in 1794. GWD, 6:174; Simpson.

thank you for your kind offer to send me a drawing on which you were employ'd on your 70th. Birthday. If not too great a sacrifice on the part of my ever kind & valued friend Mr Gibson, I will accept it & treasure it for both your sakes—as well as for the resemblance to the best of men, our venerated & dear Bishop White. I shall rejoice to see your *handy work* again, my Beloved friend, I thought you had discontinued that agreeable accomplishment. But now, since you have *recommenced*, persevere as long as it is not injurious to your eyesight.

I am at work on a screen for my darling Conrad Lewis, nine years old—it is a pattern his dear Father gave me, & I promised to work it for this dear Boy who resembles his Father I think. It represents "a Spanish Boy on a Donkey". Fortunately my patience cannot be exhausted on embroidery. This is on silk canvas with zephyr yarn. I commenced it on the 1st. Decr. One of the hind legs is badly drawn in the pattern, & I have been trying to rectify the defect by my work. You may judge of my perseverance by the fact, that I have worked & picked out that leg, *five times*. Late last evening I completed the leg as well as I can make it, tho' not equal to my wishes. Every Winter I work a large piece for one of my Grandchildren. I wish I could show them to you. I am very anxious to paint again on rice paper, but until I complete my keep sake pieces for my Grand children, I do not like to commence painting.

I live in my own room except at meals, seldom go out of the front door—work until candle light, & read as long as I can keep my eyes open. I rise always before the Sun & read my prayer Book & Bible until breakfast is ready. Is not *this* a *regular life.* Fortunately I can live without much exercise. In the summer I go down in the mail Stage, & return in August, & this fatigues me less than younger persons more accustom'd to exercise. I had letters last night from my dear Parke, my precious Boys in N.O—& dear Isabel at Belmont. All well & happy. I trust that I shall see them all in the Summer well, & doing well.

I shall hope to go to the D[istric]t in April, & to see then our truly great & good Pres[iden]t. I look upon his election as a peculiar mercy from the Giver of all good. Gen'l Taylor will be the "Regenerator of his Country." He is to me "the light of other days," He is actuated by the same noble principles, the same devoted Patriotism that distinguished The Father of his Country—& he will walk in *his* steps.

I rejoice that George Morris[21] is so fine a young man. Dear Anna Murray is a most amiable woman & she has married a very fine young man, a *gentleman* in character, appearance, & manners, & highly respected in the Navy. His Mother & Sisters are fine women & truly excellent. They received Anna as a Daughter & Sister, & she writes me, that, "she has realised her most sanguine anticipations of happiness." Julia Morris is a sweet little Girl & reminds me very much of our dear Caroline.

I regret much the continued state of suffering that our poor friend Miss Hare experiences. She has my sincere love & kindest wishes. My kind friend E Fisher too has a melancholy task, altho of great interest to her feelings. They have ever been devoted Sisters. Is poor Mrs Harrison[22] pious, has she that light from above which can make even loss of sight endurable. To me it would be the greatest of all privations. I become more deaf I think every year, & sometimes at Church I can scarcely hear at all. Have you ever tried "Moreheads magnetic machine". It is said to be a remedy for many evils, & deafness is one of them.

E unites with me in much love for you, & kind regards to Mr G. My love to your Nieces & all kind friends. May God bless you all.

Your truly attached friend
E P L

————————— ❦ —————————

Audley July 27th. 1850

Ever dearest & truest Friend,

Such you have been to me for nearly sixty years, age & infirmity cannot change you, & even to Judge from your letters & *hand writing* you have not changed in any thing. Your dear letter is most soothing & gratifying to me, you & Mr G appreciated my lamented friend, our noble & *truly* great President as he de-

---

21. George Calvert Morris (1828–1882), a lawyer, was the son of Nelly's cousin, Caroline Calvert, and Thomas Willing Morris; his sister was Julia Meta Morris (1830–1857). John W. Jordan, ed. *Colonial and Revolutionary Families of Pennsylvania*, 3 vols. (Baltimore, 1978), 1:72.

22. Mrs. George Harrison was the elder sister of Elizabeth Powel Francis Fisher. Joshua Francis Fisher, *Recollections of Joshua Francis Fisher, Written in 1864*, arranged by Sophia Cadwalader (Boston, 1929), vii-viii.

served.[23] It was a privilege to know him in his domestic relations, but to *those*, to "know him no more" adds to our regrets. He is ever present to me, that noble benevolent countenance, the most expressive I have ever seen, ever beaming with kind feeling, with noblest feelings & principles, cannot be forgotten. We were unworthy of him, & the Almighty has removed him from a path strewed with thorns, from outrage & insult never before heaped on a President, & one too, the *only one worthy* to be the successor of Washington, to everlasting happiness in Heaven. I believe *now*, many *feel* his loss, who have embitter'd his Administration, the Nation *generally* I believe do feel as they ought, but think of those in Congress, even [Henry] *Clay*, who in the last days of his life, heaped on his pure name such mean & unfounded abuse, who— from mortified ambition hated one they could not imitate, & *now* pretend to *shed tears*, base crocodiles they are, & ever will be in my eyes. I was much pleased with the speeches in Congress on the sad occasion. Mr Conrad has promised to send me a pamphlet of all the proceedings, & I will try to procure a copy for you.

His poor Wife[24] & family have my deepest sympathy. No one has ever presided at the W House, so graceful, so charming as Mrs Bliss,[25] Mrs Wood[26] I love dearly, her Father whom she resembles in heart & in countenance, told me before I saw her, "I am sure you will love Ann." The poor Son[27] was far away in La. poor fellow it was a dreadful shock to him. Dr Wood, Col Bliss, & his Brother Col Taylor,[28] were all worthy of his love & to *all* his loss is irreparable.

You appear my friend not to be aware of my having had an attack of Paralysis. During the winter I suffer'd great inconvenience from weakness in my hips, all my joints were loose, & when I moved in bed, it was like the rattling of a *bag of bones*, when I walked I felt like falling to pieces. At last I could not get

---

23. Zachary Taylor died 9 July 1850.
24. Zachary Taylor (1784–1850) married Margaret Mackall Smith (1787–1852), a member of a prominent Maryland family, in 1810.
25. Taylor's youngest daughter, Mary Elizabeth, married his aide, Col. William Wallace Smith Bliss, in 1848. The couple lived at the White House with the Taylors. Elbert B. Smith, *The Presidencies of Zachary Taylor and Millard Fillmore* (Lawrence, Kans., 1988), 66–67.
26. Taylor's eldest daughter, Ann Mackall, married Robert Crooke Wood (1799–1869), an army surgeon. Smith, 67.
27. Richard Taylor (1826–1879) managed the Taylor plantations; he became a Confederate general.
28. Col. Joseph Pannill Taylor (c. 1796–1864) was a career military officer.

into a carriage, or walk out of doors. A kind friend procured me Mrs Betts supporter hoping it might restore me, but before I could try it, I lost the use of my left side from paralysis. My face was drawn on one side so that I could scarcely speak, & the Dr dreaded a still more serious attack.

For the first time in *sickness*, I was depressed, & being utterly helpless, I pray'd for death—rather than such dependence & uselessness. I required 2 women to assist me, I could not rise from my bed or my chair, or turn in my bed, could not comb my head or cut up my food, & the pain I suffered in lying down made me dread the night. My good Pastor Mr Peterkin,[29] a saint in countenance & in character, & my former Pastor Mr Wilmer pray'd for me, visited me, wrote me the most consoling letters, & I felt convinced that I ought to feel *grateful* to God for his mercy in sparing my *mind* & my *right* hand. I felt that great as was my trial I had often *deserved greater*, & that it might have been far worse. My face was restored & my voice, I could write to my children & friends altho it was very fatiguing as I could not hold my paper with my left hand. Esther was very attentive & kind to me, & my neighbours evinced unwearied sympathy & kindness. My sight was as good as ever I could read books & the dear kind letters of my absent children & friends, I bowed in submission to the will of God, I had still much to live for, & I resolved to do all the Dr prescribed for me. He said that my age & my size were against me, but he hoped I might recover partially. Moreheads Galvanic machine, the flesh brush, & divers medicines, have enabled me to use my hand, to work for my Darlings, & *now I walk alone*, but like a child learning to walk—very unsteady, I cannot go up & down steps, I cannot get into a carriage, or turn in my bed, or comb my hair without assistance but I can cut up my food, & do much I despair'd of ever doing again. My limb still swells very much. At my age it is consider'd a wonderful amendment.

My Darling Parke has suffer'd much on my account, but she cannot come to me this Summer. They are all well. My Darlings C & L Conrad have just left me, they have not been well this Spring & I am still anxious about them. All E's Boys are well. May God bless you & Mr G.

Ever most truly & affectely yours
E P L

---

29. Joshua Peterkin, D.D., (1814–1892) was rector in Berryville 1848–1851. *Journal of the Ninety-Seventh Annual Council of the Protestant Episcopal Church in Virginia held in Epiphany Church, Danville, on 18th, 19th, 20th, and 21st of May, 1892* (Richmond, 1892), 97.

Audley Decr. 1st. 1850

My Dearest Elizabeth,

Your most dear & precious letter of Augt. 12th. has been long unacknowledged, but has been my constant companion. In my left pocket with one from my absent darling child, & one from my precious Boys in Washington, often perused with heartfelt pleasure, but [for] some cause or other I have not until now been able to answer it. Altho I can use my hand, & walk in the house with a cane; yet I am far from being restored to my usual *comforts*. I am still too dependent, too helpless to be able to *enjoy* life, altho' most grateful to the Father of Mercies that I *am as I am*—able to read & work, [to] help myself in some trifling respects. The weeks pass rapidly, but I can do very little in them profitable to others, or to myself. This beautiful Autumn I cannot participate in, I cannot go out of the house or in a carriage; I stand at the door, & seeing the green wheat, the beautiful mountains, inhale the sweet air, but my limbs are weak & I despair now of ever recovering entirely.

My only child & hers are far from me, I cannot feel otherwise than anxious about them. It is impossible for me to go to *them*, I fear they will never be permitted to visit me. B will always have some excuse. If she is not permitted to come *next Summer* we may never meet again. *Before* the warm season I cannot wish her to come, the risk would be too great for one accustom'd to that climate for so many winters. They were all well at the date of her last letter, B's Sister Mrs Donelson,[30] my childs best friend in *that* family, had just died at Nashville, stricken with Paralysis, at once insensible, & in 3 days closed her life. How very common that disease has become. Mrs D is deeply regretted by many friends.

My precious Boys reside with their Father in Washington very happy & with every comfort. He is devoted to them, & they are much pleased with their school. My precious Lewis is subject to attacks of catarrhal fever & hoarse cough which make me always anxious about him. My Beloved friend, you cannot conceive the aching anxious feelings of a Parents heart, especially when at a *distance*, & with the impossibility of *going* to a sick & suffering child. When I had perfect use of my limbs, distance,

---

30. Eliza Eleanor Butler (1789–1850) married Rachel Jackson's nephew, Captain John Donelson IV, in 1823. Pauline W. Burke, *Emily Donelson of Tennessee*, vol. 1 (Richmond, 1941), 98–99.

fatigue, difficulties were *nothing* to me, I had energy for *all*, but *now*, I am incapable of exertion—*useless*.

E & her dear children are well & happy. Since I last wrote to you, I had the sad satisfaction of receiving a letter commenced but *unfinished*, which Col Bliss found among the papers of my lamented revered friend Gen'l Taylor. He twice sent me a message that "he was writing to me", but his time was so constantly occupied that he had very little leisure for his friends. The letter was commenced on the 4th. of March. He described his journey to Richmond to lay the corner stone of the Monument to Washington—His kind feeling for me when my Brother pointed out "Woodlawn" in the distance—he could but think of the happy years I had passed there surrounded by my family, & friends—his hope to go at no distant day to visit Mt Vn. & Woodlawn with some one who has known those places & their owners in our palmy days, & could describe all to him, & point." It was a long letter, closely written, most kind & excellent & I need not say, how beyond measure it is precious to me. How much I regret that he could not complete it. His honor'd Remains are safe with his Parents in their Tomb in Kentucky, his family now in Louisiana. "Does he *live*, as he deserves, with the "Father of his Country"— in the *hearts* of his Countrymen." I fear they are too fickle, too mad, too *unworthy*, the greater number of them, to *feel* as they ought, all *his* excellence, & *their* obligations. It is a pleasure to remember that he thought I resembled his *Mother*, & Dr W believed that he was much attached to me. I can never forget, or cease to love & honor the most noble of all except Washington.

You regret, dearest friend, that you have never seen me at *Audley*. Cannot you venture so far in the Spring. The journey by rail road is very easy to Charlestown Jefferson County, where safe carriages are to be had to bring you here, or if you prefer to continue in the cars to the "Depot Summit level"—nine miles from us, E's carriage would be sent for you with great pleasure, if you informed us what day you would be there. What a gratification it would be to us all to welcome you & Mr Gibson here—to see my earliest, & dearest, & *truest* friend again would almost renew my best & happiest days. I could show you the cup dear noble Zach gave me. He said, "that you may think of me when you drink your coffee", I have never required *any thing* to remind me of *him*—his letters, his *bust*, (Mrs T's Gift). I am sure we could be *mutually* happy in such a meeting. I *too* am *very deaf*, it is painful since all appear to *whisper* when they speak to me. & E would attend you & Mr G to see all that could gratify you near us.

My own dear & fondly remember'd friends, Maria Nixon, Mrs Fisher, Patty Hare, Mrs. Jackson, Mrs Deas, Mrs Palmer, & others, how truly happy I should be to see them all again. They live in my memory as if we had never been separated. Dear E Mifflin & all her family—& is dear Mrs Bradford still alive. Neither time or Paralysis can destroy my love for those so dear to me in my days of happiness. When *all* was *bright*. I beg you to assure them all of my affecte remembrance. Our united loves & kindest wishes for you & dear Mr G. Mr & Mrs McCall & Mr Gs family.

Ever most truly & unchangeable Your affecte friend
E P Lewis

————————————❧————————————

Audley Janry 21st. 1851

My Beloved friend,

When I refer to the date of your last most affectionate & welcome letter, Decr. 12th. I can scarcely realise the passage of time. I have so frequently been on the point of commencing a letter to you, & some evil influence has prevented the accomplishment of my wish, to thank you for this new proof of an affection which in so many years has never varied, has been proved by so many kind acts to me & *all mine* to those beloved ones so long removed from all earthly care & kindness. Did I not with *my whole heart return* that faithful devoted friendship, altho' I never had opportunities to *prove* it by acts of kindness as *you*, my dearest Elizabeth had, yet it has never been less devoted than your own, & my gratitude will be as glowing, as imperishable as my affection. How often I have lamented that my lot in life was so far removed from yours, & that adverse circumstances divided us so many years.

Memory still restores to me the dear scenes of our youth, Union Street where I have passed so many happy hours, where the *Sun always appears to shine* as it did in our hearts in those happy days. Your dear rever'd Father, & Mother, dear Elizabeth Allen & all our intimates. All have passed away. Before I went with my Darling Parke to place her at school, I dream'd continually of being in Phi[ladelphi]a & trying to reach Union Street to see my dear Betsey Bordley, but I never could accomplish getting to your house. What a happy fortnight I passed in Phi[ladel-phi]a—almost constantly with you, I was at least 3 years younger for those two weeks. When at Woodlawn I could always recall those happy times, & all I loved & liked in that favorite City. Now, I scarcely know who are yet living of those I once called my friends. May I never have to mourn your loss, dearest friend, altho' I am persuaded that you will still go to happiness eternal when you resign the comforts of this life so full of the memory of good & kind deeds to your fellow mortals.

I often think of dear Mrs Powells expression in regard to our children, "They are careful comforts." My Darlings in La. & even my precious Boys in Washington, are sources of constant anxiety. When I could use all my limbs, could bear stage travelling at a moments notice, I could go to them if they required me; but since my attack of Paralysis *that comfort* no longer remains, I can walk about the house with a cane, can read, write, & work, but I cannot get in & out of bed without assistance. As a *nurse*, my "occupations's gone". This is to *me* a sore trial, I can only pray to God to preserve & bless my precious ones. They are at present well, my Boys very happy in their Fathers house, & he is devoted to them. Perhaps my darlings from La. may be permitted to visit me next Summer if I live. We all wish that you & Mr Gibson were well enough to visit Audley when the Summer makes travelling pleasant. I fear I can never cross the mountain again.

I cured myself some years since of Erysipelas by taking Seidlitz powders as a medicine, & rubbing the eruption with equal parts of bolted meal & flour—avoiding all *cold* applications, or exposure to cold air. Physicians are less partial to Seidlitz powders than I am, they have been almost my only remedy for *every* disease for nearly 30 years.

Dr Coxe writes Esther that poor Andrew Allen is dead. What was *his* disease by which he suffer'd so much. Did he leave any children. I have heard that his last wife was a charming woman. I am happy to hear that he was so pious. I trust he has obtained eternal happiness in Heaven. Do you remember the day he dined with my Daughters & self at your house. How ill he looked then, yet still how witty & agreeable he was. I recall him to my mind *now* when only 18—how handsome how healthy, how witty & how agreeable he was, more so than any one I ever knew. He gave me a beautiful ode on my 15th. Birthday & altho I committed it to the flames 57 years ago just before I was married, & never copied it it has never been forgotten. I can repeat it now perfectly. I never saw anyone who was so congenial in taste & disposition as Andrew Allen, & I certainly should have loved him, had I not been too happy & too gay to be susceptible. I have never seen any one in my life who possessed so much to excite admiration, at least according to my taste. What were his pursuits, & how did he use the brilliant talents he possessed. What was his character in domestic life.

Dear Elizabeth [Allen] what a charming girl she was. Ann was beautiful I always thought, but not so brilliant as dear Elizabeth. Is Mrs Hammond alive & did she leave children if dead. Do tell me all you know of the family. How like a magic lantern now appear to me the years & the persons I once knew so well. They were many of them *most precious*. I am very deaf, but the softest note of music I hear, but not a *word* of a song. But it is time for the mail.

Accept for yourself & Mr Gibson my affectionate attachment. Believe me ever your devoted friend

E P Lewis

Love to all friends.

[Audley March 16, 1851?][31]

My Dearest best friend, How much I thank you for your most affecte & interesting letter. The account of dear Andrews years of suffering, of which I knew nothing until your letter before the last received gave me the first intimation. I asked Dr C[oxe] & Marcellus[32] about him, they said nothing of his bad health. I am most anxious indeed to know the cause of his suffering, & how long he has been so great an Invalid. I was surprised to see him look so dark & badly when I dined with him at your house, but I supposed it only temporary. He objected so much to my *Turban* & "said I had never been so becomingly dressed as when the Schuylkill [River] was my mirror, & he my femme de chambre." How much I regret that I could not have seen him after his return from Palestine & Wales. What a *feast* to me to hear him converse & see his beautiful views. Your letter brought him so vividly before me, blessed with health & such charming spirits. I have never known

---

31. Fragment of a letter attached to a poem not reproduced here.
32. Esther Lewis's brother, Marcellus Coxe (1820–1850). *Descendants of Colonel Daniel Coxe.*

his equal in wit & conversation. I can scarcely realise the sad sad change, that he is now gone from us forever, altho' I bless the goodness of the Almighty that he was so well prepared for the change, & is now blessed forever in Heaven. Do write me all you know of him, however frivolous you may think the anecdotes of his youth. Have you any of his poetry, & do write me his "monumental prose"—& do tell me if he ever spoke of me at all, & what he said—of me & my dear Girls. I am not surprised that he was admired & caressed in Boston, there are those who could appreciate him there. Have you a likeness of him late in life, my *mind* contains a perfect likeness of his youth.

I am busily engaged in working keep sakes in chenille for *you*, M Nixon, Mrs Fisher, Mrs Palmer, Mrs Deas, Patty Hare, dear E Mifflin &c. I shall send them all to you to select your *favorite*, it must be the *best*, next to *you*, M Nixon, Mrs Palmer, B Fisher, Mrs Deas, dear Patty. I have worked 3 of them. I trust I may be spared to complete *all* before my 72nd. birthday. Is Mrs Bradford alive, she is one of my oldest friends. My true love ever to my ever dear kind friends.

I do not *forget* your welcome visit to my sweet home, but you could not recognise it *now*. I went to see it when last in Alex-[andri]a. All the trees, the hedge, the flower knot, my precious Agnes's Grove, the tall pine Washington, *all gone*, in front a few trees & vines, but sweet recollections "linger there still". If I live & recover to cross the mountains *again*, I will again like a poor exile visit my ruined home.

Let me hear soon again from my beloved & ever true friend. May God bless you & dear Mr G & all I have cause to love. All are well & unite in kindest love & wishes ever most truly yours

E P L

———————————❧———————————

Audley Augst. 4th. 1851

My Dearest Elizabeth,

Your very affecte & welcome letter of July 17th. deserved a more prompt reply, but the excessive hot weather & other circumstances prevented. Accept my most sincere acknowledgements for the kind & cordial reception of my "keepsake," & all your affectionate expressions of approbation. You are mistaken in your recollections of *Nelly Custis*, she was only *17*, The original of the Portrait was *25* & had been the Mother of four children—& *8* yrs in such circumstances, had certainly produced a considerable change in figure &c. I wish *I had* a correct likeness of your *old friend*, but in the *inner man*, as (poor Mrs Macpherson once said to me,) *time* has made *no change*. Memory could not be otherwise than *faithful*. I owe too much gratitude to my unchangeable friends in Philadelphia, *ever* to forget them—or cease to love & feel deep interest in their welfare. As I could not hope to see them again, I wished to prove, that I felt the same at *72*, as at *10* or *12* years old. With all the cares & trials of my long life, I have been the same in heartfelt affection for the friends of my *brightest days*. How could I *forget* that "such things *were*, & that they were most precious."

I regret my beloved friend, to hear that you are feeble in health, but I trust that bracing Oct. will renovate & enable you to take the exercise so necessary to renew your strength. My limbs I fear will never bear me [to] walk again. Altho' I am better than I once expected I could ever be again, & feel most grateful to the Almighty for his mercies, yet I believe that beyond the present *improvement*, I cannot anticipate. E thinks I have improved since she left me, I was *then*, *far* from *well*, my limbs were much swelled, the use of the flesh brush has reduced the swelling considerably, but my knees are very weak, & I totter when I attempt to stand, or move without my cane. My rolling chair is a pleasant change, & if I can get to the gravel walk below the Portico steps, & roll into the Garden, I shall rejoice, but I fear to attempt it yet. The weather, since the rain has made it cool & damp, gives me rheumatism. I am nearly as deaf as you are, & only my eyes & hands are efficient.

I have yet many calls on me for work of different kinds, Grandchildren, nieces, nephews, & kind friends; so that except answering letters, I write not at all. I have had a blank Book several years, to copy in it my verses for my *only* child, & have only copied *one* piece. I dislike of *all things* to copy *my own verses*. "The Battle of Bladensburg," "Mt Vernon"—"On my lamented darling Agnes", I think you must have in your Trunk. I have very few that would be *worth* sending you. I thank you very much for the verses you sent me, they shall be carefully preserved. You are happier than I in being yet *capable* of *inspiration*, I have not for *many* years made even a rhyme. Anxious cares occupy my mind too much.

I wrote to my Darling Parke, & told her your kind message, & all your affecte expressions to me & mine, & Mr Gs. Her children have been sick, but I trust are now well. Butler had gone to N.Y by Sea, to recruit, & expected to return in 3 weeks. My child had been sick but was then well, altho suffering excessively from heat & unusual continuance of drought. Nearly all her neighbours had left her for the North. My Darlings Conrads are well & happy. My Boys & E all well, but we miss poor Lawe. very much. My Dearest Mary Lee, & 3 children are with us, & we expect my dear good Sister & 3 grandchildren this week. My Dear Niece offers best respects & wishes for you & Mr G. She has a son at W. Point, *worthy of his Father.* In my opinion, he needs no other eulogy. Col Lee is detain'd by his duties in Balt[imor]e.

You & Mr G are very kind in having a copy taken of my portrait—but I am sorry to say that Root[33] has disappointed me most grievously. It is a very poor affair indeed, not better than one taken by a very inferior artist here. I admired Roots likenesses so much, I prefer'd him to *Brady,*[34] but there is one in N.Y whose name I do not know, whose Daguerreotypes are like miniatures. I regret having employ'd R. He has not done me justice, I hope you have been more fortunate in *your* copy.

I regret your disappointment in regard to your letter from Miss Allen, but I have sustain'd a greater loss. Oscar Lafayette[35] wrote to me immediately after the death of his excellent Father, my faithful friend & Brother, giving me all the particulars of that event. I have never received it, nor can it be recover'd. & Edmond [Lafayette] could not come to see me as he wished to do. He was some days with my children in La. They were charmed with him. In heart & mind he resembles entirely his Grandfather & Father, in person, a handsome resemblance of his Father. I regret much not seeing him.

Will you excuse Dearest friend, this miserable letter & accept for Mr G & your dear self our united love & every kind wish

---

33. Either Marcus Aurelius Root (1808–1888) of Philadelphia or Samuel Root (1819–1889) of New York, brothers who were outstanding daguerreotypists and photographers. Philadelphia Museum of Art, *Philadelphia: Three Centuries of American Art* (Philadelphia, 1976), 327, 351.
34. Mathew Brady (1823–1896) was a well-known daguerreotypist and photographer with a portrait studio in New York; he became famous for Civil War photography.
35. Oscar Thomas Gilbert du Motier Lafayette (b. 1815) and François Edmond Gilbert du Motier Lafayette (b. 1818) were the sons of George Washington Lafayette.

& prayer for your happiness & believe me *ever* most truly & affectely Yours

E P L

———————————— ❦ ————————————

[Audley] Octr 14th. 1851

My Beloved old friend,

Your dear kind letter of *Augst. 23rd.* makes me regret my
long silence but I have been too anxious & unsettled to write at all
since I received it, & I wished to send you the verses on my Angel
Agnes. Esther has copied them for me, with my translation of
some french verses, which I hope you will like. I thank you sincerely for your beautiful verses, I read them repeatedly, & then
enclosed them to my darling Parke. She & her dear Girls admire
them extremely, & they will encourage their industrious propensities. My darling child, & her Mother & children, inherit a love
of the *needle*, & *all its uses* from my Beloved Grandmother who
was, in *all* things, a model for her sex.

Do not *apologise* for sending *me* verses, The only regret I can
feel is that I cannot emulate you now in that respect. *My* life has
had too much of care & painful anxiety to admit of poetic inspiration, much as it *once* brighten'd my dear home Woodlawn. Now, I
feel unable very frequently to write a letter. My *only one* of *eight*,
has a life of sorrow, privation, anxiety, almost always, *this* Summer more than ever. Her children have all been sick even *ill*
repeatedly, her servants 20 at a time, ill, 4 or 5 of her house servants at a time when she most required them, her kind friends all
travelling for health or pleasure except very few confined at
home by sickness or sorrow. All her unhappiness in being unable
to see me in my precarious situation, bad crop, excessive heat &
suffocating drought, myriads of mosquitoes—all this in addition
to my helplessness to relieve her in *any* way. My friend, in never
having been a *Mother, you cannot conceive* a Mothers trials. You
have *cause* to rejoice in your fate. Long may you have reason to
rejoice in your *destiny*.

My Darling Boys C & L Conrad passed three weeks with me.
They left me a week since, & arrived safely in W[ashingto]n. For
them I am always anxious. I am as helpless as ever, & no hope of
being better.

Barton Stout[36] first came to W as an agent for distributing *maps*. Mrs. Fitzhugh & P made some observations & he politely differ'd in opinion, which they thought *presumptious*. On that hint I wrote the verses "I pray thee Ladies do not pout". He made a second visit & we invited him to remain a week. We had several young Ladies with us, & he composed verses for *all* & a beautiful piece on "Woodlawn" for me. At the end of the week, I wrote for him "Stranger rest &c. He was amiable & very grateful for kindness. When in after years he became a member of the N.Y Legislature, he sent me his "Maiden Speech." I have never heard of him since. "Woodlawn" was published in a Phi[ladelphi]a paper signed "Barton". E McClellan told me she had seen the paper. You are right my dear friend in selecting the "Cross & Wreath, that is the *favorite* with us. I hope *all* my friends will like their pieces. I shall be much pleased to see dear Elizabeths verses, altho' ignorant of the fact until I received your letter, I knew that she was capable of every thing, bright & beautiful in feeling & expression, with a "heart that might be shrined in chrystal & have all its movements scanned."

My kindest love to all my dear friends, & best wishes. We are looking out for our Sailor Boy. E & all her Boys well. Our loves & every kind wish for you & Mr G. May God bless you both now & ever prays your devoted friend

E P Lewis

Excuse this miserable scrawl.

---

36. Z. Barton Stout of Ontario County served in the New York State Assembly in 1839. New York *Civil List*.

In the last year of her life, Nelly lived for letters. She awaited the mail eagerly and read the letters she received again and again. Despite her debility, she continued to write to friends and family. Her last letter to Elizabeth was written in June 1852. On July 13, 1852, Nelly apparently suffered another stroke. That night, letters arrived from many of her favorites—her daughter Parke, her sister Martha Peter, and Robert and Mary Lee. She was never to read those letters. Alternately delirious and in a stupor, she was devotedly nursed by her widowed daughter-in-law and one of her unmarried half-sisters, probably Arianne Stuart, who described her last days in a letter to Mary Lee. Nelly lingered for two days, unaware that she was dying and leaving no deathbed messages. She died July 15, 1852, seventy-three years old. In death, her long life completed the circle to its beginning: she was buried at Mount Vernon next to George and Martha Washington's tomb.

She had little to leave in her will, property and slaves having already been divided among the children. One old slave, Sam, was freed at her death with $50 "as a remembrance from his old mistress." Her "memorandum of my Wishes" detailed the disposal of her personal effects: books, relics, paints and paint boxes, needlework, engravings, keepsakes of Mount Vernon, small pieces of furniture, china, her poems. Her principal heirs were her beloved Charley and Lewis Conrad, the sons of Angela; Parke and her children were also substantially remembered. Little mention was made of Esther Lewis and her sons, but likely enough, since they lived together, Nelly had already given the Lewises their keepsakes. She closed the will with her "devoted love & blessing to all my Darling children," and that they had had in full measure. Better than belongings, she left the memory of her love to family and friends.

In August 1852, Elizabeth wrote a five-page draft statement (probably not published) expressing some of her thoughts on her friend, "having had the happiness to know her intimately fifty eight years." She extolled Nelly's beauty, wit, piety, and devotion to family and friends. Elizabeth summed up Nelly's character: "Her character was emphatically her own,—simple and independent, excellent in itself, and not to be classed with those who look only to this world's passing advantages. Whether in the retirement of domestic life, or in society, she was always the same—fair and open as the day—she never assumed a sentiment that she did not feel—she was sincere, & content to be known only as she really was."

Elizabeth and James Gibson grew very old together, quietly charitable and devoted to their nieces and nephews. James died in 1857; Elizabeth continued to live in the house on Walnut Street. Shortly before her death, Elizabeth, assisted by her favorite niece, edited her history of the Bordley family (written in 1826); it was privately printed after her death. On August 23, 1863, eleven years after Nelly's death, Elizabeth died at nearly eighty-six. She left a considerable legacy of real estate and money: over thirty relatives and several charities received substantial bequests. She was buried in the graveyard of St. Peter's Church, Philadelphia.

In preserving Nelly's letters, Elizabeth preserved her friend's life story. Without their record, George Washington's beautiful Nelly would be a shadowy figure, the last fifty years of her life all but unknown. Because Nelly and Elizabeth's friendship lasted a lifetime, Eleanor Parke Custis Lewis emerges from the pages of these letters a fully realized woman.

Bibliography

Adams, John Quincy. *Memoirs of John Quincy Adams.* Edited by Charles F. Adams. 12 vols. New York, 1970.
"Address Delivered by Rev. Clement M. Butler, at the President's mansion, on the occasion of the funeral of Abel P. Upshur . . . ." Washington, D.C., 1844.
Alberts, Robert C. *The Golden Voyage: The Life and Times of William Bingham, 1752–1804.* Boston, 1969.
Alexandria *Gazette.*
Allis, Frederick S., Jr., ed. "William Bingham's Maine Lands, 1790–1820." In *Publications of the Colonial Society of Massachusetts*, vols. 36–37. Boston, 1954.
Ames, Kenneth. "Robert Mills and the Philadelphia Row House." *Journal of the Society of Architectural Historians* 27 (1968): 140–46.
Ammon, Harry. *James Monroe.* New York, 1971.
Appleton's Cyclopaedia of American Biography. 7 vols. New York, 1887–1900.
Armes, Ethel. *Stratford Hall: The Great House of the Lees.* Richmond, 1936.
Baltimore: Its History and Its People. Vol. 3, *Biography.* New York, 1912.
Bemis, Samuel F. *A Diplomatic History of the United States.* New York, 1936.
———. *John Quincy Adams and the Foundations of American Foreign Policy.* Westport, Conn., 1981.
Betts, Edwin M., and James A. Bear, Jr., eds. *The Family Letters of Thomas Jefferson.* Columbia, Mo., 1966.
Bevan, Edith R. "Druid Hill, Country Seat of the Rogers and Buchanan Families." *Maryland Historical Magazine* 44 (1949): 190–99.
Bingham, Theodore A. *The Bingham Family in the United States*, 3 vols. Easton, Pa., 1927–30.
Binney, Charles C. *The Life of Horace Binney.* Philadelphia, 1903.
Biographical Dictionary of the Maryland Legislature, 1635–1789. Edited by Edward C. Papenfuse, Alan F. Day, David W. Jordan, and Gregory A. Stiverson. 2 vols. Baltimore, 1979.
Biographical Directory of the American Congress. Compiled by James L. Harrison. Washington, D.C., 1950.
Biographical Directory of the Governors of the United States, 1789–1978. Edited by Robert Sobel and John Raimo. 4 vols. Westport, Conn., 1978.
Biographical Directory of the South Carolina Senate, 1776–1985. Edited by N. Louise Bailey, Mary L. Morgan, and Carolyn R. Taylor. 3 vols. Columbia, S.C., 1986.
Blaustein, Albert P., and Roy M. Mersky. "Bushrod Washington." In *The Justices of the United States Supreme Court, 1789–1969*, vol. 1, edited by Leon Friedman and Fred L. Israel. New York, 1969.
Bobbé, Dorothie. *Fanny Kemble.* New York, 1931.
Bond, Henry. *Family Memorials.* New York, 1855. Microfiche.
Bordley, James, Jr. *The Hollyday and Related Families of the Eastern Shore of Maryland.* Baltimore, 1962.
Bowie, Lucy L. "Madame Grelaud's French School." *Maryland Historical Magazine* 39 (1944): 141–48.

Breck, Samuel. *Recollections of Samuel Breck*. Edited by H. E. Scudder. London, 1877.
Bridenbaugh, Carl, and Jessica Bridenbaugh. *Rebels and Gentlemen: Philadelphia in the Age of Franklin*. New York, 1962.
Brief of Title to Several Tracts of Land. Philadelphia, 1863.
Brighton, Ray. *The Checkered Career of Tobias Lear*. Portsmouth, N.H., 1985.
Brissot de Warville, J. P. *New Travels in the United States of America, 1788*. Cambridge, Mass., 1964.
Britt, Judith S. *Nothing More Agreeable: Music in George Washington's Family*. Mount Vernon, Va., 1984.
Brockett, F. L. *The Lodge of Washington: A History of the Alexandria Washington Lodge, no. 22, A.F. and A.M. of Alexandria, Va., 1783–1876*. Alexandria, 1876.
Bronson, William White. *The Inscriptions in St. Peter's Churchyard, Philadelphia*. Camden, N.J., 1879.
Burke, Pauline W. *Emily Donelson of Tennessee*. 2 vols. Richmond, 1941.
Burke's Presidential Families of the United States of America. London, 1975.
Burt, Nathaniel. *The Perennial Philadelphians*. New York, 1975.
Butler Family Papers. Historic New Orleans Collection.
Callahan, Edward W., ed. *List of Officers of the Navy of the United States and of the Marine Corps from 1775 to 1900*. New York, 1901.
Capers, Gerald M. *John C. Calhoun, Opportunist: A Reappraisal*. Chicago, 1969.
Carter, Hodding, and Betty W. Carter. *So Great a Good: A History of the Episcopal Church in Louisiana and of Christ Church Cathedral, 1805–1955*. Sewanee, Tenn., 1955.
Cary, Wilson Miles. "The Dandridges of Virginia." *William and Mary Quarterly* 5 (1896): 30–39.
Chastellux, Marquis de. *Travels in North America in the Years 1780, 1781 and 1782*. Translated and edited by Howard C. Rice, Jr. Chapel Hill, 1963.
Cheves, Langdon. "Izard of South Carolina." *South Carolina Historical and Genealogical Magazine* 2 (1901): 205–40.
———. "Middleton of South Carolina." *South Carolina Historical and Genealogical Magazine* 1 (1900): 228–62.
Clark, Allen C. "James Greenleaf." Columbia Historical Society *Record* 5 (1902): 212–37.
Clark, Thomas D. *Travels in the Old South: A Bibliography*. 2 vols. Norman, Okla., 1969.
Cline, Rodney. *Pioneer Leaders and Early Institutions in Louisiana Education*. Baton Rouge, 1969.
Cloquet, Jules. *Recollections of The Private Life of General Lafayette*. London, 1835.
Conkling, Margaret C. *Memoirs of the Mother and Wife of Washington*. Auburn, Ala., 1850.
Cope, Thomas P. *Philadelphia Merchant: The Diary of Thomas P. Cope, 1800–1851*. Edited by Eliza C. Harrison. South Bend, Ind., 1978.
Copeland, Pamela C., and Richard K. Macmaster. *The Five George Masons*. Charlottesville, 1975.
Corson, James C. *Notes and Index to Sir Herbert Grierson's Edition of the Letters of Sir Walter Scott*. Oxford, 1979.
Corson, Richard. *Fashions in Hair*. London, 1984.
Cox, Ethelyn. *Historic Alexandria Virginia, Street by Street: A Survey of Existing Early Buildings*. Alexandria, 1976.
Cullum, George W. *Biographical Register of the Officers and Graduates of the United States Military Academy*. 3 vols. New York, 1879.
Cushing, Grafton D. "Typescript of Cushing family genealogy, especially the family of John Perkins Cushing (1787–1862)." Massachusetts Historical Society.

Dangerfield, George. *Chancellor Robert R. Livingston of New York, 1746–1813*. New York, 1960.

Delancey, Edward F. "Chief Justice William Allen." *Pennsylvania Magazine of History and Biography* 1 (1877): 202–11.

Descendants of Charles Willing. Historical Society of Pennsylvania.

Descendants of Colonel Daniel Coxe of New Jersey. Historical Society of Pennsylvania.

Detail Map of the Lower Mississippi River. [Washington, D.C.?], 1894.

Dictionary of American Biography. 22 vols. New York, 1928–58.

Dictionary of Louisiana Biography. Edited by Glenn Conrad. 2 vols. Lafayette,1988.

Dictionary of National Biography. 63 vols. London, 1885–1901.

du Bellet, Louise Pecquet. *Some Prominent Virginia Families*. 4 vols. Lynchburg, 1907.

Dunlap, William. *Diary of William Dunlap, 1766–1839*. Edited by Dorothy C. Barck. 3 vols. New York, 1930.

Eckhardt, Celia M. *Fanny Wright: Rebel in America*. Cambridge, Mass., 1984.

Emery, Noemie. *Alexander Hamilton*. New York, 1982.

Encyclopedia of American History. Edited by Richard B. Morris. New York, 1982.

Fisher, Joshua Francis. *Recollections of Joshua Francis Fisher, Written in 1864*. Arranged by Sophia Cadwalader. Boston, 1929.

Fisher, Sidney George. *A Philadelphia Perspective: The Diary of Sidney George Fisher*. Edited by Nicholas B. Wainwright. Philadelphia, 1967.

Flexner, James T. *George Washington*. 4 vols. Boston, 1965–69.

"Flitcraft, Harley, Meiligh, Roberjot, and Wheatcraft Families." Historical Society of Pennsylvania.

Forbes, Abner. *The Rich Men of Massachusetts*. Boston, 1851. Microfiche.

Fortier, James J. A., ed. *General Zachary Taylor: The Louisiana President of the United States of America*. New Orleans, 1937.

Freeman, Douglas S. *R. E. Lee: A Biography*. 4 vols. New York, 1934.

Genealogical files, Tudor Place.

Genealogies of Pennsylvania Families from The Pennsylvania Genealogical Magazine. 3 vols. Baltimore, 1982.

Genealogies of Pennsylvania Families from The Pennsylvania Magazine of History and Biography. Baltimore, 1983.

Genealogies of Virginia Families from the William and Mary College Quarterly Historical Magazine. 5 vols. Baltimore, 1982.

Gibbs, George. *The Gibbs Family of Rhode Island and Some Related Families*. New York, 1933.

Gibson, Elizabeth Bordley. *Biographical Sketches of the Bordley Family of Maryland, for their Descendants*. Philadelphia, 1865.

Gibson, James. "Family Statement." Historical Society of Pennsylvania.

Grande Encyclopédie. 31 vols. Paris, [1886–1902].

Greve, Charles T. *Centennial History of Cincinnati and Representative Citizens*. 2 vols. Chicago, 1904.

Groce, George C., and David H. Wallace. *The New-York Historical Society's Dictionary of Artists in America, 1564–1860*. New Haven, Conn., 1957.

Hamilton, Holman. *Zachary Taylor*. 2 vols. New York, 1941, 1951.

Hamm, Margherita A. *Famous Families of New York*. 2 vols. New York, 1902.

Hanson, George A. *Old Kent: The Eastern Shore of Maryland*. Baltimore, 1876.

Happel, Ralph. *Chatham: The Life of a House*. Philadelphia, 1984.

Harkness, Robert H. "Dr. William B. Magruder." Columbia Historical Society *Record* 16 (1913): 150–87.

Hayden, Rev. Horace E. *Virginia Genealogies*. Baltimore, 1959.

Hervey, John. *Racing in America, 1665–1865*. 3 vols. New York, 1944.

Hidy, Ralph W. *The House of Baring in American Trade and Finance.* Cambridge, Mass., 1949.

Hinshaw, William W. *Encyclopedia of American Quaker Genealogy.* 7 vols. Compiled by Thomas W. Marshall. Ann Arbor, Mich., 1936–77.

Holgate, Jerome B. *American Genealogy.* Albany, [N.Y.], 1848. Microfiche.

Jackson, Joseph. *Encyclopedia of Philadelphia.* 4 vols. Harrisburg, 1932.

Jenkins, John S. *The Generals of the Last War with Great Britain.* Buffalo, 1849. Microfiche.

Johns, John. *A Memoir of the Life of the Right Rev. William Meade.* Baltimore, 1867. Microfiche.

Johnson, Edgar. *Charles Dickens.* 2 vols. New York, 1952.

Jones, Howard M. *America and French Culture, 1750–1848.* Chapel Hill, 1927.

Jordan, John W., ed. *Colonial and Revolutionary Families of Pennsylvania.* 3 vols. Baltimore, 1978.

Journal of the Ninety-Seventh Annual Council of the Protestant Episcopal Church in Virginia held in Epiphany Church, Danville, on the 18th, 19th, 20th, and 21st of May, 1892. Richmond, 1892.

Judd, Jacob., ed. *The Revolutionary War Memoir and Selected Correspondence of Philip Van Cortlandt.* 3 vols. Tarrytown, N.Y., 1976.

Juettner, Otto. *Daniel Drake and His Followers.* Cincinnati, 1909.

Keith, Charles P. "Andrew Allen." *Pennsylvania Magazine of History and Biography* 10 (1886): 361–65.

Knight, B. Hoff. Mullanphy Family Data. Historical Society of Pennsylvania.

Lanman, Charles. *Biographical Annals of the Civil Government of the United States, during its First Century.* Washington, D.C., 1876.

Last Will and Testament of Elizabeth Bordley Gibson, Deceased. Philadelphia, 1863.

Leach, Frank Willing. "Philadelphia Families." Historical Society of Pennsylvania.

———. "The Philadelphia of Our Ancestors: Old Philadelphia Families." *The North American.* Scrapbook of articles arranged alphabetically by surname, Historical Society of Pennsylvania.

Leach, Frank Willing, and Alexander Du Bin. *The Coxe Family.* Philadelphia, 1936.

Lee, Edmund J., ed. *Lee of Virginia.* Baltimore, 1974.

Lester, Malcolm. *Anthony Merry Redivivus.* Charlottesville, 1978.

Lossing, Benson J. *Mary and Martha: The Mother and The Wife of George Washington.* New York, 1886.

Low, Betty-Bright P. "Of Muslins and Merveilleuses: Excerpts from the Letters of Josephine du Pont and Margaret Manigault." *Winterthur Portfolio* 9 (1974): 29–75.

———. "The Youth of 1812: More Excerpts from the Letters of Josephine du Pont and Margaret Manigault." *Winterthur Portfolio* 11 (1976): 173–212.

MacBean, William M. *Biographical Register of Saint Andrew's Society of the State of New York.* 2 vols. New York, 1922–25.

McCall, Charles. "The Chronicles of the McCall Family." Philadelphia, 1873.

McCarty, Clara S. *McCartys of Virginia.* Richmond, 1972.

McCue, George. *The Octagon.* Washington, D.C., 1971.

McDermott, John F. *The Lost Panoramas of the Mississippi.* Chicago, 1958.

McGinnis, Karin H. "Moving Right Along: Nineteenth Century Panorama Painting in the United States." Ph.D. diss., University of Minnesota, 1983.

McMaster, John B. *The Life and Times of Stephen Girard.* 2 vols. Philadelphia, 1918.

Madariaga, Salvador de. *Spain.* New York, 1930.

Martin, John H. *Martin's Bench and Bar of Philadelphia.* Philadelphia, 1883.

Maryland Genealogies: A Consolidation of Articles from the Maryland Historical Magazine. 2 vols. Baltimore, 1980.

Mason, Frances N. *My Dearest Polly: Letters of Chief Justice John Marshall.* Richmond, 1961.

Meade, Bishop. *Old Churches, Ministers and Families of Virginia.* 2 vols. Philadelphia, n.d.

Memoirs and auto-biography of some of the wealthy citizens of Philadelphia by a merchant of Philadelphia. Philadelphia, 1846. Microfiche.

Merrill, John H. *Memoranda Relating to the Mifflin Family.* Philadelphia, 1890.

Mitchell, Mary. *A Short History of St. John's Church, Georgetown, from 1792 to 1968.* Washington, D.C., 1968.

Monaghan, Frank. *John Jay.* New York, 1935.

Moore, Charles. *The Family Life of George Washington.* Boston, 1926.

Moreau de Saint-Méry, [Médéric-Louis-Elie]. *Voyage aux États-Unis de L'Amérique, 1793–1798.* Edited by Stewart L. Mims. New Haven, 1913.

Morris, Charles, ed. *Makers of Philadelphia.* Philadelphia, 1894.

National Cyclopaedia of American Biography. 60 vols. New York, 1892–1972.

New York *Civil List.*

Newport *Mercury.*

Niemcewicz, Julian U. *Under Their Vine and Fig Tree.* Translated and edited by Metchie J. E. Budka. Elizabeth, N.J., 1965.

Norris, J. E. *History of the Lower Shenandoah Valley.* Chicago, 1890.

O'Connor, Rachel. *Mistress of Evergreen Plantation: Rachel O'Connor's Legacy of Letters, 1823–1845.* Edited by Allie B. W. Webb. Albany, N.Y., 1983.

Oliver, Vere L. *The History of the Island of Antigua.* 3 vols. London, 1894–99.

Otis, William A. *A Genealogical and Historical Memoir of the Otis Family in America.* Chicago, 1924.

Park, Lawrence, comp. *Gilbert Stuart.* 4 vols. New York, 1926.

Penman, John S. *Lafayette and Three Revolutions.* Boston, 1929.

Perkins, Bradford, ed. "A Diplomat's Wife in Philadelphia: Letters of Henrietta Liston, 1796–1800." *William and Mary Quarterly* 11 (1954): 592–632.

Peter, Mrs. Walter. "Peter Family Genealogical Notes." Mount Vernon Library.

Philadelphia City Directories (PCD), 1795–1851.

Philadelphia Museum of Art. *Philadelphia: Three Centuries of American Art.* Philadelphia, 1976.

Philip, Alex J. *A Dickens Dictionary.* London, 1928.

Pollock, Thomas C. *The Philadelphia Theatre in the Eighteenth Century.* Philadelphia, 1933.

Proceedings of the American Philosophical Society 22 (July 1885).

Proceedings of the Massachusetts Historical Society, 1835–1855, vol. 2. Boston, 1880.

Ramke, Diedrich. "Edward Douglass White, Sr., Governor of Louisiana, 1835–1839." *Louisiana Historical Quarterly* 19 (1936): 273–327.

Records of Spring Grove Cemetery. Cincinnati, Ohio.

Rensselaer, Florence van. *Livingston Family in America and its Scottish Origins.* New York, 1949.

Riffel, Judy. *Iberville Parish History.* Baton Rouge, 1985.

———, ed. *Iberville Parish Records.* 2 vols. Baton Rouge, 1981–82.

Rivlin, Joseph B. *Harriet Martineau: A Bibliography of her Separately Printed Books.* New York, 1947.

"The Road to Rome." Alexandria, 1860.

Rogers, George C. *Charleston in the Age of the Pinckneys.* Norman, Okla., 1969.

Rosengarten, J. G. *The Early French Members of the American Philosophical Society.* Philadelphia, 1907.

Salley, A. S., Jr. "The Calhoun Family of South Carolina." *South Carolina Historical and Genealogical Magazine* 7 (1906): 153–69.

Scharf, J. Thomas. *The Chronicles of Baltimore*. Baltimore, 1874.

Scharf, J. Thomas, and Thompson Westcott. *History of Philadelphia, 1609–1884*. 3 vols. Philadelphia, 1884.

Schmit, Patricia Brady. *Nelly Custis Lewis's Housekeeping Book*. New Orleans, 1982.

Schoonover, Janetta W. *The Brinton Genealogy*. Trenton, N.J., 1952.

Scoville, Joseph A. *The Old Merchants of New York City*, vols. 1, 3. New York, 1889.

———. *The Old Merchants of New York City*, vol. 2. New York, 1863.

Seilhamer, George O. *History of the American Theatre*. 3 vols. Philadelphia, 1888–91.

Shockley, Martin S. *The Richmond Stage, 1784–1812*. Charlottesville, 1977.

Silva, Innocencio Francisco da. *Diccionario Bibliographico Portuguez*. 22 vols. Lisbon, 1858–1919.

Simpson, Henry. *The Lives of Eminent Philadelphians Now Deceased*. Philadelphia, 1859.

Smith, Elbert B. *The Presidencies of Zachary Taylor and Millard Fillmore*. Lawrence, Kans., 1988.

Sorley, Merrow E. *Lewis of Warner Hall*. Baltimore, 1979.

"Taylor of Southampton &c." *Virginia Magazine of History and Biography* 24 (1916): 213–14.

Thane, Elswyth. *Potomac Squire*. Mount Vernon, 1963.

Thornton, Anna Marie. "Diary of Mrs. William Thornton, 1800–1863." Columbia Historical Society *Record* 10 (1907): 88–226.

Tilghman, Oswald. *History of Talbot County, Maryland*. 2 vols. Baltimore, 1915.

Torbert, Alice C. *Eleanor Calvert and Her Circle*. New York, 1950.

Tracy, Berry B. *Federal Furniture and Decorative Arts at Boscobel*. New York, 1981.

Traveller's Steamboat and Railroad Guide to the Hudson River. New York, 1857.

250 Years of Painting in Maryland. Baltimore, 1945.

United States Census for the State of Louisiana, 1850. Washington, D.C. Microfilm.

Vernon, Edward, comp. and ed. *American Railroad Manual*. New York, 1874.

Warfield, J. D. *The Founders of Anne Arundel and Howard Counties, Maryland*. Baltimore, 1967.

Washington, George. *The Diaries of George Washington*. Edited by Donald Jackson and Dorothy Twohig. 6 vols. Charlottesville, 1976–79.

———. *The Papers of George Washington*. Edited by W. W. Abbot. *Presidential Series 2, April–June 1789*. Edited by Dorothy Twohig. Charlottesville, 1987.

———. *The Writings of George Washington*. 39 vols. Edited by John C. Fitzpatrick. Washington, D.C., 1931–40.

Webber, Mabel L. "Dr. John Rutledge and His Descendants." *South Carolina Historical and Genealogical Magazine* 31 (1930): 7–25.

———. "The Thomas Pinckney Family of South Carolina." *South Carolina Historical and Genealogical Magazine* 39 (1938): 15–35.

West Virginia: A Guide to the Mountain State. Works Projects Administration. New York, 1941.

Westcott, Thompson. *A History of Philadelphia*. 5 vols. Philadelphia, 1886.

———. *The Historic Mansions and Buildings of Philadelphia*. Philadelphia, 1877.

Wharton, Anne H. *Salons Colonial and Republican*. Philadelphia, 1900.

White, G. Edward. *The Marshall Court and Cultural Change, 1815–35*. Vol. 3–4 of *History of the Supreme Court of the United States*. New York, 1988.

Wildes, Harry E. *Lonely Midas: The Story of Stephen Girard*. New York, 1944.

Willing Collection. Historical Society of Pennsylvania.

Winsor, Justin, ed. *The Memorial History of Boston*. 4 vols. Boston, 1881.

Witcher, Robert C. "The Episcopal Church in Louisiana, 1805–1861." Ph.D. diss., Louisiana State University, 1969.

Woodward, William E. *Lafayette*. New York, 1938.

Worst, Helen N., Collection. Historical Society of Pennsylvania.

Zahniser, Marvin R. *Charles Cotesworth Pinckney*. Chapel Hill, 1967.

Index